Cognitive Energy Healing

MAGGIE MCLAUGHLIN

Copyright © 2018 Maggie McLaughlin.

All rights reserved. No part of this book may be used or reproduced by any means, graphic, electronic, or mechanical, including photocopying, recording, taping or by any information storage retrieval system without the written permission of the author except in the case of brief quotations embodied in critical articles and reviews.

The information, ideas, and suggestions in this book are not intended as a substitute for professional medical advice. Before following any suggestions contained in this book, you should consult your personal physician. Neither the author nor the publisher shall be liable or responsible for any loss or damage allegedly arising as a consequence of your use or application of any information or suggestions in this book.

This book is a work of non-fiction. Unless otherwise noted, the author and the publisher make no explicit guarantees as to the accuracy of the information contained in this book and in some cases, names of people and places have been altered to protect their privacy.

Balboa Press books may be ordered through booksellers or by contacting:

Balboa Press
A Division of Hay House
1663 Liberty Drive
Bloomington, IN 47403
www.balboapress.com
1 (877) 407-4847

Because of the dynamic nature of the Internet, any web addresses or links contained in this book may have changed since publication and may no longer be valid. The views expressed in this work are solely those of the author and do not necessarily reflect the views of the publisher, and the publisher hereby disclaims any responsibility for them.

The author of this book does not dispense medical advice or prescribe the use of any technique as a form of treatment for physical, emotional, or medical problems without the advice of a physician, either directly or indirectly. The intent of the author is only to offer information of a general nature to help you in your quest for emotional and spiritual well-being. In the event you use any of the information in this book for yourself, which is your constitutional right, the author and the publisher assume no responsibility for your actions.

Any people depicted in stock imagery provided by Getty Images are models, and such images are being used for illustrative purposes only.
Certain stock imagery © Getty Images.

Print information available on the last page.

ISBN: 978-1-9822-0799-1 (sc)
ISBN: 978-1-9822-0800-4 (hc)
ISBN: 978-1-9822-0801-1 (e)

Library of Congress Control Number: 2018908178

Balboa Press rev. date: 07/23/2018

Awakening

Remain
ever mindful
an inner light glimmers
within our hearts
to guide us all
together
and as
one

Hush and be still
Hear
the silent whisper

Love is the key
Love is the key

Trust this truth

Resume
your journey
anew

–MM

To John, always

CONTENTS

PREFACE xiii

INTRODUCTION: MY STORY xvii
A Gift of Life xvii
Enlightened Guidance xxvii

PART I: COGNITIVE ENERGY HEALING 1
Healing Body, Mind, and Spirit Naturally 1
A Glimpse into What to Expect 9

PART II: CONCEPTUAL FOUNDATIONS OF COGNITIVE ENERGY
    HEALING 13
Cognition and the Mind 13
Energetics and Spirals 15
Spirals and Energetics 22
On Spirit, Transcending the Material World 26

PART III: THE DYNAMICS OF CHANGE 29
Understanding Change 29
Enabling Change, a Perceptual Shift 30
Initiating Personal Change 35
An Invitation to Think Outside the Box 37

PART IV: SENSING AND PERCEIVING 47
The Body's Perceiving Systems 47
Perceiving Energy 48
A Look at How These Systems Work 49

The Sensory Nervous system	49
The Vital Energy System	50
The Immune System	54

PART V: THE COGNITIVE ENERGY HEALING PERSPECTIVE ... 57
On Perception, Pain and Health	57
The Pain Response as Processed and Delivered by the Brain	58
Physical and Emotional Injury	60
Autoimmune Diseases	62
Epigenetic factors	64
Finding a Diagnostic Tool	66

PART VI: MUSCLE TESTING, A DIAGNOSTIC APPLICATION ... 69
Word Power and the Power of The Word Meaning, Intention and Perception	69
The Power of Words in Muscle Testing Applications	72
Coded Muscle Responses	77
CEH Muscle Testing Techniques	80
The MT Technique When Working with Others	80
MT Strategies with Words, Questions and Statements	84
Response to a Single Word	87
Yes and No Code Response to Questions	88
Response to True and False Statements	89
Four Self-Testing MT Techniques	90
The O and Pincer Fingers Method	90
The O and One Finger Method	91
The Back of the Hand Method	92
The Two Finger Method	92

PART VII: COGNITIVE ENERGY HEALING MODALITIES ... 95
Taking a Quantum Leap	95
Methodology for the Cognitive Energy Healing Modalities	98
Energetic Healing Hands	98
The Temporal Attunement Modality	100
The Centering Attunement Modality	102
The Release and Reclaim Modality	105
The Body Energy Attunement Modality	106
Blocked Energy Release	107
Energy Streaming	108
Bridging Energy Flow	109

Where Cognitive Energy Healing May Help 111
Case Studies: Cognitive Energy Healing Helping Others 114
Where Cognitive Energy Healing Has Made a Difference 134

PART VIII: FROM SELF-AWARENESS TO SELF-EMPOWERMENT 137
Our Inner Resources 137
A Pathway to Freedom 141
Creating a Balanced and Happy Life 142
Healing as a Team Effort 152

APPENDIX: A SPIRAL JOURNEY 155

AUTHOR'S NOTE 161

REFERENCES 163

SUGGESTED READINGS 165

PREFACE

The principles and practices of Cognitive Energy Healing came to me when I desperately needed healing help beyond the scope of what was available at the time. And I must add this inspired knowledge came as a gift of life from a source beyond my resources, one I believe to be Sacred.

This new healing modality based on communication with the conscious and unconscious mind and the restoration of healthy body energy flow has not only healed me, it has since proven effective in the treatment of others dealing with a broad range of unresolved health concerns as well. This natural and non-invasive approach bridges the communication gap between the holistic body and the cognitive mind, enabling healing for a considerable number of unresolved health concerns. It has proven effective in addressing certain healing concerns such as inflammation and pain responses, emotional stress, physical and emotional trauma, as well as some autoimmune and epigenetic related diseases. This practice has also proven helpful in supplementing and supporting other on-going treatments.

Cognitive Energy Healing employs both verbal and energetic communication with the client to identify the underlying causes of health concerns. This is followed by a case-specific treatment protocol to initiate the desired healing outcome. The energetic aspect of the healing process employs both subliminal communication and the stimulation of the body's energy flow systems. In most cases this holistic body, mind and spirit approach serves to remove energy blockages to healing, freeing the body to heal itself as only it can do.

In regard to the well-being and safety of the body and its ability to reproduce, the brain runs the show. Everything that is perceived from the body's internal and external environments informs the brain of the body's holistic safety and well-being. Within this dynamic, the brain's executive function is to oversee, manage and maintain homeostasis, and to initiate a protective response to perceived threats. And as both the conscious and unconscious mind are part of the cognitive processes, the brain acts to oversee and respond to these aspects of its own operation.

Cognitive Energy Healing treatments can be effective in correcting or eliminating the root causes of a significant number of health concerns. Through conscious communication with the cognitive mind, and the energetic and physical body, corrections can be made to maladaptive or harmful responses impacting a person's physical, emotional, and spiritual well-being.

~~~~~~~~~~~~~~~~~~~~~~~~

Cautionary notes

- *The application of Cognitive Energy Healing attunements requires training and certification in the practice.*

- *The information presented in this book is to be utilized with cautious self-awareness and discernment. It is in no way intended to remove the need for seeking professional medical and/or mental health attention as required. Ultimately, and as always, you must be aware when medical treatment or other professional treatment is to be sought out. All references to "healing unresolved health issues" refers to concerns that have been first addressed by a medical professional and are not the result of extended or permanent physical damage. The healing methods provided in this book come from my personal healing journey, and it is from this perspective I will be sharing what I have learned.*

- *Cognitive Energy Healing is a spiritually-inspired method of healing. Qualified training in the CEH Practice is required for anyone wishing to become a practitioner. Besides offering an introduction to self-healing, training and certification for practitioners is also available.*

- *Going forward and threaded throughout this narrative, stories of successful healings will be included to help provide a practical understanding of the scope, methods and effectiveness of CEH. Please note that names of participants whose healing stories are shared in this book have been changed to protect their privacy.*

INTRODUCTION

My Story

A Gift of Life

"We must be willing to let go of the life we planned so as to have the life that is waiting for us." —Joseph Campbell

We never know where our lives will lead us or what challenges we will encounter and learn from along the way. This is a story of learning to see with new eyes, of discovering a new way of being, and of developing a new healing method to restore holistic wellness. Passage from my early life pathway to the one I am happily enjoying now required a profound change in who I was and what I believed my life's purpose to be at the time. In effect, the impetus for such a dramatic change is usually brought about by a significant life-altering jolt of some kind. Mine came in the form of trauma and illness.

Little did I know I was setting out on a twenty-year journey of research, study and experience beyond anything I could have ever imagined. Initially this is a story of survival and my determination to get my life back during years of living with environmental illness, autoimmune disorders, and other related physical and emotional health concerns caused by a prolonged exposure to environmental toxins.

The turning point in my healing journey came with the realization that no medical remedy was available to enable me to be well again. While medications helped to lessen my symptoms minimally, I found myself in the inescapable grip of pain and illness with despair making inroads daily. Gratefully, this reality remained true only until that fateful day when I was inspired or should I say guided to learn a new way to heal myself and be well again. It is through this and other healing revelations that I have come to experience personally a healing story worth sharing, one that offers hope to others in need of healing for a significant number of unresolved health concerns.

Since that time, not only has this healing enlightenment led to the creation of the new healing practice I call Cognitive Energy Healing, a non-invasive, comprehensive body, mind, spirit approach to healing, it has also helped restore the health of an ever-increasing number of people. Beyond its initial application for allergy elimination, the breadth of health concerns that can be helped effectively or completely alleviated by this modality continues to grow. And so now in this writing, it is my intention to share this message of hope for restored wellness with a broader audience of people in search of help for their unresolved health concerns.

In and of itself, life is the greatest gift one can ever receive. This became all too real for me when suddenly I found myself in an ongoing battle to save own my life. The initial three years proved to be unrelenting and challenging. Eventually, however, the menacing shadow of my illness had to relinquish its power as I came to learn some amazing insights about how to heal myself. As I healed and was able to move my focus beyond healing myself to the healing of others, my life was set back on a new and vital pathway. Today, it is my greatest joy to report that the scope of what is possible through Cognitive Energy Healing has grown far beyond anything I could have ever imagined.

So now let's go back to the beginning of my story to have a closer look at how all this unfolded from the initial environmental accident that led to a life threatened and derailed, and then onward to a life restored, revitalized and impassioned to help others. My story begins following a prolonged exposure to environmental toxins, potentially lethal at elevated levels. Nothing in my life to this point could have prepared me for the trauma and the health challenges that ensued.

It began in the fall of 1997. I was forty-eight, happily married with three terrific children transitioning into the world of adulthood. All was great on the home front. I was however, becoming increasingly unwell. I had developed a number of persistent health concerns including viral and bacterial infections, body pain, migraines and fatigue. My immune system struggled to cope with what was eventually identified as a hazardous exposure to toxic molds and sewer gas.

Finally, it all came to a head one afternoon I found myself having difficulty breathing and my heart was racing frighteningly fast. Then my mind simply went blank. I vaguely remember managing to get myself home that day, collapsing as soon as I got in the door. From that day onward, daily survival became my all-encompassing focus.

Environmental illness in its many manifestations proved to be nothing like the time I broke my ankle when, following surgery and a recovery period of a few months, my life quickly returned to normal. This time, I found myself on a life-threatening precipice dealing with inflamed lungs and vocal cords, unrelentingly pain and allergic reactions, as well as random asthma attacks. The onset of hypothyroidism followed shortly thereafter. Engulfed in illness and the emotional trauma of the whole experience, my life was completely derailed.

Living in this my new reality, I had absolutely no hope of ever being able to return to work or a normal life of any kind. Indeed, it was from this devastating new reality with the odds stacked against me that I mustered the determination to find a way to be well again. Along my journey I was challenged like never before to change and to grow as a person, and ultimately my efforts paid off as I came to learn self-healing and to experience results beyond anything possible at that time.

My home was the safest place I could be, and yet I wasn't even safe there. I was in a constant state of allergic reaction as my immune system was being triggered by everything I came in contact with. Stuck in trauma mode from the initial toxic exposure, it now identified everything in my environment as an alien threat. And no one and nothing was able to turn off this abnormal response. I was frightened by what was happening to me, and I knew that this was truly a battle for my life. At that time and for the next few years I had no hope of ever escaping this devastating health nightmare. It saddens me now looking back, to think of the horrific impact all this must have had on my family as well.

My day to day world had suddenly became very small, not even being safe from reactions in my own home. And while some symptoms remained constant, others surfaced randomly in reaction to any number of things, sometimes identifiable, other times not. Besides reacting to everything I ate and came in contact with, grocery stores, shopping centers, hair dressing salons, restaurants, and places of public gathering of any kind had become dangerous places to be due to their scents, chemicals, and other environmental concerns. Going outdoors was fraught with hazards as well, including pollens, grasses, molds, car emissions, etc. Survival meant limiting my exposure as much as possible.

So, I struggled to find foods I could eat with the least possible reaction, I cut my own hair, avoided all cleaning products other than vinegar and baking soda, all shopping was done by my husband, a social life was no longer an option, and yet somehow, we carried on. I remember one day driving home from a visit to the doctor when I suddenly realized nothing in this city I had lived in most of my life looked familiar. I was completely lost and disoriented while being but a few blocks away from my destination. Fortunately, I was able to pull into a parking lot to wait for this spell of brain fog to pass. Oh my, how frightening, and what next?

I saw doctors who did what they could, however I was not getting better. My autoimmune concerns could be managed only somewhat with medications, and a cure was clearly nowhere in sight. It wasn't until I finally sought alternative healing through energy treatments that I experienced any degree of real healing. From my experience with the then new energy healing modality, I discovered that the effective elimination of allergies was possible. This approach employed a combination of acupressure, spinal stimulation and controlled breathing in combination with exposure to vials containing the energy of potential allergens. These treatments, of which I received a great number, proved to be significantly helpful and encouraging.

Meanwhile, and with respect for the healing I had received with this energy healing practice, I grew increasingly aware that this approach was falling short of meeting my particular range of concerns. Progress was very slow as only one allergy treatment could be delivered per session, and some of these had to be repeated numerous times before they would hold. Also, my case was unusual as I was dealing with an endless and ever-growing list of allergens with no end in sight. It became pressingly evident that this approach would take more than my lifetime and my current bank account for me to be well again. And in addition to these concerns, out in the world I continued to remain at risk of random and severe allergic reactions wherever I went. I needed to find some other way to access the healing I needed.

With this awareness, the answers I was seeking did eventually come in response to a newfound resolve to find a way to heal myself. It was with this shift in mindset to self-healing and a renewed determination to be well again that a new healing pathway began to open before me, the one that has since led to the creation of Cognitive Energy Healing.

This learning did not come as a one-off insight, but rather as a process. Being more spiritual than traditionally religious, my initial leap of faith was to simply and sincerely ask for help. In offering a verbal prayer, my request was not to be miraculously healed, but rather to be guided in some way to heal myself. And very much to my amazement help did come, however not in the instantaneous miraculous way one tends to imagine such things.

The guidance I received came in response to my questions regarding my changing healing needs as they arose over time. So, rather than a quick fix cure all, this learning to self-heal was a process that would in time form the foundation of a holistic practice for the healing of self and other. And as this new approach was based on verbal communication with the cognitive mind to state the desired healing outcomes, I independently researched whatever health area was being addressed to better apply what I had learned. This approach of being actively engaged in learning as much as possible about a healing concern has proven to be invaluable in my healing work, and remains an on-going part of the practice.

Whether the enlightened knowledge I was receiving was awakened from my higher cognitive awareness or was revealed by a sacred source remains beyond proof. Either way, it is a tremendous gift of healing and I am profoundly grateful to the source, whatever it may be. Awakening to my new reality of healing and newfound hope stirred in me a profound emotional and visceral shift, as I stepped out of desperation and hopelessness into a world of boundless possibilities for healing and for good.

As there is something mystical about the sense of being uplifted beyond our earthly bounds, my creative side led me to eventually express my own sense of this on canvas in a painting and in written form as a poem. Both works are called *Living on the Wind*. I will share the poem with you here.

Living on the Wind

Divine silence
descends
Quiet stillness
embraced

Lifted up
on gentle breezes
Upon the wind
we soar

Wings glide
on golden light
Silken waters
flowing

> Toward
> a crimson fire dance
> as sunset boldly beckons
>
> Great mystic bird
> We fly
>
> —MM

Beyond the ephemeral passage of time, within that fleeting period there can be hope, beauty, joy and passion. My words here are to say that all this had been restored to my life, and more than ever before I was now awakened to the majesty of every precious moment.

Along with this very big knowing that enabled my healing, came renewed hope as fear and desperation lost their power over me. I knew the healing guidance I was receiving came mysteriously from within me and yet somehow at the same time from another place, one that was greater than me. Curiously, this awe-inspiring awareness was tempered by a calm knowing that all is as it should be.

Bit by bit, through my thoughts, dreams and writings, I came to intuitively know the healing techniques that would save my life, and eventually form the foundation of the Cognitive Energy Healing practice. Inspired guidance sometimes came in the form of dreams, and I would try to learn their metaphorical meaning by asking for clarification. These were made clear either intuitively through spiritually-inspired thought or writing, also known as automatic writing. Whenever a question was asked, the answer would come either immediately or shortly thereafter. My queries were generally healing focused, sounding something like the following: Can I be guided to know how to heal myself? What can I do to stop/eliminate a severe allergic reaction? What types of healing do I need to learn so I can once again be safe in the world? And how can I free myself from almost constant pain? As each question was asked, the answer would come in a timely fashion, so I was able to heal myself each time, as the need arose.

For me to apply this great gift in a healing way, all I had to do was give myself permission to recognize and engage my own innate healing ability. Amazingly, as it turns out, the only essential tools for Cognitive Energy Healing practice are always with us and readily accessible. These include healing hands to engage and restore normal energy flow, and the practitioner's conscious subliminal healing directives to engage the executive power of the brain to make corrections that enable the holistic body to heal. Absolutely no testing devices, appliances or energy vials are required. While my early treatments were primarily allergy focused, the scope of the practice has grown holistically to address the significantly broader body, mind and spirit scope of healing concerns.

As the need arose in treating myself and others, I discovered the Cognitive Energy Healing techniques worked to halt allergic reactions and eliminate the allergen as a potential trigger. While a treatment takes only seconds to perform, it effectively works to stop even a life-threatening anaphylactic reaction within seconds. By treating reactions as soon as they occur, complete recovery from the established symptoms is usually realized within minutes. Such things as tearing will stop, and inflammation and congestion will subside and clear. However, if for whatever reason treatment is delayed, the reaction will develop into full blown symptoms, and once these become fully entrenched they will take longer to clear.

I learned that should an allergen have an emotional association its complete elimination requires that they be treated concurrently. I recall two of my allergic concerns that persistently resisted elimination until I was able to identify and release their associated emotion. These were mustard and carrots, and they were successfully eliminated once I released their childhood association of fear, a fear of my father's temper outbursts at the dinner table. As this allergen/emotion association is essential for the effective elimination of certain allergies, this will be explored in greater detail later.

Eventually, as my health improved I came to a place where I wanted to help others in the way I had been helped. Initially, I ventured to share a small part of this journey of recovery with family and a few of my closest friends. As they came to learn about my self-healing practice, I was surprised to discover that this sharing didn't cause the stir or the negative reaction I had expected. In fact, for the most part, they were relieved that I had found a way to make myself well again. At that time, it had never occurred to me that someday I would take this sharing to a significantly larger audience in the hope of helping others as I have been helped.

Initially, as the occasional need for healing arose, I was able to offer help for a number of minor health concerns affecting my inner circle of family and friends. Later as my skills and confidence in the healing practice grew, I was able to move on and work with more demanding concerns. While the type of healing I dealt with as a novice healer was less challenging, it served as a wise place to begin. Later, as my experience and knowledge grew, I was better able to take on more complex healing concerns. These will be presented as case studies in Part VII.

For the moment, I would like to share a few of my earliest healing experiences, with the caveat that all names in these and any ensuing healing stories have been changed for privacy reasons.

One evening Sandra, a guest at our home, was getting dressed to attend a formal gathering. After applying her make-up, she came to me in distress as she was experiencing a full blown allergic reaction to the mascara she had just applied. Her eyes were red, swollen, and tearing. I offered help, and as she knew about my own self-healing work, she readily accepted. Within minutes of receiving the treatment, Sandra's eyes started to return to normal as the burning, redness and inflammation lifted. A short time later, with all traces of the reaction having gone and still wearing that same mascara, Sandra headed out for the evening. It felt great for me to be able to help someone in this way.

Also, in those early days I occasionally offered help to a number of people suffering from insect bite reactions. It was known that Melissa's usual reaction to mosquito bites had always resulted in a significant inflammatory response. On this occasion, we were seated on her back deck when she remarked that she had just been bitten by a mosquito. Knowing about her concern, I suggested I might be able to help, and with her permission I proceeded to treat her. Since that time and in the years since, Melissa has not experienced any further allergic type reactions to mosquito bites.

From this experience, I learned a couple of things: the quicker the treatment is delivered after the bite, the greater the chances of reducing the inflammatory response; and as I learned later, the treatment was effective in preventing future allergic reactions to mosquito bites as well.

The following experience serves as further confirmation that the sooner a treatment is administered, the less the inflammatory reaction tends to be. While working outdoors, Sam was swarmed by wasps and was mercilessly stung seven times on one arm. Being nearby, I was able to respond immediately, treating him within seconds of the attack. Amazingly and to the surprise of both of us, Sam didn't experience any visible swelling whatsoever. Admittedly, I had no idea whether he was allergic to wasp stings or not, however what we both remarked following the treatment was that there was no evidence of an inflammatory response.

These are just a few of my early healing experiences as I reached out to help others when they were in need. This gift of healing that has helped me to regain my health had awakened in me a growing awareness that it must be made available to help others as well. In this writing, my hope is to bring this life-changing healing message to all who hear my words. It is my firm belief that the ability to heal resides in all of us, and is readily accessible to those who are open and willing to access it. And yet, interestingly, it is not necessary for a client to believe in this healing approach for it to work.

Before moving on, it is interesting to note that my learning of the Cognitive Energy Healing modalities was guided by some well-established teaching principles. As I transitioned to more advanced applications of what I had learned, it became increasingly evident that my healing-related questions were being answered in an interesting way. The responses I was receiving were geared to my level of readiness to apply the information provided, a process similar to how a child's learning progresses from the simple to the more complex. Indeed, one could say when I entered the whole process of learning to heal myself I was as a child, a novice to this new world of healing. In the years since, my learning continues to grow in order to address an ever-increasing body of healing knowledge, and I gratefully embrace the challenge.

Life can be wonderful, sometimes challenging, but always precious. Today, I find myself generally well, working to heal others, and writing this book to pass along this healing message. My life is active and happy, and I am doing all the things I love to do. And now, having arrived at the place in my life where it is time to share this healing message, I offer along with an introduction to the Cognitive Energy Healing modality the possibility of restored wellness for a significant number of unresolved health concerns.

In bringing this part of my story to a close, I remain ever conscious and grateful to all those who stood beside me on my challenging journey back to wellness. This includes my family and friends, medical practitioners, health care providers, and alternative healing practitioners. And daily, my gratitude is expressed with my every living breath to the sacred source that taught me the Cognitive Energy Healing modalities and enabled me to be well again.

Enlightened Guidance

When the time came for me to begin my self-healing journey, I was guided forward by a divinely inspired passage:

Save the children

Divine light is your guide

Love is the key

The phrase **"save the children"** came to me at a point when I was finally able to consider shifting my focus from self-healing to offering healing help to others as well. The healing gifts I had received were clearly intended to help others, for who are these "children" in need of help but all of us. No matter what our age, we are all children of a higher source, and as such it is our sacred duty to care for and help those in need to the best of our ability.

From my perspective, the accompanying two phrases are to be understood in reference to the first. The next phrase **"Divine light is your guide,"** offered assurance that I would be guided in my healing practice. My personal belief is that spiritual help and direction is available and accessible for those with real needs, recognizing that needs and wants are not in the same camp. As I understand it, the desire for a second car in the garage or a bigger, grander house don't seem to quite make their way into the higher spiritual plane as these are matters of want rather than of need.

Some words, either through overuse or misuse, can lose their essential meaning, and *love* is one of those. Surprisingly, and for this reason, **"Love is the key,"** touched an uneasy chord with me. I decided to try to understand the meaning of the word love as it was intended within the context of the Divine message. In an effort to conjure up a list of synonyms that are associated with both healing and love, I came up with the following list: trust, appreciation, caring, understanding, kindness, concern, compassion and forgiveness. Immediately the cloud lifted: Love, as manifest through compassion for self and others, is essential to being a healer.

Inspired by this message, I purposely moved forward onto the pathway of energy healing. And, as we are wisely advised in air travel to place the oxygen mask on our own face before helping others, healing myself was without question my first priority. Looking back on the initial and overwhelming task set before me, I must celebrate this incredible gift: what an amazing classroom I have found myself in! Though at times painful and frightening due to my illness, this has been experiential learning beyond my wildest dreams.

Admittedly, living with my daily health challenges has not been easy. However, with hindsight I now know my illness had been necessary to redirect my path onto this purposeful journey. Fortunately, and all the while, there has been and continues to be great comfort in knowing that even beyond the love and support of friends and family, I am not alone. In this writing, I am moved by the awe-inspiring belief that once shared, the Cognitive Energy Healing body of knowledge and its practice will come to be recognized by many as a significantly beneficial healing resource.

What an amazing classroom I have found myself in!

PART I

Cognitive Energy Healing

Healing Body, Mind, and Spirit Naturally

This book introduces a new approach to healing and the journey of learning and discovery that led to the practice called Cognitive Energy Healing. For many, it offers a story of hope for restored wellness.

Cognitive Energy Healing is an energy based, natural and non-invasive approach to healing body, mind, and spirit. The aim of this healing practice is to identify and eliminate the root causes of health concerns so healing can take place, rather than the reduction or masking of symptoms with medication. For the many living with unresolved healing concerns, this holistic practice provides a non-invasive way to restore physical, emotional and spiritual well-being. And as verbal communication both conscious and subliminal is fundamental to the practice of Cognitive Energy Healing, the acronym CEH, pronounced as "say," will be used for brevity's sake going forward.

My ongoing research through access to a tremendous amount of scientifically based health and wellness information has enabled CEH to be at the forefront of addressing a growing range of healing concerns. As new health-related scientific discoveries are surfacing all the time, this knowledge can be readily integrated into the practice. Breakthroughs in the areas of autoimmune and epigenetic diseases have been topics of significant discussion in recent years. My research into health discoveries is always with an eye to determining how this new knowledge may provide a viable application within the CEH practice.

This book provides an overview of the CEH methods and techniques used in the healing of both oneself and others. By acting to correct and eliminate the physical, emotional, psychological, social and spiritual underlying causes of a broad range of health concerns, these modalities provide an effective and reliable approach to healing. This holistic body, mind, spirit approach promotes healing by engaging both mind and body to release the specific causes of energy blockages to healthy energy flow. Usually a single treatment takes only seconds to perform, and outcomes have proven to be amazingly successful. Clients usually report feeling energized following a treatment session. And for those who have completed a treatment regime, the vast majority report their healing results as being positive, significant, and for some, life-changing.

The term *modality*, as used here, refers to either the comprehensive CEH practice itself, or the particular methods used within the practice. As well, the acronym BMS will be used in reference to the body, mind, spirit continuum, the dynamic and interactive earthly trinity of one's being. Body refers to the physical being, mind to the conscious and unconscious being, and spirit is our energetic being of the soul, the crucible that holds our emotions, intentions and conscience. Spirit is also our energetic connection to our higher selves, and/or a Divine source.

In the years since receiving my first healing revelations, many more such insights have surfaced, serving either to meet a specific healing need or to provide a refinement to an existing modality. Amazingly, these healing practices are neither complex nor difficult to perform. While the pathway to learn a significant truth can be a long and challenging one, often times once resolved the final answer turn out to be surprisingly straight forward and uncomplicated.

From my personal experience in working with both my own healing concerns and those of others, I remain confident that this practice offers effective and lasting benefits for a host of unresolved healing concerns. As Cognitive Energy Healing came to me as a life-saving gift, it is my intention in this writing to bring this message of hope to others who are also in need of healing help. While self-healing of minor concerns can be practiced with only a brief CEH introductory program of instruction, more significant healing concerns are best addressed by a trained practitioner. CEH practitioners work from a significant and essential body of knowledge and experience.

While skepticism toward any new healing approach is natural and indeed wise, I encourage you to read on to make your own informed decision as to whether this approach is right for you. This modality is not offering miracles; it is offering healing possibilities through cognitive and energy practices that have proven effective for many. This is an opportunity to learn about the CEH's broad range of healing applications. It is heartening to report that this modality is realizing cures for a number of concerns that to this point have only been managed to varying degrees by medication.

Looking to the broader health care arena, energy medicine, which is also known as vibrational medicine, along with other energy healing practices still remain largely outside the physical and mechanical body-based practice of Western medicine. It is however interesting to note that going back to ancient times, energy medicine was one of earliest healing practices. Anthropological prehistoric evidence indicates that shamanic traditions were being practiced as far back as 30,000 years ago. Ayurveda, whose origins date back to 5,000 BCE India and continues to this day, is an integrated medical practice that incorporates the holistic body, mind, spirit as one within both nature and the cosmos.

Historically, the move to the practice of Western medicine, with its focus on the physical rather than the energetic body is a relatively recent phenomenon. And as with any significant paradigm shift, the pendulum tends to swing full course rather than half measure; the primacy of the Western medical model served to largely discredit energy healing practices in the Western world. This trend however is changing with an ever-growing interest in energy medicine.

I find it puzzling that such a vast resource of early healing knowledge came to be almost entirely eradicated from Western healing practices to make way for modern medicine. This model shift from energy healing to the Western physical body medical model gives rise to a few questions: What happened to moderation when making such a drastic change? Were all energy healing methods perceived to be completely without merit? Was any consideration given to the possibility that the proverbial baby might be tossed out with the bath water? Could we not be better served with an integrative, physical and energetic medical model? Fortunately, all was not lost for the sake of the other.

Today, even though science, and quantum physics in particular, has argued for the existence of energy as the basic manifestation of all that is from the tiniest energetic particle to tangible masses of solid matter, there remains a real and significant lag in bringing the energy healing model into the current practice of medicine. All the same, big change related to energy is coming! Medical researchers, if not practitioners as of yet, are increasingly choosing to take a fresh and less protracted look at the potential benefits of energy medicine.

The forces behind this shift in thinking are driven not only by the findings of quantum physics and such concomitant tools as electromagnetic imaging, but also by the need to find cures for illnesses that have not been resolved by the current practice of medicine. One indication we are awakening to energy healing as a valid practice is the growing number of health professionals offering acupuncture, an ancient Chinese energy healing practice. Advances such as this help lay the groundwork for emerging new developments in energy healing. I am certainly not alone in believing that a flood of medical breakthroughs will follow the eventual incorporation of energy medicine into the practice of modern medicine.

Returning to the overview of the CEH practice, it is important to emphasize that energy and cognitive based procedures are applied in a safe, and non-invasive way to engage and initiate healing. There are absolutely no medications or medical procedures, manipulation, acupuncture or acupressure involved in this practice. Rather the approach is to enable the body to initiate healing corrections as identified by the practitioner and delivered in the form of subconscious and energetic directives. Ultimately the intention is to effect a cure for any number of unresolved health concerns in a painless way and in a surprisingly short period of time. Even in those cases where a cure cannot be fully realized for whatever reason, it is often possible to bring about noticeable improvements in the client's symptoms. Also, as the underlying causes of an illness, pain, or malfunction in one person may be and often are entirely different in another, healing strategies and protocols within the practice are and must remain case specific.

Fundamental to the CEH practice is the belief that the body will heal itself once all energy blockages to the desired healing are released. Healing is a process, and it can only be fully realized by addressing all related concerns impacting the comprehensive BMS dynamic. Depending on what is being addressed, the task is either to identify and eliminate the cause of energy blockages impacting a person's well-being, or to release and correct any of a broad range of causative dysfunctional concerns. The goal is to restore normal and healthy body, mind and spirit function for the holistic well-being of the person being treated. Depending on what is being treated, healing can take place almost immediately, while in others the healing process can require anything from a few minutes, to a few days, and sometimes even a couple of weeks. In this latter case, it is usually because the body requires more time to clear any accumulated toxins and make the necessary healing repairs.

The scope of healing concerns successfully addressed by Cognitive Energy Healing is significant and growing due in large part to the tremendous resource of new and readily accessible health-related information. As regards autoimmune diseases, CEH acts to correct the misinformation that has caused the immune system to incorrectly identify essential body components as a threat to its well-being. A maladaptive immune attack on the body is destructive and potentially even life-threatening. The attack can target anything in the internal environment of the body, including organs, glands, tissues, bones, hormones, nerves, lymph and blood components, enzymes, and so on. To prevent a misguided immune system from inflicting permanent damage on the body, it is essential to identify and correct the misinformation it is receiving as soon as possible.

The body's well-being is contingent on its ability to properly monitor both its internal and external environments, and to respond protectively as required. Beyond surveilling the inner workings of the body, the immune system also responds to any threats from the physical, chemical and energetic environment of the outside world. From the external environment, for example, an irritant in the air may cause sneezing, coughing, or eyes to tear up. The presence of an invading virus, parasite, or bacteria will trigger an immune battle to eliminate it. Meanwhile, in the case of a misguided immune system, anything from the outside world can be wrongly identified as a threat to the body, triggering either allergic or asthmatic reactions.

The body's sensory systems perceive everything in the external vicinity and respond defensively as required. This includes everything that is inhaled, ingested, touched through contact, injected (needles, insect bites, etc.), or experienced energetically (energy frequencies experienced with or without direct contact with the source). For the environmentally-sensitive or allergic person, the list of possible irritants and allergens is virtually infinite, though some are more common than others, including such things as scents, pollens, molds, and chemicals, and even something as innocuous as a carrot or an apple. Virtually anything that is identified as a potential danger to the body from the external environment, whether real or misguided, acts to trigger an immune response or initiate a conscious defensive or protective action. Some additional factors influencing the severity of an autoimmune response include the intensity and the duration of the exposure. An immune reaction can range from a mild irritation such as a rash to anaphylactic shock (anaphylaxis), a potentially life-threatening response.

A healthy autoimmune system, acting as the body's own first-responder system, plays an essential and life-sustaining role. One is left in awe of how complicated the body is, and how vigilant it must be to survive in relationship with both its internal and external environments. And yet, for most people on any given day, the body manages all this without giving it even a conscious thought.

Beyond correcting a number of autoimmune concerns, CEH has proven effective in healing certain causes of physical and emotional pain and dysfunction. One particular concern that is very much part of our modern reality is the impact of prolonged exposure to stress. Some harmful effects include anxiety, gastric and intestinal digestive problems, headaches and migraines, fatigue, high blood pressure, irritability and sleep issues. Prolonged exposure to stress is to be taken seriously as it is also a recognized cause of cancer.

In addition to immune concerns, there remain many other factors that can significantly impact one's well-being. When one's health does go awry, either physically, chemically, emotionally, or energetically, the full spectrum of the BMS network can be impacted. Holistic wellness requires the balanced and uninterrupted functioning of these dynamic and interrelated systems. In relationship to the body and to the outside word, the complex workings of the mind cannot be overlooked or dismissed. The cognitive brain receives, interprets, processes and responds to situations as they are perceived, understood and stored as traumas, emotions, memories, and beliefs. And significantly prolonged exposure to negative experiences and the memories of these can potentially have serious and lasting health consequences.

Beyond these concerns, the complexities of the body/mind relationship go further still when you include such influencing factors as self-generated thoughts, and indirectly experienced events that have been witnessed, observed or learned about by word of mouth or through the media. It's no wonder in today's world that digestion is impacted by watching the news or reading the morning paper over breakfast. Sometimes the stress of just being in the world can negatively impact a person's health, as when the repeated swallowing of one's words (suppressing feelings and thoughts) results in painful clenched jaw muscles, and living with long-term anger results in heart health concerns.

Throughout a person's lifetime, the body's surveillance systems remain on duty to keep us well and safe. Other than trying to get the sleep we need and maintaining a healthy diet and exercise regime, it's natural for us to go about our daily lives without giving a moment's thought to the body's significant and challenging task. Besides working to keep all its systems running smoothly, the body on its own can heal minor cuts and abrasions; it can work to eliminate viruses and bacterial infections; it can clear certain types and levels of inhaled or ingested toxins; and it can mend properly aligned broken bones. However, while the body does know how to heal itself, sometimes it needs assistance in getting to a place where it can effectively complete the healing process on its own.

As responsible adults, we know it is our responsibility to maintain a healthy level of body awareness in order to recognize a symptom as a message calling for or demanding attention. Though we aren't issued an operator's manual at birth, we have fortunately learned a few things along the way about how to take care of ourselves. When a person feels unwell due to illness or some other kind of dysfunction, the body manifests any of a broad range of symptoms to (in part) trigger an awareness of a health concern. Symptoms can include anything from the discomfort of a stuffy nose or vertigo, to searing debilitating pain, anxiety or depression. Pain, inflammation, and other forms of physical, mental or behavioral dysfunction are generally recognized as a cause for concern and possibly even a call for help.

When it comes to wellness, due diligence rests on the individual person or caregiver to access the best available healing resources. Once alerted to a health concern, it is usually up to the person involved to decide on the appropriate action required. Perhaps this is something the person can handle on his or her own, while in other instances, medical assistance or some other type of healing help is required.

There is a growing awareness that the best and most effective path to wellness isn't always through medication, medical intervention or surgery. Sometimes it is wise to consider other avenues such as massage, physiotherapy, naturopathic or chiropractic help. Also, other alternative healing methods such as Cognitive Energy Healing may augment the healing benefits of the medical treatments being received. In order to make an informed choice of how to proceed in addressing a health concern beyond the conventional medical approach, it is advisable to first do a little research to find out as much as you can about the practice or modality that you are considering trying.

Later in this book, you will be introduced to CEH modalities, as well as some of the many types of healing that have been realized within its scope of treatment. You will also learn about the methods used to effectively access the body's communication system as this enables the practitioner to determine the root causes of such symptoms as pain and disease, as well as the causes of mental and physical malfunction.

The overarching aim of the CEH practice is to enable holistic wellness through the application of case-specific modalities and protocols. It addresses a broad range of health concerns, offering help and even the possibility of a cure for some autoimmune concerns, such as the effective elimination of allergies. Also, its applications can reduce or eliminate the stress arising from physical and emotional traumas.

A new area that is currently being addressed by CEH is epigenetically caused illnesses and disorders, as it acts to restore normal gene function. Epigenetic concerns are the result of a maladaptive gene expression that causes certain genes to be turned off erroneously or left on indefinitely. This is caused by prolonged exposure to external stress factors. These can be heritable from ancestral origins, and can be caused by such mental or physical traumas as poverty, loss, illness, famine, war or genocide.

A Glimpse into What to Expect

Hopefully you are now curious to learn a little about what a person is to expect from a CEH treatment. Amazingly, besides some training in this modality, everything else that is required, you already have readily at your disposal: hands to direct energy flow, a heart as the source of love and compassion, a mind for understanding and communication, and breath for its life-sustaining ability to cleanse and to heal.

Following the release of an energy blockage, the time required for the restoration of normal energy flow can vary depending on what is being treated. When a practitioner is using CEH to eliminate any of a list of allergens, the correction for each takes place instantaneously at the time of treatment. This is also true for self-treatment of an allergic reaction that is in progress; however, in this case it takes a minute or so for the symptoms to completely clear, recognizing that more severe reactions usually take a bit longer. Pain relief from certain types of physical and emotionally-caused pain are usually realized following around ten to twenty minutes of treatment.

While correction of an autoimmune malfunction takes mere seconds to perform, full healing of such a health concern can take anywhere from a few minutes or up to a week or more for the body to complete the healing process. It all depends on what has been corrected and how much healing is required. This said, it is also important to mention that in cases where permanent damage to the body has already occurred, the extent to which healing is possible will be limited. In regard to the Release and Reclaim Modality, treatments to release harmful beliefs and behaviors in favor of healthy ones will take effect as soon as the concern has been fully and properly addressed. Meanwhile, indications that the desired change has taken place will be noted later when the usual trigger(s) no longer result in the undesired response.

From my early self-healing practice, I have gained a few insights which I will share with you here. Should the immediate treatment to stop an allergic reaction be delayed for whatever reason, symptoms such as congestion, coughing, and choking may increase in severity once they are activated. Postponing treatment for an allergic reaction will also extend the time needed for a full recovery. **Best practice is to apply the treatment immediately following exposure to an allergen, or as close to the onset of symptoms as possible.**

Once an allergy is extinguished, it is not likely to recur, that is unless it needs to be treated in combination with something else. This combination could include something internal to the body such as a hormone, a physical or emotional trauma, or certain external environmental factors. A CEH practitioner is trained in identifying such relevant associations, so that the allergy can be treated and permanently eliminated.

To better understand this process, let's consider a combination involving an emotion:

A young child, while finishing her last bite of apple in the schoolyard, is harshly scolded by a teacher in front of friends for some kind of misbehavior. A few weeks later the child, who loves apples, discovers eating an apple makes her feel unwell. Eventually, the reaction develops into an allergy causing her to avoid eating apples all together.

Upon seeing a CEH practitioner for treatment to eliminate the apple allergy, a number of things may have to be included in the treatment besides the apple itself. This could include such emotions as the *fear* the child felt when the teacher scolded her, the *embarrassment* of being scolded in front of her friends, the *shame* for having done something wrong, or the *indignity* and ensuing *anger* at being wrongly accused. This is all to say an allergy treatment may require a combination involving one or more associated concerns to effectively release the energy blockages causing the allergy.

With this glimpse into a very small aspect of the practice, we now move on to an overview of the conceptual foundations of Cognitive Energy Healing and to consider some of its other healing applications.

Note: If you are convinced of the potential effectiveness of Cognitive Energy Healing and would like more information about certification to become a Cognitive Energy practitioner, please consult the contact information at the back of the book.

PART II

Conceptual Foundations of Cognitive Energy Healing

Cognition and the Mind

The brain is the dynamic and interactive control center of the holistic body, and is responsible for the oversight and direction of all its operations, behaviors and responses. While the higher cognitive processes take place in the frontal lobes, other cognitive functions take place in other regions of the brain. The cognitive mind, comprising both our conscious and unconscious awareness, is responsible for such cognitive processes as being attentive to our perceptions for learning, decision making, planning, problem solving, thinking, and understanding all we experience.

While some memory is stored in the executive cognitive location of the brain, it is also stored in the temporal lobes. The cognitive brain is aware of and responsive to our emotions as they act to influence our perceptions and how we respond to them. Emotional responses originate primarily in the limbic system and act to involve the entire nervous system. And as we are all too aware, depending on the type and intensity of a negative emotion, its effects can be physically experienced in the head, heart and/or gut. Further to this experience, it may later manifest as pain and/or disease anywhere in the body, depending on the intensity and the duration of the experience. This is to say that unresolved emotional issues can be harmful to a person's health and well-being.

Everything that is learned through the cognitive experience is stored as memory, including our core beliefs learned in early childhood. And as we work our way through our personal, social, physical and sensual experience of the world, our cognitive memory influences and directs our various responses and behaviors arising from them. Language is a behavioral skill that serves our cognitive processes by enabling us to communicate with ourselves through thought, and with others through speech, writing, gesture, code, sign language and even subliminal communication. These means of representing and expressing our cognitively perceived world enable us to share our thoughts, solve problems, state our intentions, express our desires and improve our personal and shared understanding of the world.

Each word thought, no matter how it is communicated, carries the same energy charge as what it represents. A word unto itself is energetically neutral: it simply carries its meaning. However, its perception depends on a number of variables including the intention and the manner of its delivery, as well as the recipient's personal emotional associations with the word. In other words, the degree of positive or negative association with a word depends on the person's cognitive perception of it. While words such as sadness, anger, jealousy, and betrayal will not have a significant energetic effect on most people, others will feel their energy impacted negatively on both a cognitive and visceral level. And while words such as joy, love and caring have a positive association for most, their impact will most likely be negative for those who are lacking in these areas.

Let's now move on to look at how the processes of the cognitive mind, language and behavior factor into the practice of Cognitive Energy Healing. To briefly address how this is done, initially, the practitioner applies an energy testing technique to determine the body's response to subliminally communicated messages. This not only engages the cognitive aspect of the client's brain to identify those concerns negatively impacting their holistic health, it also produces a noticeable and readable physical response. This approach can determine for example whether the word *stress* in and of itself has a negative health-related impact on the person being tested. Such information-gathering identifies the underlying causes of health concerns as well as which CEH modalities applications will best serve the client's particular healing needs.

Energetics and Spirals

With increasing research into the electro-chemical processes of the human brain and the bioenergy of the cell, science has come to recognize the importance of understanding how the physical body's transmitted information about itself is perceived, processed and responded to. Through magnetic resonance imaging research, it is now possible to identify and map the electro-chemical energy responses in the brain in reaction to stimuli.

Fundamental to the Cognitive Energy Healing practice is the belief that along with the comprehensive neuro-networks of the physical body, a vital energy system with its own function and energy flow operates both independently and in tandem with the body's electrochemical network. These two systems are understood to be in constant communication with each other, as both work to maintain the well-being of the interactive and dynamic BMS continuum.

Energy is essential to all life. The vital sensations of living energy are felt in its vibrational, pulsating and streaming flow. The biologist Neil Lane in his book *The Vital Question* acknowledges that the fundamental life-giving force is energy and expresses concern at the lack of research in this area. Lane takes this head on as he proceeds to investigate such big questions as *what is life* and *what is living*. He explains that the life of every cell of the body is dependent on proton energy to stimulate the production of adenosine triphosphate (ATP), the fuel source for the operation of the miniscule mechanisms in the cell's nucleus, known as nanomachines. These extremely small machines perform the life-sustaining functions of the cell, and indeed for all of the trillions of cells in the human body. Lane also speaks about other energies fundamental to life including bio-energy that enables the contraction of muscles and the operation of the heart, and the electro-chemical energy processes of the brain for managing body operations, as well as its own cognitive processes.

Beyond these known sources of energy, are there other body energy systems yet to be scientifically recognized? The following recent scientific breakthrough demonstrates that science is ready and increasingly able to explore this exciting new area of life energy research.

The Telegraph,
Bright flash of light marks incredible moment life begins when sperm meets egg, Sarah Knapton, Science Editor

Refer to: http://www.telegraph.co.uk/science/2016/04/26/bright-flash-of-light-marks-incredible-moment-life-begins-when-s/

Hitting the newsstands across the UK and the world on April 16, 2016, The Telegraph published an article on a scientific report released by researchers at Northwestern University. Fluorescence microscopy has made it possible to observe what happens at the very moment of fertilization of the human egg. The zinc spark discovery was made by Francesca Duncan, an assistant professor and researcher in Obstetrics and Gynecology. This breakthrough was first revealed in an article entitled Radiant Zinc Fireworks Reveal Quality of Human Egg.

Refer to: http://www.northwestern.edu/newscenter/stories/2016/04/radiant-zinc-fireworks-reveal-quality-of-human-egg.html#sthash.0REoEiJh.dpuf

The scientific explanation is that an enzyme from the sperm activates the egg cell when it penetrates the plasma membrane, sparking an explosion of light. As only the healthiest fertilized eggs emit the greatest spark, the current scientific application of this discovery is to determine which are the healthiest eggs to implant for in vitro fertilization.

For a spectacular visual of this event, please see _The Scientist (the-scientist.com)_, May 3rd, 2016, Image of the day: Fertilization Fireworks.

There now, we have it: verifiable evidence that human life begins with a fireworks light show. How simply beautiful and amazing! It's truly wonderful that there is now scientifically observable and measurable evidence of a burst of light energy at the moment of fertilization, and that there is also a practical application for this knowledge.

And yet looking at this discovery from another perspective, many of us would remark that while recognizing how truly significant this discovery is, we have known all along that life force energy is in all of us; it's as a real as the air we breathe. Life force energy is essential for human life, and its processes are in operation within us all the days of our lives. Our internal energetic body is constantly sparking, flowing and transforming, while the body's external energy is radiating both inward and out from itself as it relates to both its internal and external environments.

Flow systems, patterns and directions of flow for air, water, sediment and energy are ubiquitous. These include such things as the pathways of rivers, the wind, lava, spiral nebulas, and the body's blood and lymph circulatory systems, as well as its energy flow systems. The CEH practice is fundamentally engaged in maintaining a healthy balance and flow of all the body's energy systems, from the electrochemical energy flow systems of the brain and the network of neuropathways throughout the body, up to and including the body's subtle energy flow systems of the meridians, chakras and auric field.

Dr. Sally Goerner in her essay _The Science of Energy Flow Systems_, discusses a number of interconnected flow networks that are essential to the existence of the cosmos. How they circulate affects function of the whole, whether this be a living organism, the universe, matter, ecosystems, etc. She also notes that these networks are governed by universal patterns and principles, and that this is relevant to holistic wellness.

Knowledge of the body's subtle energy flow systems and its relationship to wellness is not a recent discovery. Indeed, several energy healing practices have been around for a very long time. These include the Chinese practice of acupuncture, the Hindu yogic chakra and auric field healing practices, and the Ayurveda practice of integrative medicine. A brief overview of some these practices will help lay a conceptual foundation for the CEH approach to energy healing.

Within the ancient practice of Chinese Medicine, *Qi (Chi)* is the name for life force energy. The Hindu word *Prana* and the Japanese word *Ki* (as in Rei*ki*, the hands-on healing energy practice) also refer to life force energy. *Qi*, meaning breath, is the essential life sustaining system of the body in Chinese medicine. Within the body, a healthy, balanced and sustained energy flow is essential to holistic well-being.

Qi life force energy is fundamental to Chinese medicine and has led to such healing practices as acupuncture, qigong, and yoga. The underlying belief of these practices is that any disruption to the body's vital energy flow can result in illness or other types of body/mind dysfunction. Acupuncture, which dates back at least two thousand years, involves the insertion of tiny needles into the skin at various body energy points along the energy flow pathways known as the *meridians*. The spiraling flow of energy through the meridians serves to nourish the body's vital energy requirements. Its ascending directional flow is called the yin, and the descending the yang. Acupressure, a more recent application of the acupuncture practice involves the manual stimulation of these same energy points.

Yoga and Qigong are approaches to energy healing that employ posture and breathing techniques, as well as various meditation practices, to restore and balance energy flow. The yogic traditions of Hinduism and Buddhism also have identified another body energy channeling system known as *chakras*. The word chakra is Sanskrit for wheel, signifying the vortex or whirlpool-like motion of energy flow. And like the meridians, the chakras are an energy flow system serving to receive and transmit energy throughout the body.

Though identified as separate, the seven chakra pools of energy circulate along the vertical axis of the spine, flowing through each other along a continuous, interconnected and cyclic pathway. Each of these spiral flowing energy pools emits a unique energy frequency that produces a rainbow refraction of white light. The pathway of Chakra energy flows upward from the Root Chakra (red) at the base of the spine, to the Sacral Chakra (orange) at the lower abdomen, to the Solar Plexus Chakra (yellow) in the stomach area, to the Heart Chakra (green) just above the heart, to the Throat Chakra (blue) at the throat, to the Third Eye (indigo) at the middle of the forehead and slightly above eyebrow level, and then on to the Crown Chakra (violet) at the top of the head.

It is important to note that each of the chakra locations is in alignment with the physical body's projections of nerve bundles extending out through the spinal vertebrae to the various organs and glands in their area. The energy flow through the chakras nourishes and restores the life force energy requirements of all the glands, organs and tissues within the respective region of their associated chakra vortices. There are different ways to determine body health through the chakras. Interestingly, perhaps the most straight forward is doing a pendulum reading. This is done by suspending a pendulum in front of or over each chakra. A healthy energy flow will move its swing in a full clockwise circle.

Each chakra's well-being is responsive to a particular range of emotional issues. To provide a brief overview of these, the Root Chakra relates to survival issues, the Sacral Chakra to well-being and sexuality, the Solar Plexus Chakra to self-worth and self-esteem, the Heart Chakra to love and inner peace, the Throat Chakra to communication and truth, the Third Eye Chakra to intuition, imagination and wisdom, and the Crown Chakra to spiritual connection, beauty and bliss.

The Chakras serve as a kind of BMS health barometer manifesting the state of wellness through the intensity, direction and/or shape of the energy channel flow as it passes through each of from them. While there are different approaches to correcting irregularities in Chakra energy flow, the primary CEH approach is to communicate directly with the cognitive processes of the brain to initiate the healing changes required. This is achieved by releasing energy blockages arising from physical and/or emotional trauma. Healing is indicated by improvement in chakra energy flow which is readily discernable, observable to both the practitioner and the client when pendulum readings are taken. As mentioned earlier this is but one way of assessing the state of chakra energy flow. Muscle or Energy testing is another; this approach will be presented in detail later.

Auric field and chakra healing are often offered in tandem, as functions of these systems influence each other. The auric field is the oval shaped energy flow system that surrounds the expansive exterior of the body. Its subtle energies protect the body by the eliminating harmful internal energies, and by shielding it against harmful energies from the external environment. Like the Chakras and the meridians, the auric field is in continuous energetic communication with the brain, informing it of any irregularities or threats to well-being.

Cognitive Energy Healing recognizes the comprehensive vital energy system, comprised of the energy flow channels of the meridians, chakras and auric field as a real and an essential component of the physical and energetic body. Beyond nourishing and reflecting the holistic health of a person, these systems are energetically accessible to the practitioner to enable healing. Disruption in energy flow anywhere within this system can be identified and corrected with CEH applications.

The vital energy system is essential for life and is sustained by breath. The system's life-force energies first develop and grow within from the moment of conception and continue to flow and radiate throughout a person's lifetime. And though the length of a lifespan varies, it is always finite, coming to a close as the last life-sustaining breath is exhaled from the body. The practice works to identify and address vital and spiritual energies in a healing way. This spans from ancestral influences up through gestation and birth, and throughout a lifetime, up to and including the moment of death. This is not to say that the story of life in the spiritual sense ends here, it is only to say that this is the framework within which the practice is able to address health and wellness matters.

The finite nature of the physical life cycle is a reality that evokes any number of questions about energy and spirit following death. While some question whether energy and spirit or either of these even exist, others remain uncertain or curious about vital energy and where it might go following death. Many believe these energies in the form of spirit leave the body to become one with a Divine being, to experience some form of afterlife, while others speak of a reunion with a Universal Consciousness or Sacred Source. And still others maintain that spirit moves on to live life anew on a journey of learning from one lifetime to the next toward a higher state of being. And while thoughts and beliefs about such matters vary considerably, there is inspiration and wonder in exploring the mysteries of our spiritual being.

Within the context of the CEH practice, its fundamental and guiding principle is to determine the cause(s) of dysfunction in the BMS continuum and to restore and maintain wellness. The causes are determined through a series of non-medical investigative methods that will be presented in the section on methodology. The practice then applies a range of healing modalities to restore a healthy and balanced energy flow in both the internal and external energy body. Referring back to the earlier discussion of energy flow systems, any form of injury or trauma, whether physical or emotional, can cause an interruption or a complete blockage to healthy energy flow in the body. This in turn can result in a broad list of possible symptoms including pain and inflammation, fatigue, mental illness and disease, to name a few. And while healing usually follows naturally on its own, an entrenched energy blockage can act to delay, inhibit or even prevent healing.

An analogy comparing the workings of the human body to music may assist in explaining the impact of disruption or blockage to flow, the one being energetic and the other melodic. Not unlike a musical performance, the body in all its amazing complexity has its own dynamic flow, its own orchestration of harmony, rhythm and balance. While an interruption in melodic flow is jarringly unpleasant to the ear, disruption to energy flow in the body is the cause of dysfunction and/or disease.

Any disruption to energy flow within the body triggers health related symptoms, and when these are consciously perceived they serve as an alert system to inform the body of a concern. Symptoms are the body's way of issuing a call for help and for this reason should be given due consideration. In many cases, assuming the health condition has been addressed by a medical practitioner, CEH can assist and promote healing by re-engaging and stabilizing a healthy and healing energy flow.

Realistically, depending on the health issue being addressed, there can be circumstances limiting the amount of healing that can take place. This includes such concerns as how advanced a disease is and whether permanent damage has occurred. This is to say, the pre-existing deterioration of body tissue particularly in degenerative diseases may limit how much healing can actually take place with a CEH intervention. It may however help to prevent or abate further deterioration.

Having discussed the spiraling flow of energy throughout the body, we are now ready to move on to a brief exploration of spirals, and their role in the practice of CEH.

Spirals and Energetics

> "To see a World in a Grain of Sand
> And a Heaven in a Wild Flower,
> Hold Infinity in the palm of your hand
> And Eternity in an hour."
> ...
>
> William Blake
> *Auguries of Innocence*

Inspired by William Blake's vision of the wonder and the mystery in what lies before us, we begin our journey into the fascinating world of spirals. Our explorations, as they relate to energy flow patterns of the body, will take us first out into the universe as it carries Earth and all creation in its spiral flow. While there is fascination in knowing that you are star dust, there is awe and wonder in knowing you are that and so much more.

Through the mystical images from the Hubble Space Observatory we are able to see beyond our earthbound view, to discover that the spiral is no secret to the greater cosmos of which we are but an infinitesimally small part. These photographs bear witness to a spectacular display of the spiraling energy flow out from older stars into the ever-expanding universe surrounding Earth's cosmic neighborhood. And as our galaxy, the Milky

Way, like other spiral nebulas provides a brilliant light show of distant young stars moving outward into the universe on their spiral journey, we on planet Earth are silently carried along the pathway of this majestic flow.

Earth itself abounds with countless manifestations of spirals patterns and vortices. The forces of nature are constantly at work creating spirals, whether through the movement of the wind in a tornado, the seemingly sculpted shapes of the conch, nautilus and giant tritan shells, the silk weave design of a spider's web, the path of a leaf floating downward on the wind, the whirl flow of eddies of water in a swift current, the geometric arrangement of the seeds in cones and flowers, even the coil of a snake resting on a rock.

Spirals abound both naturally and in our created world of architecture and design. And for millennia both the circular and the rectangular version of the iconic spiral design have been created by humanity for their symbolic value to represent such spiritual and energetic forces as life and seasonal cycles, growth, and the eternal journey of spirit. With this awareness and from my experience, once you become aware of spirals in any of their manifestations, you will start to discover them everywhere!

While we encounter spirals almost daily in nature and in crafted design, their story promises to lead us on an intriguing journey of enlightenment as well. On a superficial level spirals are a controlled expanding or retracting line, shape, or movement that can be described as winding, coiling, unfurling or whirling and are found both in nature's designs and vortices as well as architectural designs, motifs, and patterns. In any and all its manifestations, the spiral is perceived as a cyclic and dynamic geometric shape implying or describing movement, whether expanding outward from its central point and progressing toward infinity or moving inward toward its center point. Besides delineating an inward or outward direction, the spiral movement can also rotate in an upward or downward direction, as well as in a clockwise or counterclockwise direction.

The dynamic line of spiral is a recognized symbol of birth, growth and change for nature's cycles, as well as for the feminine cycles of fertility, rebirth and procreation. Within the human body, the spiral is deeply rooted in both our physical and energetic realities. Probably the most well-known spiral in the body is the DNA double helix, a wonder unto itself containing a phenomenal amount of genetically coded information coiled efficiently into the nucleus of every cell of the body. To consider other less obvious examples of spirals in the body, look no further than your hand and notice as you make a fist, the thumb and index finger curl in to form a perfect spiral. Also, the outer ear and the cochlea concealed within the inner ear are spiral shaped. Many, albeit not all, people have spiraling whorl pattern fingerprints. And of particular wonder is the delicate spiraling pattern of the tiny hairs on the crown of a newborn infant's head.

Ancient traditions symbolically ascribed different characteristics to spirals depending on the direction of their movement. The clockwise moving spiral was recognized as having a creative force, while that of the counterclockwise spiral was identified as being destructive. No doubt nature, in its various manifestation of the spiral, influenced this distinction. In the Yogic tradition, which is thousands of years old and continues to be practiced, the clockwise spiral represents breath and spirit. And the yin-yang symbol of energy flow, represented as one within a circle, is a double spiral of cyclic and complementary forces with a seed of the other contained within each to form a balanced and equal relationship.

In primitive dances for healing and incantation, the spiraling or whirling movement were and continue to be performed to awaken a connection with spirit. These dances are intended to induce a state of ecstasy, as the dancer experiences a sense of connection with the mystic center of their being.

The renowned Sufi dancers, the Whirling Dervishes, exemplify this energetic and whirling kind of dance. The purpose of this dance goes far beyond the superficial aspects of being a visually-stimulating performance and tremendous workout for the performer. Rather it a sacred ritual performed to induce a religious trance bringing the dancer closer to God. The clockwise whirl (yang) has an energetically outward moving sensation, while the counterclockwise movement (yin) creates an inward moving feeling of energy flow. The whirling dervish dance offers two insights worthy of consideration, the first being the direction of energy flow, and secondly the spiraling movement itself instills a sense of transcendence to a higher state of consciousness.

There is wisdom to be gained from these dances, as well as from the powerful weather phenomena of tornadoes, hurricanes and typhoons. They both offer a compelling story of how the spiral movement creates a calm at the epicenter of a storm and brings a centering and mystical experience. These phenomena have practical energy flow applications in the CEH treatment for pain, inflammation and other health concerns. This will be addressed in greater detail in the section on methodology in Part VII.

Spirals, besides being identified as one of the sacred geometries of our world and the universe, also define the pattern of the energy flow within body. This principle is applied in the practice of CEH to restore healthy energy flow to the interactive and integrated systems of the body. Its applications engage, activate and direct energy flow as needed.

Earlier, it was mentioned that energy flows in a spiral path through both the meridians and the chakras. This directional flow is significant. For one thing, as energy spirals through the body, it is able to come into more intense contact with the territory covered than if it traveled directly straight through. The spiral energy delivery system provides the most effective and efficient way to accomplish the mission by servicing the greatest amount of territory with the greatest amount of energy distribution during any given energy flow cycle. Upon identifying or detecting a malfunction within the body's energetic dynamic the Cognitive Energy Healing applications act to enable and initiate the necessary healing corrections.

The spiral is of the universe, of the Earth and of all creation. From the cosmic bodies of outer space, to the flora and fauna of Earth, including we humans, there is evidence the universe knows something big about spirals. From the inner core of our being we are indelibly linked to all that is, and the spiral is significantly and magnificently part of this. It is perhaps no small wonder that its energetic application so effectively serves a healing purpose as well.

I remain in awe and grateful for the spark that awakened me to the profound significance of the spiral in its many manifestations, and in particular to its energetic application to promote healing. This awareness grew from a desire to be well again, from my dreams, my readings and travels, my mindful contemplation of nature and the Hubble's magnificent images of the cosmos. For me, the redirected path of my life's journey has shifted from what initially felt like a complete derailment to a joyful pilgrimage on a spiraling pathway of learning and enlightenment.

And should you wish to continue the journey, more inspiring insights about spirals await in the Appendix.

An inspirational thought for a significant other kind of healing, from *Ancient Knowledge and Moderns Science* by Robert J. Gilbert:

In sacred geometry, the artificial split between physics and metaphysics can be healed, and the foundations for a new healing science of the future can be established. http://www.sacred-geometry.com/ancientknowledge.html

On Spirit

Transcending the Material World

I am that I am

(God's response when Moses asked for his name)
- King James version, Exodus 3:14

~~~

> Except for this point, this still point
> There would be no dance,
> And there is only the dance
>
> T. S. Eliot
> *The Love Song of J. Alfred Prufrock*

The interplay of our experiences and perceptions, of our choices, intentions and actions are part of the complex dynamic of who we are, who we aspire to be, and how we choose to be in the world. And within us all, we possess the power to change, to create, to heal, to make a difference, and to know our highest selves in a spiritual way.

The renowned French archaeologist Jean Clottes, through his extensive research into Paleolithic cave paintings, engravings, and stone sculpture, concluded that these art works show evidence of shamanistic beliefs and rituals going back hundreds of thousands of years. He called these early humans *homo spiritualis*, observing that their art demonstrates a level of abstract thinking beyond a purely material existence. The archeological evidence found in these caves from funerary offerings to cave paintings suggests that even these earliest humans were capable of a certain level of spiritual awareness. Apparently, the human capacity for thought, awareness, and introspection has been with us for many thousands of years.

One can only imagine this time when the first cathedrals were not constructed by the hand of man, but were caves sculpted by nature's elements. As part of a spiritual ritual, these early humans entered the mysterious nether world of the cave to create paintings on the cavern walls. Drawing on such archaeological evidence, it is believed that even the creation of these images, mostly of animals, was a spiritually-inspired experience rendering them sacred upon sanctuary walls. One can only imagine these forms illuminated and animated to life by glowing firepit embers and flickering torch light. These paintings were more than mere images; they were emotionally charged with a shared meaning and purpose that enhanced a mystical and spiritual experience.

Today, large portions of the world's peoples have come to know, value and nurture the spiritual aspect of their lives. For some, this is experienced through ritualistic dance, drumming or chanting, while a great many others find spiritual communion through the practice of a particular religious faith. Whether in church, or in nature, through prayer or meditation, in solitude or in community, many among us have experienced spiritual transcendence. Some would describe this as a connection with the "I am" of the Divine, that aspect of the sacred which resides both within and beyond. Others may know this as a sense of elation or a connection with their highest selves when experiencing the beauty of a musical piece or an ocean sunrise, the love and joy of a newborn child, or the cleansing breath of fresh mountain air. For those who have known such moments, you may have experienced the sense of having your breath taken away, caught in a moment of transcendence between breaths: ever so real, and yet beyond words.

In an attempt to address this link between ritual and the spiritual, let's look once again to the sacred and ritualistic dance of whirling dervishes. How is it that the spiraling movement of the dance heightens the dancer's spiritual connection? In referring to T.S. Eliot's poem, I propose that perhaps the vortex of the dance creates an inner "still point," a place of calm at the dancer's physical center, a place where body, mind and spirit come together as one in a sensation of spiritual ecstasy. This movement also reminds us of the powerful forces of nature during a hurricane where a calm is created at the center of the storm. Perhaps the power of the vortex to create stillness at its center works in a similar way.

For Cognitive Energy Healing, the pathway to healing is founded in the belief that *Love is the key*, love being the symbolic key that opens the portal to our sacred and highest selves. This is not a stagnant kind of love, but rather one that requires a compassionate intension for the well-being and wellness of oneself and others. Such unconditional love opens the energetic pathway to the cognitive mind while aligning it with an infinite source of healing energy. And as illness, pain and suffering melt away, we can come to know BMS wellness and experience the calm at the center of our being, this place called "... the still point", so then we too can know at the highest state of our being "... there is only the dance."

PART III

The Dynamics of Change

Understanding Change

Change is an inevitable part of the human experience. Core beliefs, religious beliefs, mores, values and vested interests, all play a role in how a particular change is perceived. Whether experienced individually, societally, culturally, or institutionally, the way we perceive and respond to change influences our experience of the world. Conscious efforts to embrace change while respecting both individual and societal preferences can be a delicate balancing act of complex variables and associated challenges. And, whether seen as friend or foe, reactions to change can be strong on either side of the argument.

Within the context of this work, change will be discussed from two radically different perspectives as they relate to the practice of Cognitive Energy Healing. Initially, we will explore the dynamics of change within a societal context to gain some insights as to how these may relate to the introduction a new energy healing practice. Then under a more finely tuned lens, we will shift our focus to look at change as it relates to the health and well-being of the individual CEH client. This perspective will look at concerns arising from harmful behaviors, attitudes and beliefs and how certain CEH applications can address these to enable beneficial change and healing.

Enabling Change, a Perceptual Shift

The most difficult subjects can be explained to the most slow-witted man if he has not formed any idea of them already; but the simplest thing cannot be made clear to the most intelligent man if he is firmly persuaded that he knows already, without a shadow of a doubt, what is laid before him.

LEO TOLSTOY

All truth goes through three stages.
First it is ridiculed.
Then it is violently opposed.
Finally, it is accepted as self-evident.

SCHOPENHAUER

Dreams, both conscious and sleeping, help us visualize our goals and desires, and can often set us on a path to achieve them. Conscious dreams, those experienced in our waking hours, can motivate us to think and explore beyond what is, to imagine what could be. As our thoughts, dreams and discoveries act as the seeds of change, they help define the way forward and frequently improve the quality of our lives.

Change is an essential and ongoing aspect of life. From our earliest beginnings, we have been spurred on to explore beyond our known world and to follow our dreams of what could be. Humanity's natural determination to know and understand ourselves, our world and our place in it has shaped our past and present, as in this moment it is actively working to shape our future.

For countless generations people have chosen to venture into the unknown territories of this planet and outward into the vast regions of the universe. Our passion for exploration has also drawn us inward to discover and learn about the functions and processes of nanoparticles, molecules and cells, as well the inner workings of the brain. These natural human tendencies for discovery and invention continue to shape our understanding, perception and experience of the world. And as new truths are discovered, attitudes, beliefs, and ways of being in the world evolve to align themselves with this ever-changing reality. Worthy of consideration in this process is the significant and persistent tendency to resist change driven by our established norms and beliefs.

Both the Russian novelist Leo Tolstoy, and Albert Schopenhauer, the German philosopher, were all too well aware that new ideas, and new ways of doing things such as those proposed by CEH almost always encounter varying degrees of resistance. It is human nature to prefer the comfort and security of the status quo over some unfamiliar way of doing things. And yet, with new knowledge and the time being ripe for change, new truths and models for understanding the world are eventually adopted to help shape and potentially improve the pathway going forward. So, while a degree of resistance to change can and often does have value, let's now venture a look at some of the cultural and social aspects of living in our ever-changing world, and how these might influence the acceptance of a new healing modality such as Cognitive Energy Healing.

Generally, people are well served by the societal forces acting to protect the individual and the greater good. And even beyond the comfort of the familiar, promoting and maintaining the status quo does impose a measure of caution to protect society and its institutions from rashly accepting poorly planned and ill-fated change. At first glance, it may appear easier to circumvent change all together in order to prevent rocking the proverbial boat. Fortunately for the advancement of humankind, this approach would be anathema to our natural and innate drive to explore, discover and learn about ourselves, the world and the universe. And while advances in knowledge and understanding do engender change, entrenched resistance often results in creating a time lag before it becomes accepted and established as the new reality.

To better understand the dynamics of change and how they play out in the real world, let's see what can be gleaned from the following real-life experiences of change. This is a frequently cited story of how the process of change played out in a significant event in history.

Up until the mid-sixteenth century, both Church and State believed Earth to be the center of the universe, and any thoughts to the contrary would have been considered heretical, unlawful and downright preposterous. Then came the day when the Polish astronomer Copernicus did just that. And to further aggravate the situation, his findings were later confirmed by the Italian astronomer Galileo, who consequently found himself arrested for heresy. Though Church and State vehemently resisted accepting their findings, they eventually had to give way to the sound evidence that placed the Sun at the center of our galaxy. Unquestionably, this was a dramatic game changer for the institutions of the period, as when you change the game, you change the rules of how it is to be played as well.

To further explore this concept of change from today's perspective, let's look to the need for change on a global scale to protect the environmental well-being of our planet. No one country, group, or individual can claim innocence for actions that continue to negatively impact our planet. Many of us are just now opening our eyes to such urgent and pressing concerns, having for too long perceived Earth's resources as limitless and ours to use as we see fit. Awareness is growing that we all bear the custodial responsibility of taking care of our environment and its limited resources. This shift to recognize our interdependent relationship with our planet has brought about significant efforts to preserve and protect our home planet.

A significant advocate in this story of change, James Lovelock, a scientist, naturalist, and author, has spent a lifetime addressing such concerns by rallying significant support and awareness for Earth's well-being. Lovelock's Gaia hypothesis was first formulated back in the 1960s, and served to promote a change in our understanding of our individual and global responsibilities as residents of our challenged and suffering planet. The Gaia hypothesis described his vision of our planet as an interconnected, dynamic, and living organism. He achieved this by conferring Earth with a new name: he called it Gaia, the name of a Greek goddess. Through this simple and purpose driven act Lovelock sounded a wakeup call, garnering attention on a global scale.

So, what's is it about this name Gaia and the renaming our planet that caught our attention? The act of giving Earth the name of a vital being and the particular name choice itself, the name of a Greek deity, worked amazingly to ascribe Earth with both living organism and sacred characteristics. This exemplifies the power of myth, as Joseph Campbell has so eloquently addressed in his works on the subject. Humanity understands and relates to our created narrative as it brings order and understanding to our lives. And in this case, the name Gaia carries within it the power to shift our perception of Earth as a place existing purely to serve our needs, to that of a sacred living organism deserving of respect and nurturing. So, what's in a name? Well, Gaia for one, has struck a global and empathetic chord.

And yet, further to this story, it is worth noting that it was not Lovelock himself who first conceived of the idea of Earth as a "living organism." Rather this concept dates back at least to Alexander von Humboldt, a renowned Prussian naturalist, who first presented this concept back in the early 19th century. While Humboldt's bold new vision of Earth was recognized as significant by the scientists and academics of his time, it did not rally the troops to action as the Gaia hypothesis has. Perhaps the difference is that Earth was not as challenged then as it is today.

As regards the dynamics of change, what then are we to conclude from the stories of Copernicus and Galileo, and Humboldt and Lovelock? We can recognize that change is a process, as it takes its own time to overcome any number of challenges before becoming entrenched as the new reality. Also, the push for change frequently has to wait quietly in the wings only to resurface when the need for it and the time are right.

This brings us now to consider the concept of change as it will impact the establishment of CEH as an accepted healing practice. My hope in this venture is twofold: that many unresolved health issues will be addressed effectively by this modality and secondly, that it will come to be accepted increasingly as an authentic and reliable healing practice.

Perhaps eventually, even Western medicine will come to incorporate at least some aspects of energetic holistic health into its practice.

These stories illustrate how new knowledge can initiate change in our assumptions about ourselves, the world, and our place in it. Admittedly, it takes time to spread the word and deal with resistance to change on all its personal, societal, cultural and institutional levels. While the seeds of change are being planted all the time, only those that come to be accepted as viable, take root and potentially flourish. The promise of energy healing is just such a seed, and I am encouraged as signs of this new way of perceiving and addressing health concerns are taking root today even within the practice of Western medicine.

Significant inroads in this regard are being made today. Such practitioners as Siddhartha Mukherjee, a physician, spoke to this in his TED Talk presentation on October 7, 2015 as he addressed the current need for a perceptual shift in the practice of medicine. He argued that change is not only coming, it is happening now and it promises to transform the way we heal. He noted that as antibiotics are losing their effectiveness to kill bacteria, physicians are becoming increasingly aware that new approaches are needed. Mukherjee added that it is now recognized that depression is best treated not by medication alone but combined with talk therapy. And that physicians now recognize that immunotherapy at the cellular and genome level is the new frontier for cancer treatment. He then ventured to add that environmental factors should be included in the creation of this evolving new model of medicine. One can only hope that in addition to this recognition of the influence of environmental factors, that significant attention will also be given to the influence of emotional factors, as well.

Relating directly to this is the growing area of research known as epigenetics, the study of how experience and environmental factors can shape genetic expression by determining which genes are turned on and the regulation of their on/off sequencing. Ultimately, healthy gene expression is essential to wellness. And while epigenetically-caused changes can be positive, certain long-term exposures to harmful environmental and emotional factors can lead to disease and dysfunction. Also, it is important to note that epigenetically caused changes can be heritable. This is to say for example, that the emotional and environmental trauma of a famine can negatively alter gene expression not only for the affected population but for generations to come.

We can only hope that someday there will be a more holistic medical standard that includes an awareness and understanding of emotional and environmental factors on wellness. Until recently, the areas of energy and shamanic healing have been the only practices honoring these realities of the human experience. It has been my experience in the practice of Cognitive Energy Healing that these factors play a primary role as the underlying cause for a number of our health and healing concerns.

Initiating Personal Change

In shifting our focus from the larger arena of societal concerns, we now look to addressing the concerns of the individual CEH client who needs help to change harmful behaviors, attitudes and beliefs. Once the practitioner identifies the causative forces driving such concerns, the relevant modalities are applied to release these harmful concerns, replacing them with healthy options that are consistent with the client's current beliefs and values.

From birth to about the age of six, our core beliefs are established and registered in our subconscious mind. These beliefs form the foundational code of who we are, and how we are to live our lives. This spectrum of acceptable behaviors, attitudes, and values is usually learned from parents, family, and community. And not surprisingly, behaviors and beliefs falling outside this established framework are viewed skeptically as being unacceptable, wrong- minded, ineffectual, or even harmful.

Certain core beliefs can be limiting and potentially even harmful. As adolescents and young adults become increasingly engaged in the outside world, they come to form their own beliefs, values, and attitudes. When these are out of alignment with the core beliefs acquired in early childhood, they can cause internal conflict and turmoil, and they can be limiting by acting as stumbling blocks to achieving personal goals. Besides preventing a person from being true to themselves and their aspirations, the resulting stress and frustration can notably impact a person's physical and emotional health. To address this concern, CEH offers a Release and Reclaim protocol that can, in most cases, effectively identify and release limiting and harmful beliefs, while replacing them with healthy ones that are in alignment with a person's current belief system. Naturally, all of this can only be achieved with the client's collaboration and consent.

Whether on their own, or with professional help, some people come to an awareness that some of their core beliefs are working against their well-being and preventing them from realizing their full potential. The subconscious mind, the enforcer of core beliefs, is believed to hold as much as 95%, or the lion's share of control over how we are in the world. This leaves the conscious mind with only a flailing 5% of a voice on any relevant matter. Even with a strong, persistent and determined personal effort, lasting change is very difficult to achieve on one's own. In confrontations between the elephant and the mouse, the mouse rarely wins on its own, but rest assured there are ways and help of some kind is usually available.

One of the significant factors influencing well-being includes any of the range of insecurities instilled in early childhood. These can manifest in adulthood as low self-esteem and low self-confidence, resulting in such debilitating behaviors as timidity, second guessing oneself, being indecisive, and lacking the courage to stand up for what you want and what you believe in. Such behaviors can be very stressful, demobilizing and even debilitating. They can essentially close the door to career choices requiring decisive and confident decision-making.

Insecurities stemming from childhood can impact work performance, relationships, the management of personal and financial responsibilities, to name a few, and any stressors associated with these can directly impact a person's physical and emotional health. Harmful core beliefs can be addressed in a safe and beneficial way with the help of the CEH Release and Reclaim Modality. The methodology for this practice is presented in Part VII.

As parents, teachers, coaches, and counsellors, we all bear the responsibility of awareness when speaking to children. The impact of negative words directed at a child should never be underrated, as they can have a lasting and harmful effect throughout a lifetime. Positive words and perceptions generally and within reason, tend to have the beneficial effect of being encouraging, empowering and confidence-building. When a frustrated and irritated parent berates a child with such words as, "it's a waste of time to expect anything good to ever come of you," while probably not intended to last beyond the adult's anger of the moment, the impact on the child can potentially inflict lasting and pervasive emotional damage. Words have power ranging from positive to negative, and we all bear the responsibility of intention in how we use them.

This same awareness of the power of words should extend to our personal and work relationships, as well as to how we speak to ourselves. Berating oneself for one thing or another can become a harmful and debilitating habit. Thoughts of being a failure, not much good at this or that, or calling oneself stupid repeatedly takes its toll on a person's self-concept, and ultimately on their own health. Clearly, a pattern of such negative words directed at anyone else besides yourself would be considered abusive and unacceptable. For some, such behavior can become a habit, and realistically self-abusive habits are difficult to break. Here once again, CEH can offer some possible solutions to correct this behavior.

The CEH Release and Reclaim protocol, sometimes in combination with other healing modalities of the practice, can help release a range of harmful behaviors, beliefs and attitudes. And for those who have experienced these treatments, they frequently describe them as being a tremendously freeing, and self-empowering.

An Invitation to Think Outside the Box

Recognizing that the incorporation of energy medicine into Western medical practices is only in its very early days of development, you are invited to join me as I reflect on my journey to healing and the rather circuitous pathway that eventually led me there. And though my established beliefs about health and wellness were challenged along the way, I now know the decision to find a way to be well again has made all the difference. This determination spurred me on to explore healing options I would never have considered before, such as energy-based healing. Ultimately and ever so gratefully, my less than conventional shift from the physically-based medical modal to address my particular healing concerns has resulted in the creation of Cognitive Energy Healing. The self-healing benefits of the practice on their own have offered me a life of wellness, and a future that would not have been possible otherwise.

It is only natural for each of us to want to live our lives to the fullest, as free as possible from illness and suffering. Realistically, even with all the current advances in Western medicine, certain health concerns, autoimmune diseases among them, continue to remain a challenge often beyond the scope of what they can adequately address. And yet from my experience with CEH, real and sound solutions to a number of such health concerns are accessible and, depending on how far along the disease has progressed, beneficial amounts of healing can still be realized.

For many of us, a medical diagnosis can mean a lifetime of invasive testing, medications, and a variety of therapies to help manage a chronic or degenerative health concern. And frequently, even with all the excellent medical help available, the patient is left with ongoing and unresolved healing needs. While pain management with medication can help a person get through the day, it does not offer a cure for chronic pain nor does it dispel the real concern over its potential side effects. For these reasons among others, a growing number of patients are supplementing their medical treatments with the help of alternative approaches to healing.

First and always, it is recommended that your health concerns be addressed by a medical practitioner, prior to making the move to explore alternative or supplementary options. However, should you at some point find that your needs are not being fully addressed, you may wish to consider supplementing your care with alternative healing methods.

It is always advisable to do some research prior to trying something new. Learn as much as you can about the particular practice you are considering: ask friends what they know about the practice, search websites for descriptions of various practices, and review any testimonials provided. And then ultimately, if your intuition has steered you right in the past, trust it. Our initial gut feelings deliver an important message arising from subliminally perceived and processed information well before input can be analyzed and logically addressed by the conscious mind.

It was only as I became increasingly aware that my health challenges were moving beyond the scope of the medical help I was receiving, that I began my search to find another way. Significant and unrelenting health challenges proved to be a strong motivator. And so began my determined search for a healing practice that might offer some hope. Choosing whom to see from the extensive list of healing practitioners available came to feel like an overwhelming task. Perhaps sharing a bit of my own search for healing will help.

My first foray out to look for help was not so bold. On the advice of a friend I went to see another medical practitioner, one who was practicing a new allergy testing and desensitizing approach modelled somewhat on that of an allergy treatment center in Dallas, Texas. And even though this new practice did not bode with my doctor at that time, I was determined to give it a try.

This allergen testing approach, unlike the conventional skin test method taking only minutes to complete, required weeks of day-long visits involving subcutaneous injections every fifteen minutes to determine my tolerance levels for a seemingly endless list of allergens. This battery of extensive testing determined that I was in allergic reaction to everything I was exposed to during testing with the exception of distilled water, while showing only a minimal reaction to lettuce. However disturbing this information was, it made perfect sense, as it explained why I was in a constant state of pain and experiencing an unrelenting variety of symptoms. And even though the list of identified allergens was extensive, it didn't cover everything I was reacting to, as I would soon learn.

After completing this extensive testing procedure, I was prescribed a case-specific allergen desensitizing serum. This serum was to be self-injected from three to four times a day, the fourth injection being reserved as an emergency back-up shot to be used only as required. During the period that I followed this regime, rarely did I see a day that this last injection wasn't required.

This treatment approach did prove to be superior to anything I had experienced before. However, over time these injections started to lose their effectiveness. This ominous new awareness forced me to realize I needed to act soon to address this concern. Should I continue with the same medical regime and return for yet another program of testing, or should I search for another approach? As if guided, I decided on the latter, and fortuitously within days I bumped into a friend who spoke encouragingly about a new *alternative energy healing* approach that had effectively eliminated a number of her allergies. Encouraged, I decided to give this approach a try. And without a doubt, this move proved to be a significant game changer.

As farfetched as my friend's claims had sounded initially, this naturopathic and energy-based allergy elimination approach helped significantly. The treatments I received did provide some real healing solutions, and my quality of life improved for periods at a time. This approach was far beyond what anyone would have thought possible, and yet here I was getting some real help. This move from conventional medical to an alternative energy healing approach was a huge perceptual shift for me. Going forward this new awareness of energy healing was to make a significant difference in my life.

From my experience of this new-to-me procedure, allergen desensitization required the client to hold a glass vial of water infused with allergen energy while the practitioner applied acupressure to a number of energy points along the meridians of the body. Following this manual stimulation was applied along the spinal column, while the client was guided through a pattern of controlled breaths. Over the next year and a half of usually twice weekly appointments, one by one *a number* of my allergies were successfully eliminated, and my health improved noticeably. However, in my case this *number* was small, as I was allergic to virtually everything, and new allergens were surfacing all the time.

However grateful for the help I was receiving, this approach proved to be a very slow and costly process. Only one allergen could be addressed per visit, with no more than two treatments being possible per week. And while many of the treatments I received proved to be successful, a number of them required multiple repeat treatments before an allergy could be completely eliminated. Added to this, I had a personal and practical concern that this healing method was not readily accessible to protect me when out on my own. I randomly experienced asthma attacks and allergic reactions, anywhere and at any time. I needed something that could quickly and effectively rescue me on the spot wherever I was. I needed a reliable treatment that would hold, preventing me from having a repeat occurrence in the future.

There were brief stretches of time when I was able to manage fairly well, then, out of the blue, a variety of new allergies would randomly appear with some of these being frighteningly severe. It felt like I was running down a road just ahead of a speeding bus, wondering whether I would be able to survive the latest onslaught of reactions. I desperately knew I needed to find another way.

I needed to find a way treat myself quickly and effectively, no matter where I was or how severe the reaction.

With this new awareness came a growing sense that the type of healing I was searching for was soon to be within my reach. With hindsight, it is my belief that this initial introduction to energy healing had set me on a new and vital pathway, the one that has since enabled me to heal myself and others.

The inspiration, the one I believe to be spiritual and sparked my journey toward a new energy healing practice, came while I was seeking relief through meditation on a particularly challenging day. My thoughts had shifted to a kind of prayer as I found myself asking for help, healing help that would enable me to be well again. Not having prayed in such a way since childhood, this was new for me. My request was not for a miracle that would provide an instant cure, rather it was for direction and knowledge of what I needed to do to heal myself.

Surprisingly and for the first time in my life, I finally felt that my words were being heard, as the guidance I needed did come. And as though a veil had been lifted, the knowledge essential to my survival became readily available. From then and to this day, this guiding source continues to be accessible to me as I work to heal and to train others in this practice.

This initial knowing as a one-off experience could be called an epiphany, however, the revelations that continue to provide effective healing information suggest that this is something more. My sense of it is as though a mentor, a very informed guiding and teaching mentor, seeds my thoughts with knowledge that goes beyond intuition. And as mentioned previously, this communication comes through either in the form of thought or through automatic writing. I am not hearing a billowing and all-powerful voice or experiencing some type of visible or audible intervention, rather it is a subtle and quiet kind of knowing. Have I simply awakened an aspect of my subconscious that is a source knowledge far beyond that of my conscious mind? Am I tapping into a universal consciousness, or am I receiving spiritual guidance? All I know for certain, is that this experience is real, and awe inspiring. Never once has it failed to address my need for healing.

After I learned the first healing technique, nothing could have prepared me for what was to follow. Out of the blue one day I was violently stopped in my tracks by an anaphylactic reaction to something I had just eaten. This was the first time I had ever experienced such a severe and life-threatening reaction. Strangely, while this terrible thing was happening to me, I managed to maintain an uncanny sense of calmness while confidently utilizing my newly learned self-healing technique. Amazingly, and with such natural simplicity, it worked! Up until that time, I did not have an EpiPen*, however since that day I carry one as back up just in case. While my treatment method has always worked for me, one can never be too careful when it comes to such matters.

During this severe reaction, I wasn't able to breathe as my throat had swelled and filled with mucous. And yet, it was only seconds following my treatment that my throat relaxed, the mucous started to clear and I was once again able to breathe freely. It had both stopped and corrected a dysfunctional autoimmune response. In this case, the allergen was a type of seafood I had never eaten before.

A treatment requires only seconds to perform and brings an allergic reaction to a halt almost immediately, however the body will require some time to clear the established symptoms. The time it takes for these to completely dissipate depends on the type and severity of the reaction. Let's take the simple example the non-stop sneezing in reaction to pollen. Shortly after the treatment sneezing will stop, then following this any lingering congestion will clear. Naturally, depending on the type of reaction or its severity, it may take somewhat longer for symptoms to fully clear. Nevertheless, the healing process to halt the manifestation of symptoms in all causes is initiated at the moment the treatment is properly completed.

In a clinical setting, the CEH practice is able to proactively heal and eliminate allergies in an effectively and timely manner. During the healing session, there is no specified limit to the number of treatments that can be effectively administered, and each treatment is checked to assure that it has taken successfully.

From the earliest beginnings of my quest to be well again, I could have never imagined that the answer would come in the form of a sacred healing gift. And yet, there it was! This self-healing revelation would never have come to be had I not chosen to break with tradition and step into a new and unfamiliar healing territory. Since that day, this self-healing method has proven effective in halting and eliminating allergic reactions not only as they occur, but as a preventative treatment for identified allergens in a clinical setting.

It is significant to note that the range of what can be treated by this practice has grown far beyond allergy-related concerns. In addition to correcting allergic reactions to external stimuli, this practice has enabled healing to correct autoimmune reactions against the internal body itself as well. CEH can effectively address or noticeably improve such autoimmune and deficiency diseases and disorders as psoriasis, various types of arthritis, and gout, to mention but a few. Also, this modality has helped reduce or eliminate sleep disorders, anxiety, migraines, and phobias. And adding to this range of healing applications, the CEH Release and Reclaim protocol has proven effective in healing concerns caused by emotional and/or physical trauma, while the Body Energy Attunements can in many cases noticeably reduce or eliminate pain and inflammation.

Moving forward, it is my hope to guide you to understand and learn about the healing practice I call Cognitive Energy Healing. And while recognizing that for some this will be a significant leap into unfamiliar territory, let's try to imagine a healing model that offers both noninvasive and pain-free healing. By freeing your mind from entrenched boundaries as to what can be, give yourself permission to explore new healing possibilities never thought possible until now. Then guided by the highest intention for holistic wellness, we venture to consider such challenging healing concerns as cancer, diabetes, dementia, heart and lung disease, as well as other diseases thought to be incurable at this point. The masking, controlling and suppression of symptoms are not to be part of this newly envisioned healing model. Once liberated to think beyond the established models, you are invited to explore the mysteries of the unknown, for it is in this place that new answers and solutions are to be discovered.

Some may ask, should we not wait for scientific validation of these new healing methods before putting them to use to meet our current needs? Historically speaking, any number of healing methods were adopted medically prior to having scientific proof or a clear understanding of how they worked. Early examples of this is the use of alcohol or ether. What doctors knew at that time was that these substances worked to calm and/or anesthetize the patient so an operation could be performed. As this relates to the practice of CEH, currently there is no available scientific explanation of how energy healing works. However, in the interim, I would argue that the healing benefits of the practice should be accessible to those in need of help for their unresolved heath concerns.

We will now move on to explore how the body experiences, responds to, and copes with its physical, energetic, and emotive relationships with the external world.

As a word of caution regarding serious allergies, I do encourage anyone at risk of a serious allergic reaction to carry an EpiPen, as I do. Life is too precious; it is wise to keep all your bases covered.

PART IV

Sensing and Perceiving

The Body's Perceiving Systems

*We shall not cease from exploration
And the end of all our exploring
Will be to arrive where we started
And know the place for the first time*

T. S. Elliot, "Little Giddings"

Everything that is perceived is relevant to our subjective experience for our continued safety, well-being and ability to function in the world. The body's safety and well-being in both its internal and external environments is protected by its sensing/perceiving systems. All perceived information is transmitted directly to the brain where it is received, processed, and acted upon when necessary to initiate an appropriate and case specific response.

Information perceived by our sensory organs and the autonomic nervous system (ANS) is electrochemically carried along the body's nervous system's network of neurons to the brain where it can be acted upon as required. The central nervous system is comprised of the brain and the spinal column, while the peripheral nervous system extends into the body's extremities. Whereas the sensory organs perceive data from the external world of the body, the role of the ANS is to oversee and maintain the smooth functioning of the body's organs including certain muscles, and to respond as directed by the brain when required.

In addition to these medically acknowledged information perceiving systems, and consistent with the energetic model espoused in this writing, I will include the life force energies that make up our vital energy system. This system of subtle energies is comprised of the chakras, meridians and the auric field. Its purpose is to monitor the comprehensive energetic experience of the body and like the other systems mentioned earlier, its job is to communicate perceived information to the brain for processing. As these systems energetically perceive the energy frequencies relevant to body safety and wellness, this information is received and transmitted electrochemically through the peripheral and central nervous system to the brain for processing. This is to say that all perceived information, whether sensory or energetic, is managed by the brain.

Perceiving Energy

Quantum physics has proven that energy is the fundamental component of all that exists. Everything we perceive from the inorganic to the organic, from the nanoparticles in the mitochondria of a human cell to the basic H_2O water molecule, and from ants to elephants, no matter what the configuration, everything is an expression of energy and as such emits its own unique *energy frequency*. This frequency serves a practical purpose in that it an identifying energy signature of whatever it represents. So, as this relates humans in all their diversity, the spectrum of energy signatures lies within a definite and distinct range of frequencies. The same is also true for plants, animals, and ultimately everything that is, in all their diverse manifestations. Amazingly, with every new human birth, a new and distinct energy signature is added to the list of human energy frequencies.

Our energy driven world of televisions, mobile phones, computers, and other electronic devices demonstrates that energy is an extremely efficient and fast way to transmit information. Furthermore, it is important to remember that all these energy systems are physical manifestations conceived of by the human brain, the ultimate receiver and processer of information. Energetic information from thoughts, memories, emotions, beliefs, and traumas, from the internal and external environments of the body is processed and managed energetically by the brain, enabling us to be well and to function as physical and cognitive beings in a complex and ever-changing world.

A Look at How These Systems Work

The Sensory Nervous system: Perceptions from the sensory nervous system enable us to see, hear, touch, taste, smell and maintain control over spatial positioning, movement and balance (the vestibular sense). The vestibular sensory organs are located in the temporal bone in the inner ear near the cochlea. Once the data perceived by these *six* senses is processed by the brain, we are able to have a conscious experience of the external world. Importantly, the sensory system also keeps us apprised of any perceived threat to the body's well-being.

The information perceived by the sense organs is electrochemically transmitted along neuro-pathways to the brain for processing. Should any of this data be identified as a potential threat, the brain immediately calls for a case specific protective response from the body. And as the feed of information from the senses is in our conscious awareness, we can be alerted to take defensive/protective action in such ways as blinking to keep dust out of the eyes, stabilizing one's footing to restore balance, moving quickly to step out of harm's way, pinching the nose to avoid inhaling a foul or harmful odor, covering the ears to protect the ear drum from damage by loud noises, protecting the mouth from hot foods, and calling out for help in the case of a hearing or seeing signs of an emergency situation.

Should a person suddenly find themselves in real danger such as in an attack by an intruder, the brain, while consciously coming up with a strategy to deal with the threat, is also alerting the autonomic nervous system (ANS) to initiate the *fight or flight response*. This response provides an energy boosting infusion of adrenalin into the bloodstream, while temporarily suppressing immune function in order to channel the additional energy required to address the threat at hand.

The ANS is comprised of two main components: the sympathetic and the parasympathetic nervous systems. The parasympathetic system works to maintain the smooth operation of all bodily functions. And while the sympathetic nervous system is also engaged in maintaining the body's homeostasis, its primary function is to initiate the fight or flight response mentioned earlier. The ANS, besides overseeing such involuntary functions as breathing, sleeping, digestion, heart function and perspiration, can also be called upon to trigger such protective reflex responses as blinking, choking, coughing, and sneezing to clear irritants as required.

Upon receiving information of a threat to the body, the brain sends a directive to the autoimmune system to initiate a defensive response against such pathogens as bacteria, viruses, parasites, and antigens including toxins and other harmful agents including allergens. In order to eliminate an invading organism or substance, the autoimmune system sends a defensive army of antibodies comprised of white blood cells, known as lymphocytes. While pathogens include all invading disease-causing microorganisms, an antigen is any foreign substance that is harmful to the body. And in the case of an allergic response, the response is triggered by normally safe external stimuli being mistakenly identified a threat.

The Vital Energy System: While the sensory systems glean information about the world external to the body, and the ANS conveys information about the internal body, the body's vital energy system informs the brain about both environments concurrently. Energy frequencies emitted by anything that exists in the body's vicinity, whether from within or external to it is perceived and transmitted instantaneously to the brain for processing. The vital energy systems serve a perceiving function that can be compared to a type of energy-sensing radar system, one that is relentlessly on duty surveilling our environments to protect our well-being all the days of our lives.

From quantum physics research, we have learned that everything, absolutely everything whether organic or inorganic, liquid, solid or gaseous, from this planet and speculatively the entire universe, has its own unique energy frequency, or energy signature. The body's *vital energy systems* serve to perceive and inform the brain of any perceived threat to the safety and well-being of the body within its internal and external energetic environments.

The energy flow channels of the meridians monitor the central and peripheral areas of the entire internal body as the flow moves from the head to the finger-tips and toes and back again. The chakra system is also a cyclic flow system. It differs from the meridians in that its energy flow is along the spinal column, pooling in seven distinctive areas to nourish the organs, glands and tissues in their respective regions located from the tip of the coccyx to the crown of the head. Notably, the energy pools of the chakras are situated in those areas along the spine where nerves extend out into the body. By contrast to these two systems, the auric field surrounds the external body. Besides releasing harmful energies from the body, it serves as a two-way surveillance system to protect the body by perceiving and responding to the body's energetic environments.

The range for perceiving energetic information varies, however the brain as receiver of this data is most responsive within a perimeter of approximately five feet (just less than a couple of meters). By energetically linking into the body's electrochemical neuron pathways to the brain, these three systems communicate relevant energy information affecting the body's vital energy function.

Perhaps a few stories of energetic information being consciously perceived in everyday life would be of interest at this point:

- *Having received a time sensitive phone message for my husband, I was finally able to locate him down the street talking with a neighbor. As they were looking in the opposite direction, and from my standpoint my options to get his attention were either to call out in the hope of being heard, or to try another less disruptive approach, one that has worked well for me in the past. Choosing the latter, I sent a focused gaze his way, and immediately sensing this "energy message," he turned to make visual contact. Voilà I had his attention.*

It is my belief that we all have this amazing ability to communicate energetically, should we choose to engage it. However, I would add, as with anything, this ability improves with practice and can become a lost skill if not put to use at least once in a while.

- *The sense of knowing something energetically is not an uncommon experience. You may have had the experience of feeling someone's gaze upon you from a distance. A mere look back over your shoulder is the usual confirmation that what you are sensing energetically is real. And should you know that person, the encounter is acknowledged with a smile or a wave, otherwise you are left wondering what that focused attention from a stranger could have been about.*

In addition to the perceiving energetic sense, a person's energetic state of being can be influenced by others, even in a brief and superficial encounter. Generally speaking, most people find social encounters to be a positive and mutually energizing experience. And yet it is not uncommon to personally experience or to hear about a person feeling energetically drained following even the briefest encounter with certain people.

Certain energy draining people are sometimes referred to as energy vampires, as they prey on others to replenish their depleted energy supply. Christian Northrop, in her book *Dodging Energy Vampires*, addresses this topic along with the concern that empaths, caring and helpful people, are particularly vulnerable to their manipulation. Northrop explains that though not usually immediately obvious, energy vampires are aware to a certain degree that they are preying on the energy of others. Fortunately, for most people these types of encounters are not a frequent occurrence, and usually those who are able to pick up on this patterned behavior make a point of avoiding contact as much as possible. Awareness is the first step to protecting yourself if you find yourself being made a target in this way.

Another influence can be a person's negative energetic polarity as it too can influence the energy levels of others. Energetic polarity can be influenced by many factors including hormone balance, attitude, habits, diet, emotional state and stress levels. A scale of this polarity can range from high negative to high positive. Not only is this phenomenon real, but it can temporarily have a negative impact on other people's energy levels, leaving them feeling inexplicably physically and emotionally fatigued, sometimes to the point of exhaustion. When given the choice, people naturally prefer to engage with those who are in the energetically positive range. Further to this, those people who consistently register on the negative side of the scale may be emotionally unwell and in need of some kind of healing help to address the cause of this concern.

- *Many amazing and emotion stirring stories have come out of the hair-raising experiences people have had. Usually such events happen in response to an energetically perceived threat. The following is my own hair-raising story, from a trip to Bhutan, a remote kingdom in the Himalayas. On the night of my arrival, while sleeping in a hotel room with completely open, glassless and screen-less, windows I awakened to the alarming sight of a large insect resting on the wall just a few feet from my bed. In the moonlit room, this creature cast a magnified and menacing shadow as it slowly moved its elongated sensing antennae back and forth to assess its own safety.*

    While still groggy from sleep and before opening my eyes to this sight, I had the hair-raising and unsettling sensation that I was not alone. Frozen in fright and with eyes suddenly wide open, I saw what I now believe to be some kind of large beetle. I wanted to call out for help, but I couldn't find my voice. Meanwhile, my husband who was sleeping in a twin bed across the room from me awakened and asked what was going on. As I had not made a sound, had he perhaps picked up on the sudden energy shift in the room? I pointed speechlessly at the insect, he grumbled

> *something, then less than gallantly signaled for me to move to his bed as he settled fearlessly into mine. My disgruntled hero!*

The experience of hair rising up on various locations on the body, like the back of the neck, is a brain initiated visceral response to an energetically perceived sense of impending danger. This reaction has served humanity over the ages, particularly as an alert system to protect people from attacks by wild animals. Today, this response can happen when a person has a sense they are being stalked, or that some intruder has entered their home. The hair-raising phenomenon is usually experienced prior to an actual encounter with the potential threat and serves to heighten the body's awareness of a threat, as well as to set the fight or flight response at the ready.

We have all witnessed this warning system in cats and dogs. And though less observable, the tiny hairs on the sensing antennae of insects such as butterflies and the one I encountered on my trip also deliver a message of energetically-perceived threats.

The Immune System: While the body's various *intelligence-gathering systems* actively provide feedback about any potential threats from its internal and external environments, the autoimmune "defense" system remains on ready alert for direction from the brain to respond as required. This takes us beyond mere reflex responses such as eyes tearing up to wash away minor environmental irritants and sneezing to keep breathing passages open, as well as such other involuntary responses as gas or indigestion.

The autoimmune system is in the business of sending out antibodies to protect the body by eliminating pathogens and antigens, which, as mentioned earlier, include viruses, bacteria, toxins, and any substance identified as harmful to the body. For example, once perceived, an invasive virus becomes the immediate target of immune antibodies as they act to eliminate the foreign threat as quickly as possible. Besides these concerns, immune responses can also be triggered by exposure to certain energy fields such as magnetic, electrical, nuclear and ultraviolet energy emissions. Elevated exposure to such energies can cause the growth of tumors and certain cancers.

Sometimes, for some people and for whatever reason, a person's immune system can malfunction resulting in a variety of immune diseases. This all begins with an error made by the brain in its role of processing perceived information, and can be likened to a bug or a virus in a computer system. In other words, autoimmune diseases such as allergic reactions are triggered when the brain incorrectly identifies an otherwise harmless substance or material as a threat to the body's well-being. Interestingly and not so unlike an allergic response to external stimuli, the immune system can also be misguidedly sent to attack essential components of the body itself. So, whether in response to stimuli from either the internal or external environments of the body, maladaptive and disease-causing responses come about as a result of a glitch in the brain's information processing system. Fortunately, communication with the cognitive brain through CEH applications has proven effective in correcting many of these concerns.

The complete list of autoimmune diseases is a long one, with at least eighty identified to date. A brief list of some of these diseases includes allergies, asthma, arthritis, eczema, psoriasis, diabetes, multiple sclerosis, lupus, chronic fatigue syndrome, fibromyalgia, scleroderma, Graves' disease, celiac disease, Crohn's disease and even cancer, to name but a few. The CEH practice in its focus on lasting healing, goes beyond the identification of the immediate causes of many of these diseases to include such influencing factors as negative emotions, stress, traumas and harmful environmental exposures.

The following section will explore the Cognitive Energy Healing perspective on perception, pain and the body's efforts to protect itself. This will open the way to addressing how CEH as well as a number of other healing modalities work to determine the causes of illness in a non-invasive way.

PART V

The Cognitive Energy Healing Perspective

On Perception, Pain and Health

The dynamic and interactive nature of the holistic person speaks volumes to just how complex we are. The who and the how of the way we are in the world at any given moment is the result of many contributing factors and goes back even farther than the fetus in the mother's womb, to include ancestral influences as well. On a polarized scale ranging from positive to negative, who and how we are in this, our experience of the moment, our now, is a reflection of a lifetime of experiences, perceptions, emotions, reactions, relationships, our stressors, our successes and our failings, and so much more. Within this complex dynamic, even epigenetic factors can influence a person's experience and perception of the world.

How we are in the world is influenced by so many different factors, including: our core beliefs instilled in early childhood, our sensory perceptions of the world, our emotionally laden social experiences including our memories of these, the challenges of learning new things, adapting to change, and just generally coping and dealing with the ups and downs of everyday living. The human experience can range from ecstasy and joy to misery and severe pain, and a prolonged experience of the negative side of this spectrum can eventually lead to any of a number of health concerns. The sensory experience of pain is delivered as a message from the brain to alert a person to the areas of concern and to get help as required.

The old expression that God will never give you more than you can handle is nothing more than a placating fallacy. Realistically, certain of life's challenges can truly be unbearable and insurmountable. Fortunately, at least for some, there is help. The kind of assistance I'm talking about does not involve medication or years of therapy, as I have personally experienced both in working with my own concerns as well as those of others. My message is that Cognitive Energy Healing does have some real solutions to a number of unresolved health concerns. And these can significantly improve person's quality of life in a timely fashion, oftentimes within just one treatment session.

The Pain Response as Processed and Delivered by the Brain

Protection of the holistic body requires that everything perceived in its internal and external environments, including what we eat, breathe in, hear, touch, observe and experience physically, emotionally and energetically be processed by the brain. Naturally, this requires that due attention be given to such health concerns as emotional and physical injury and trauma, malfunction, and illness. Besides processing all pertinent perceived information related to the body, the brain in its executive function also delivers the call for action to address any possible threat to the body's health and well-being. Both the autonomic nervous system and the autoimmune system stand at the ready to respond to the brain's directives to protect and defend the body.

A Healing Gift

The brain receives and interprets sensory information about an injury to any part of the holistic body. It then determines the intensity and duration of the pain response within a polarized scale ranging from pleasurable to painful. Pain is more than a hurting sensation; its intensity and duration usually indicate just how serious the concern is, though there are exceptions which will be discussed later. In a clinical setting when a client/patient is asked to describe their level of pain, the usual approach is to place it on a scale from one to ten, with one being just barely noticeable and ten being unbearable.

Besides describing pain as it relates to its intensity, it can also be described as acute or chronic, and primary or secondary. Acute pain is experienced while healing is taking place, whereas chronic pain can occur once healing is complete. The experience of chronic pain is a condition that can be continuous or intermittent and is usually easily provoked. Primary pain is the pain experienced at the site of the injury, while secondary pain can occur elsewhere in the body as a result of its attempt to cope with the primary injury. An example of this would be a back injury eventually leading to inflammation in the hip or the knee joint.

To explore the concept of pain a bit further, some experiences of pain can be transient as when you stub your toe on the sidewalk, while pain arising from exercise can be sporadic. Emotional pain does share some similarities with physical pain in that it can be fleeting or influenced by past experiences. It can also manifest as physical pain at any number of locations within the body. Ultimately however, severe persistent emotional or physical pain delivers a commanding message to pay attention and get help.

Beyond mere irritants which are unpleasant, personal preferences for such things as the type of music or how loudly it is played (soft vs loud, classical vs rock), food options available (vegetables vs meat, peas vs lima beans), and types of behaviors (eating quietly vs crunching audibly) etc., can lead to painful experiences for some. Within the pain/pleasure range of experience, we can breathe in the scent of the rose, turn down loud music, avoid touching the flame, tread cautiously near the edge of a precipice, enjoy the sound of the surf, and choose to seek help for persistent or severe pain.

Pain is a subjective experience. Some people have a lower pain tolerance than others, and consequently feel pain more intensely. Also, certain people may experience a disproportionally severe pain in response to a notably minor injury. Possible reasons for this response could be that a previous injury remains hypersensitive because it has not fully healed, or a *default trauma response* is triggered by a residual neuronal memory of an earlier trauma. This is to say that under these circumstances, no matter how minimal the current injury to an area may be, the brain will always interpret it as serious and initiate a full-on trauma-level response. Further insight into this concern can be found in the case studies in Part VII.

Physical and Emotional Injury: Besides the experience of injury caused by physical or emotional trauma, pain can also be caused by certain types of mind/body malfunction, and illness. The brain, as the body's information processor, delivers the site-specific pain message to the consciously mind. And while an awareness of a mild pain gets a person's attention, a severe or persistent pain is a call for help. Clearly, a pain from a stitch in the side while running delivers a very different message than that of a broken bone. While one is probably transient, the other demands attention.

Our emotional experiences of stress and trauma are real and are not to be dismissed as insignificant. Negative emotions and trauma function as an integral part of the holistic body and as such influence its health and well-being. Neurological studies have indicated that long-term exposure to emotional stress can result in permanent brain damage and can also be the cause of certain cancers. Even our negatively-laden emotional memories reside seemingly dormant in the sub-conscious mind, and as such though out of mind still have an impact on the mind/body continuum. Also, such memories can be sparked to life by our day to day experiences or may inadvertently surface in disturbing and/or recurring dreams. So, while the conscious mind may be convinced that all is well, it can be unexpectedly jolted out of this illusion to the awareness that certain unresolved issues and concerns have yet to be addressed.

Memories of past experiences, both good and unpleasant ones, can easily be brought to mind by everyday experiences. The pleasurable scent of lilacs may bring back memories of a visit to a grandparent's home, a musical piece may awaken memories of a special evening shared with a friend, and a taste of lobster may rekindle happy childhood memories at the family cottage. Real life also includes a significant number of unpleasant experiences as well, including such things as the loss of a loved one, financial concerns, suffering from illness, or any of a long list of possible traumatic experiences such as loss of a loved one, neglect, abuse, war and famine, etc.

Unresolved negative memories live on seemingly dormant in the subconscious mind, covertly exercising their own kind of harmful impact on a person's health. It is significant to point out that the effect of living with a number of unresolved negative memories is like carrying weighty stones in a backpack, as they act cumulatively to take a toll and can eventually become "knee buckling"! And when their impact becomes too much to bear, help beyond one's own resources is often required.

While many among us are able to comfortably live with the full scope of our memories and associated emotions, others, for any number of reasons, find themselves overwhelmed, frustrated and unable to cope. Feeling powerless to address certain concerns is often dealt with by avoidance or denial. Meanwhile, left to unconsciously fester in the subconscious, their residual impact manifests in illness and/or pain. On the up side, the CEH Release and Reclaim Protocol, performed during a Centering Attunement, can be very effective in addressing such concerns by releasing the harmful impact of memories and their associated negative emotions. With treatment, while the memory itself remains intact, its power to harm or to cause pain is released.

Whatever is perceived by the senses can impact the holistic body in real and significant ways. To help put this in perspective, let's consider all that the eyes can see and the ears can hear. This includes all that is visually perceived through personal experience, witnessed from a distance, and observed through such things as literature and the media. In the case of witnessing a traumatic accident, though perceived on a conscious level, the subconscious mind is alerted, potentially leading it to protectively set up energy blockages to conscious memory. It is also significant to note what the eyes perceive, and the mind processes can impact the body physically, energetically and/or emotionally. In other words, our senses communicate perceived information and stimulate the necessary responses to protect the holistic wellness and safety of the body.

Research by Laura Redwine of the University of California has found significant links between attitude and physical well-being. Indications are that attitude has a notable impact on such things as heart health, the level of pain experienced by the body, one's ability to sleep, and brain function. And interestingly, Redwine's research team has also found that a life practice of daily gratitude significantly reduced levels of C-reactive protein and other markers of inflammation.

In addition to the body's sensory awareness of the external world, it is also finely attuned to the state of its various internal systems including its glands, organs, bones, internal fluids, enzymes and hormonal secretions, etc. Imbalances and malfunctions within the body are usually accompanied by some type of perceivable symptom such as pain, discomfort, malfunction or other irregularity in body function.

The Cognitive Energy Healing practice recognizes that attitudes and emotions influence our well-being. For this reason, emotion is an integral part of this healing practice as it is indelibly linked to the holistic experience of the body.

Autoimmune Diseases: The body's sensory and autonomic nervous systems are responsible for perceiving the body's safety in both its internal and external environments. For whatever reason, should the brain's processing of this information be erroneous, the autoimmune system will be wrongly directed to attack the body's own tissues as a foreign pathogen. This misguided immune attack on the body's own tissues can result in painful disorders and diseases, a number of these being serious and even life threatening. There are over eighty autoimmune diseases identified including asthma, allergies, rheumatoid arthritis, psoriasis, celiac disease, type 1 diabetes, Hashimoto's thyroiditis, lupus, scleroderma, multiple sclerosis and the list goes on.

Looking first to the body's relationship to its external environment, the following is an overview of potential allergen sources. These include anything we eat (food and drink) or inhale (scents, fumes, airborne substances such as dust and pollens); viral, bacterial, microbial and parasitic infectants; anything that is injected subcutaneously such as drugs, vaccines, insect bites and stings; any materials or substances that the skin comes in contact with; and anything in the body's external environmental range of energy perception (radiant/electromagnetic, magnetic, electric, nuclear, heat, chemical and solar light energy, ultraviolet light energy and all energy frequencies emitted by organic and non-organic materials and substances).

As I understand it, allergic reactions and autoimmune diseases in general occur when the brain misinterprets sensory, autonomic nervous or vital system information. To gain some insight into the perception side of this operation, let's visit an outdoor picnic experience to get an idea of what the readily alert and energetically misinformed immune system might be called on to address as a potential threat.

In the case of the allergic person, their energy sensing system will be hyper-vigilant, actively scanning for any potentially harmful energies in the body's external environment, and this list is seemingly endless. Readings could include the soil underfoot, the creatures in and on the soil, the grass, plants, scents, hydrocarbon fumes, smoke and molds, insect bites, etc. In addition to these potential antigens, the body will be energetically aware of everything worn that day including such things as the fabric of the jeans, any detergent residue left in them, the chemical dye that gives the jeans their signature color, a copper penny left in a pocket, and even the tannins in the leather sandals. Beyond this and when within range, it also energetically perceives the plastic of cups, plates and utensils, including any food that the person eats or comes in contact with. And this is just a superficial list of possibilities.

Should no threat be perceived from any of these energies, the body's defense system remains at ease. However, as soon as a threat from any of this myriad of potential allergens is detected, the brain processes this information and acts immediately to send an electrochemical message to the immune system, whose job it is to respond defensively, in an allergen-specific way. This is to say the response to something ingested is different from the response to a mosquito bite and so on. And the severity of the response could be anywhere from mild to life threatening.

So, now looking to autoimmune diseases internal to the body, an autoimmune attack is triggered when the brain incorrectly identifies some component within the body as a foreign or invading threat to its well-being. And as with allergic reactions, this experience can be both painful, and even life-threatening. From my perspective, I see this misguided autoimmune response as similar to an allergic reaction, with the main difference being that the enemy, the antigen, is something internal to the body rather than external to it. And essentially not so unlike the outdoor picnic story where the scanning process for potential threats takes place outside the body, the scanning process in this case takes place internally. The brain upon receiving and processing the data in both cases and as required, issues the order to initiate autoimmune defensive attack. Internally, as the body is a world of complexity unto itself, the number of organs, tissues and secretions that could be wrongly identified as a threat and potentially attacked by the immune system is infinitesimal.

As regards all autoimmune responses, CEH directives to the brain have proven effective in making corrections to maladaptive immune system behaviors. While reactions to antigens can be halted, the body may be unable to restore or regenerate tissues that have been destroyed under autoimmune attack. Treatment applications may still be beneficial in stopping further damage from taking place. In addition to this and in many cases, the body does have unto itself an arsenal of resources to heal and regenerate certain autoimmune damaged tissues once the misguided attack has been halted following treatment.

Epigenetic factors: Genes carry in their DNA the information of how the BMS is to *act,* and it takes generations for alterations to occur in their sequencing makeup. Epigenetic influencing factors from the natural and social environment of a person can generate changes to how genetic information is expressed or acted on. These changes take place during a lifetime, and while some can be beneficial, some are harmful. And once established, these changes also can be heritable.

Beyond the usual causes of pain such as injury, viruses and microbes, certain epigenetic changes to gene function can make a person physically and/or emotionally unwell. A number of epigenetically linked diseases have been identified, including certain types of cancer, obesity, heart disease, autism and a number of syndromes. Some epigenetic factors that can negatively influence gene behavior include such things as famine, nutrient deficiencies, emotional and/or physical abuse, genocide, or the lack of adequate food and shelter. In other words, epigenetically-linked health concerns arise as a result of long term exposure to physical and/or emotional trauma, causing alterations to normal gene expression.

And while epigenetic changes do not alter the genes themselves and the information they carry, these do alter their behavior and their sequencing. A gene's normal expression may become inappropriately switched off or stuck in the on position. In other words, an epigenetic change to a gene can result in it losing its normal *on/off* sequencing, causing it to remain *on* when it should turn *off* or vice versa. For example, a gene may lose the ability to stop producing a certain hormone, leading to a harmful overproduction or it may be unable to turn on the production of an essential hormone. Such epigenetically related concerns can significantly have a negative impact on body health. Cognitive Energy Healing can in certain cases identify the original cause of the epigenetic concern, release its negative impact and direct the brain to restore normal gene behavior.

Whenever the brain is made aware that it can make a beneficial correction to gene expression, it is proactive to initiate the necessary change.

As we now find ourselves at a significant turning point, we will move on to address the following question: With all the physical, emotional, energetic and epigenetic factors involved in determining the root causes of health concerns, how does the CEH practice manage to access the diagnostic information essential to healing? The answers lie in the range of investigative and diagnostic methods employed by this modality.

Finding a Diagnostic Tool

For some, it will come as a surprise to learn that a diagnostic tool, or rather technique already exists and has been in practice since it was first discovered in the mid-1960s. Others may already be familiar with the practice known as *Muscle Testing or Energy Testing*, a biofeedback technique that enables an assessment of the mind/body interface in response to stimuli to determine which of these pose a threat to the body.

Muscle Testing, a branch of applied kinesiology, is an existing and effective practice that has been in use for several decades. Dr. George Goodheart, first discovered this technique in his chiropractic research practice back in 1964. His findings revealed that the body's muscles exhibit a strong response when exposed to safe physical stimuli, while a weak muscle response was triggered by contact with harmful physical stimuli.

By the 1970s, Dr. John Diamond was working to expand on Goodheart's findings when he discovered that Muscle Testing for cognitive and psychological influences showed responses similar to those provided by physical stimuli. He called this new discipline *behavioral kinesiology*. To further clarify this approach, Diamond learned that the body exhibits the same weak/strong muscle response to thoughts or emotions as it does to such physical things as food or materials. His research showed that subjects exposed to positive or negative thoughts or emotions, as experienced either verbally or through gestures, exhibited the same relative strong or weak response to safe or harmful stimuli.

As we don't all respond to our internal or external environments and experiences in the same way, MT (Muscle Test/Testing) continued to be recognized as a tremendous resource to determine an individual's personal responses when exposed to a selection of physical, chemical, thought, and emotional stimuli. MT has proven to be a particularly effective approach in detecting allergens (the food, substance, or energy causing an allergic reaction), for identifying other autoimmune concerns, as well as the root causes of physical and emotional pain.

Ultimately, the MT technique provides the body with an effective method of communicating a broad spectrum of information about itself by identifying not only what is happening to negatively impact wellness, but also the underlying causes of the problem.

The MT diagnostic technique is currently used by chiropractors, naturopathic doctors and other healing practitioners as well as some medical practitioners. This approach is a painless, non-invasive way to determine the root cause of the body's healing concerns and serves as one of the primary investigative methods employed by the CEH practice.

A brief description of this practice is presented below, while a more detailed explanation of the CEH muscle testing application will follow in Part VI.

Muscle Testing: This technique identifies a person's reaction to safe and threatening stimuli. A strong muscle response indicates the stimuli is safe, whereas a weak response indicates the body perceives it as a threat. (The person being tested will be referred to as the client.)

Procedure: The tester has the client extend their arm out at shoulder level and is asked to hold firm. The tester, with their hand resting on the client's forearm and wrist over the client's wrist, applies a light downward pressure. The client should test strong for this, with their remaining arm firmly in place. Next, the client is exposed to a particular stimulus, let's say the word apple*. Should they be allergic to apples, their arm muscles will weaken and drop uncontrollably in response to the threatening stimulus. Should this person be allergen free apples, the mild pressure applied by the tester should not be sufficient to push this person's arm down.

* *Certain modalities use an energy vial approach that contains the energy of the stimulus, while CEH employs only its word name.*

For those not familiar with MT, this technique provides a readily accessible way to gain information about health-related concerns affecting a person's health and well-being. The weak/strong muscle response supplies both readable and reliable biofeedback about anything that is perceived as a threat by the body.

The CEH approach offers an enhanced version of the application described above. Rather than testing by exposing the client to stimuli perceived by the senses, this modality employs cognitive and energetic-initiating stimuli as delivered through the subliminally communicated thought of the practitioner. By enabling access to the body's response to its holistic experience, this approach significantly increases the spectrum of what can be investigated in the search for root causes of health concerns.

Besides responses to the physical, chemical and energetic world, testing areas also include responses to emotive, social and personal experiences. While guided by a focused investigative MT protocol, the practitioner is able to seek out and identify the root cause(s) of a significant number of body/mind health concerns. Information gathered in this way provides the basis for the case specific CEH treatment modality.

Wherever possible, the ultimate goal of Cognitive Energy Healing is to enable lasting healing by addressing factors negatively impacting the client's overall health. Should these include matters of a private concern, healing can be enabled by identifying and releasing the associated negative emotions. This does not eliminate the memory of this experience, rather it releases and takes away its negative power to cause physical and emotional pain and illness. Should the client be unable to recall a traumatic concern because it has been suppressed by the subconscious, all that is required to identify it is to determine by MT when it occurred. Further to this, regarding matters of client confidentiality, all CEH practitioners are bound by an oath of client confidentiality and this is taken seriously.

The following section will provide a detailed explanation of the Cognitive Energy Healing approach to the practical application of Muscle Testing.

PART VI

Muscle Testing, A Diagnostic Application

Word Power and the Power of The Word Meaning, Intention and Perception

"Words have energy and power with the ability to help, to heal, to hinder, to hurt, to harm, to humiliate, and to humble." -Yehuda Berg

"Your words have power. Speak words that are kind, loving, positive, uplifting, encouraging, and life-giving." -Unknown

Words communicate our perceptions, feelings, thoughts and ideas. Their message is delivered through speech, writing, sign language and gesture, thought and subliminal thought communication. In order to avoid interference from the conscious mind and to obtain objective responses during muscle testing, Cognitive Energy Healing uses subliminal thought communication with the subconscious mind.

Irrespective of the method of delivery, word communication is processed by the cognitive brain/mind located in the frontal lobe area. This is the site of higher cognitive function that enables us to solve problems, understand and formulate our thoughts and ideas, as well as to receive, interpret, and understand verbal communication in a meaningful way.

Words identify objects, materials, substances, places, plants, animals and people. Action words describe what is happening; descriptive words elaborate on the particular qualities of a thing; and demonstrative words indicate such things as distance and time. Prepositions and articles expand on what is being stated, while conjunctions connect related thoughts and ideas. Though some languages have variation in their application, these parts of speech comprise the basic components of the more than five hundred languages of the world.

From the quantum perspective, energy is the foundation of existence. And as words are energetically-charged with meaning and intention, their power can vary dramatically depending on how they are delivered and how they are perceived. The power of the signature meaning of a word can be intensified based on its intention, how it is delivered, and its ultimate impact is determined by the subjective perception of the person receiving the message.

Perception of a communication can vary greatly from person to person for any number of reasons. Some factors that can influence one's perception include stress, past experiences, core beliefs, habitual behavior, attitude and sensitivity. And naturally, the nature of a person's perception influences their reaction or response. While a negative comment may spoil one person's day, this may not even register as a blip for someone else - the effect being "like water off a duck's back." Even the salutation "have a nice day," may be received with a smile by one person or a grumble by another.

Depending on the meaning, intention, delivery, and perception of words, their potential impact ranges on an emotive polarity scale from creative to destructive, kind to distressing, engaging to oblivious, sensible to absurd, gentle to abrupt, calm to anxious, patient to frustrating, playful to serious, and so on. Our words can bring tears of sadness or of joy, they can carry love and appreciation or anger and hate, be enriching and encouraging or menacing and even frightening. And as words have the power to influence our experience of life with the potential to have a significant and lasting impact, it is wise to remind ourselves from time to time that we all bear the responsibility of using them wisely. Words can be helpful or harmful, and how we choose to use them impacts both ourselves and a broad spectrum of others.

Let's take for example the word *fire*, which carries the meaning of burning or combustion. The essence of this word from this definition is neither positive nor negative. This word carries a positive energy charge when used in reference to the warmth of a campfire; however, its charge becomes negative when referring to a destructive forest fire.

The emotive power of words resides in the way they are delivered. The power of the written word can be intensified in many different ways including font size and boldness, as visually experienced here:

fire.......... *versus*.......... **FIRE!**

While the emotive power of a spoken word is communicated and intensified through the application and modulation of tone, volume, gesture, action and facial expression.

As words have the power to hurt or to heal, being mindful of their intention is essential to the practice of Cognitive Energetic Healing. Also, through MT, the practice can determine the client's personal emotive association with a word. For example, not everyone has a positive association with the word *love*, or a negative association with the word *alone*. The practice employs both spoken and subliminal communication to determine the root causes of health concerns and in the application of its various healing modalities.

At this juncture, I would like to briefly explore another aspect of the power of words, specifically the power of *the Word*. Believer or not, religious and spiritual beliefs form a significant part of the Western cultural fabric, and for this reason I am drawn to consider *the Word* as used in the spiritual/religious context of Judeo-Christian and

Islamic belief in the infinite power of God. On first glance, the MT energetic weak/strong response to any word from the lexicon of possible choices, appears entirely different from the concept of the Word as used in scripture referring to revelation and creation by an omnipotent Divine being, one who is also omniscient of the hearts and minds of all humanity. This scrutiny of the intention behind our words and behaviors by one so powerful as God, Yahweh, Elohim, Allah or other Divine being holds us accountable for all we say, think and do.

Clearly *the Word* within the Divine consciousness, and *the word* as expressed in human communication reside on two very different planes, one spiritual and the other secular. And though these are separate realities, my understanding is that they come together as one in the holistic body, mind, spirit experience of each of us in our responsibility for an awareness of the intention behind our thoughts and actions. In other words, both within and outside of religious doctrine, we are spiritual and secular beings charged with the responsibility of the intention to do good for both self and other.

This attempt to address these two seemingly disparate concepts is intended *to focus our attention on intention*, specifically those on the positive side of the spectrum. Compassionate love of self and other, and a mindful intention for good is essential to the practice of CEH, as therein lies the source of healing energy.

I would be remiss if I did not add that neither spiritual nor religious beliefs are a prerequisite to receive the healing benefits of Cognitive Energy Healing.

The Power of Words in Muscle Testing Applications

Whenever exposed to safe or threatening stimuli, even that carried by words, the body knows immediately whether it is friend or foe and responds accordingly. To tap into this source of information about the client's well-being, the CEH practitioner employs subliminally communicated words, statements and questions that cause the body's muscles to produce a readily discernable and readable response. Words can cause an MT to test strong or weak, and this response is subjective, meaning specific to the individual client. This investigative approach requires a trained and informed method of inquiry.

While information provided personally by the client, as well as subtle energy flow readings offer insight into possible healing strategies, Muscle Testing is the primary investigative method used by the practice. No matter which testing method is applied, it is essential to maintain an ongoing collaboration with the client throughout the session as this provides an invaluable source of information throughout the investigation.

The CEH application of muscle testing is directed toward determining the underlying causes of health concerns. This method provides an effective, efficient and non-invasive way to identify the root causes of malfunction and illness. During an MT session, a strong response indicates there is no concern related to the word being tested, while a weak muscle response indicates this word has a negative or threatening association for the client and further investigation can determine why.

So, while such words as mother (love, nurturing), chocolate (delicious), dopamine (necessary hormone), calcium (an essential nutrient and electrolyte) generally have a positive association and result in a strong muscle response, these same words may unconsciously be perceived as a threat by others, resulting in a weak MT response, as seen in the following:

Mother!...... stress due to unresolved issues

Chocolate!...... allergy to a food item incorrectly identified as an antigen, also possible negative emotional associations

Dopamine!...... hormone incorrectly identified as an antigen causing its production to be suppressed

Calcium!.......... allergy to an essential nutrient causing a mineral deficiency - wrongly identified as a harmful substance, it is eliminated from the body

In response to the practitioners informed protocol of investigation, the body knows which energies are negatively impacting its well-being, and it is able to communicate this information during MT. Interestingly, this is also true even if the client at least consciously doesn't understand the meaning of the word. Clarification of an unfamiliar word is provided following the test, and then retested to confirm the reading.

Note: While autoimmune responses to physical injury, invading bacteria and viruses are normal and healthy responses to protect the body from real concerns, the last three examples listed above indicate abnormal autoimmune responses triggered by perceived information being processed incorrectly and consequently misinterpreted by the brain.

In order to gain an understanding of the body processes that cause the muscles to exhibit weak or strong responses, we will look at what is taking place in the body at the time of exposure to a threatening stimulus. Once the brain has processed information of a perceived threat of any kind, it immediately sends a directive to the body's defense systems (the autoimmune system and the autonomic nervous system) to initiate a protective/defensive response. As these systems require a significant and focused energy boost to fuel an immediate and strong response, certain other demands on this resource are temporarily suspended including the energy feed to *the muscles,* immune system function and the production of certain hormones. This explains why exposure to a harmful energy results in a weak MT response at the moment of exposure to negatively impacting stimuli. As energy from the muscles is temporarily repurposed to address the immediate threat at hand, their weak bio-feedback identifies the trigger.

Muscle Testing has proven itself to be a reliable investigative technique to identify which aspects of the body are under attack, and the source of the threat. In a clinical setting, the CEH practitioner through subliminal verbal testing is able to check from extensive lists of physical, emotional and energetic health-related factors to determine concerns that need to be addressed. With this MT-acquired information, along with insights acquired during dialogue with the client, the practitioner develops and applies a focused healing strategy. Through the application of CEH attunements, the practitioner informs the cognitive brain of identified concerns, thereby enabling it to make healing corrections where needed.

As mentioned earlier, the only stimulus employed by the CEH approach to muscle testing is the subliminally-communicated thought of the tester. This direct communication with the subconscious mind provides an objective response, free from the client's conscious interference to promote personal preferences. A person's conscious response, for example, may incorrectly deny being overwhelmed by stress to avoid being seen as weak or a failure. So, in order to obtain a reliable response, as Dr. John Diamond initially stated in the title of one of his books about muscle testing, *The Body Doesn't Lie.*

When subliminally communicating the *word name* of anything through thought while muscle testing, bear in mind that the word name, whether expressed out loud or in thought, carries the same energy signature as the actual person (Audrey, ...), food (lobster, ...), substance (mercury, ...), material (plastic, ...), emotion (rage), trauma (near drowning, ...), memory (neglect), belief (self-worth, ...), or behavior (alcohol abuse, ...) being referred to. In other words, the MT response to a subliminally-communicated word name is the same as the actual experience of it. In the case of a person who is allergic to ragweed, they will exhibit the same weak MT response to the physical presence of ragweed, as to the subliminally-communicated word name for it.

While the MT for the name *Audrey* will test strong should it have a positive association such as being the name of a loving aunt or a close friend, the name will test weak if there is an emotionally-negative association with this person. The word name *lobster* will evoke a strong MT response for test subjects who are not allergic to it and a weak one for those who are. And, although *mercury* is a toxin, it will test weak only if it is a current threat to the subject's well-being, such as if there are elevated mercury levels in their blood or if there is an established allergy to it. Plastic in its various forms is virtually in every modern home and office, and for most people except for those allergic to it, the MT for this material will be strong. The person living with the emotion of *sadness*, the trauma of *drowning*, memories of *neglect*, or beliefs of being *unworthy* will test weak for these words. And a weak MT to an essential nutrient such as a vitamin or a mineral, requires further investigation to determine if the cause is the result of a dietary deficiency, an allergy or a digestive enzyme deficiency.

The task of the practitioner is to continue the investigation to identify the primary cause/s of a health concern, and once determined, to then apply the appropriate modalities to alleviate, eliminate and/or correct whatever is causing the problem. Naturally, all responses to stimuli are subjective, meaning that what negatively impacts one person may be perfectly fine for another. The word *love* for example will show a strong MT response for the person who has a positive life experience in this area, while the person experiencing such negative associations as loneliness, betrayal or loss, will probably test weak. As CEH acts to release energy blockages caused by negative emotions, memories, traumas, beliefs, and behaviors, healing can then take place.

Generally speaking, when a person has an *extreme like* or *dislike* for a particular food item, this can be seen as a possible red flag for an allergy to the particular food item. The person who absolutely loves chocolate to the point of finding it irresistible, may well be allergic to it. And the person who has an extreme dislike for broccoli, may be allergic to it, however this reaction can simply stem from a dislike of its texture or smell. Besides a knowledge and understanding of the concerns being addressed, MT detective work often relies on the experienced practitioner's insight and intuition, as tapping into these inner resources can lead to answers and solutions that otherwise would not be readily accessible.

When searching for the root causes of health concerns internal to the body itself, there are a number of possible avenues to explore: physical, chemical, emotional, energetic, and epigenetic. While allergens from the external environment trigger autoimmune reactions, the immune system can also launch a destructive attack on the internal components and secretions of the body causing a significant number or diseases and disorder. As in both cases the autoimmune system is acting on misinformation to identify and react defensively to stimuli perceived as a threat. In this sense the internal immune response can be likened to an allergic reaction to an external antigen. And while incorrect information in both cases can result in a range of concerning health symptoms, with some being potentially fatal, only the internal autoimmune reaction is fully dedicated to the destruction of the body's own tissues and secretions.

For many, it is difficult to understand that something as nutritious as a carrot or as essential as insulin can for whatever reason come to be incorrectly identified as an antigen. The organic stamp of approval does not make the food item safe for a person who is allergic to it, no matter the purity of its growing conditions. And yes, a person can be betrayed by their body: it can turn destructively on itself in an autoimmune reaction. With this profound awareness, I hasten to add there is hope for people living with either of these health concerns. The CEH attunements and modalities have proven both efficient and effective in correcting such challenges by restoring a healthy normal response to safe stimuli.

Coded Muscle Responses

Since the initial discovery of the weak/strong muscle response to safe or threatening stimuli, a number of other MT techniques have been developed to further improve our ability to communicate with the body. In addition to learning that the word names for anything and anyone are as effective in initiating a muscle response as a physical exposure to them, we now know that subliminally-communicated *thought messages* also act to initiate muscle responses as well.

Beyond the fundamental weak/strong response to words and thoughts, practitioners are also able to attune the subconscious mind/body connection to provide a *muscle code response*. By subliminally establishing codes for weak and strong MT responses, the body is able to provide yes and no answers to questions, and true/false responses to statements. This broader spectrum of communication with the body significantly increases what can be learned by the MT investigative process to determine the cause of health concerns.

The established code response for a yes/no reply to a question is a weak muscle response for a *yes* - think of it as a kind of affirmative arm "nod", while a strong MT response serves as a "firm" *no*. So, in response to the question, "is there a trauma associated with Sally's allergy to apples," the code response is either weak, exhibiting a downward arm movement for a yes, or strong as the arm remains firmly in place for a no. With further investigation in this case, it would be possible to determine when the trauma occurred, what exactly caused it and who was involved.

Similarly, a communication code can be established to indicate the true or false nature of a statement, with a strong response indicating the statement is true, and a weak response indicating it is false. For example, the MT statement, "Ted's allergy to pine trees is associated with an emotion," the body's code response is strong if it is true, or weak if it is false. A true response indicates that both the pine trees allergy and the emotion must be treated together for the allergy to clear completely. The next step then, is to determine what the emotion is and if it involves someone else. It could be that something disturbing happened to this person or someone they care about in the vicinity of pine trees. Perhaps it was a mountain biking accident that took place in the area of a pine grove trail.

During the investigative MT process, the practitioner is to ensure that all questions or statements are clearly and succinctly communicated. The information gathering sequence proceeds in a structured and rational way, working from broad categories down to the specifics. Initially, for example, it can be determined if the concern being addressed is energetic, physical, chemical, emotional, or spiritual, or a combination of these. Each of these has their own subset of areas of investigation including the who, what, when, where, why and how as they pertain to the search for underlying causes. Information gathered in this way identifies specifically what needs to be addressed during treatment to enable healing.

When formulating questions or statements for MT, it is important to be aware that the subconscious mind interprets these communications literally. Unclear questions such as the following need to be reformulated: "Did Paul drop the ball on that one?" could be restated "did Paul keep his commitment to take his mother to the doctor?" Similarly, "was Paul held back for no reason?" could be rephrased "did Paul have a good reason for the delay in responding to his friends call for help?" Also, through hypnosis research, we know the subconscious mind does not recognize negative words such as *no, not,* or the *n't* contraction within the context of a sentence. Where possible try to reformulate statements and questions to avoid incorporating these negative words, as they will confuse the process with wrong answers. To help clarify why this is so, consider the following situation:

Before playing a tennis match, should your opponent say, "I will try *not* to hit you," the subconscious mind will understand only, "I will try...to hit you", causing that statement to be perceived as a threat. This psychological and tactical ploy serves to subconsciously put you in a defensive mode, and consequently at a disadvantage in the game. As strange as it may sound, had the opponent awkwardly placed the word *not* following the statement, as in "I will try to hit you, not," the subconscious mind would understand the whole phrase as being negated and interpret your opponent's words as being well intentioned. Obviously, your conscious mind would be suspicious of this unusual way of talking.

Hopefully, this example provides you with some understanding of another strategy to communicate with the subconscious mind. Simply put, the preference is to rephrase what you want to say without using *no, not,* or *n't,* or try another interrogative strategy. Should this not be accomplished easily, the alternative is to move the negative word from within the context of the phrase and relocate it to the end of the sentence: *Robert perceived this as a threat, not.* Though the conscious mind perceives this as an awkward formulation, it does provide clear and effective communication when the subconscious mind is involved.

You are now aware of three ways of communicating with the body during an MT investigative session: by word, statement, or question. Practical applications of these will follow to help clarify the process.

In the following section, MT methods for testing others, as well as for self-testing will be presented. You will discover MT to be a tremendously valuable information-gathering technique, as it enables access to the holistic body, mind, and spirit's vast resource of information about itself at any particular point in time. Ultimately, the effectiveness and reliability of these methods significantly depends on the investigative knowledge, training, skill and insightfulness of the practitioner.

CEH Muscle Testing Techniques

The MT Technique When Working with Others

All communication during the application of the muscle test is subliminally communicated through the practitioner's conscious thought.

CEH practitioner's position for Muscle Testing:

A fictitious client named Peter will serve our purposes in this presentation, and the practitioner will be referred to as the tester.

With client/testing partner Peter standing at ease in front of you, ask him to extend his right arm straight out in front of him so that it is level with his shoulder - see suggested variations below*. The tester moves to the left to align their right arm with Peter's, while stepping back just far enough to rest their right hand on his forearm. The tester's wrist should be positioned on top of Peter's wrist.

The tester gently holds Peter's arm while subliminally communicating whatever is being tested. Peter is informed that the cue for him to hold his arm firmly in place is provided when the tester opens their hand out flat, as this is immediately followed by an application of downward pressure of approximately two pounds (slightly less than a kilogram).

The client's resulting strong or weak muscle response is then interpreted by the tester.

Let's assume you are the tester, and Peter is your client: On your initial MT session with Peter, you consciously and subliminally establish a code link with his body for a *yes* and *no* answers by conveying the thought message that a strong MT response indicates a *no* answer, while a weak one indicates a *yes*. Then, to determine whether this coded response is established, you MT for the thought message "show me a *no*" by pressing firmly downward (remember no more than two pounds of pressure) with your open hand positioned on the forearm, wrist over wrist. Peter's arm should test strong, indicating a *no* response code is established. Next, MT for the thought message "show me a *yes*." This time as you press down, Peter's arm should test weak, dipping downward as in a head nod indicating a *yes*, confirming the *yes* code response is understood. Once established, this code of communication remains established for this client for all future MT sessions.

This "show me" Yes/No communication test should be done at the start of every testing session to determine if the energy of the person being tested is balanced, and whether their MT is providing reliable and clear responses. During future sessions, remember to vary the order of your "show me" requests to avoid establishing a consciously remembered patterned response. You can vary this "show me" statement approach by asking questions to which you already know the answers: Is this Sally? Is this Dick? Is this Peter? Was Peter born in the month of July? In Peter's case the only *yes* answers would be to the last two questions. Though Peter is not consciously aware of your questions or statements or questions, he is subconsciously attuned to the message and your communication code to provide reliable MT responses.

* Note: The tester and the partner/client may be seated to accommodate either a height differential or a personal preference – the general position remains the same, with the right arm of the tester aligned with the right arm of the person being tested.

Also, should the use of the partner's left arm be preferred, align your left arm in front of your partner's extended left arm, and proceed as described above.

Ways to address concerns leading to incorrect responses:

1. Confirm that both the tester and the person being tested are well hydrated. A drink of water may be required to re-establish normal energy flow. It's a good practice for both the tester and the person being tested to have a drink of water prior to beginning the MT session.

2. Confirm that both the tester and the person being tested have not crossed their legs, as this interrupts normal body energy flow, resulting in consistently weak MT responses.

3. Should MT answers be persistently stuck on either a *no* or a *yes* response, irrespective of the question being asked, or simply if the response appears to make no sense, it is possible the subject may be experiencing *an energy imbalance.* Energy balance can be readily restored in a number of different ways such as by having the person gently clap their hands a few times while alternating the top hand from the left to the right. Another alternative is to walk on the spot with arms swinging back and forth as in normal walking. And remember hydration could be a factor should the concern continue.

4. The following MT questions can help determine how the practitioner should proceed: does this treatment need to be done in combination with anything else? Is there an underlying internal or an external concern that needs to be released along with a particular treatment? Does this treatment need to be repeated, or has this treatment taken 100%?

Following the MT detective work to identify the cause of a particular health concern, a case specific CEH treatment is applied to enable the body to complete the healing process. There are three avenues to explore: the holistic body (BMS), the energetic, and the genetic/epigenetic.

Additional troubleshooting advice:

- Initially, the client being tested may need to be reminded to hold their arm firm, "steady as a beam," discouraging the tendency to push upward in an effort to overpower the tester as this negates the reliability of the response. Remind them that the pressure applied will be only about two pounds (less than a kilogram).

Inform the client that this test is to assess the impact of certain energies on the body's well-being. While some energies are perceived as safe and test strong, others are identified as a threat and elicit a weak response. This test information helps the tester determine whether or not a CEH treatment is required.

Remember to address everything that is discovered at the time of its discovery or as soon as possible following its detection, as any exposure to a harmful stimulus, even if it's just its word name, initiates a defensive response.

- Sometimes an allergen will not clear because it has an *emotional or a trauma-related association*. In this case, both the allergen and the emotion or trauma are to be treated back to back within the same treatment session. Say for example, something upsetting happened while a person was eating a hotdog with mustard. This person, whose MT indicates an allergy to mustard may have received disturbing news about someone close to them while eating the hotdog – a breakup of a relationship or the death of a friend, for example. The body, for whatever reason, can be misguided to wrongly associate mustard with this stressful news, resulting in it being identified as something harmful to the body.

MT Strategies with Words, Questions and Statements

Responses to a word name: In the application of the CEH muscle testing method the word name for something carries the same energetic signature as the substance or the emotion being tested.

To start, the tester assumes the MT position, placing their right wrist on top of the client's outstretched right wrist while gently holding their forearm. As the word name of whatever is being tested is subliminally communicated through the tester's thought energy, the tester immediately opens their hand to apply a light downward pressure. Should the client subconsciously perceive this word as a threat, the applied pressure will result in a weak muscle response. As you will recall, this occurs because the body's muscle strength energy is diverted to engage a defensive autoimmune or *fight or flight* response. Otherwise, the MT response to this word will remain strong.

Should a practitioner want to determine the cause of a client's pervasive stress, testing can begin with such general categories as a person, work, family, finances, etc. Once a category is identified, the tester can explore further to determine specifics. For example, if the stress is due to a person, the subcategories would include family, friend, colleague etc. If a family member is identified, further investigation could include gender, spouse, parent, sibling, child, aunt, uncle, cousin. From here, personal details will identify the source of the stress. Associated emotions would be the next category to explore in order to determine the cause of the stress and to initiate a CEH treatment to release its negative impact on the person's health.

Sometimes, what a person is allergic to seems to defy logic. As strange as it may sound, a person can MT strong for car exhausts, while testing weak for carrots, even organic ones. When carrots are wrongly identified as an antigen by the body, they can cause significant allergic reactions. While being tested in a clinical setting the subliminally communicated word *carrot* would cause in a weak MT for the person who has such an allergy. And while breathing car exhausts are not good for a person, they won't necessarily be identified as an allergen even if they are an irritant. Following my toxic environmental exposure, I randomly became very allergic to raw carrots, while curiously having no noticeable reaction to cooked carrots. This natural and normally healthy vegetable triggered an escalating and frightening response of choking, gagging, and throat swelling. Fortunately, the CEH allergy elimination treatment in combination with an associated emotional trauma has stopped this allergy from recurring.

When MT for emotions such as anger, envy, resentment, regret, etc., a weak response indicates this emotion is causing an energy blockage that is negatively impacting the person's well-being. Conversely, an MT to any emotion whether positive or negative, tests strong if it is not perceived as posing a threat. Between discussing concerns with the client and focused MT detective work, the root causes of health concerns can be identified. Information acquired in these ways informs the practitioner of the specifics for the healing treatments to follow. And please be reminded that any and all physical and/or emotional trauma associations must be administered concurrently with the allergy elimination treatment.

Testing by making a statement: Establish the code of a strong muscle response for a true statement and a weak response for a false one, saying the client's name in a statement, "this is Jack." The MT response will be strong as this is a true statement. Should you say some other name such as "Mary," the statement will test weak, as this is a false statement. The statement "Fred is allergic to beets," tests strong if Fred is truly allergic to beets and weak if this is a false statement. The response to the statement, "Mary feels unworthy," will test strong if true and weak if false. At times, responses to statements may indicate the need for further investigation, as well as providing some idea of which avenues to pursue.

Testing by asking a question: The practitioner establishes a set MT response code for answers to questions to indicate a *yes* or *no* reply. A strong response indicates a *no* answer, while a weak response is a *yes*. The next step is to establish this same code with the client. This is achieved by first subliminally communicating the established yes and no responses, then proceed to MT for the statement "show me a no" - this muscle response should be strong. Then say, "show me a yes" while applying the MT, and this response should be weak - the arm dips downward as in a nod. Assured that the code is established and that you are receiving correct answers, proceed to ask the question, "Is John allergic to bee sting?" A yes answer is indicated by a weak MT, while a no answer provides a strong response. Once again, information gathered in this way, besides helping to determine the root causes for health concerns, also provides insights into developing an appropriate protocol for treatment.

The three information-gathering MT methods of using words, asking questions, and making statements provide investigative options for the practitioner, as well as helping to cross-check response reliability. This is to say some investigations lend themselves better to true and false statements, while others are best addressed with questions to obtain yes and no answers. The tester is free to apply any one or a combination of all these approaches during a testing session. It is also important that the communication is clear and focused. The tester should be aware that the subconscious mind interprets verbal communication literally. This requires that the tester be vigilant in scrutinizing the delivery for both meaning and intention. "Is Jill under the weather?" for example, is open to the ambiguity of a literal interpretation, whereas, "Is Jill feeling stressed, ...worried, ...ill?" provides a clear and discernable message.

Occasionally, it happens that the MT response to a question results in only a slight release at the shoulder rather than a clear firm arm or downward dip. This vague response can be described as "spongy" and is not reliable, indicating that further investigation is required. The tester should first review the question to verify that it is clearly stated, and if deemed to be so, the same test question is repeated to determine if they are on the right course. If not, this question can be reformulated as required until clear responses are received. It is also possible to change the format from asking questions to making statements to determine if this improves the reliability of the responses.

Unlike the conscious mind, the subconscious mind has no reason to tamper with the body's truth about itself. The self-interest aspect of the conscious mind renders it is an unreliable source of information about the body. In order to circumvent the subjective preferences of the conscious mind, MT communicates directly and subliminally with the dependably objective resources of the subconscious mind.

And now, we will move on to some practical applications of these testing procedures. During the muscle testing aspect of the diagnostic investigation, communication is transmitted subliminally by the practitioner. Information gathered in this way can, at any time, be shared and discussed with the client, to further inform and guide the on-going search for underlying causes of health and wellness concerns.

MT Application 1: Response to a Single Word

This approach of testing for the word name of something lends itself particularly well to allergy and emotion testing.

The following session addresses an allergy

Sherry is dealing with a persistent and irritating rash. MT can begin by addressing the list of possible causes, starting with broad categories, then working toward the specifics.

The MT for the subliminally communicated word thought *ingestant (anything taken orally)*, immediately evokes a *weak* muscle response, indicating something that was eaten is probably the cause, or at least part of the cause. Starting with the first meal of the day, the word *breakfast*, also provides a *weak* response. When asked verbally, Sherry informs the tester what she had for breakfast. This includes coffee with milk, oatmeal with milk, cinnamon and blueberries. As the MT words *coffee* and *milk* both test strong, they are ruled out as a possible cause of the problem. Then voilà, the word *oatmeal*, tests weak. The culprit has been identified. Now is the time to MT to determine if this allergen needs to be treated in combination with anything else such as a *trauma* or an *emotion*. Should the answer be *no*, the CEH treatment for oatmeal is performed. Following the treatment, MT is repeated to determine if the treatment has taken completely.

Should a combination treatment be required, the tester can MT to learn if the treatment for oatmeal needs to be treated in combination with such things as an *emotion*, or a *trauma*. In Sherry's case let's say she tests weak for an emotion. Working from a list of possible emotions, the word *grief* is identified to be in association with her oatmeal allergy. The tester can then test for grief caused by the loss of something or someone. As the word *someone* tests weak, the investigation moves on to determine if the association is with a work associate, a friend, a family member, etc. Let's say the words *family member* test weak, as does the gender determinant, *female*. This then is enough information to speak with Sherry to ask her if she is grieving for the loss of someone in her family. Let's say she replies that her grandmother passed away recently.

When tested on their own and in combination, the words *grandmother and oatmeal* test weak. This information makes sense to Sherry, as she explains that her grandmother had always made oatmeal for her during her childhood visits. As grief due to loss of a loved one had become associated with oatmeal, Sherry is given the CEH treatment for the release of this allergy and the associated emotion of grief. The follow up check on this combination treatment holds strong. Now finally, with these energy blockages lifted, it takes Sherry's body only a couple of days to heal the red and itchy rash.

Note: There can be more than one emotion or trauma associated with an allergy. In Sherry's case, perhaps such emotions as regret, anger, or loneliness could also be a factor. Also, remember the body completes the healing and this is a process that can take varying amounts of time depending on what is treated - usually anywhere from a few minutes to a couple of weeks.

In other cases, an allergy can be in association with a physical trauma, a memory or a belief or even something internal or external to the body. By including both MT and dialogue with the person seeking help, healing concerns can be identified and addressed as they appear. Facility in the investigative aspect of this work comes with practice, and yes, the practitioners' intuition can prove to be an invaluable resource.

MT Application 2: Yes and No Code Response to Questions

On an initial visit, the tester establishes the body communication code for yes/no answers with the person to be tested, a *yes* indicated by a dip down of the arm, a *no* by holding firm.

Paul has been experiencing persistent headaches without being able to determine their cause. The tester, while holding Paul's arm asks silently: "Do Paul's headaches have a physical cause?" The MT provides a *no* response. The following questions could be: "Are Paul's headaches caused by stress, …. a hormone, … a nutrient deficiency?" A **yes** MT response to the question about stress can be fine-tuned by following up with questions about money, work, family, etc. A hormone, might include stress hormones and/or neurotransmitters, for example. And a nutrient deficiency opens an investigation into vitamins, minerals and phytochemicals.

MT Application 3: Response to True and False Statements

The client will respond strong to a *true* statement and weak to a *false/untrue* statement about anything that relates to them. The response to statements is distinctly the opposite of the yes/no responses to questions.

Paul is upset and stressed about something, however, he is having difficulty explaining the cause. Initially, the tester verifies that Paul is giving accurate MT responses to the subliminal statements. The statement "This is Sam" provides a weak response indicating this is false, while "This is Paul" tests strong, which is true. As reliable responses have been received, testing can proceed.

Sometimes, people find themselves feeling upset and yet unable to pinpoint the reason why. By running through a range of statements, such as "Paul is upset because of something he did, or something someone else did" it is possible to zero in on the person and the situation that caused him to be upset. The first statement tests weak as it is false, while the second statement, something someone else did, tests strong as it is true. Working through other statements additional information is acquired, when both "this happened at work," and "betrayal by a colleague" test strong. This provides enough information to release the emotional energy blockage caused by the betrayal, freeing Paul to be able to address his work-related concern in a calm and reasonable fashion.

Four Self-Testing MT Techniques

During self-testing sessions, it is essential to keep your conscious mind out of the equation, as this can compromise the reliability of the responses, especially for emotionally charged personal concerns. Though there are some techniques that may help get around this concern, for the present, should you become aware that this is happening, you are encouraged to find an impartial testing partner.

As there are a number of ways to self-test, I will offer a few approaches to consider. You are encouraged to try these techniques and decide which one feels right for you. As the first three methods require the use of both hands, and are more visible in a public setting, they are recommended for use in private testing sessions. The most discreet technique and my personal favorite is the technique requiring only one hand, as it can be easily used while driving the car for example or be carried out unnoticeably while in the company of others.

Self-Testing Technique 1, the O and Pincer Fingers Method: With your left hand, form an O shape by bringing the index finger to the tip of the thumb. Then with your right-hand form a pincer by placing your index finger on the pad of the thumb. Next, place the pincer fingers inside the O. You are now ready to test the strength of the O. Hold the O firmly as you try to push the thumb and index fingers apart by opening the pincer fingers as far as you can. You should **not** be able to separate the fingers forming the O.

Test for a word: You are now ready to test for a word. To suggest a few: anger, disappointment, happiness, apples, pears, turnip, physical or emotional trauma. To begin, place the right-hand pincer fingers in the center of the O shaped by the fingers of the left hand. Push open the pincers fingers and try to break the O formation while thinking or saying the word being tested. A strong response with the O formation remaining unbroken and intact indicates there isn't a concern with the word being tested, while a weak response, as shown by the fingers forming the O being pushed apart, indicates there is something in need of attention. Should further investigation be required, I suggest you move on to the statement or question approach to gain more information.

Test Using Questions: All questions must be formulated for yes/no answers. Consciously establish the code, with the thought a strong response indicates a NO answer - the O remains firmly closed under the pressure of the pincer fingers pushing against it. Now repeating this same thought-process a weak response indicates a Yes – the O breaks open. To test that this code is established, say, "show me a NO" – you should not be able to break open the O formation. Then say "show me a YES," and this time the O should break open as the index finger and thumb separate under the pressure of the pincer fingers pushing against them. You are now ready to start asking questions that provide yes or no responses.

Test Using Statements: Remember that true responses to statements test strong, and false responses test weak. Should you make a false statement, the pressure of the pincer fingers will overpower your ability to maintain the closed O formation. A true statement will provide a strong response, as the O shape will hold firm.

You are encouraged to practice this O and Pincer Finger Method before moving on to try the other methods. Avoid investigating anything that is emotionally charged, as your conscious mind will attempt to give you the answers you want to hear.

Self-Testing Technique 2, the O and One Finger Method: As in the previous method, form an O shape by placing the index finger of your left hand on the end of your thumb. Then place the index finger of your right hand in the O. You are now ready to test the strength of the firmly held O, by directing the thrust of the inserted index finger at the weak point of the O, where the thumb and finger come together. You should not be able to break the O.

Word MT: Weak responses are indicated when the O shape is broken. This occurs when the word has negative or threatening association, while a strong response results when the word has a positive and safe association.

Question MT: Should the right index finger not break through the O shape, the strong test response indicates a *no*. If the index finger breaks through, a *yes* response is indicated.

Statement MT: A firmly held O is a strong response, indicating the statement is true, conversely a weak response indicates it is false.

Self-Testing Technique 3, the Back of the Hand Method: With your elbows bent and held next to your body, place the first two fingers of the left hand on the back of your closed right hand, just slightly in from the first two knuckles. The right hand should remain firmly in place when pressure is applied by the two extended fingers.

This method may also be performed while seated with your elbows resting on your knees or while resting your right arm on a table or the arm of a chair.

Word MT: When a word carries the message of a threat, a weak response occurs: the rigid wrist gives way and the hand bends downward under the finger pressure. A non-threatening message provides a strong response: under pressure, the hand remains firmly in place.

Question MT: The hand bending downward under pressure is code for a *yes* response to a question. A *no* response is indicated when the hand remains firmly in place.

Statement MT: A firm hand response indicates the statement is perceived as truthful, while a weak response shows the statement is perceived as false.

Self-Testing Technique 4, the Two Finger Method: As mentioned earlier, this is my preferred approach as only one hand is required, freeing the other hand to do something else. It is also the least conspicuous method for use in public settings. Admittedly some people have difficulty gaining facility with this approach, as I did initially. It took me several attempts before it felt right. Be patient and stay motivated, as the benefits of this method far outweigh the challenge of mastering it.

It doesn't matter which hand you choose to use, and your arm can be bent at the elbow or held straight down. Now close your fist and point your index finger out from your hand. Next, place the adjacent middle finger on top of the index finger, resting the end of this finger on the fingernail, or between the first knuckle and the fingernail.

To perform the MT, hold your index finger firmly straight out in the pointing position while pressing downward on it with the middle finger. You should not be able to overpower the pointing index finger with this downward pressure. Note: in this application the index finger for self-testing applications functions like the arm MT when testing others.

Word: A weak response occurs when the downward pressure of the middle finger overpowers the pointing index finger causing it to bend downward: an indication that the word being tested has a negative or threatening association. A strong response is exhibited when the pointing index finger remains firmly in place: an indication that this communication is not perceived as a threat.

Question: A *no* response is indicated when the pointing index finger remains firmly in place under the pressure of the middle finger. A *yes* is indicated when the pointing index finger is easily pushed downward under the pressure of the middle finger. Think of this movement as a nod for a *yes*.

Statement: When the pointing index finger under the pressure of the middle finger tests weak the statement is *false*. A true statement is indicated by a *strong* response.

You are now ready to begin this journey of discovery to learn what your body is now able to communicate to you. Always be aware that reliable self-testing requires that your testing list avoid including emotionally charged concerns; the self-interest of the conscious mind will naturally overrule the objectivity of the responses. Also, you are free to choose which method of inquiry best suits your needs at the time.

Awareness is the first step toward healing, whether it be obtained through your own self-testing, with the help of a CEH practitioner or through some other type of professional help. These are but a few tools that hopefully will prove of some use to you.

And now to begin exploring the energetic healing applications of CEH.

PART VII

Cognitive Energy Healing Modalities

Taking a Quantum Leap

We now move to largely unfamiliar territory!

The Cognitive Energy Healing approach to healing is based on the premise that once the body is freed from blockages to normal energy flow, it is enabled to heal itself. As a balanced and uninterrupted flow of energy throughout the body is essential to holistic wellness, the CEH modalities, through engagement with the cognitive brain, release the root causes of the energy blockages that prevent or obstruct the healing process.

How can real healing be achieved through this restorative and non-invasive approach? The answer is twofold as either one or both of the following approaches can be employed to enable healing. First, once a healing concern is identified, the subconscious aspect of the cognitive brain is subliminally informed of the healing concern being addressed, and is given directives to initiate whatever changes are required so the desired healing outcomes can be realized. Then the brain, as overseer and manager of all body operations, once aware of what needs to be addressed, is amenable to make whatever corrections are required to support the holistic well-being of the person being treated.

This is achieved through the application of CEH cognitive energy and healing hands attunements to engage, stimulate, direct and restore normal energy flow throughout the body's vital energy systems. Frequently, these modalities are used in tandem, as one can enhance the effectiveness of the other. Also, it is important to emphasize that the use of pressure or manipulation during any of these applications is never required or permitted in any of the Cognitive Energy Healing modalities.

Cognitive Energy Healing attunements employ three basic modalities to address the needs of the client. While all three modalities employ hand movements to stimulate and direct energy flow, the first two establish a communication link with the subconscious mind enabling the practitioner to deliver subliminal healing directives. These modalities will be presented in detail along with a description of their practical application in the ensuing chapter.

The following is a brief overview of the three Cognitive Energy Healing modalities:

The *Temporal Attunement modality* came to me early in my self-healing journey while dealing with multiple, severe and random daily allergic and asthmatic reactions. It involves establishing a temporal energetic link through the energy portals at the temples on either side of the head, located slightly above and in front of the ears. This is achieved by focused hand energy movements and conscious directives for the desired healing. In this regard, it is interesting to note that the word *temporal* has two meanings, both relevant to this application: the one meaning being of this Earth, or Earthly, and the second refers to the physical location of the temples on either side of the head which is the stimulation site of this CEH application.

The *Centering Attunement Modality* came to me years later and has since taken precedence in my practice, as it is the most effective and efficient method of the two. The energy portal for this attunement is at the third eye, also known as the inner eye. It is located at the sixth chakra, in the horizontal center of the forehead, slightly above the juncture of the eyebrows. Hand movements over the third eye area are applied to stimulate and direct energy flow, while the practitioner subliminally communicates the intention for healing. This communication is received by the subconscious aspect of the cognitive mind, and is acted upon by the brain within the parameters of its charge to assure the holistic well-being of the body and all its operations. Its arsenal of resources that enable the body to heal itself, include the autoimmune system, the autonomic nervous system, and the vital energy system.

The *Body Energy Attunement Modality* is focused primarily on releasing and relieving pain and inflammation and to promote physical healing, as it works to eliminate energy blockages caused by injury and/or trauma. Recognizing that the memory of physical and emotional trauma stored in the body's cells can result in painful physical symptoms, this attunement can also be effective in releasing their negative impact on the physical body as well. Temporal or Centering Attunements have proven effective in supporting this body energy modality.

These three modalities offer access to a powerful and effective source of restorative healing energy. And as no one aspect of the BMS continuum operates independently from the other, energy work in any one area benefits the comprehensive well-being of the person receiving treatment.

It is important to mention that while the material in this section provides an understanding of the basic modalities and procedures of the Cognitive Energy Healing, their practical application is based on a significant body of knowledge, and for this reason should not be practiced without proper training.

Methodology for the Cognitive Energy Healing Modalities

Energetic Healing Hands

Diagram a. The Open Energetic Hand

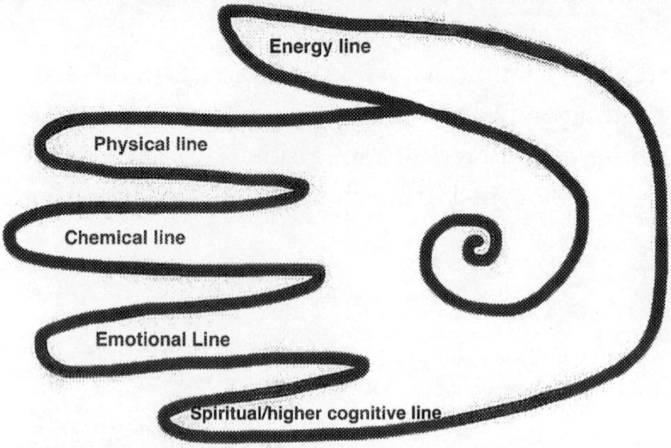
Energy line
Physical line
Chemical line
Emotional Line
Spiritual/higher cognitive line

Diagram b. The Energy Channels of the Hand

The open hand position has the fingers aligned beside each other; the palm of the hand is usually placed in the auric field over the area of the body being worked on. The energetic connected hand position is formed by first aligning the fingers beside each other, then drawing them slightly inward so that the tip of the thumb touches the pad of the middle finger; the tips of the fingers are placed over the treatment site.

Prior to beginning a treatment session and to enhance energy flow, take a couple of deep, cleansing and relaxing breaths. To facilitate optimum energy flow through the hands during treatment sessions, they should be held in a relaxed position. Tense hand muscles only slow down the flow of energy. And only the opened hand or the connected hand positions are employed. During a treatment session the hands are usually placed within the client's auric field or just slightly out from the site being treated. On occasion healing hands may also be rested gently directly on the body, such as on the client's head, arms, shoulders, back, legs or feet.

Description of Hand Positions and the Energy Pathways

The Energetic Hand: *The body's extremities including the hands, feet and crown of the head are the portals for vital energy flow either into or out from the body. Within the body, energy travels along energy channels or pathways known as meridians. Each meridian has a specific type of energy flow as seen in diagram b showing the energy channels of the hand. This energy can be consciously engaged, tapped into and directed for healing purposes. The connected hand position as described below, enables the practitioner to focus and stream healing energy.*

The Connected Hand Position: *The thumb is the on the main energy circuit line of the body's energy meridians. In the connected hand position, with the fingers together and the thumb touching the middle finger, all the energetic connections are linked to form a focused and concentrated energy sourced flow system engaging all the energy channels of the body. Together the thumb and index finger establish a physical energy link, thumb and middle finger a chemical energy link, thumb and ring bearer an emotional energy link, and thumb and small finger a spiritual link.*

The Open Hand Position*: All body energy channels flow through the palm of the hand. During treatment, the open hand receives and delivers a broader more dispersed pool of the same energy that flows through the connected hand position.*

In practice, the connected hand position is used for the Temporal and Centering Attunements, while both the connected and open hand positions are engaged during Body Energy Attunements.

The Temporal Attunement Modality

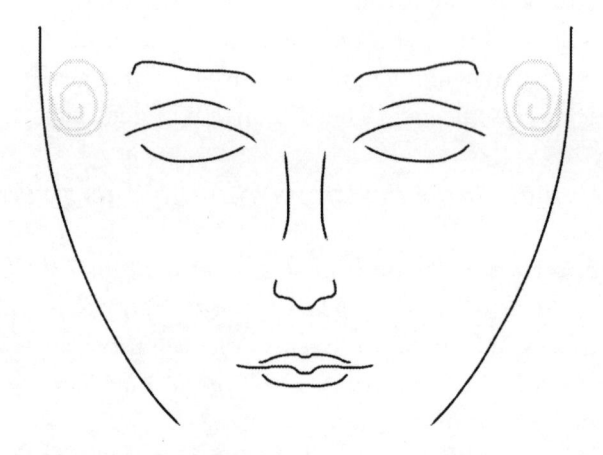

The temples, located on either side of the head just forward of and above the ears, are an energy gateway or portal that can be readily accessed for healing purposes. In fact, massaging the temples is a common practice to release tension and to relieve headache and migraine pain.

The Temporal Healing modality is intended to eliminate any identified energy blockages, and to balance and restore normal energy flow in the body. This modality not only enables a subliminal communication link between the practitioner and the healer to engage healing energy flow, it also stimulates and restores normal energy flow to the body. Throughout the treatment session, the practitioner works collaboratively with the client to assure that their desired outcomes are clearly communicated and addressed.

Procedure: The practitioner positions both hands in the *connected hand* position to create a full circuit healing connection. This is followed by a couple of cleansing relaxing and energy stimulating breaths. This breathing practice should be repeated off and on during the treatment to stimulate and maintain energy levels. Next, the fingertips of each energetic hand are held in the auric field just out from the temples by about an inch (2-3 cm) and placed at the center of each temple. This establishes an energetic link between the healer and the person receiving the treatment.

During this following step of directing and stimulating flow, the practitioner subconsciously states clearly and concisely what is to be released or corrected. Starting from the central point of the temples, begin an outward spiraling hand movement: the rotation is upward and around toward the face and back around again for twenty to twenty-five rotations. Once the outer extremity of the temples is reached, continue rotations over the same area to complete the cycles.

When treating yourself, think of this cyclic motion as wheels rolling forward. This same forward movement is employed when working on others, however it is from their front, rather than your own. In other words, the rotation is up and around and toward the practitioner standing in front of the client.

The closing step following the completion of the spiral rotations is intended to maintain and stabilize the newly restored healthy energy flow. This is accomplished by centrally placing one connected hand over and just out from the third eye located in the center of the forehead, slightly above the juncture of the eyebrows. Hold this position for at least five seconds. This closing step is intended to stabilize energy flow while the requested healing is being acted upon. During this time, it is also possible to re-state the desired healing correction.

And though not usually necessary, a supplementary closing step may be added as reinforcement for a particular treatment. This simply involves moving the hand slightly further out from the previous stabilizing position and bringing the hand into the open position with the palm in alignment with the third eye.

This position can be held for an additional few seconds before closing.

All attunements are followed by MT to verify if the treatment has taken, whether it needs to be repeated, or whether a combination treatment is required. A combination treatment could include a memory, an emotion, a trauma, an internal component of the body, an epigenetic factor passed down the ancestral line, etc.

While the Temporal Attunement approach works for all the same BMS concerns as the Centering Attunement Modality approach to be presented next, its limiting factors are that it takes more time to perform and requires the engagement of both hands and sometimes this is not always possible, especially if self-treating while driving the car, for example.

The Centering Attunement Modality

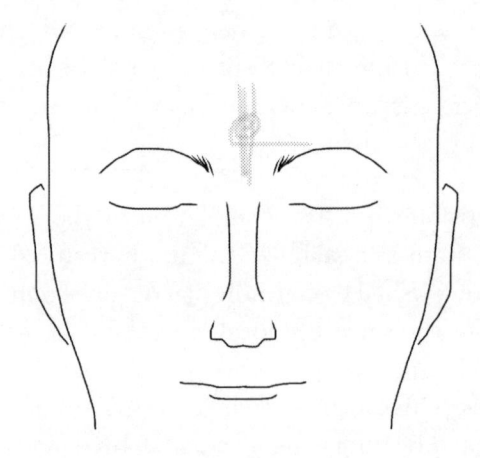

Currently, this is the most powerful centering and healing technique I know. The centering aspect refers to the balancing, alignment and modulation that is required to re-establish normal energy flow. This method connects directly with the brain, the body's energetic command center, through the third eye energy gateway, also known as the sixth chakra. The modality also links the practitioner's healing directive into the subconscious aspect of the cognitive mind. Only one hand is required for this application, which usually takes about ten seconds to perform.

Procedure: The Centering Attunement differs from the Temporal Attunement in that there is only one direct energy link, the one established over the third eye. The practitioner engages the cognitive brain with a brief invocation stating the intention for good and for healing, while energetically stimulating and directing energy flow over the third eye area. These hand gestures are performed within the auric field, about an inch (2-3 cm) out from the area.

Stroking hand gestures are employed to stimulate energy flow, while the spiral hand movement directs and engages this flow to initiate a connection with the subconscious cognitive mind.

For clarity purposes, I will explain the invocation, which is the statement of intention for healing on its own, then I will explain the hand gestures on their own, and finally I will explain how the gestures and the statement are integrated as they are performed in unison.

The invocation without the hand gestures:

The following invocation is recited subliminally to cognitively communicate the practitioner's good intentions for the client's healing and well-being. And, depending on the client's preferences, the word *Highest* can be used in the place of the word *Divine*. It is important to emphasize here as well that a belief in a sacred spiritual being is not required for this treatment to be effective.

The invocation: Highest or Divine love, light, and healing, through the Earthly plane to where "I am", or "the name of the client is."

The hand gestures, only:

This gesture serves to draw healing energy into the center of the energy portal.

With the connected hand placed just above and out from the third eye, begin by tracing three vertical energy-stimulating downward strokes. Then move the hand to just above the left eyebrow, level with the center of third eye. From this position draw a horizontal straight-line through and across the center of the third eye to then fluidly curve back on itself in a *clockwise* motion. This inward spiral motion is to intersect three times with the vertical strokes and end at the central point of the third eye.

Procedure:

1. To engage and stimulate energy flow, trace three downward strokes through the center of the third eye, starting just above and ending just below the site.

2. Starting over the middle of the left eyebrow, trace one fluid horizontal line across the center of the third eye to the other side, then without interruption spiral this movement back over itself drawing *three inward curling spirals*, completing the gesture with the middle finger centered at the middle of the third eye. This establishes the energetic link between the healer and the client.

3. Hold this central position over the third eye as you subliminally state the desired healing for person receiving the treatment. This stabilizes the energetic link during the delivery of the healing message.

4. As an option, this can be followed with a couple of additional clockwise spiraling movements to reinforce normal energy flow during the healing process.

5. To close and to stabilize the restored energy flow, position and hold your connected hand centered in place over the third eye for about five seconds. The desired healing can be restated at this time. And if deemed beneficial for this particular treatment, the supplementary reinforcing open hand closing can be added for a few additional seconds.

The integrated Centering Attunement, incorporating both invocation and hand gestures:

Note: With the treatment hand in the connected position, perform each gesture, while silently saying the accompanying phrase.

Highest or Divine love (starting just above the third eye make the first downward stroke through the third eye)

Light (make the second downward stroke through the third eye)

And healing (make the third downward stroke through the third eye)

Through the earthly plain to where <u>I am</u>, or <u>the name of the client</u> is. (starting above the middle of the left eyebrow trace a horizontal line slightly below the third eye. Then without interruption spiral this movement back on itself by tracing three inwardly directed spirals over the third eye, completing the rotation with the middle finger at its center).

While holding the energetic hand still over this central point, the desired healing is subliminally communicated. This can be followed by a couple of additional spiraling movements to further promote the restoration of normal energy flow., Then, close by holding the connected hand in place over the site for five seconds or so. The supplementary closing with the open hand can be added if felt beneficial. This is followed by MT to ascertain if the treatment as stated in the subliminal communication is holding strong.

The Release and Reclaim Modality

As this treatment is performed in conjunction with either the Temporal or Centering Attunement, it is included here to provide some insight as to its application and purpose. This protocol releases beliefs and associated behaviors that are harmful or limiting, while at the same time replacing them with healthy and beneficial ones that are consistent with the client's current values and belief system. So essentially, one belief or behavior is released to reclaim another, one this is both good and beneficial.

This modality is also effective in releasing negative emotions that cause mental and physical pain and in correcting emotional concerns that negatively affect chakra energy flow. Throughout this process and in ongoing collaboration with the client, the practitioner works to determine how best to address the concern. Ultimately, it is the client who decides on the phrasing and intension of the release and reclaim statements that best suits their need for beneficial and healing change.

A prime example of this application is the release of a fear. Fear, besides its self-preservation benefits arising from our primal need for survival, is associated with a significant number of associated negative emotions, including such things as fear of disappointing, failure, responsibility, success, confrontation, abandonment, loneliness, rejection, loss, death, physical pain, etc. In addition to these different types of fears, we can also include the pathological fears known as phobias. The list of phobias is very long, however to name a few: heights, open spaces, germs, dentists, flying, cats, dogs, snakes, spiders, bats, cemeteries, thunder and lightning, and even clowns. Whether rooted in emotions or phobias, the negative emotional association with the fear must be released for healing to take place. The void left by this release is filled with a range of reclaimed positive emotions such as love, trust, confidence, worthiness and forgiveness.

The Body Energy Attunement Modality

The three basic methods included within this healing category are Streaming, Bridging, and Releasing. These applications are intended to restore normal vital energy flow to the body by enabling stalled or blocked energy to return to normal flow rates and patterns, re-establishing homeostasis within the holistic body.

The negative impact of physical, emotional and/or spiritual concerns can manifest as blockages and disruptions to normal energy flow within the body and are usually associated with varying degrees of pain and/or malfunction. The application of Body Energy Attunement modalities has proven effective in promoting healing by reducing anxiety, stress, tension, inflammation and pain, while enabling the body to restore its structural and circulatory balance. And besides releasing the impact of physical trauma, this modality has proven effective in releasing that of emotional pain and trauma as well. During the application of this modality, my clients frequently report experiencing a cooling or cold sensation with an emotional release, and a warm to hot sensation when a physical healing is taking place.

The practitioner usually works within the client's auric field, as well as on the body itself by resting hands on certain areas such as the head, neck, shoulders, arms, hands, thighs, calves and feet for brief periods of time. **While Muscle Testing does involve the application of a light pressure on the client's arm, all Cognitive Energy Healing treatments are performed without the use of massage, manipulation or pressure of any kind.**

A variety of hand positions and movements can be employed to free stalled or blocked body energies, to re-establish normal energy flow, or to enable the body to re-align itself structurally or energetically. Only two hand positions are employed, these being the *connected hand* and the *open hand positions.* One or both hands may be engaged during a treatment as they remain either at rest over an area to channel energy flow or rotated in spiral clockwise or counterclockwise directions to engage and promote energy flow. Besides giving direction to energy flow, spiraling energy also draws out blocked or stagnant energy from the body to re-establish a healthy energy channel. During such applications, healing subliminally communicated directives can also be delivered to state the desired healing outcomes.

Blocked Energy Release: This procedure requires the use of only one hand.

Spiraling energy with the connected hand and/or the open palm over an area of concern in a *counterclockwise* motion serves to draw out blocked or stalled energy caused by physical or emotional trauma or injury.

Drawing energy out and away from the site establishes the *"still point"* at its center, as in the eye of a hurricane or the centering point for the whirling dervish*. This energy flow is flicked off the fingertips before proceeding to the next step.

With the still point established, the body is ready for the activation and restoration of normal energy flow. This is achieved by bringing the open palm of the hand back over the area of concern, this time moving in a clockwise motion. The hand can then be drawn back into the connected position for five to ten more rotations, finishing with the open palm resting in place just above the area of concern for approximately five seconds. Once normal energy flow is restored, the body should be able to complete the desired healing.

This complete procedure is performed in a fluid and uninterrupted way. Depending on the severity of the concern, this treatment can be repeated, or the application of one of the following two approaches may also be beneficial.

Energy Streaming: This procedure engages both hands, starting initially with one hand; the other is brought in to complete the treatment. The energy stream can either be directed to flow out from the body to release blocked energy, or into the body to bolster and restore normal energy flow.

The two-part process:

a. To stream blocked energy out from the body, hold the energetic connected hand above the treatment site for a second or so to establish an energetic link, then proceed with five to ten counterclockwise movements. Continue with this motion as this hand is then opened to a relaxed position for a few additional rotations before being held in place above the site.

Now, with the second hand in the connected position bring it in to rest just slightly above the center back of the opened hand. Hold still in this position for a few seconds to establish this second energetic link, then trace five or so counterclockwise spirals in the space above the back of the first hand. Once complete, draw the upper hand outward to about a foot above the site (30 centimeters), and hold this position for a few seconds to maintain the established outward flowing energy stream. Then, finger flick this stream of blocked energy flow out and away from the treatment site to release the blocked energy from the body. Now open this hand and hold it in place over the site for about ten seconds. Maintain this position as it is the starting point for the next part of the application.

b. The purpose of the next step is to stream healthy energy into the body to restore and re-establish a normal energy flow. Continue from the previous position with both hands open, one located over the site and the other above and further out from it. Move the upper hand back into the connected position and begin a clockwise rotation, spiraling inward towards the back of the opened hand. Hold this position for a few seconds to establish an inward energy stream. Then open this upper hand, holding it in place in the air just above the lower hand for approximately five seconds to stabilize the energy flow. This completes the Energy Streaming Treatment.

The body's normal flow of energy should now be restored and able to sustain itself. This treatment may be repeated as required.

Bridging Energy Flow: This procedure employs both hands. It is usually performed in the auric field just above the surface of the body, or the practitioner may rest their hands gently on certain parts of the client's body such as the head, neck, back, chest, abdomen, arms, hands, legs or feet.

Bridging energy flow can be achieved in a couple of different ways. Hands held in the open position can be placed on either side of various parts of the body such as the head, neck, shoulder, leg, foot, the chest and back or the mid-body region of the abdomen and back. From this position, various treatment combinations can be employed, including holding the hands in place over the site, or by engaging one hand in a counterclockwise or clockwise motion over the site, while keeping the other hand still. The counterclockwise motion can be applied to push back stalled energy before moving it forward in a clockwise motion.

Remember a treatment is always completed with a clockwise spiral followed by the stabilizing open palm resting just above or on the site.

Another bridging approach involves placing hands in the connected position equidistant from each other on the same side of the body as the afflicted site. Say, for example, the location of concern is the spine. Begin by centering each hand together in the auric field just above the site, then move them out from each other in opposite directions along the spine until they are each four to five inches from the original location. The hands can then remain in the auric field or rest on the body. Various hand positions and rotations can be employed from these locations. Remember, always to close the session by working directly over the site, with a clockwise motion followed by the open palm of one hand held at rest to stabilize the established energy flow.

For a variety of practical reasons, a complete and effective presentation of these applications can only be achieved in person, as demonstration and hands-on experience are essential to learning the proper procedure for these modalities.

A note of interest, before moving on:

A number of people who have experienced the centering power of whirling around in one direction or the other report having experienced an interesting phenomenon. The general consensus is that whirling in a counterclockwise position causes a feeling of energy flowing out from the body, while the same movement in a clockwise direction produces a sensation of energy being drawn inward.

Should you wish to try this for yourself, first place your left hand over your chest while the right arm is gently arched outward from the side of your body. Then turn around on the spot in a counterclockwise direction for two or three rotations while maintaining an awareness of energy flow. Did you sense a directional energy flow while doing this exercise?

Then following a brief and stabilizing rest to avoid vertigo, place your right hand over your chest and extend your left arm out as in the previous exercise. Now rotate in a clockwise direction for two to three rotations. Take note once again whether you sensed an opposite directional energy flow, and if so is it as described above?

I don't expect that everyone will pick up on these sensations. There may indeed be something to this phenomenon, or perhaps the power of suggestion may influence the perception of the experience.

Interestingly and possibly related to this flow experience, the right side of the body has been described as the "giving side" and the left side as the "receiving side". Perhaps emotional concerns associated with giving and receiving may explain why some people experience persistent and recurring health problems on one particular side of the body. Muscle testing can be applied to help determine if there is indeed a negative association with the experience of giving or receiving.

The following section is intended to provide a brief overview of those concerns that have demonstrated either significant improvement or complete healing through the application of CEH modalities.

Where Cognitive Energy Healing May Help

All experience of the present moment occurs within a period of time we refer to as *now*. In this sense of the word, now is not an isolated and insular moment of time, it is rather a triad inextricably comprised of the past, present and future of our being. It is but one spot along a related and interactive continuum reaching back from one's ancestral roots, to encompass a life lived from birth to death. It is from within this comprehensive framework of now that Cognitive Energy Healing strives to identify and resolve the underlying causes of concerns negatively impacting the health and well-being of its clients.

Prior to presenting a series of CEH client case studies, a brief summary of some the healing concerns addressed by the practice is presented below.

- Auto-immune diseases: These diseases occur due to a misguided immune system wrongly identifying stimuli from the internal or external environment of the body as a threat. The source of this malfunction originates in the brain, and this malfunction can be corrected through CEH applications. When something is wrongly identified as an antigen (a toxin, or a dangerous foreign substance) the body's response can range from a minor discomfort, to debilitating or severe, and can even be life threatening. Examples from the very long list of auto-immune diseases include allergies, asthma, multiple sclerosis, arthritis, type 1 diabetes, Hashimoto's thyroiditis, Grave's disease, celiac disease, cancer, and lupus.

- Emotions: Our emotions occur in response to our experience of the world. Their impact can range from positive to negative as they act upon our perceptions, attitudes, temperaments, behaviors as well as how we relate to ourselves and others. Negative emotions can be stressful and harmful to our health, particularly if held over long periods of time. And even when buried in the subconscious, unresolved negative emotions continue to take their toll on a person's physical and emotional state of being. Once the negative emotions impacting a client's well-being have been identified, the CEH attunement protocol are applied to discharge their negative power. And though the emotion remains real and is remembered, it loses its ability to harm a person's physical and/or mental well-being.

- Traumas: Physical and/or emotional trauma can cause serious energy blockages that manifest as pain, inflammation, disease, and maladaptive behaviors, as well as a range of mental disorders including anxiety, depression and post-traumatic stress disorder (PTSD). It is now recognized that once a trauma has been experienced, the brain's default response to any level of injury, no matter how minor, can become locked into a trauma-level pain response. Once identified, this trauma default response pattern can be released with CEH applications to enable responses that are in alignment with the severity of injury. The practice also has a range of applications to address and release the physical and mental symptoms of trauma.

- Memories: Both conscious and unconscious memories of unresolved life experiences can negatively affect a person's physical and emotional well-being. Even while lying dormant in the subconscious mind, negatively charged memories can weigh heavily on a person's emotional well-being. Such memories can even be carried over from a person's ancestral line in the form of epigenetic heritable diseases and other types of maladaptation, including anxiety and depression. CEH applications are able to identify harmful memories and release their power to negatively impact the mind/body continuum. And where epigenetic concerns are identified as the underlying cause of dysfunction or disease, the certain applications may be able to restore normal gene expression.

- Beliefs: Throughout our lives, core beliefs formed in early childhood until about the age of six remain established as our dominant belief system guiding our values, attitudes and behaviors. Naturally, as we grow into adults our increased engagement in the world results in the formation of new beliefs that can come into conflict with these core beliefs. These can then become stumbling blocks to a person's ability to achieve their full potential, resulting in frustration, conflict, stress, self-doubt and failure. While an awareness of the need for change is the first step to initiating a desired change, CEH protocols can facilitate and expedite the process to replace harmful beliefs with healthy ones.

- Behaviors: Certain harmful behaviors can arise from habit, addiction, attitude, phobias, fear or obsession. These can be rooted in such things as trauma, anxiety, anger, fear or stress, and are associated with an identifiable cause or trigger. During a Centering Attunement many such concerns can be addressed by the Release and Reclaim protocol.

- Epigenetics: Unlike genetic mutations which take place over generations, epigenetic changes take place within a person's lifetime in response to social and environment experiences, and these can be heritable. These changes to gene expression can be either positive or maladaptive, and in the latter case can lead to a range of diseases, syndromes and disorders. In order to adapt to the changing dynamic of the internal and external factors affecting the body, expression of normal gene function is either turned *off* or *on* as required. Malfunctions occur when the sequencing of this function is left on too long or is erroneously turned off when it is needed. CEH, by informing the cognitive brain of an epigenetic concern causing maladaptive gene expression, communicates healing directives to enable the correction of misguided gene behavior.

With this understanding of the CEH practice and its healing mission, we now move in for closer look at how its various modalities have been applied to help a number of clients dealing with a broad range of healing concerns. How best to do this, but with a selection of case studies.

Case Studies: Cognitive Energy Healing Helping Others

While working on this book, my healing practice has been entirely voluntary. I asked but one thing in return, and this was always clearly stated on the initial visit with each of my clients. In return for my efforts to help address their health concerns with CEH, I asked permission to share in this writing anything I learned from our sessions that could be helpful in the healing of others. They were also informed that should any of their healing experience be included in the book, their privacy and anonymity would be respected.

Naturally, our fee-for-service culture left many of my clients wanting to reimburse me somehow, so I suggested that should they wish, they could make a donation to a charity of their choice. And, as writing a book is a time- intensive activity and not wanting to be overwhelmed with requests for help, I asked my clients to be discreet about spreading the word, and thankfully they were. My healing work with these people has been a rich and rewarding experience, as most of them including myself were amazed by the healing that ensued from the CEH treatment sessions.

The following are a few cameo glimpses of Cognitive Energy Healing at work both in the practice and in random encounters while out and about. A variety of health-related concerns will be addressed, and each study will include some valuable healing insight learned over the period of working with the client or the person who accepted my offer of help.

- In public settings, excluding emergency situations where medical help should be sought, a CEH practitioner may consider offering help to a person experiencing a health concern. Prior to offering assistance, the practitioner must decide whether an energy treatment would be of any help, and if so, proceed only with the express permission of the person, parent or guardian involved.

Case I: I was standing poolside when Sarah, a little girl just learning to swim, came out of the water bent over holding her stomach. She went directly to her mother for help. As Sarah had been in the water for a rather long time enjoying her newfound swimming ability, I thought perhaps she may have swallowed more than a healthy amount of the pool water. Shortly afterward, recognizing her condition wasn't improving, I asked her mom if I could help and she agreed.

Within less than a minute of a CEH Body Energy Attunement, this little girl was fine again. Sarah popped up from her poolside chair, smiled and commented in a surprised kind of way as she headed off for another dip: "I'm fine, and you didn't even touch my stomach."

Sarah was right, I hadn't touched the physical site of her pain, rather I had worked in the energy field just above her stomach to restore her body's normal energy flow.

Case II: It was a beautiful autumn day and a great day for a barbecue at a friend's cottage. At some point, I noticed that Alice was not quite looking or feeling herself. When we chatted, she mentioned that seasonal allergies were causing her a lot of discomfort. Alice's nose was red and constantly running, and her eyes were red and irritated as well. When I mentioned I might be able to help, Alice was keen to give it a try.

We met privately for a brief session and MT revealed she was in allergic reaction to golden rod, rag weed, thistle, and leaf mold. Once treated, the runny nose and teary symptoms cleared up within an hour. She let me know later on that she was well and finally able to get a relaxed night's sleep.

With an allergy elimination treatment, Alice's allergic symptoms were readily stopped. Following this correction, it naturally follows that the swelling and irritation in the nose and eye area were able to begin healing. And assuming no additional allergies emerge in the future, Alice's experience of fall should be much more enjoyable going forward.

- Anxiety can have many different causes: physical, chemical/hormonal, emotional or any combination of these.

I knew Jenny from previous appointments, so I was surprised to see her arrive in considerable distress. Her body was rigid, turned inward tightly on itself, while she looked fixedly downward to avoiding eye contact. Jenny's anxiety and desperation were palpable.

MT revealed that the driving force behind Jenny's anxiety was stress arising from anger, guilt, and a self-imposed need for perfection. The way she held her body and avoided eye contact indicated she was protecting herself from exposure to any further external stressors. Jenny explained she felt exhausted, overwhelmed and powerless to help herself. As the CEH Centering Attunements released each of these concerns, the rigidity constricting her body melted away, her eyes lit up and she returned to a relaxed state. Jenny was back to her usual self, once again able to engage in the world. It was amazing to see this transformation take place within a brief fifteen minutes or so.

An anxiety attack such as this one can be triggered by a current or a past stress or trauma. Surprisingly, the seeds of anxiety can remain dormant for years, or even decades, surfacing when triggered by any number of possible stressors or memories. As seen in this case, intense anxiety can push a person into a state of protection causing them to shut down engagement with others in a desperate effort to prevent exposure to any additional external stimuli.

The emotional impact of a traumatic experience can be carried unconsciously for decades. Such things as a child's fear of being abandoned by a parent, the premature death of a sibling, or a teenager's guilt from an undesired sexual encounter can be carried silently, dormant in the subconscious mind, only to resurface years later sometimes in response to only a minor stressor. Unresolved emotional concerns can resurface when awakened by something as simple as a touch, a taste or a smell, the sound of someone's voice, or some other random and seemingly insignificant experience that serves as the proverbial "last straw," the one that breaks the camel's back.

Some will say, "Oh, I've dealt with that," seriously believing that they have freed themselves from the negative impact of something they have experienced either recently or at some time in the past. However, MT, on a number of occasions, has revealed that this is not always the case; sometimes this is just a story people tell themselves so they can move on with their lives. The reality is the emotional impact of memories, especially traumatic ones, can remain dormant in the subconscious mind, carried like weighty stones over the span of a person's lifetime, and rarely is this without consequence to a person's well-being and health. CEH can help lighten the load by identifying and releasing the cause of such health-harming negative memories and emotions.

Fortunately for this type of healing to occur, CEH does not require the client to relive the negative experience or to share their personal details with the practitioner. Once MT has identified such relevant factors as the time period of the event and/or the emotions associated with the experience, the appropriate modality is applied to release the energy blockages and their associated harmful impact on wellness. As mentioned previously in this regard, healing is enabled during treatment when the subconscious mind is made aware that the harmful concern has been identified, addressed and released. Though the memory of the traumatic experience remains, it loses its power to continue its negative impact on the person's well-being. Following such a treatment, clients have repeatedly described this particular CEH experience as being tremendously freeing, enabling them to once again move forward with their lives.

- The following stories involve treatments to eliminate a particular allergy in combination with an associated emotional and/or physical trauma.

Case 1: *Sandra's initial MT testing session indicated she was allergic to tin, and she was treated for this at the time. However, her follow up visit indicated the treatment hadn't held. Further investigation revealed that a combination of associated emotions needed to be released for the effective elimination of the allergy to tin.*

MT identified that both "sadness" and "regret" were associated somehow with the tin allergy. Upon sharing these findings with her, Sandra became silently introspective for a moment, clearly moved by what she had learned. She then went on to reveal that these findings had awakened a childhood memory of her mother having returned home from a trip with some beautifully painted "tin" Christmas ornaments. After reflecting on this memory for a moment, Sandra went on to say that she wished she had been more appreciative of her mother growing up, expressing regret for this and sadness at missing her now deceased mother.

The tin allergy was successfully eliminated in combination with the release of the associated emotions of sadness and regret.

It is only natural that we make associations between our emotions and our physical environment. Who would have thought that a person could have an allergy to tin, and furthermore that it would be associated with emotional blockages going back decades to early childhood? In Sandra's case this was more than opening the proverbial can of beans, and a "tin can" at that, as any contact with this metal either by touch or by ingesting food contained in it would trigger an allergic reaction.

While on the subject of allergies to metals, it is interesting to note that allergies to gold, silver, nickel and copper, the metals used for coins, often have a money-related emotional association such as financial stress or fear of not being able to make ends meet. MT can determine if a combination treatment for emotions is required in association with the treatment for these metals.

Case 2: Michelle requested help with some chronic digestive problems. Testing revealed an allergy to milk and lactase, the digestive enzyme for the lactose in milk. In addition to these, an associated emotion of fear related to her father dating back to her childhood was identified. As soon as Michelle was informed of this, she paused momentarily, as if watching the pieces of a puzzle fall miraculously into place. She then proceeded to share the following memory:

Michelle had grown up in a small town on the coast. She recalled walking with her dad on Sundays to the town wharf. On the way, he would treat her to an ice-cream at the local dairy shop. Little Michelle enjoyed her treat as they continued their walk down the wharf, however as they went further out over the water she could sense her father's fear growing. He was terrified his precious little girl would fall off the edge.

Unconsciously, Michelle had come to associate milk (ice-cream) with her father's fear. Releasing the associated emotion of fear in combination with the milk allergens (lactose, a milk sugar and lactase, the digestive enzyme for milk) had worked to successfully correct her digestive concerns caused by milk.

The external and internal environments of the body can and do influence our well-being. Such things as life experiences, our emotions in response to these, and the reactions of others can impact our health and well-being. As seen in Michelle's case, combination treatments can include factors from both internal and external environments of the body. And once all associations have been identified and included in the treatment, the allergy to the particular substance will be effectively eliminated.

- Household pets, such as cats and dogs are frequently considered part of the family. Challenging concerns can arise when a family member becomes allergic to the family pet. And sometimes the MT investigation reveals that the spectrum of allergens a person is dealing with is greater than initially anticipated.

Jack, a boy of about eight, came to see me with his mom. The hope was that I could eliminate his allergy to the family's cats. His mother was concerned about his ongoing allergies, noting Jack had to carry tissues everywhere he went to deal with his constantly running nose.

Jack's eyes and nose were notably irritated, and this little guy just looked tired. MT indicated he was very allergic to cats, and further testing indicated he was also allergic to a number of other environmental concerns and dietary nutrients. As each of these allergies was identified in turn, they were released with a Centering Attunement. The following day, I was very pleased to see Jack doing much better; the energized spark of the little boy had returned. About a month later, his mother gratefully reported in that Jack was doing very well and the persistent cat allergy was completely gone.

Remarkably, all this was accomplished within just one treatment session.

Sometimes a constellation of allergens can affect a person concurrently. During a treatment session, the practitioner will test to identify and treat as many of these as possible, while clearing any associated emotions or traumas as they are identified. At the beginning of the next treatment session, these treatments are checked to confirm that they have held completely, not needing to be repeated.

- The following brief story reveals that in rare cases allergies can happen at anytime and anywhere, both randomly and unexpectedly.

Kirk had joined a group of friends, including myself, for a seafood treat at a rural coastal restaurant. At that time, he didn't know he was allergic to lobster as he had eaten it before without any notable concerns. Shortly after the meal however, it was alarming to suddenly see him turn deathly pale and sink down to sit on a nearby step. He looked like he was about to faint. As others were present and ready to call for help, I offered Kirk a Centering Attunement for a possible allergy to lobster. There was no time, nor was he in any shape for muscle testing. He accepted and seconds later, to the relief of all present, he came around, stood up and regained his composure. The emergency was defused.

In this case, the allergic reaction occurred in a remote area; it came on suddenly and was completely unexpected. Fortunately, this scenario of a random and sudden appearance of a serious allergy is not a common occurrence. Usually, mild symptoms such as sensitivities arise to provide an early warning sign that an allergy could be developing.

With hindsight and if Kirk had known he had a serious allergy to lobster, he should have avoided this food option, notified the server of his seafood allergy, and as an added precaution he should have been carrying an EpiPen.

From my experience and that of those I have helped, the CEH Temporal or Centering Attunement treatment should be in everyone's survival kit. **Like the Heimlich Maneuver, these treatments can save lives.** Anyone can self-treat if they are on their own and able to do so, otherwise with permission, someone else can perform the attunement. And should a person be aware of a serious allergy, they should always carry an EpiPen, as one can never be too careful in such cases.

- Though amazed at the results that have been possible through Cognitive Energy Healing, realistically, a complete cure for certain unresolved healing concerns is not always possible. Often, in such cases however, this modality can provide pain relief, and calm muscle tension and inflammation to enable a degree of relief and healing to take place. The practitioner can also suggest some energy healing strategies for self-help while working with clients with chronic pain concerns.

This client, while not able to receive a complete cure for her health concern, did benefit and continues to be ever so grateful for a tremendous healing break though made during her treatment that drastically reduced the intensity and duration of her pain. It relates to the release of a *default trauma response.*

Ever since her car accident several years ago, Rachel continued to experience recurring episodes of severe back pain. She has been bedridden on numerous occasions, as anything from light lifting to a random movement could send her into intense pain and wrenching muscle spasms, and this could last for days. Rachel was very aware that emotional stress has been a significant factor in making her more vulnerable to such painful bouts.

Though CEH has not as yet been able to completely correct the cause of her back issues, it has provided Rachel with considerable relief from pain and the associated and exceedingly painful muscle spasms. In addition to Body Attunements, related emotional and physical causes of the back pain were addressed with Centering Attunements. And as Rachel indicated an interest, she has also been instructed in some self-help energy streaming techniques to help relax her muscles and relieve her pain.

On an amazingly positive note, ever since I addressed the default trauma-level muscle spasm response to back injury, Rachel has repeatedly and gratefully told me that her painful muscle spasms have completely stopped and have not recurred since. This remains the case for a couple of years since. Knowing that the brain initiates the pain response, I had subliminally told it to stop its default trauma response to every back injury, no matter how small. Amazingly since that time back pain responses have normalized and Rachel no longer experiences intense muscle spasms and their associated severe pain.

In treating a chronic pain response as a default response that can be corrected, CEH has been able to arrest the brain's habit of perceiving all ensuing minor injuries to an area as trauma. This said, sometimes there are limits to how much actual healing can take place due to a pre-established condition. In Rachel's case, a recent X-ray of the injured area indicated fusion of the vertebrae and bone spurs would continue to result in some level of ongoing back pain. Nevertheless, and even in such cases, energy healing can help relieve the pain of a flare up, reduce the intensity of the pain response, calm inflammation and help minimize further tissue damage.

In addition to this, these concerns can be better managed by providing the client with some energy-based muscle relaxing self-treatment techniques to address a concern as soon as it arises, before it escalates into a more painful situation. Whenever possible, should the client be interested, self-help energy healing techniques can be taught during a treatment session.

- People often assume they have no choice but to live with a condition either because it is not regarded as very significant, or that it has been deemed not medically treatable.

Early on in my self-healing practice, I noticed that a friend's hands shook uncontrollably whenever he carried a cup or a glass full of some beverage; interestingly, this shaking did not occur while carrying an object such as a book. As Dan was in his late forties at the time, I was concerned that this might be an early sign of some chronic disease that would need medical help. Hoping to gain some insight into what might be happening, we did some muscle testing. And thankfully, what had appeared to be a symptom of a potentially serious concern, turned out to something that could be easily remedied.

Testing revealed that Dan was allergic to the stress hormone cortisol, a response triggered by a worry about spilling the contents of the glass or cup he was carrying. Indications were that this worry was rooted in a stressful childhood experience, perhaps an embarrassment over the spill or for being scolded at the time. Attunements for cortisol, a stress hormone, and the associated childhood negative emotions experienced when the incident occurred, proved to be a success. The hand shaking stopped immediately and there has been no further concern in this regard ever since.

Sometimes a solution can be so amazingly simple. And to think Dan could have spent his entire life with this seemingly insignificant problem, thinking he could do nothing about it. It's surprising that such a minor emotional reaction to a mildly stressful activity could result in the naturally-occurring hormone, cortisol, being identified as a threat and an antigen to be targeted by the autoimmune system. Gratefully, this concern is and remains a thing of the past.

- Psoriasis is an autoimmune skin disease that causes red, itchy, scaly patches. There are seven different types of this disease in all. Psoriasis is believed to be caused by an inheritable genetic maladaptation leading to an overproduction of skin cells and inflammation. Episodes of psoriasis can be triggered or aggravated by stress, illness, injury or other factors. Two cases with different strains of the disease will be presented here.

Case 1: Jim's episodes of psoriasis manifested as a reddish scaly dry patch on a side of his nose and cheek, and sometimes also appeared as spots on his legs. His treatment included allergy eliminations for some dietary nutrients as well as for some stress hormones. Within about a week, Jim's symptoms had disappeared completely, and for years since he continues to remain psoriasis-free.

Case 2: Marci suffered from the pustular type of psoriasis, with flare ups occurring on her hands and on the bottoms of her feet. Testing revealed that the causes were work and personal stress, some dietary allergies causing a nutrient deficiency, some allergies to topical creams she was using and to cotton. She wore cotton socks most days. When treated, Marci's condition improved significantly though it was not completely eliminated. There is a growing awareness, for both Marci and myself that as her load of emotional baggage decreases her psoriasis condition improves. Stress and stress management appear to be significant factors.

The skin is an organ of the body, and its health can be negatively impacted by both internal and external factors. By identifying and releasing the causes of an immune response such as psoriasis can result in a cure, at least for some, and for others the severity of the condition can be significantly reduced. And stress management is a significant factor.

It is also relevant to that an allergy-caused nutrient deficiency can lead to a broad range of diseases, and certainly can be a causative factor for psoriasis. Nutrient deficiencies can occur when nutrients essential to the body's well-being become erroneously identified as an allergen, resulting in them to being eliminated from the body as quickly as possible. The ensuing vitamin and nutrient deficiencies can result in a number of deficiency illnesses.

In Marci's case, epigenetic concerns remain to be explored as a possible causative factor.

- While under limited exposure to irritants and toxins, the body is generally able to detoxify itself through breath, exercise, a healthy diet, adequate sleep and bodily excretions. However, depending on the frequency and intensity of exposure, the body's toxin eliminating systems can become overwhelmed, often leading to chemical and environmental sensitivities and allergies.

Some people experience daily exposure to a broad range of chemicals in their work environment (e.g. petrochemicals, dyes, inks, fumigants, detergents and antiseptic cleaners, pesticides, plastics, metals, wood and plaster dust, etc.). Most can manage limited environmental exposures and remain relatively healthy, however for some, daily exposure can stress the limits of the body's tolerance level. Work environment exposures can develop into allergies triggering mild to severe responses.

Like hospital employees, petroleum workers, and many others, hairstylists and aestheticians are unavoidably exposed on a daily basis to a broad range of chemicals. Their work requires them to be in frequent contact with dyes, permanent hair treatments, shampoos, conditioners, creams, cosmetics, and perfumes. Such exposures can occur through direct contact (touch, or inhaling) and indirectly through a perception of a product's energy emissions. This is not to say there is anything wrong with the hairdressing products per se. Rather, for some people some of these products can become identified as allergy-causing antigens posing significant health concerns over time.

A number years ago Adam, a gifted hairstylist, had to take a temporarily leave from his profession after developing serious allergies to a number of chemicals in his work environment. He was determined to find a way to return to the work he loved, so he developed strategies to protect himself from the products that had caused his allergic reactions. Opening his own salon proved to be a wise decision as this enabled him to have more control over his work environment.

Having known Adam for some time, and keen to help, I suggested he might be interested in trying a CEH treatment session. We set up a meeting for an hour at the salon first thing in the morning. Even before beginning our battery of testing for the salon products, and to Adam's surprise, his initial MT tested weak. The cause proved to be an environmental allergy to the residual chemicals in the salon from the previous day. This allergy was eliminated prior to moving on to test the list of salon products.

Besides identifying allergies to a number of products Adam had been using on a daily basis, he was reacting to the chemicals and scents of the products used by the other stylists in the salon, as well as to the energy frequencies emitted by products used in his proximity. As each allergy identified was readily eliminated as indicated by a strong MT following each treatment, I felt much good had been accomplished in the brief hour session that morning. Adam's allergy load had been notably reduced in one session.

Over the next year and a half, I continued to find Adam well, enthusiastic about his work, and as determined as ever to keep his work environment as safe as possible.

What is a person to do when they are no longer able to work in their chosen trade or profession due to an allergy or asthma? Whenever possible, taking some time out as Adam had wisely chosen to do, provides time to recover from the exposure to allergy-causing antigens. Also, getting adequate sleep, being physically active, and maintaining a healthy diet are things a person can do to help the body in its natural detoxification process.

Ultimately however, should a person dealing with work environment allergies and sensitivities decide to remain in such a job, CEH allergy elimination can help. I would caution that regular allergy checks are recommended as allergic reactions place the body under stress, and long-term exposure to stress can have serious health consequences. Allergic reactions can develop over time to products experienced on a daily basis, or they can suddenly appear "out of the blue" as an immediate response to a new product.

- Besides enabling a degree of healing that was not believed to be possible, the following story acknowledges that for some, the move from the known and trusted medical model to try an alternative healing approach can be a difficult step into the unknown. I first met Ann and Don while on a brief vacation south to escape the Canadian winter. Though this story is about Ann, Don does factor in in the beginning.

Prior to our meeting, a mutual friend had mentioned to Don that I might be able to help him with his allergies to flowering fruit trees. As he was visibly in a full blown allergic reaction at our initial meeting, he readily accepted my offer of CEH help the following day. These treatments worked for those exposures, and Don remained allergy-free for the remainder of his visit to a southern climate.

Though his wife Ann had been curious about the energy treatments her husband received, she remained somewhat skeptical until she saw that CEH attunements had readily stopped his allergic reactions. Ann then cautiously decided to share a little secret with me, and this proved to be a call for help. We were alone at the time when she removed her wig to reveal she was completely hairless. In fact, she told me she had no hair on her body whatsoever, explaining she had a condition called alopecia that had started five years ago.

Without making any promises, I suggested we could try CEH to see if it could help in any way. MT revealed a few internal allergens which I treated, before I learned that some of the primary causes of Ann's condition were trauma and stress related. Ann, at that time simply wasn't ready to address this concern, so we didn't go any further. I sensed she had a tremendous fear of dealing with such concerns.

It wasn't until the following year that I saw Ann again. And voilà, much to my surprise, some patches of hair, though spotty, had grown in. Our work the previous year, though only preliminary, had produced some amazing results. Hair had grown, where there had been none before the CEH treatment. Ann still remained uneasy about exploring further trauma concerns, so we addressed some minor ones. And surprisingly, even more hair grew, though still patchy and not yet a full head of hair.

I believe for a complete correction of the alopecia conditions to take place, an outstanding trauma has yet to be addressed, and this can only happen when the client is ready. Any number of health-related responses can manifest in the body's response to trauma. Sometimes its impact can remain dormant, without any noticeable cause for concern, until something triggers it to surface. Often even just a minor stress factor is all that is required to initiate significant health symptoms to flare up in a body's call for help. Trauma, though seemingly dormant can continue to fester and may require professional help. In the interim, what has been accomplished by the CEH treatments even to this point in Ann's treatment is amazing. Hair is growing where there was not a single visible strand!

Remember that a practitioner can address only those emotional concerns a person is ready to release, and that can sometime take time. It is also important for the client to understand that energy blockages caused by trauma can be effectively released without having to relive or revisit the disturbing memory of the experience. As the subconscious mind already knows the story, CEH can free the client indirectly by releasing the impact of the negative emotions associated with the trauma experience.

- The very fabric of our physical being is interwoven with our emotional experience of the world, and as emotions can cause physical symptoms, physical symptoms can impact our emotional well-being as well. This was ever so evident when Alicia, someone I had known for some time, came to me for help. Apparently, something strange had happened to her back, and she said it was too complicated to explain over the phone. Well, that proved to be an understatement!

When Alicia arrived for her treatment session, words could not explain my surprise at what I saw. It was disconcerting to see this woman who is, or at least had been about three inches taller than I, met me face to face at my eye level. Her body was contorted with her shoulders drawn off to one side and out of alignment with her body. Then when she turned to show me her back, I saw her spinal column was in a slurred S shape. It was clear that something had caused her body to become noticeably shorter. The questions remained: what had happened? and why?

Alicia explained that she had been receiving treatment elsewhere, but her recovery had stalled. It was difficult to imagine that her condition had been any worse than what I was seeing at the time. She told me she was not aware of any injury that could have caused this, however, when asked if she had recently experienced an emotional trauma, she was taken aback. She was shaken by the realization that there may be a connection between what had happened to her, and her husband's recent prostate cancer diagnosis. She noted that sequentially her husband's diagnosis had preceded her back issue. MT confirmed that the emotional trauma of this news was the root cause of her spine losing its alignment, and that an associated energy blockage was preventing healing from taking place. Like a crumbling house of cards, her spine had given way to the impact of the trauma of her husband's diagnosis.

Recognizing that two distinctly different healing concerns were in need of being addressed, I started with the emotional release of the fears that Alicia was confronted with when she learned the threatening news about her husband's health. Once released, these were replaced with trust, hope, and an intention for healing. Further to this, MT confirmed that all emotional concerns associated with the trauma had been released. To complete the treatment, the second healing concern was addressed with a series of Body Attunements to balance and realign the spine.

The healing of Alicia's back concern took place over a period of only two treatment sessions, and as early as following the first session, it was clear that healing was already taking place. The next day, the final session was all that was required for Alicia's body to be able to make the remaining corrections it needed to complete the healing.

Negative emotions and emotional trauma can and do take their toll on the physical body. To initiate Alicia's recovery, it was essential that her emotional concerns be released prior to addressing the physical healing of her spine. The emotional trauma had been the cause, the back problem was the result. Alicia's healing took place like a miracle, her spinal column realigned itself and her body resumed its normal height. All this in just two sessions!

- People are complex in so different many ways. When it comes to CEH treatments, as one layer of concern has been addressed, others waiting in the wings can surface for attention, and it is important that each of these be addressed as they appear. Following the pathway to healing can lead the practitioner along a sometimes unpredictable and seemingly random route, as occurred in the following case.

Following years of trying to get help with traditional therapies and treatments Marya, out of desperation, decided to see if CEH might offer help for her concerns. The first time I met her I noticed she carried her body at an angle, leaning noticeably about five degrees to the one side. This could have been caused by a physical injury, however my sense was it was the result of some kind of emotional trauma. The latter was confirmed by both MT and my conversation with her, which suggested she had somehow been victimized; her emotional pain was being communicated by an injured person stance.

Traumatized by a childhood of emotional and sexual abuse, Marya's adult life continued to be plagued by betrayal and dysfunction. She revealed she had spent most of her life, from childhood on, "in hiding." This revelation proved to be very a significant clue to her healing, however this particular concern could not be addressed until near the end of her treatment regime. Healing is a process, and all indications pointed to other concerns needing attention first. Going forward, MT guided the healing path ahead.

Traumas and a seemingly endless list of painful emotions including shame, sadness, betrayal, helplessness, and anger needed to be released. Centering Attunements, and Release and Reclaim treatments were effective in addressing these concerns. Following this, a Body Attunement was successful in restoring Marya's skeletal structural alignment. Within minutes, her body miraculously shifted from listing to one side, to a point where she was effortlessly standing perfectly erect. The "victim stance" was gone and remains so for a few of years since.

At a subsequent session Marya once again brought up this persistent concern of being in hiding, as she spoke more fervently about this strange feeling of needing to hide. It was during this conversation that something unexpected and unusual happened. Her right eye, seemingly without reason, started to blink uncontrollably. Not knowing what was going on exactly, we both responded with an uneasy giggle. As the blinking eventually stopped, I couldn't help thinking that this might in some way be related to Marya's concern about being in hiding.

It wasn't until the next session that once again as Marya was talking about this inhibiting and pervasive feeling of needing to hide, the blinking eye behavior returned. As this behavior appeared to be some kind of a signal, I calmly asked if I could ask some MT questions to try to determine what this meant.

I learned that this communication came from a twelve-year old child, an aspect of Marya's consciousness that had been hiding in fear for decades. This child aspect of her personality, finally feeling safe and no longer helplessly trapped by fear, indicated through MT that she wanted to come out of hiding and be one with her adult self. Marya accepted this integration with a calm sense of purpose and joy. The combination of emotional mind and physical body attunements finally worked to reunite Marya with the fragmented and hidden aspect of herself. No longer fearful, the hiding child was able to join as one with her adult self. For Marya, this amazing transition to the new reality of being whole with the child aspect of herself freed from fear and the need to hide, was both an enriching and empowering experience.

Healing is a process! Sometimes this requires following a somewhat meandering pathway to wellness. In this case, other concerns including trauma, emotions, and memories had to be addressed initially before dealing with other pending concerns. And also, and once again, as this was relevant in Marya's case, CEH does not require the client to revisit the painful memories of trauma or abuse in order to release them and enable healing. All that is required is to determine when the trauma occurred and to release the associated negative emotions so that they will no longer be harmful to a person's health and well-being.

- Hepatitis is any of a group of diseases causing inflammation of the liver due to autoimmune disease, viruses, toxins, or alcohol.

There are five main types ranging from hepatitis A through E. This disease can be a temporary or a long-term condition, and in rare occasions it can be fatal. Symptoms include a yellow discoloration of the skin and whites of the eyes, fatigue, as well as a range of unpleasant digestive concerns.

Charlotte came to see me following an alarming concern about her liver. Her doctor had diagnosed her condition as hepatitis and in her case, the cause was undetermined. She told me the lab report indicated her liver enzymes had skyrocketed.

Thinking this disease could be the result of an autoimmune response, I proceeded to MT for potential internal allergens related to both her liver and her blood. A number of related concerns were identified and promptly addressed during a couple of treatment sessions. Of particular interest here, is that following each of the two treatment sessions Charlotte's liver enzymes count went down dramatically to level out finally within the normal range.

Though difficult to prove, CEH treatments may have been the reason for Charlotte's rapid recovery as they immediately preceded each recorded improvement. If nothing else, autoimmune responses that were targeting components of Charlotte's blood and her liver were corrected.

- In the following case, I decided to focus my initial attention on some new symptoms that had recently surfaced, and were exacerbating the client's ability to manage her ADHD disorder. What was to follow came as an amazing surprise, potentially offering hope to many.

Attention Deficit Hyperactivity Disorder (ADHD) is a mental disorder affecting millions worldwide. People with this neurodevelopmental disorder are described as being easily distracted, inattentive, impulsive, having difficulty focusing and following instructions, and the list goes on. The cause is unknown and the impact of this disorder can pervade all aspects of a person's life, including school, work, personal relationships and social engagement.

Melanie had managed her ADHD symptoms fairly well with a combination of medication and coping strategies. That was at least until recent episodes of brain fog, fatigue and difficulty sleeping left her feeling overwhelmed, exhausted and frustrated. These concerns were impacting both her work and personal life.

Recognizing that Melanie required immediate attention, we did an intensive back-to-back treatment session. Fortunately, previous visits for other health concerns had already addressed a number of factors, including such things as diet, environmental and work-related allergens, including the release of some energy blockages caused by trauma.

The treatment protocol for this session included three basic areas: brain function, epigenetic gene function, and chakra energy flow. Initially, autoimmune reactions to hormones and neurotransmitters affecting brain function were identified and corrected. Next, concerns regarding gene action were restored to the required on or off setting sequence to enable optimal brain function. And finally, malfunctions in energy flow through chakras six and seven (brain area) were identified and corrected. All three protocols were addressed with Centering Attunements.

About two and a half months following the treatment sessions, Melanie, in complete amazement, reported significant and lasting beneficial results from our healing work. Not only were her sleep issues, fatigue and brain fog concerns gone, but for the first time in her life, her constantly overstimulated and hyper-reactive brain was calm. For her, this was proving to be a new and much appreciated improvement in her quality of life.

This remarkable reduction in Melanie's ADHD symptoms came as a complete and wonderful surprise to both of us. With the CEH corrections, it had taken only twelve days for the healing to take place, which is in alignment with the standard healing period for such complex treatments being anywhere from one to two weeks.

Then, out of the blue and for a period of a few months, the old ADHD symptoms returned. When Melanie came to see me for help about this concern, a seventh chakra energy malfunction was readily identified and corrected. Melanie has since returned to her calm and focused state of well-being, significantly better equipped to manage the debilitating symptoms of ADHD.

Sometimes we put limits on what is or can be possible. Taking on the challenge of Melanie's sleep, fatigue and brain fog issues seemed to me to be well within the scope of CEH. However, my mind-set that ADHD was completely beyond the scope of what could be addressed by this modality has since been gratefully recalibrated. The impossible becomes the possible when we give ourselves permission to look beyond the boundaries of what is, and at least give it a try.

This experience of working with Melanie has been a very big learning opportunity for me, with the assurance that road blocks to new possibilities can be lifted. We just have to give ourselves permission to do so, as we move into this new era of discovery and healing possibilities.

Where Cognitive Energy Healing Has Made a Difference

Besides having made an absolutely amazing difference in my well-being and quality of life, Cognitive Energy Healing has also served the healing needs of a growing number of other people. Though I don't want to inflate the results, they have admittedly been truly remarkable, and in many cases, have made healing a reality where it was not thought to be possible.

The following is a brief list where CEH has made a difference:

- Identifying the root causes of autoimmune diseases, and helping improve or completely restore wellness

- Identifying and correcting nutrient and vitamin deficiencies caused by allergies

- Releasing causes of physical and emotional pain and trauma

- Reducing and potentially eliminating anxiety and depression

- Reducing or potentially eliminating inflammation

- Releasing harmful core beliefs to reclaim beliefs that are healthy and consistent with a person's current values and goals

- Reducing and eliminating the potentially negative impact of stress

- Correcting epigenetically-caused gene dysfunction by restoring normal gene expression for optimal health

- Identifying and releasing the triggers for certain harmful behaviors, habits and attitudes including phobias and obsessive-compulsive disorders

- Restoring and balancing normal energy flow throughout the body's electrochemical and bio-energetic flow systems, as well as the subtle energy flow channels of the auric field, chakras, and meridians

- Enabling the body to structurally balance and realign itself

- Balancing and improving brain function

- Reducing the symptoms of ADHD (at least in Melanie's case)

- Enabling clients to help themselves

And now in memory of a dear family friend Gerry who passed away a few years ago, I would like to share a story that may possibly be relevant, at least for a brief period with respect to cancer remission.

We planned to meet up with Gerry, a longtime friend from Australia, and his new bride Grace on a ten-day river-barge cruise from Budapest to Amsterdam. The trip had been organized to fulfill a dream of Gerry's to return one last time to his birthplace and home town in Holland. He had been diagnosed with terminal cancer with about three months left to live. Even with this heavily-pending reality, and including brief visits to hospitals along our journey, we shared an absolutely wonderful time together. There were glorious moments of shared laughter and joy my husband and I will treasure always.

I had told Gerry about a CEH treatment I thought might be worth trying, so one afternoon in the last part of our journey as Grace was off for a massage, we gave it a try. I hoped that this treatment, at this point untested, would enable his body to identify and eliminate the invading cancer cells. And as things turned out, this one-off treatment may have changed the direction of what was happening in his body, as on his return home, he was found to be completely cancer-free. Following this, Gerry and Grace were able to enjoy a wonderful two more years together.

Sadly, by the end of this two-year period, cancer resurfaced in a completely different part of his body than the previously diagnosed cancer. I learned about this sad news shortly before setting out on a planned visit to Australia. However, it was too late as Gerry had passed away while I was in transit.

Life is a learning journey. Looking back on that time, I recognize that our vacation together was too brief to have explored the underlying causes of why Gerry was stricken with cancer in the first place. Other questions linger as to why, when cancer had been eradicated in one organ, that it would resurface two years later as a completely different type located in another part of the body.

We have increasingly come to know that cancer always has its own reasons for being, and that it has something to do with identifiable root causes: while some may be genetic others include stress, trauma, anger, diet, obesity, tobacco, alcohol, exposure to carcinogens such as chemicals and radiation, and the list goes on. When given time and awareness, we can address a number of these concerns. This takes us back to the bottom of the listing of how CEH has made a difference, as it can enable clients to help themselves by identifying their particular health risks for cancer. It can also release the negative impact of harmful emotions, stress and trauma on the body.

PART VIII

From Self-Awareness to Self-Empowerment

Our Inner Resources

Instead of going along with the culturally driven "take a pill for that" approach to dealing with our problems and then coping with the ensuing not so pleasant side effects, the following thoughts on self-empowerment are offered as a non-invasive alternative to restoring health and balance to one's life.

People frequently tend to forget that there is much they can accomplish on their own to deal with stress, to cope with daily challenges, to correct unwanted behaviors and to change harmful attitudes and beliefs. Know that in a way not unlike our ability to change our minds, individually, we each have the power to make cathartic changes to correct harmful attitudes, beliefs and behaviors. Being receptive to the enlightening spark of conscious awareness provides an opportunity to initiate beneficial and positive change in our lives. This awareness is a fundamental part of the self-empowerment process, and can be significantly enhanced with self-healing training in Cognitive Energy Healing.

Have you ever noticed that when given a moment of solitude, the mind automatically tends to move into self-awareness and introspection? And at such times, when faced with a problem to solve it readily takes on the task. The unconscious mind on its own sets off in the pursuit of a solution without further conscious involvement. Given time for introspective thought, the mind will assess and address problems and concerns that can enable you to make beneficial changes in your life.

This self-assessment function of the brain can be thought of as a kind of a road safety check, the *vehicle* being your holistic self and the *road* ahead being your life. By engaging your own inner resources, you will learn how to work for and protect your well-being as you become aware of the oftentimes subtle body, mind and spirit signals coming your way. And as required, depending on the challenges you are dealing with, this very same self-awareness will spur you on to seek out the help of friends, doctors and other health practitioners as required.

Most of the time, the majority of us somehow manage to muddle through the daily challenges and stressors that come our way. Meanwhile, others find themselves struggling and overwhelmed with any number of challenging concerns. Some apt expressions to describe such challenges are, "I'm barely able to keep my nose above water," "I'm peddling my bicycle as fast as I can," "I feel like I'm drowning." The experience of feeling trapped in long term exposure to high stress conditions is unsustainable and dangerous to one's well-being. It can impact work performance, family and personal relationships, and ultimately can result in serious health concerns. And yet, not to despair, as there is usually something you can do about it. The first step following awareness is to give yourself permission to develop a workable strategy and then to act on it.

Body ownership comes with a number of responsibilities beyond basic safety, food and shelter. As the vehicle that takes you through life, your holistic body requires a regime of regular checks to maintain optimum holistic health. Naturally, this requires a degree of oversight of one's internal and external well-being, along with a conscious commitment to respond and make changes as required.

Log into your own self-awareness and trust that given a problem, your introspective and creative mind is at the ready to try to oversee where you are at and where you are going in your life, and will strive to address any concern that arises. By making room for your inner voice you will come to know that it is there to guide you through life's challenges. And when additional help is needed, a CEH self-healing practice can be an invaluable added resource, particularly on a challenging journey.

Let's consider some ways to fit such a regime into a busy day. For most, general oversight can take place effortlessly over the day as it unfolds, while introspection requires some quiet, personal time and inner space to listen and to think. Where can you find such a place in your day? Perhaps it may be found in the early waking hours of your morning, while showering, over your morning coffee, during a walk at lunchtime, just before sleep, or you can schedule it in by setting some dedicated time aside for introspection or meditation.

Creating one's personal space and time for introspection is indeed a growing and pervasive challenge in today's stressful and digitally-driven world. With all the amazing and valued advances in technology our lives have been transformed in innumerable beneficial ways. Living better digitally has made many of the things we value instantaneously accessible, including instant access to a boundless resource of knowledge and information. Portable PC's and hand-held devices have freed us from a stationary work station, enabling us to carry our work with us anywhere we go, and making many of our social, entertainment and media requirements instantly available at any time of the day or night.

These significant benefits, however, are counterbalanced by a growing concern for their impact on our mental and physical health. The online digital way of life has added such new and unsettling concerns as *device anxiety* and *device addiction*. Inadvertently, while immersing ourselves in the many life-enhancing benefits of digital technology, we have dropped some of our self-protective boundaries, and this has come at a personal cost. Some of the trade-offs for being electronically connected with anyone, anywhere, and at any-time have resulted in us carrying our workloads home, bringing an end the standard nine to five work day, and we have sacrificed our down time by being accessible twenty-four-seven by phone, text or e-mail. In addition to this, and something that has struck us by surprise, is the social isolation caused by the decrease in real person to person contact. Why waste your time speaking directly to a person, keep it simple and send off a text! With awareness, all of these concerns can be addressed in a healthy way by learning to set and protect healthy boundaries. When you give yourself permission to act, you have the power to create your world, so why not make it a healthy and happy place to be.

For people dealing with *device addiction,* a moment of silence or calm away from external digital engagement can be intolerable, causing them to feel anxious or on edge. The sense of losing connection with the life-affirming outside digital world can be unsettling and even frightening for them. In an effort to block the mind's natural tendency for introspection, they may seek escape by engaging in any of a number of *device addiction* behaviors such as tuning into loud thought-drowning music, obsessively playing digital games, or compulsively checking and re-checking their device screens for any sign of external attempts to connect with them. This is a sign additional help may be required. Therapist's offices are filled with people dealing with such issues.

The full on, all the time, online lifestyle is addictive and has led to a significant increase in stress, a known cause of such serious and potentially fatal illnesses as cancer and heart disease. Unconsciously, we have been sacrificing the time we need to recharge our energies in order to carry on. Additional concerns include soft tissue damage caused by frequent texting on our hand-held devices, neck pain caused by the ergonomic challenges of sitting for long periods of time at a computer, and eye damage caused by long term exposure to computer screens. Ultimately, the ball is in our court to help heal and protect ourselves as best we can, and to seek help when help is needed.

Change is possible. Take the challenge, engage your self-awareness, tune into yourself and listen, then work at taking back control of your life. And though CEH may not have all the answers, it can help with this process in a number of significantly beneficial ways.

A Pathway to Freedom

In this section, I will be speaking about ways to free ourselves from limiting beliefs about our abilities, letting go of emotional pain and trauma, and how we can help ourselves to manage and release some of the causes of physical pain. The decision to modify or correct any type of undesirable behavior on your own requires awareness, determination and a well thought out course of action. As any new strategy for achieving lasting lifestyle change is rarely easy, it may be advisable to get some additional help such as counselling, seeing a therapist or perhaps CEH may offer the help you need.

When two people meet for the first time, even before a handshake, before a word is spoken, both have subliminally and unconsciously received information about the new acquaintance. Energy readings and scents are perceived and assessed intuitively. Perceptions on a conscious level include the person's physical presence and their appearance, including how they carry themselves, the sound of their voice, their gestures, mannerisms and facial expressions, as well as how they dress. Once names are exchanged, the person's name then becomes linked with the broad scope of information gleaned during this first encounter as well as from any future encounters. Later, a simple mention of the person's name will carry with it all this previously learned information about them. And in addition to the superficial things one may notice initially such as gender, height, weight, attractiveness, etc., important assessments about personal safety and trust are also being made and registered for current and future reference.

The low vibrational energy of people overwhelmed with fatigue, stress and negative emotions impacts those people they are in close and frequent contact with. Generally, people with a positive attitude tend to pick up on such energies fairly quickly, and given the option, will try limit or avoid contact with them as much as possible. And since better things usually come from a positive approach, aligning oneself with a positive outlook will improve your day, enhance and grow beneficial relationships and friendships, and will simply make for a happier life.

Creating a Balanced and Happy Life

> The mind is its own place
> and in it self
> Can make a Heav'n of Hell
> and a Hell of Heav'n

Paradise Lost, John Milton

Personal change and growth are possible through thoughtful introspection, and a mindful awareness of how we are in the world. With eyes wide open to the truth, take the time to ask yourself why you feel the way you do or why you reacted as you did. Much can be accomplished through our efforts to learn about ourselves, and even more importantly our shadow-selves, those aspects of ourselves that we are not so proud of. Should we wish to engage it, the power to make beneficial and health-enhancing change resides within us. It begins with self-awareness, and when a need for change is recognized, the next empowering step is to give oneself permission to find a new way forward.

Knowing yourself is the first step toward creating a self-fulfilling and happy life. There is much to be learned from being mindful of how you are in your life, both individually and in all your various roles and relationships. Don't let fear hold you back from asking yourself such personal questions as am I happy, do I feel fulfilled in my personal life or at work, is my stress load manageable or is it taking a personal toll, is my body trying to tell me something through such symptoms as headaches, back pain, or digestive concerns?

And to gain a little further insight into identifying the stress-inducing factors that are negatively affecting your well-being, such questions as the following may be helpful: Why do I feel the way I do when ……, why do I always react in this way when …., why do I feel uncomfortable when ……, what can I do to break this harmful or painful pattern ……, what triggers this unpleasant reaction in me, does this problem originate with me or with somebody else, am I hindered by self-doubt? Should the answers to any of these or other relevant questions of your own indicate all is not well and a need for change is evident, the next step is to focus on developing a workable strategy to improve your quality of life. And it goes without saying, this can have a positive impact for yourself as well as your relationship with others.

Along with growing one's self-awareness, it is significantly beneficial to try to work on replacing negative thoughts about yourself and others with positive ones. A positive approach to life is empowering and attracts good things to come your way, including good and well-intentioned people and enriching experiences.

The following is offered as a few insights on how to tap into your inner resources to create a healthier and happier life:

- Love of oneself and others is fundamental to living a full and happy life. Love is key to enabling us to value and care for ourselves, and is beneficially-shared with others in acts of friendship, kindness, compassion, and forgiveness.

For most people, we have learned the word *love* evokes a strong MT response. However, for some people this same word carries negative emotional associations. There are any number of reasons why the word *love* would test weak, such as an association with rejection, abandonment, sadness, grief or loss. Such associations cause energy blockages that negatively impact a person's quality of life and in some cases, even their health. Once identified, such blockages can be readily released and corrected using a combination of the CEH Centering Attunements along with Release and Reclaim statements to bring about the desired life-healing change.

Clearings of this nature can and often do take place within a few minutes. Other cases may require more time as more layers of emotional concern are revealed. Whether it be a one-off concern, or a number of related concerns requiring sequential treatments, it is important to realize that people are complex, they react to things in different ways, with varying degrees of intensity, and sometimes there is a cumulative effect.

- It is essentially our responsibility to establish and maintain a realistic and healthy balance in our lives. Admittedly most of us at one time or another have been caught up in a stressful mire that could be related to family, friends, colleagues, work, community or financial challenges. And while this is all part of life, sometimes we can feel overwhelmed and powerlessly trapped in a prolonged exposure to stress, which, as you know, can significantly impact a person's health.

When life challenges and stress get out of balance, it is necessary at some point to stop and take stock in an effort to find some kind of a workable solution. It is worthwhile to have a levelheaded look at what types of expectations you are placing on yourself, as well as to identify those that are placed on you by others. This can help you determine how these may be affecting your well-being, and what you can do to address them.

A good strategy at the outset is to determine if your roles and associated responsibilities are out of balance and need adjustment. Life roles, what Carl Jung called archetypes, include such things as spouse, parent, care-giver, creative person, mentor, student, protector, provider, friend, hero, leader, follower, survivor, victim, etc. As all roles come with responsibilities and expectations, a review of what is happening in this area can be helpful in recalibrating and balancing such demands as you work toward getting your life back on track.

The following is a *take control of your life* kind of exercise intended to help develop strategies to manage your various roles for your well-being and that of the people you engage with. Ultimately it is about establishing a healthy and realistic balance in your life. It's a pen and paper exercise that allows you to lay out before you on paper your roles and associated responsibilities and expectations. Getting all of this out of your head this way offers an opportunity for a more objective perspective to evaluate and determine where things are out of balance and changes are necessary.

Take Control of Your Life, a review of roles, responsibilities and expectations toward making changes as required:

a. List 1: List all your roles, then prioritize them in numerical order. Highlight which of these you feel to be the most stressful and/or demanding of your time and energy.

b. List 2: Transcribe each highlighted role, leaving a few lines to include a point form description of their respective responsibilities and demands.

c. Working from list 2, categorize the identified goals and expectations as either A for *Achievable* or NA for *Not Achievable*. The NA identifier is an assessment of what you feel is beyond what you can realistically manage on your own.

d. Strategies can then be developed to address those items identified as Not Achievable. You may ask yourself if there are any possible modifications that would make this goal or expectation achievable. Is it possible to cut back temporarily on any of your lesser roles to free up some time to deal with the more pressing concerns of the moment? Do you need some additional help to carry out properly those responsibilities that can't be met? Is there someone you can ask for help or employ to assist you at this challenging time? Do you need to set in place some healthy boundaries to protect yourself from any excessive demands being placed on you by others?

Be realistic and fair in creating your new strategies for moving forward, and recognize that priorities may have to be modified to meet changing needs as time goes on. And sometimes, you simply have to give yourself permission to say no, recognizing you have reached your limit or that someone else would be better suited to the task.

- We're all guilty of having been snagged into certain habitual and negative behaviors or thought patterns at one time or another. Besides habit-driven behaviors, these can also include thought patterns driven by anxiety, worry, fear, guilt, anger, jealousy, etc. And once caught in the loop by such negative thought patterns, people tend to believe they are powerless to stop them. No matter how convinced you are that there is no way to find your way free, there are ways to take control of the situation, and the results can be both liberating and life enhancing.

Addressing negative thoughts, feelings and behaviors:

a. Not only can you learn to identify harmful behavior patterns as they occur, with practice and patience you can learn to stop them. The first step to freeing yourself comes with an *awareness* of the problem behavior. The next is to give yourself *permission to change* this behavior. By linking awareness with permission for change to take place, you can learn to identify and override the habit of ignoring the messages coming from the subconscious mind, the overseer of behaviors and intentions, or as Lucien Freud called it, the superego.

b. With awareness comes the ability to identify the trigger that sends you off into a negative behavior pattern. Pema Chödrön, in her book *Taking the Leap: Freeing Ourselves from Old Habits and Fears,* speaks in an enlightened way on this subject. She recommends that whenever you find yourself caught up in *a downward spiral,* a *worry loop,* or *harmful behavior,* recognize that these are patterns and habits that we can do something about. By becoming consciously aware of such concerns and identifying their triggers, we can learn to stop them on the spot before the cycle begins.

Ask yourself what it was that initiated the harmful response. What was the trigger? Once identified, it is then essential to have a default *plan of action* in place to divert you from engaging in your habitual response. Chödrön recommends focusing on one's breath as an immediate response to a known trigger as this helps to restore calm and control while providing time to decide how best to proceed.

The next step is to have an established default behavior plan in place to engage in, as this will defuse the controlling power of the trigger. Choose a safe alternative activity, one you enjoy and one that will work for you. Some possible ideas include going to the gym or for a run, connecting with a supportive friend, reading, playing a challenging game, gardening, meditating, etc. And whenever possible, physically move yourself away from the known trigger, as this is a positive and conscious way of taking control of the situation.

And know that should you need further help, CEH investigative and releasing modalities can help in correcting negative behavior patterns.

c. We all make mistakes, have had negative experiences, and generally most of us try to learn from these and move on. When trying to address concerns of this kind on your own, write out all the emotions you associate with the mistake or negative experience you had: e.g. shame, anger, frustration, etc. Then say "I release (say the list) ...., I forgive myself, and I reclaim my right to learn from the experience and move forward with my life. Release the negative burden by replacing it with a positive approach. Kindness begins with yourself. If you find you are unable to accomplish the "move on" part of the exercise, then a CEH Centering Attunement may enable you to do so. Oftentimes, it all starts with releasing any associated negative emotions and forgiving yourself.

- In order to reach one's fullest potential, it is important to identify and let go of limiting beliefs about oneself. On your own, you can learn to pay attention to how you speak to yourself. Beating yourself up verbally by calling yourself a failure, stupid, hopeless, worthless, etc. is a harmful pattern of self-abuse. It is important to be aware that both positive and negative statements about one's self tend to become a self-fulfilling prophecy, so out of love and kindness for your own well-being, work to take a positive approach when addressing such concerns. It is beneficial to get into the habit of making positive *I am* statements when thinking about yourself, as a positive attitude is empowering in enabling you to bring about beneficial changes in your life.

For some, breaking a self-criticizing or down-putting habit can be a difficult task, as many of these can be deeply rooted in core beliefs from early childhood. Once identified, the CEH Release and Reclaim protocol has proven to be effective in correcting these concerns.

And speaking to the power of our thoughts, did you know it is beneficial to one's health to be grateful for the good things in our life? Research into a daily practice of gratitude conducted by Laura Redwine and Dr. Robert Emmons of the University of California revealed that a daily practice of gratitude reduces the impact of fear, stress and anxiety by noticeably lowering the production of cortisol, a stress-related hormone. A positive attitude and thankfulness also improve a person's ability to sleep, as well the quality of sleep. They also found that the practice of gratitude has significantly decreased such heart failure causative factors as heart inflammation and high blood pressure. And if this is not motivation enough to consider *a daily gratitude practice*, it also reduces depression by stimulating the release of the pleasure hormones, serotonin and dopamine.

Healing can come in different forms and sometimes, something as simple as making an effort to change certain perceptions about ourselves, others and life in general can be positive and life enhancing. It seems obvious that consciously creating a positive thought environment combined with being grateful would have worthwhile health benefits. This research into how attitude impacts well-being validates and heightens our awareness that conscious choices of how we choose to be in the world do make a difference.

When dealing with an ongoing issue or a one-off incident in your day, sharing your story either through journaling or talking with a friend can be both helpful and cathartic in providing an objective and clearer perspective of what you are dealing with. Just writing about a challenging experience relieves stress and sets your subconscious mind to working on ways to deal with the concern. And while sharing a concern with a friend, partner or spouse, do let them know that you appreciate their kindness. That said however, they should not be made to feel that you are asking them to solve your problem for you, as ultimately that is your concern. Should additional insights be offered by a thoughtful listener, do receive these respectfully as they may be helpful in your decision making.

Also, remember that wherever you are and whatever you are dealing with, the healing power of your breath to help you remain calm and maintain your focus is always with you and readily accessible. Try it and see for yourself; on your own and in this moment, experience the benefits of the ocean breath*. By breathing rhythmically and more fully, you engage the ebb and flow of your breath to create a sound similar the surf, a sound created by the friction of air moving through your breathing passage. Mindfully focusing on the calm rhythmic ocean breath can be centering, cleansing and healing.

And know that when you give yourself permission, you are enabling yourself:

- to trust

- to heal

- to take care of yourself

- to seek help when needed

- to make behavior changes when needed

- to value yourself and others

- to love and be loved

- to be happy

- to be patient

- to be kind and compassionate

- to forgive yourself and others

- to celebrate the successes of others
- to be tolerant
- to move on
- to release harmful beliefs, habits, and behaviors
- to acknowledge and let go of the painful memories and traumas
- to be fully present in the moment
- to be mindful
- to value yourself and others
- to know and love yourself
- to love and respect others
- to celebrate your gifts
- to be well
- to be grateful
- to simply be

And know that any of these, and others on your personal list, can be addressed readily in an effective and healing way with a CEH self-healing practice.

* The ocean breath is always with you and readily accessible. To realize the benefits of this breath, breathe fully and calmly in and out creating the gentle sound similar to the breath used to fog a mirror or your glasses, and yet sounds so like the cleansing and calming rhythm of the ocean when performed with your eyes closed. So, close your eyes and be with the rhythmic flow of the ocean breath. As different traditions have varying approaches, you may wish to further research this on-line.

Problem solving: some thoughts on how the mind works

We are about to address two different problem-solving challenges: one, to find a lost memory and the other, to solve a problem that has not been addressed before. Let's explore both scenarios.

Allow yourself to think back to how your mind functions when you are searching for an answer to something you knew at one time in the past but have since forgotten. This memory is not lost but hidden away in those infamous dark recesses of your mind.

Most people have experienced at one time or another trying to remember the name of someone we have met in passing. Say, for example, you are in a social setting and you see someone you know; you recognize this acquaintance, however you draw a blank when you try to retrieve this person's name. While some have developed strategies to deal with such situations, generally the more pressed we feel to access the name, the less likely it will be recovered in time. Those who are best at this, having been down this path before, may choose a less stressful approach by remaining calm and trusting the name will surface when required as they listen for cues and clues to find the answer. Free of the self-imposed stress of conscious interference, the brain is much more efficient at doing its job of retrieving a forgotten memory. You reach out to shake hands and voilà, there it is, "_Sally_, it's so nice to see you."

Now let's take this one giant step further. Rather than trying to retrieve information that is already in your memory banks, let's check out how the mind functions when attempting to solve a new problem. In this case, the answer you are looking for is not stored anywhere. It is not a matter of searching for what is already in your memory; it is a matter of working with whatever resources you have accessible at the time. You can do a little research related to the concern, ask others for their insights, or even dream on it. Then seemingly out of the blue, your diligence pays off. Your "eureka" moment arrives. And rather than putting your head to the grindstone, you may have been relaxing with a book, chatting with a friend, going for a walk, or patting your cat. The solution ever so effortlessly just slips in. Don't you love it when that happens?

When the brain is freed to do its work, the answers will usually come. Being put to the task, the subconscious mind will work quietly on its own to solve a problem, find an answer or resolve an issue. Naturally, some of us are better skilled at enabling our brains to perform this research than others, and as with any skill, it can be improved upon with practice. Proceed by consciously acknowledging a concern, then relax and trust your brain to work on the task at hand.

In addition to our readily accessible information and brain resources, as well as a CEH self-healing practice, some believe that we are able to access additional help from a higher energy source such as a universal consciousness, angels, or spirit guides. Whatever the source, we can improve our problem-solving skills by consciously engaging and trusting that help in dealing with our challenges is readily available and accessible.

Healing as a Team Effort

The body/mind dynamic protects us from harm and heals us when we are injured or in pain, bearing in mind that it can only accomplish what is realistically possible. Fortunately, there are ways to expand this realm of healing possibilities through medical intervention and certain alternative healing practices. So, while a person can accomplish real and effective healing on their own, it is reassuring to know there is a broad range of outside help available when required.

The search for the right alternative health practitioner can be a daunting task. Who out there can best provide the help you need? Do your research: search online, find a book on the subject, read testimonials, speak to friends for advice and ultimately make a decision that you sincerely believe is in your best interest. If your gut feeling, otherwise known as your intuition, has served you well in the past, it is worthy of serious consideration in the final decision-making process. And it is my hope that this book has provided the insights you need to recognize Cognitive Energy Healing as a practice that can offer real healing solutions for a number of unresolved concerns.

The practice offers a team approach to healing as the practitioner and the client work together collaboratively to uncover the causes of health concerns and what can be done to address them. And should the client be interested in learning some supplementary healing techniques to assist in the healing process between sessions, the practitioner may have some valuable suggestions to offer. Engaging the client in their own healing has proven to be both beneficial and empowering during treatment, as well as over the entire period of the healing process.

In closing, I would like to offer my thoughts on how one can best be in the world with all its many challenges. Be proactive in creating the life you want to live and share with others, beginning with an introspective and mindful awareness of yourself. Build and draw on your inner courage and determination to bring about change when it is needed. Look first to yourself and know that compassionate love for self and other is key to a healthier and happier life. Only when you sincerely love yourself can you live your life in a loving and compassionate way. Others will feel your light and the world will be a better place.

My hope in this writing has been to inspire an interest in the benefits of the Cognitive Energy Healing. For those of you who would like to learn about training in self-healing techniques or practitioner training and certification, my contact information is listed below.

cognitiveenergyhealing.ca

APPENDIX

A Spiral Journey

In the most amazing and wondrous way, the spiral design is an essential part of the fabric of the universe through its cosmic expression in form, pattern, and movement. And as part of this infinite dynamic, humanity from its earliest time as sentient beings has incorporated the spiral design into its created reality for spiritual, aesthetic, and functional purposes. Besides its many applications in the energy healing practices of CEH, and the spiritually-inspired spiral movements of ritual and dance, this iconic design also serves humankind globally in surface decoration and architectural design.

While wood, stone and clay were the only available material resources for early humans, works in metal came into use later with the advent of the Bronze and Iron ages. A visit to any major museum of ancient civilization is bound to display a number of fine examples of the sculpted, carved, molded, incised or painted spiral design. From my travels to visit a number of ancient spiritual sites around the world, I have seen the spiral design used symbolically as a religious icon in architecture, sculpture, pottery, and paintings, as well as a decorative feature on a great variety sacred-objects. And beyond its spiritual application, the spiral is seen as a visually pleasing pattern used in jewelry, ceramic and fabric design, and ornamentation.

The use of the spiral pattern as a symbolic icon in spiritual and religious expression dates back thousands of years, and is believed to represent the path of the spirit on its eternal journey. This symbolism also carries the messages of growth and the cycles of life. Besides being a pagan symbol, the spiral can be found in many old world Christian churches. One outstanding example is to be found in St. Peter's Basilica in Rome, in the upward spiraling pillars of the majestic main altar. The design of these sculpted marble pillars evokes a sense of being uplifted toward the heavens. Paradoxically, images of the Garden of Eden with the spirally-coiled snake symbolically suggest the downward journey to that other place.

More than 5,000 years ago, well before the erection of Stonehenge and the Egyptian pyramids, the Neolithic people of New Grange, Ireland constructed an enormous burial mound covering an area of 4,500 square meters. This mound remains to this day, and should you be so fortunate as to visit this site, you will be awestruck by the massive boulders along its base at the front entrance to the mound. These boulders engraved with a flowing pattern of interconnecting spirals are boldly striking in their size and their ornamentation. One can only venture a guess as to their prehistoric spiritual significance.

Upon entering the narrow and low entrance passageway at New Grange and crouching down to walk through the cave-like tunnel, one is led to a central inner chamber. Visible on an adjacent stone wall is a distinctive carved tri-spiral, three interconnected spirals. One can only speculate as to the meaning of this ancient inscription. What we do know is that this mound and the area surrounding it was a spiritual place, and perhaps as the spiral symbolically may imply, a place to honor the passage of spirit on its eternal journey. Questions arise as to why *three* spirals, as opposed to another number? Do they represent a deity, a trinity in the divine sense, or could they represent an Earthly trinity of the body, mind and spirit?

For the Polynesian peoples, such as the Maori of New Zealand, the spiral is a long honored spiritual and cultural symbol. From their earliest history to this day, this design is an integral part of their daily lives. Spiral designs ornament Maori architecture, boats, clothing, pottery and jewelry. As evidenced by their preserved history, the Maori have been master carvers of both wood and jade, and remarkably the spiral has remained their primary design motif and spiritual icon. I have to say that I have never seen so many spiral designs in one place, as when I visited the Museum of New Zealand, Te Papa Tongarewa, in Wellington. This museum houses an amazing and extensive collection of Maori artifacts and honors the wisdom of the spiral in its outstanding display of these works.

On the remote islands of the Orkneys off the Scottish mainland, an increasing wealth of standing stones and ancient sites can be explored as new locations continue to be unearthed. The Neolithic stone circle, The Ring of Brodgar, is but one such site and is truly spectacular in its own right. The standing stone ring of now twenty-seven remaining standing stones, the original number was probably sixty in all, is about one hundred and fourteen yards (over one hundred meters) in diameter. The Ring is believed to have been used for the purposes of ritual and astronomical observation of such things as the summer and winter equinoxes.

Standing within this stone ringed area, I was moved by the experience of simply being in such an ancient site, with thoughts of how this place was once a significant gathering place for ritual celebration of such things as rites of passage and the changing of the seasons. Along with the other visitors that day, I was naturally drawn to walk along the inside circular path defined by the stones. And though following a circular path as defined by the standing stones and not a spiral one, I became aware during this short journey around its inner periphery, that the clockwise direction I had unconsciously chosen to walk in seemed somehow significant to energy flow, and to life's and nature's cycles.

Continuing our voyage around the globe, let's move on to the distant and mountainous Buddhist kingdom of Bhutan, nestled high in the Himalayas just south of Tibet and north of India. This fascinating small country is a profoundly spiritual place, and for many it is a place of pilgrimage to visit its many sacred sites and monasteries. While traveling through the Himalayan Mountains to the Haa Valley on narrow and seemingly endless switchback dirt roads, I was delighted to come across a colorful array of prayer flags strung haphazardly at the peak of the highest mountain pass. From this high-altitude vantage point, with its breath-taking vistas, one can look out to the majestic Mount Everest in the distance. Buddhists believe the prayers written on these small colorful squares of fabric are carried forth, blessing the countryside and all who reside there as they flutter in the mountain breezes. This leads us to prayer wheels, which perform a similar function, however blessings are sent forth along a spiraling pathway.

Prayer wheels are cylinders containing sacred texts. They come in various sizes from the small hand-held version on a stick, to medium sized ones turned by a water mill, and to much larger ones found at monasteries. It is believed that the sacred prayers contained within these cylinders are sent forth by the manually or otherwise propelled spiraling motion of the prayer wheel. Of particular significance is the direction of the spin of these wheels - they are spun in a clockwise motion.

Remaining with this concept of the spiral and the importance of its directional movement, I learned while out for a walk around Bhutan's small capital city Thimpu that it is respectful and expected that you walk in clockwise path around a stupa, a Buddhist sacred commemorative monument. Spirituality is palpably present everywhere in everyday life in Bhutan, and the direction of your path, as with the direction of the spinning prayer wheels, is significant. This wisdom of the ages is consistent with the directional flow of energy in the body.

Exploring some of our Earthly wonders large or small, material or energetic, the spiral is revealed to be powerfully present in many natural forms. Evidently, even nature in its glorious variety of flora and fauna seems to know something big about the spiral. The dynamic spiral formation of the conch and nautilus shells, as well as those of the humble snail are all a natural earthly wonder to behold. Even the Australian trigona beehive is built in a spiral formation resembling a compressed spiral ramp. And looking to our forests, a spiral design emerges in full geometric perfection in the seed arrangements of the cones of such conifers as the spruce, fur and pine trees. Also, many flowers, the sunflower to name but one, have central seed arrangements displaying a similarly perfect spiral pattern. Even the rose in a time lapse view reveals its spiral secret, growing from bud to full bloom as petals unfurl outward to reveal a spiral pattern.

On a summer's day, walking through a field or a garden, you may have spotted the spiraling dance of a couple of tiny white butterflies as they take flight toward the sky. Have you noticed something special about their ascending pathways? These butterflies trace a double helix pattern, uncannily resembling the double helix of our DNA.

Such is the inspiration, the joy and the wonder of the world we live in.

AUTHOR'S NOTE

When it comes to saying thank you words sometimes seem to fall short, though I will try my sincere best to express what is in my heart.

To John, my friend and life companion, and the person with whom I have shared life's greatest joys and challenges, thank you for believing in me and for your invaluable help in mentoring me as I moved into the unfamiliar territory of writing this book.

To my three wonderful and inspiring adult children, thank you for your love and encouragement as I worked to share my gifts in pursuit of my life's passions, first being your mother and now a grandmother to five beautiful and loving grandchildren, a teacher, an artist, a writer and a healer.

To my friends, know that your interest and encouragement were a source of strength through my illness and recovery, and a valued support as I shifted my focus to sharing my story and the healing practice that grew from it. Thank you in every way, hugs included!

To my delightful Scottish friend and travel companion Jane McLaren, thank you for your valued insights and encouragement in my early days of approaching this book writing task.

To my devoted editors Susan Montague and Lisa Hrabluk, a sincere thank you. Your wisdom, knowledge and insight were a trusty beacon as I worked to find my way forward to the completion of this book. And above all thank you for your warmth, kindness, and enduring friendship.

To Shannon Jensen, who scrutinized my rough copy with her keen proof reading skills: I thank you for your kindness and patience with this novice writer and your sincere interest in my message.

And to the many people who have come to me for healing help, thank you for trusting me to share my healing gift. Your well-being is a testament to the benefits of Cognitive Energy Healing.

REFERENCES

Bejan, Adrian and Zane, J. Peder (2013). *Design in Nature, How the Constructal Law Governs Evolution in Biology, Physics, Technology, and Social Organization.* New York: Doubleday.

Campbell, Joseph (1991). *The Power of Myth.* USA: First Anchor Books. USA.

Chevalier, Jean and Gheerbrant, Alain (1996). *Penguin Dictionary of Symbols.* New York: Penguin Putnam Inc.

Chödrön, Pema (2010). Taking the Leap: Freeing Ourselves from Old Habits and Fears. Boulder, CO: Shambhala Publications.

Clottes, Jean (2016). *What is Paleolithic Art? Cave Paintings and the Dawn of Human Creativity.* translated by Oliver Y. Martin and Robert D. Martin. Chicago: The University of Chicago Press.

Doidge, Norman (2007). *The Brain That Changes Itself.* USA: Viking Penguin.

Goerner, Dr. Sally (2015). "The Science of Energy Flow Networks". in John Fullerton. *Regenerative Capitalism.* Greenwich CT: Capital Institute.

J. E. Cirlot, J. E. (1962). *Dictionary of Symbols.* Toronto and New York: Philosophical Library.

Kirkey, Sharon (10/10/2015). *Health Trouble? Give Thanks?* The National Post. Toronto: Postmedia Network, Inc.

Laine, Neil (2015). *The Vital Question. Energy Evolution and the Origins of Complex Life.* W. W. New York: Norton & Company.

Northrup, Christiane (2018). *Dodging Energy Vampires,* New York: Hay House, Inc.

Wulf, Andrea (2015). *The Invention of Nature: Alexander von Humboldt's New World.* New York: Alfred A. Knopf.

SUGGESTED READINGS

Campbell, Joseph (1991). *The Power of Myth*. USA: First Anchor Books. USA.

Diamond, John (1979). *Your Body Doesn't Lie*, New York: Warner Books.

Diamond, John (1990). *Life Energy,* Using Your Meridians to Unlock the Hidden Power of Your Emotions, St. Paul, Minnesota: Paragon House. St. Paul Minnesota.

Doidge, Norman (2007). *The Brain That Changes Itself,* Stories of Personal Triumph from the Frontiers of Brain Science, USA: Penguin Books.

Judith, Anodea (2016). *Chakras, Seven Keys to Awakening and Healing the Energy Body.* New York: Hay House.

Judith, Anodea (2004). *Eastern Body Western Mind.* New York: Random House.

Hawkins, David R. (2012). *Power vs Force,* The Hidden Determinants of Human Behavior. USA: Hay House.

Lipton, Bruce (2008). *Biology of Belief,* Unleashing the Power of Consciousness, Matter and Miracles. USA: Hay House.

Lundstrom, Meg (2010). *What to Do When You Can't Decide*, Useful Tools for Finding the Answers Within. Boulder CO: Sounds True, Inc.

Myss, Carolyn (2017). *Anatomy of Spirit.* New York: Penguin Random House.

Northrup, Christiane (2018). *Dodging Energy Vampires,* New York: Hay House, Inc.

Pert, Candice (1997). *Molecules of Emotion.* New York: Touchstone.

Printed in the United States
By Bookmasters

T4-ADN-682

BOY OVERBOARD

Peter Wells' first book *Dangerous Desires* won the 1992 New Zealand Book Award for Fiction and the 1992 PEN Best First Book in Prose Award. He has published a second collection of short stories, *The Duration of a Kiss,* and co-edited New Zealand's first anthology of gay fiction, *Best Mates*. He is also an acclaimed film writer and director of such productions as *Desperate Remedies* and *A Death in the Family.* This is his first novel.

BOY OVERBOARD

PETER WELLS

V
VINTAGE

Vintage New Zealand
(An imprint of the Random House Group)

18 Poland Road
Glenfield
Auckland 10
NEW ZEALAND

Sydney   New York   Toronto
London   Auckland   Johannesburg
and agencies throughout the world

First published 1997

© Peter Wells 1997
The moral rights of the Author have been asserted.

Printed in New Zealand by GP Print
ISBN 1 86941 319 9

All rights reserved. No part of this publication may be reproduced
or transmitted in any form or by any means, electronic or mechanical, including
photocopying, recording, storage in any information retrieval
system or otherwise, without the written permission of the publisher.

CONTENTS

Book One
DREAMS OF THE NIGHT SOIL PEOPLE *1*

Book Two
LIES AND THEIR NECESSITY *101*

Book Three
STRAIGHT IS THE GATE *121*

Book Four
OPEN SESAME *155*

Book Five
THE MISSING WORD *209*

CODA *255*

Acknowledgements

The author gratefully acknowledges the assistance of Creative New Zealand Toi Aotearoa, whose writing grant made the existence of this novel possible. I would also like to thank Harriet Allan, managing editor of Random House NZ and Ian MacNeill whose close reading was invaluable. Shonagh Koea, a writer with a curlicue pen and a sharp wit, was an inspiration.

Sookysong
　cissyspeak
　　hissing along
　　　deep dark leap.

BOOK ONE

DREAMS OF THE NIGHT SOIL PEOPLE

Eel

It was Carrot who trapped the eel.

'Look what we've caught!' Carrot kept on yelling. He slid it into Keely's hands, goon-grinning. 'Hold it,' he says. 'Feel it. It wants to feel you.'

That moment under the trees. The dump to our side, a mantle of periwinkles in the dark, glistering lights overhead. We are in a tropical jungle and it is that moment when, holding it, wriggling, mouth open, teeth bared, he, Keely, says to me:

'Go on, take it take it take it.'

And Carrot beside him starts up the murmur, like a wind in tree murmur, 'Take it take it, Noddy, take it.'

I am inside Keely's brown bowl eyes, I am swimming inside them. There are small straws there, floating on lagoons of gold, I can feel the warm widdly water fluttering through my legs as I watercrawl. His lips, my life-raft. He nods now impatiently, all the world rocks to a stop (the whole world is still, as still as that time in the bathroom), and I reach forward, out, leaning towards him. As soon as I touch, my fingerpads skim the skin-slime and, inside, muscles rotate, bulge and its tail thrash-crashes towards me. Keely and Carrot jump back. Carrot is bent over double, pain in his stomach, letting out this strange punctured sound: eeeeeeeeehhhhhhh!

But I am blind. I am blinded by Keely as I have been all along. All my skin changes into scales, stiff as dead fish as its tail wipes over me. My blood runs ice as far away, in the distance, over the hill, across the plain, beyond the sea, I see the small figure of Keely waving to me: waving goodbye.

'We tricked you, see.'

It is Carrot now raising himself up to laugh into my face. He hates me, Carrot, because he *knows*. CarrotnKeely spend all their time together, dive-bombing each other's pants, feeling for their stiffs, comparing them. Keely's is like a sausage, a fat sausage. So Carrot tells me in a scientific moment, struck into truth.

But . . .

'We tricked you, see,' Carrot whinnies to me now, opening wide his thin-lipped, rotten-banana-smelling mouth so I look inside and see his stunted baby snag teeth looking right back at me. Slumboy Carrot, with his little finger broken and wrapped in a dirty black bandage. In-turned finger, crouch-back digit.

Keely?

I don't say this. My eyes say it for me, because I am in electric shock. I can't stop the surge and rush of electricity which the eel is sending into me: dark forks, dagger thrusts. I feel its thick tube head flick around to stare up at me. It eats my eyes, the eyes which look at Keely saying: *Why Keely, why?* Because your eyes look at me too much. I feel your eyes as I walk across the asphalt, the shock of your glance as it takes up afresh each morning when you first see me. I smell the fireworks, see them in your eyes. All this he doesn't say to me as his smile slowly dies. His smile slowly dies.

He can see me now, Keely, he can see me being eaten by the eel in front of his eyes. The thick snout has come towards me, drinking me into its opened mouth — two sharp needle fangs glitter on each point as the mouth opens wider, fits over my head. *Save me, Keely.* I am inside now, inside the chill darkness, covered in spit-slick, all thick as sick, slithering me into his tightness which coils roundround, squeezing me down.

Keely. Save me.

As I begin my journey into the chill black, I half-hear Keely call out to me, *'Jamie, I didn't mean to.'*

But I know he is lying.

MY NAME IS Jamie Caughey. I am in a special class for underprivileged hyper-intelligent children. I'm meant to be a genius. I heard my parents talk about it. Better than this: I am *highly strung*. It is better to be highly strung than a genius. You get off more.

Mr Pollen, assistant headmaster, is our teacher. 'IA Accelerate is our name.' We are so intelligent we can be trusted to use our own time 'productively'. Sometimes we debate the uses of the United Nations. Other times, like now, we slope off down the creek, to the gullies which run like a moat surrounding our school. We conduct our own study of nature.

In our class there are four girls (Zeena, Angel, Stumpy, and Cora-Lee). There are also four boys. There is Winkie, who doesn't count, CarrotnKeely, and me. So short and brief those two letters, like two bits of mismatching bikini: me. M E. Just like my age. 11. Like a ladder with no rungs. How am I to climb up there? Up to where all the knowledge lies, the truth is —

This is how Carrot tricks me, perhaps. Because the me doesn't seem to be there some times. It is cellophane floating in the air. It's like me doesn't know itself, it is so busy knowing everybody else. Finding out —

'He has a Rolls Royce,' I say offhandedly. 'He has a chauffeur
'Who does?'
'My uncle in Australia.'

CarrotnKeely, Winkie don't know whether to believe in me. But my face is a shining mirror, flashing back at their disbelief. Winkie hovers on the edge.

We are sitting, legs through the bridge, creek down below a broken thread falling through the trees. This is before. There is a warm rotten smell from the dump. Wind is blowing our way. Occasionally, from the zoo, comes a lion roar. This is where we live. A no-man's-land where everything nobody wanted is put. The zoo the dump the bin. We don't live in the eastern suburbs where the tide goes out and reveals, like a necklace of pearls, whitewhite sand.

At our beach the tide goes out and then keeps on going, chasing itself forever, as if it wants to drain away, flee, hide, sink in the depths, leaving behind a huge empty battlefield where only the bodies and broken spears remain. Out into the mud threads the broken sewers: the mud and the smell mix together, warm, a crab heaven, a silent pock. This is our stain, our tribe. We are the bin people the tip people the mud people the dirt people. We do not have white sand. (But we have something else, our own secrets.)

'Does he . . . ?' says Winkie. He lives nearest the beach. I know I am safe. Winkie's face is like a mouse, all alive and twitching. His ears, you can see the veins through them, throb and rinse with pink veins of blood. Winkie has tiny hands, like pointed shoes, long as a piece of elegant Chinese carving. Winkie plays the piano with these hands.

'What sort of car does your father have?'

Carrot is catching me out. I look at his face in the light, his yellow-brown skin, grey eyes. He takes out a comb and swiftly runs its teeth (some broken) through his snot hair. He does this nervously. Trying to hide his broken finger, filthy bandage.

But his eyes catch on something.

Able Fainell is walking along. In contemptuous silence, we watch the grind of his tight shorts and skin like puff pastry. Fine scalloped hair.

'Look how he walk,' breathes Carrot, luxurious and slow.

Fainell's backside-bum waddle-sways from side to side, pertly. Juicily. In silence we watch. Then Carrot wakes up and breaks our trance. He picks up a stone and sends it scalding across the air. This breaks Fainell's saunter. He turns round and feels in his pocket. His face, I notice, is redred. Turning carefully away from us he says *fuckycunt icatchyoudie.*

I don't hear this.

CarrotnKeely lean in together, flesh rubrubbing as they laugh. Then Carrot, his hand sliding down Keely's trunk, skimmeys down and mouses into under Keely's pants. Keely's pants. Bright blue, new, boxers made to airily encase his brown legs. Keely's pants with the pocket always open, ready to receive. Keely is neat, Keely *is* neat.

But Carrot won't let go.

'What sort of car does your father have?'

I know this is the crunch, I must be careful how I lie. Or rather, how I make up the truth. I see their faces paused in front of me, pricked still and waiting and then my brain joins my mouth and my body goes loose and I feel a speed of warmth, red zigzag lightning course all up and down me until I am sitting inside, yes, inside a red poppy.

I glance away from them, so that my eyes seem to glimpse a far horizon: one they will never see (but Keely's father is a salesman, he can just see it).

On Carrot's face I see a blank refusal, a recognition he will never get there. He is working out how to hate, whether to kill me, but clouds have already choked his horizon, light falls from his face. He lowers his gaze till it hits his penknife. Blade is out, blade is gouging the wood, chips fleck the air. He is gouging into the wood KILL SHIT KILL.

Winkie, timid mouse Winkie, his whiskers twitching, turns from each of us, to each of us, trying to learn; but I have seduced Keely, I can see it, his brown eyes open wide for me, and into him I swim.

'O, me?' I say all curved as a piece of wrought iron sitting by the side of the Richmond swimming pool. 'My father has a . . . Jag,' I murmur the word, drop of pollen, formed honey. 'A Jag. Yes, we have a Jag.'

The word echoes through the narrow tunnel of our world, forming its own echo on which I ride, amplifying myself until I am not just this thin me M E sitting there, untogether, two bits of mismatched bikini. Now I am M G M cinemascope curved screen with line after line of chairs facing towards me.

But Keely is clever, he has followed me into the tunnel, I can feel his warm breath all over my face, he is right beside me now, he is fitting himself into me, he is trying my body to see how it fits into his: maybe soon we will wrestle? *Yesplease. Fit your hips onto mine, your legs through mine, we will roll together over and over inside this tunnel, our faces close together, eyes into each other's as we —*

But Keely has taken his glance away, dragged his glance away, he looks far way, to another horizon. And Keely, clever and casual, nifty and treacherous, all at the same time, says to me:

'Two-door or four-door?'

I am almost lost. The Jag. Two-door or four-door?

'Four.' I say all casual.

Pass.

'What year is it?'

'1960.' I breathe.

'What colour is it?'

And in the middle of our silent wrestle, Carrot and Winkie left at our side, I try and decide: the money or the bag?

What colour is it?

I look round me: everything here is black and white like an old worn-out film from Before-the-War. I look at all the worn-down scuffed and marked views. Everything is exhausted by the weight of so many people letting their eyes rest on what they see. Exhausted eyes, blank eyes which no longer even see the huts of the transit camp where refugees stay, the barbed wire on the top of the zoo walls to keep everybody out, the animals in. *This isn't the real world. It can't be.*

'What colour is it?'

'Red,' I say. Poppy red. Like skiing inside a poppy. Like when you've been swimming all day long then you flop down half-dead on the sand and start licking a soft blackberry ice-cream. Like closing your eyes when you look into the sun. Red as Sabrina's lips, as Technicolor is only an echo of it. That red. *Redred*. Not only red, merely red: *scarlet*.

AND UNCLE AMBROSE is driving up our street in a bright red, no, a scarlet Jaguar.

I smile.

Please take me with you. I want to escape.

RED SATIN, THE table is covered in red satin. I love to run the pads of my fingers over its smoothness, while I'm waiting. It is chill, this satin, quilted and laid flat — picture-theatre curtains ironed and placed behind glass, kept forever perfect. Improved, made better. You can wipe this red satin clean. EZY-cleen. This is because it is Formica, a wonderful word.

This is how different my life is at Uncle Ambrose's. At home our kitchen table is wood, lovingly painted and repainted by my father till you almost lose the brushstroke: we place a cloth on it each morning, each evening. To eat a meal on the bare wood would make my mother grow angry with despair, as she lowers her head, then raises it, screaming up to the flypapers dangling from the ceiling overhead: *Why are we living here?* Staring at my father.

But here, at Ponky's, *Don't call her that* (Uncle Ambrose), *her name is Priscilla*, the table is so beautiful we do not need a cloth. We revel in the fact it is EZY-cleen. The Casements are modern. Uncle Ambrose Casement is going places. He sells refrigerator after refrigerator, he has his own store. Uncle Ambrose, Aunty Gilda and Ponky live in their little rented flat, ready to, at any moment, take off. That is why, now, Ponky goes to a private school. She is on the starting blocks, about to take off. This is her first year at Richmond View, School for Young Ladies.

'WHY CAN'T I go to Ponky's boarding school, Mum?' I say. '*Why?* Ponky and me are always together. That's what it's like.'

Mum looks down at me like she's wondering what she's purchased. Then I remember something. 'Didn't you have boys at your school, Mum, your private school?'

Crafty logic.

'Yes, we did,' says Mum, 'but that was different. It was the Depression, and the boys were the sons of the headmistress. It was the middle of the country. There was nowhere else for them to go.'

'I don't care. It doesn't matter,' I say, 'to me. I want to go. I want to be with Ponky.'

'But you don't always get what you want,' my mother says slowly and sadly, raising her eyebeam to flash into the future. Her hand reaches down and ruffles through my hair. I feel her fingerpads warm and solvent, melting me down, like a caramel, until I have almost lost my hard centre. But it doesn't go. It won't ever go. I know this. This is me, this hard irreconcilable centre.

'But Mum,' I say. 'It's Ponky and me. We're always together. Butmum.'

I don't care I don't care I don't care.

LATER, MUCH LATER, she says to me (sharpening her spearpoint: it leans in-between us, holding us apart; if I move closer, it pierces through the skin): 'But isn't it what you wanted? *You said,*' she says, 'You said you always wanted to be with Ponky.'

'But,' I say, looking at her, my eyes inside her eyes, *don't send me away.*

'It's for your father.'

Better than this.

'It is a golden opportunity.'

I know gold. I am going to be a gold-digger when I grow up. I know this. I have seen it at the pictures. Gold-diggers are fun. They are crafty and plot and plan never to do any work.

Gold as in her wedding ring on her finger, gold as in sunset.

This is what happened.

THE GOLDEN OPPORTUNITY.

My father had his teeth out and the dentist's needle made him sick forever. He turned into an old man, lying in bed. His brother, his richrichrich brother across the Tasman sent him a first-class ticket to come and stay. It would be a break. He could get better. My mother could come along too. Most welcome. Thank you.

A golden opportunity.

But what about the kids? My brother, Matthew and me.

'We can't go,' says my mother who wants people to know. 'So kind of them really, most considerate but of course we . . .'

. . . into the small dots leap Aunty Gilda (no real relation) and Aunty Birdie (ditto). They live down the road. 'The kids can stay at our places. One each.'

'This is the kind of place we live in,' my mother says, fierce pride singing through her veins. 'Not good enough,' says your Aunty Margaret-Rose in Richmond, and here my mother makes Richmond sound like a windy tunnel of snuff blowing down her nose which grows longer and more aristocratic by the second, more dismissive of Hungry Creek with its dump up the road, and the loony bin, and mangroves.

So . . .

'Aunty Gilda and Uncle Ambrose will have you.'

And . . .

'. . . *You can stay with Ponky!*'

You can stay with Ponky?

But when I say: 'I don't want to, Mum,' she looks at me and the bridge between us turns caramel stiff. 'Sorry, dear, what was that you were saying?' her lips say but I see her eyes lift up and she is looking elsewhere. Why is it everyone is looking elsewhere, to other places? Once we were all together but now . . . .
. . . . the dots have become a train track, a prison line leading out of here.

Everyone joins in and wishes Mum and Dad good luck.

Good luck.

After all, it is a golden opportunity.

Ponky, Matthew and I stand out at the airport, behind the barrier and the plane takes off. It disappears.

And that is the end of it, they are gone, and I know she has finally got away and I am left in this foreign land.

Time stops and stretches and goes on forever.

EVERYTHING AT THE Casements' is different, and done differently. They do not have tablecloths on their Formica. The cutlery (stainless steel) sits on the tabletop nakedly. A tomato sauce bottle sits on the tabletop. Mashed potatoes are scooped out of the pot by a glamorous ice-cream server. This is how different the world can be.

And this is what allows me to lie, to tell a different form of truth: that I drive in a poppyred satinsmooth Jaguar, not one kept in prison, to stamp round its cage, smelling of its own dirt, covered in flies and letting out forlorn cries which die before they even reach the ocean.

No.

This Jag, Jag, Jaguar is a metal animal, a chariot which will drive me out and away from here.

This is my world at Ponky's.

FOR-MY-CAR.

'H̲E HAS THE biggest,' says Keely matter of factly, a natural authority. 'He has the biggest in the world.'

Keely and Carrot have just come back into the class. They have been out in the boys' toilets, together, alone, doing I don't know what, but I want to know, I do.

'It's sooooo big,' takes up Carrot, his face flushed pink, eyes dancing. His eyes dance a polka in front of me.

I smell him freshly now, at this moment, his banana-smell is like a robe all over him, investing him with a strange dignity.

'How big?' I say, trying not to sound interested.

We are down the very end of the metalwork classroom, hidden by a wall. It is another day. Time lies all round us, like a still ocean.

'He has the biggest cock in all the world,' says Carrot, assured and matter of factly. 'Erroll Flynn.

The way he says cock it is like he has swallowed it and brought it back up, inside himself.

'It is . . . yards . . . long,' says Keely, nodding, reeling me in. Keely and Carrot exchange a smooth glance.

'Yards and yards and yards and yards long,' sings Carrot.

I think of this. I feel very small. I look between them, they are so married. Their eyes keep catching each other's and returning, like a ball, their glance. Licked ball, goobyball, a gobstopper sucked down smooth, exchanged between them, lip to lip.

'Foursquare,' I say, knowing this will catch them out. 'Can I play at lunchtime? With yous? I'm good,' I say. 'Betternyou.'

'Maybe,' says Keely all cool as a winter draught right into my face.

He turns his shoulder to me. He leans down and brushes something off his shoe. Something he has just seen. I see all of him, all over, in one piece.

Please, I don't say.

Keely is down there, polishing his shoe with his pullover sleeve. He leaves it shiny black, mirror-sleep, in which I read our three faces, looking down as if into a pool. I see our faces, flushed, staring at the same point, frowning.

What do we see?

My feet. I'm watching them in my pedals as I push. Down the slowhill, smoothhill, away from the shops. This is when I know I'm almost in the clear. Left Winkie at the top of the road, by his mousehouse, which is across the road from the convent. Blackbird nuns coast along the streets, beaks glittering, gathering in little skeins of Catholickids, off to hell, ring the bell.

Plastic shoes push in rhythm. Winkie is a Catholic. I know this. My eyes flick sideways, shuttling the knowledge to the back of my head.

I have to be careful here. Because one afternoon, one long still afternoon as I gazed down at my feet in the pedals, lost in the rhythm, the peaceful surging circle of the cycle, the click-clicking as the chain fell in and sat sweet and squat on the spike, sending the spokes flickering and silvern, blurring everything around me into a sweet swoon, I — forgetting there was even an I, a fleshly sac — went splat into the hooped back of a parked car.

The car rode into my flesh invading me with white shock. It tore the breath out of my throat. For one moment my body died. I know this.

Forever after I carry on the bridge of my nose not only a strange sort of hollow but a tiny scar, shaped like the continent of Africa. This scar started out as a weeping flower, all scarlet, throbbing. It grew into a husk, stitched into my skin. Finally it dropped off, leaving behind a naked whiteness. So this is me, this tiny identifying mark, this nakedness. Alone on my body this is the pure essence of who I am. All else is excess, unnecessary, an exterior. But if you wish to look into my heart, see that tiny continent of Africa: in memory of the moment when, daydreaming, I crashed into the hard wall of reality.

She is not home when I get there. Hot from my bike-ride, I go out into the wash-house and feel up the suede insides of the weatherboards, still warm and damp from the sun. Locate the key, which fits into my palm strangely.

I unlock the backdoor, invade the still space of Ponky's house.

When I get near her room, a small crease of paper tells me: *she is there*. She looks up at me silently. She does not exactly breathe out heavily, but I feel her big strapping body lull out a sigh . . . of disappointment that I have come back.

'. . . Go, Ponky,' I go, hesitating on the frill-edge of entering her boudoir.

Floral carpet strands me.

Ponky does not answer, or she is leaving a small hesitation, large enough for me to fall into. Ponky is listening to her own transistor radio. The first one I have ever seen. Is hers, natch. as if she cannot quite hear me above the radio noise, she sighs, eyes shuttling back to her comic.

She buries her eyes.

She must have taken off her uniform for Richmond View as soon as she was inside the door, shedding it like a skin she cannot wait to get off, the hat, the gloves, the stockings, the shoes, the dress, the jacket: the weight of her private girls' school education now lies scuffed on the end of her bed, abandoned.

She is lying back, being Elvis. Slow cud of her chuddy.

On the radio I hear Connie Francis sing 'Don't fence me in'.

Nose wrinkling up like stink, Ponky reaches down, eyes never lifting from the page, turns Connie down.

She sigh-sighs.

Ponky chews concentratedly, allowing only a bubble to pop out as a sign that she is aware of my presence.

Pffflock! goes the bubble. The easement of air is her real greeting. She wrestles over, with a grunt, presenting me with a broad empty cliff of a back. Flick over page of comic.

Silence.

I put my bag down by my end of the bed, careful not to muck up her room.

'How'rrrre ya been.' She doesn't even make it into a question. She drags out all the rrrrrrrs, like they're a growl. Often she talks American. Either Elvis or John Wayne.

'I'm . . . ,' I start up, all bird-squeak. I unravel my day in loose spools all around me, carefully leaving out anything important.

Suddenly, she gets up. Without another word, she walks out. Straight into the bathroom.

Door shuts in my face. I don't understand this. She is always going in there. Hiding.

I look at the pink-painted door, thick pink, lustrous. Doorknob, a thin skitter of chrome, in ziggurat. *What is happening in there?* I sleep in her room every night, across the carpet from her. Our dreams entangle. Seaweed round a corpse. Or like something from summer long ago: an old ice-cream carton, the writing just about leached off it, so you can hardly read Tip Top. We have eaten all the ice-cream, forgotten, almost, its chilly soft taste — but there it lies, trapped in seaweed, surrounded by the bones of a fish, a sprat. A long forgotten sprat.

Me.

AFTER A LONG while, the toilet flushes, but late, like it's an afterthought. She comes back, face blank. I notice she does not swagger so much. She sinks down on her bed with a groan.
She turns a half-eye over to look at me.

'Ja wanna play . . . softball?' She half-whispers this.

I eye the baseball bat, wooden and stiff, leaning just inside her door. This is the only one in our district. Who has ever heard of anyone possessing anything so American? Ponky does, Ponky, whose father Uncle Ambrose is the source of all gifts, all objects, all things beyond our power. She even has a real American baseball glove, made of sweet-smelling oleaginous leather. But Ponky is alone. An only child. A child alone cannot play softball. So, to her who is given everything, these things are precisely useless.

Ponky's boudoir is all frilly and lacy, laid out like an ideal girl's room by Aunty Gilda for the imaginary girl that Ponky isn't. Ponky puts up with it all, silently, a soundless groan.

I know what I have to do.

'O, yesm,' I say all hollow enthusiasm. 'Yesm.' I'm earning my way. 'That would be really neat.'

'Follow me,' says Ponky, which I always do, dancing in her shadow, trying to follow the rolling ball of her feet.

BUT SOFTBALL TURNS out to be no good because there's only the lonely two of us. And the blank green of the park accentuates this fact. Cruelly.

'How about . . . tennis?' I mumble brightly. She looks over at me, thinks for a long hard second, then gives me the verdict.

'OK,' she breathes, like it's all my fault the baseball glove and bat turn out to be useless.

IT IS PART of Ponky's power that she has the right to play tennis on the only private tennis court in our area. The court belongs to the shut-down hotel, the only hotel ever to operate at Hungry Creek. This was in the days Before-the-War. When people living on the main road would ring ahead when they saw the police heading out. By the time the police got there, all the alcohol had been hidden. Or drunk. There were coloured bulbs in the night, and a dancing platform way out to sea. Spotlights used to rake the still waters. When the tide was in, of course.

But ever since the Accident, the hotel has been closed. They took the ropes off the maypole, the swings just hang there, never used. Rusting in their sockets. And old Mrs Kirk lives alone inside the hotel. Sometimes, on the seaward side, you see some washing hanging out. There are rooms and rooms there, locked up. You never know quite who's living in there. Sometimes old Mrs Kirk takes pity on some hard-up honeymooners. Mum says one day she half-expects to find Mrs Kirk lying there, inside, with her throat cut. Not that anyone would know for a while. For a long time. And then imagine the smell, says my mother, wrinkling up her nose as though she can already smell it.

The hotel is built right slap up against the beach. One day, everyone knows, the sea will claim the whole building. This is because the bottom rooms of the building are already open to the tide. These rooms were where Mr Kirk kept his boat. This was before the Accident, which my mother says was no accident at all.

Mr Kirk simply swam out to sea and drowned, is the official story. My mother says (backed up by certain other locals) he was seen being picked up by a launch that very night. Mrs Crickwood's daughter claims she saw him walking down the main street in Everton. Bold as brass. He had the same roll-your-own cigarette dancing on his outer lip. Unlit. 'Common as,' says my mother, even though they built the only hotel at Hungry Creek, and called it The Regina and had their own private cinema and a cocktail bar on the roof of the hotel. 'Built because the building leaked,' says my mother.

It has been locked up all my life. Only Ponky has been inside.

WE PLAY SILENTLY, with the enforced oddness of children near a sickroom. The few comments we make to each other are turned into quotations, as if surrounded by a listening silence.

At one point I think I glimpse the mask of old Mrs Kirk dissected by the venetians. The next second, the window returns to sky. And the sound of our ball rises up, hollow and somehow sad, dying out as it is absorbed into the plaster which is turning green, in its folds, and flaking off, on the seaward side.

UP THE DRIVE stumbles Mrs Randford, sweetheart from the American movies, bright blonde hair tied in a snood, cupid lips carved on her face, powder white in the afternoon light as she, unsteadily, a little, rehearses a smile — a vague wave in our direction, clutching her eternal brown-paper parcel under her armpit.

'How's your game goin', kids?' she murmurs to us, as she slips up past the tennis court, wire-netting embroidering and letting slip the iron thread of itself as she wavers her way to her anemone home.

'Mmmwinnin' two sets,' says Ponky who is sweating, to win.
We play on urgently.
It is important to win.
It is terrible to lose.
Uncle Ambrose knows this.
But someone must always lose.

Gradually, as if understanding, as if seeking to soften and smudge, and blur the harshness of all definitions, the sun starts to intensify its shadows, then string them out along the asphalt, joining small lump of gravel to the wire-end of weed.

Birds sprinkle their shade over the tennis court, softening our faces. Buses run up and down the road like clockwork speeded up. And the sun runs down the bank to embed itself in a pure line of sea.

We are in shadow.

'Mumndad won't be home for a while,' mutters Ponky wiping a look off her face. This look is crestfallen, naked, alone. 'OK, Mutt,' which is her pet name for me, 'time for the Pause that Truly Refreshes.'

INSIDE THE WASH-HOUSE her fingers play over the crate of Coca-Cola which is delivered each week for Ponky's delectation. Here I glimpse the scale of her wealth, the true dimension of Uncle Ambrose's ambition. Not one bottle of Coke like any other kid at Hungry Creek might aspire to, but an entire tray of them. They lie there obediently waiting the moment when they leap up into Ponky's grasp and she, carefully, levers the lid off each one so the precious foam does not sliver down the glass.

At this moment her fingers try to intuit the correct bottle. For there is a correct one.

The fourth from the left, two down.
No.
The seventh along, four from the right.
She opens the bottle.

In the dark, her eyes rest on me, so — for this second now (in the silence before a trolley bus, somewhere, miles away, announces its advent with an eery whistle down the wires) — I realise I exist, and she leans forward and offers me a slug from her bottle.

'But only two slurps,' she says to me sternly.

I glug down the gold and grab all the aeration which I need to keep me afloat, bubbling in the torrent of her regard. While it exists. She takes the bottle back, wiping its mouth carefully, twice, with the underside of her T-shirt. Now she lifts the bottle back and in one long draught she drains all the brown-gold inside her. I watch the bubbles sink. In silence, I appreciate the strength of her insides that they can drag into themselves so much all at once. I feel her need. She pulls the bottle away from her lips with a sharp smacking pofft! and she stands there, slightly wavering, as immense as a giant kauri tree which has been cut through and, for one instant of shock, celebrates its final moment of verticality.

We both wait.

Then, as we know it will, from out of the pit of her stomach, up through her soundpipe, crashing out of the crater of her mouth comes the entirely satisfactory sonic shape of a burp. Its sounds echo up and down the corrugations of the shed.

She grins at me. I grin back.

'Good one, Ponky.'

She lowers her glance to the Coke top. I sense the gambler in her gathering her forces in — for this is Uncle Ambrose speaking through Ponky's fingertips. She almost closes her eyes and withdraws. I feel the tremble of all her nervous oscillations in the air.

'It better be . . . ,' she half-murmurs to herself. 'It bally well better be . . .'

She reaches for the small screwdriver she always uses to prise the cork out of the undersides of the Coca-Cola cap. For Ponky is searching for the eternally elusive letter L which will complete the spelling of COCA-CO—A (the letters of which are randomly distributed under all Coca-Cola lids) thus winning for Ponk an *All Expenses Paid Trip of a Lifetime to Honolulu, a Teal Blue Plastic Carry-on Suitcase, a Year's Supply of Coke* and, better than all of this, a guaranteed photo in the *Evening Star* of our friend, Ponky, alias PK, alias Davy Crockett, Happy Little Priscilla Casement (aged 12), grinning into the camera as she climbs up the airplane stairs into the air.

True happiness always resides elsewhere.

'Take me with you?'

'I might. I'll think about it,' Ponk says coolly, keeping all her options open.

But.
And.
If.
The cork splinters back.
She holds in her hand a 'C'.
Ponk hardly lets out a sigh.

With one derisory flick of a thumb, Ponk sends the little metal object off into oblivion, signifying that from now on it is condemned junk. Its crinkle rings in the dark. Falls behind the concrete copper, to lie beside a wooden clothespeg and the skeleton of a mouse hunched into a foetal curve.

'It's a con,' I say, eager to defend Ponky's honour.

'OK,' says Ponk, stretching out to her full size, five foot eight and a half. 'Time to hit the beach.'

WE THREAD DOWN the overgrown steps, by the closed-up hotel. Hit by the smell of sand, and mud, and the fainter gossamer of sewerage, redolent of secrets, shame and pooh. The tide is right out and the sun runs a thin gilt glass over all the mud so that what is looking at us is a giant ballroom floor of gilded crystal.

I see this.

We are surrounded, suspended, briefly, in space, as we climb downwards staring out.

I squish my eyes shut.

Into this I breathe.

This is my home.

Clatter of our footsteps as we fall.

Beside us, locked doors, barred windows, boards tacked over: TRESPASSERS WILL BE PROSECUTED. Two such big heavy words falling like the judge's gavel, clang of prison door, sharp yank of hand round the back of your shirt pulling it tight against your neck.

Trespassers will be Prosecuted.

'Do you reckon Horton might be in there?'

I like to frill the rill of nervousness.

Ponk jumps. For someone so big, she can be surprisingly light on her feet.

'No. Ah. Why?'

'He could be inside there,' I say, authoritatively. 'Holding a knife. Waiting to slit your windpipe. Scarlet flower.'

'Yes,' says Ponk, breathing out heavily, no longer so intrepid. 'When he escapes.'

For we know a mass murderer cannot be held in the bin up the road. It is as natural as the tides going in and out that he will escape.

And come for us.

It is only a question of time.

A murderer cannot escape from the end of Hungry Creek. There is nowhere to go. But the same grandeur of illogic which has made him into a killer will send him down the long straight road which leads straight to our houses.

We know this.

Some part of us is always preternaturally waiting.

We know he is inside the coal shed, behind the door, under the bed. He doesn't need a key; he will simply flow out through the keyhole and come, like a lover, like a father, looking for us.

This much we know.

So we carefully keep an open distance between us and the locked-up hotel doors. Instead, we hear drops falling in heavy moist percussion onto a soaked floor. We listen for any difference in the soundfall.

Nothing.

We select some long grass and, testing it for glass or jagged tin, stretch out.

'What you thinking of?' breathes Ponky after a while.

She is lying there, hands behind her head. Looking up at sky. She smokes a grass straw. There are times she wants to know. Like now.

'Plane crashes,' I say, looking far out to sea. Sunlight toffees us all over.

'What plane crash?' she sounds doubtful. For one moment she struggles up and looks.

'O, nothing,' I say, carefully. Then, 'If a plane crashes . . . people have insurance.'

She looks at me in silence. Waiting. I like this about Ponky. She listens and can hear things that other people don't hear. Besides, her ears always prick up at the sound of money. Money is serious. Money is important. But money is also a trick. A conjuring trick which a magician like Uncle Ambrose can summon up. This is Uncle Ambrose, dispenser of halfcrowns, ten shilling notes, double-decker ice-creams, crates of Coca-Cola.

'My parents have insurance,' I say casually.

'How much?' she almost doesn't say. But her voice is interested.

'O,' I say airily, looking far out to where the sea is, rolled right back to a thin line of gold. Sun is a plane crash hurtling into the distant line of the Waitaks. I watch this blinded, numbly. Looking into it sates me. Eases me. Fiery it falls, plummets, with the ease of a dream. I smile.

'O, twelve thousand pounds. Six thousand each. Enough,' I say slowly, 'to live on for the rest of my life.'

I will be free then.

A small dagger runs down her face. She picks up a stone, fast.

A braille of birds lifts up from a tree, hurls a net, flings backwards, joyously, squawking. They attach themselves to another tree which comes bird alive. Have they heard me?

Ponk is looking right into me.

'You doan know what you're talking about,' she says then. Seriously.

She throws the stone far far away from us. After a long while, we hear it fall: plop! onto mud.

A series of metallic sounds, clicking and minute whirrings, indicate crabs are quickly scuttling away.

'Yes I do,' I say quickly. I have thought about it a lot, lying in bed. It comforts me.

Ponky picks up another stone, takes aim.

'I doan know,' I say then. My voice has a different tone, a catch. 'They left me behind. They coulda taken me. I woulduv gone. They haven't even written. Like they said they would.' I don't say, *I'm abandoned. I never knew time could be this slow. I miss them. I miss her. I wish they would come back, mumndad.*

'It's twelve thousand pounds,' I say. 'Enough to get away.'
'Where would you go?'
I think about it for a while.
'Paris,' I say. 'Yes,' more convinced. 'Paris.'
'Why Paris?' she asks, interested. I might know something she might want to know. Find useful.

'So I can go and see the collections. Dior. I'm going to be a famous dress designer,' I say then. Naked. But airily. 'One day.'

On the ballroom floor I can almost see it. Shadows. Dior gowns. A chandelier burns.

'Or an opera singer. I haven't decided yet.'

Ponk doesn't say anything. She doesn't have to. But then this is Ponky, too. She doesn't laugh at me, call me names, accuse me. She just listens. And if she thinks differently she keeps a John Wayne silence.

We lie there and let the silence dissolve us. Far out to sea is a little pickpocking sound as a single tern dipducks and tries to find a pipi. We can hear its footsteps, echoing right across the bowl of the empty beach, which we know, inch by inch, every part of it, like the insides of our hand, or as if our bodies were cut open, there it would be, inside us, shaping every organ in our body.

'I can't wait for it to be summer,' I say lying back.

Inside the ballroom I hear a fallen drip.

'We can go swimming at night again. Eh, Ponky? Full moon. King tide,' I say, waiting for Ponky to join in, and help erect the fluttering flag of all pleasure of our agreed-upon summit. 'We can go bottlefishing. We can do . . . anything. Eh, Ponk?'

I listen.

But she doesn't answer.

T HE BELL HAS slung its rung and we all tauten, turn and form into patterns. I watch: across the playground, the girls thread away in a snake, to sewing class. We boys have to join up with Form 1B and file off to woodwire metalhorror. Both the teachers here are unlike any other teacher I have met. Mr Adams is commandant of woodwork, and he is like Mr Brunt at church, the verger, tight-lipped, back rigid with anger, eyes little bullets spraying round the class.

'A poor workman blames his tools.'

Glue is made from horses' hooves. I think: Auschwitz. Already I have sneaked into the library, covenant of books, and taken a look: photos of stacked skeletons, lampshade of skins, tattoo numbers. I know all this to be true. Why doesn't anyone say it? Instead it hides inside the walls, under the floorboards, in the silences. Behind people's eyeballs from the transit camp. I know this. It is under the tip, over the back fence, being buried. Bodies under the grader.

Mr Blanney, the metalwork teacher, is no different. His room is down by the darkhorror creek, where the wet seeps into the wood. Shade cruels down the windows; everything in the room of metal is ice-cool to touch, you think your skin might leach onto metal and when you pull your hand away the skin is left behind.

Mr Blanney, surrounded by the smell of solder, little blue fires burning, paces the room, angry, angry. Nobody ever knows how he will take things. He has never been known to have a pet. Going into the room is like going into death. To be his pet would be a terror. He is balding. On the top of his head are thin sheaths of hair which look like they have been fried by sitting up there, sizzling. Sometimes he is barely shaved, and then it is as if the prickles are fighting to get out of the loose folds down by his chin.

He has no eyes.

This is why he is so angry. He barges about the room, screaming with pain.

Nothing is done well enough.

One day he lined us up. We had to sit very still. He opened his mouth wide and, pacing back and forth in front of us, he took up each of our metalwork projects (a teacaddy spoon we are making for MUM, a toast rack, an ashtray) and, laughing deeply, bitterly, loose strands of hair flying off his balding head, he turns sharp on his heels and throws the metal pieces crashing round the room.

Silence.

Silence of fear, ice dripping down all our backs. Faces white, hardly a breath among us, we all change into an octopus of fright. Will he come towards one of us?

Another piece of metal whistles through the air. Much, much later we hear it crash, dash and dribble its tears across the floor. But this is later, for in that moment we have looked into his eyes and seen there an animal from the zoo, chained. Lion-angry, pad's sore. What makes an adult human so furious? He is not furious with us. Or rather, he is furious with us, but we are not what is before his eyes. He can see none of us.

But wait!

Carrot has turned half his body, awkward with pain, towards Keely. He is trying to nuzzle his body into Keely's, out of fear. He is frightened of this spray of acid, which douses all of us, melting the flesh off our bones till we are a tiny stack of skeletons sitting there, neat, dead. *Play dead,* that is the only way. Pray he will go away. It will end. Everything ends in the end. I know this. Just stay there. Close your mind off. *I know. I know.*

'Woodley!' Mr Blanney screams into Carrot's face. Carrot wilts down inside himself, into a pool of fear running across the floor. We all, as a body, brace.

'Come here,' whispers Mr Blanney. He is smile-smiling.

The room is dark now. We are in Russia. Far away: everyone, every adult is far away. Nobody can help us.

'I have to do this, I hate to do this, why do you make me always have to do this?' Mr Blanney is keening. Broken veins on his forehead, a shimmer of sweat inside his eye pocket. Pupils turned inwards.

'Woodley, bend over.'

None of us breathes now, as we allow Carrot to be executed.

Mr Blanney sings: *Whywhywhy?* He smiles at us all the terrifying smile of a disappointed man, one driven insane.

I feel a start behind me: surely nobody is going to answer him? But it is knees pressed into me, shaking. We listen to Mr Blanney's footsteps going to his drawer, in which, we know, lies the strap.

The drawer slowly unfolds its magic.

I see the strap, which is a thin file of leather, balancing now in Mr Blanney's hand. He dangles it before our eyes, to emphasise its liveliness. It is living. It is this which has dictated Mr Blanney's actions all this half-hour. It is to this he has been driving. Hard. Remorseless. He turns abruptly to us, grinning. The strap holds him.

'Why do you always make me do this? You boys?' he whispers to us, lips stretched tight, white. His eyeballs now roll in his head and skim over each of our faces, lips: but I am ice, I know how to do this.

I can see Carrot's face, down below. Already it is crunched into fear: this waiting is worse, as worse as the possible pain which will come. His eyes are tight. Fingers clasped white round his knees. The leather of Mr Blanney's footsteps as he paces towards Carrot. Now a soft flow comes from the boys. Yes, we feel silently, seditiously, yes: *hurt Carrot*. Punish him. If you punish him, we will all be safe. For a while. But hurt him. Hurt him good. This is a terrible power, and knowledge, we all pass around amongst ourselves, silently. All of us feel shit-dirty, suddenly. But eager as crystal, sharp, pierce-point of thrill.

Ah, Mr Blanney is now behind Carrot, his footsteps gather up their pace, a sharp intake of breath among our body; now all we boys are onebody, onebreath, onehugeeye, shining, and bulging, basketball-size. His steps run towards Carrot who, crouched, tight, scrunched still, goes blank: then the shock, I realise he has relaxed. Just before the blow, he has relaxed. I remember Whopper, Carrot's brother, told him that (the secret message), don't tense up, it makes it worse, it hurts worse. Just relax. I receive this miraculous wisdom at that moment.

But Mr Blanney, swishing the strap over Carrot's body, just whisking him with the whiplash of its wake, so Carrot, uncertain whether he has felt already the blow, or whether it is still to come, turns a tragic mask towards us: is the blow still about to fall?

Mr Blanney has sauntered away from him. He has suddenly lost interest. He lets out one spurt of a bitter laugh.

'All you fuckykids get back to your work.' Something has snapped. Something is over. In that second, we hear clocks tick, voices outside the room, a distant gull and, beyond that, the living breath of other humans. We are back in the world. Poor Carrot, still crouched there, doesn't know what to do. He has never been stripped so remorselessly before, for the delectation of our pupils. We all feel mysteriously happy, as if we have witnessed a miraculous event. Carrot is — momentarily — history.

'Youboy, get back to your soldering.'

This is Mr Blanney to Carrot. It is strange, his voice is almost tender; or as if he has, at last, glimpsed a far sight. Mr Blanney has returned to being inside his body. Our voices take up, thatching over the terrible silence we have just witnessed: the hole, the black hole which lies in the centre of the globe, I have seen it. I think this of the world: inside it is a black source, and the night is simply its echo. I know this.

I say nothing. And soon, we have all forgotten it.

'I KNOW,' I say, a secret smile on the corner of my lips. Mona Lisa. *I know.*

'Know what?' says Winkie, coming into our conversation late.

I press my lips together, lower my lids. If I close them just so, like curtains, they cannot get into them. But I see, sparking between Keely and Carrot, the trapeze of their glance. They hang off it, dangling. Goon-dangle.

We are dawdling, kick-kicking our way back to our classroom. School lies in the far distance like a sleeping animal snoozing. Inside it, though, we hear the distant hum of voices. Everyone else in there is trapped, learning. We are free. We are Form One Accelerate, so clever we can walk at random, plucking learning from the air.

Like now.

'You never have,' Carrot kicks the dust with his pickers. He has this pair of old dented winklepickers, I know, everyone knows, they are handmedowns from his brother. Whopper, also known as FuckingBigCunt. Just as Carrot is a runt his brother is a bigcunt. That is what they call him. Carrot hides under Whopper's shadow, walks, trembling, inside his shoes. Which, natch, are several sizes too big. Sometimes, when he struts, pushing the frame of his hips forward, out, lying back on his pelvis as if he's carrying down there some good juicy secret so great we're all lucky to be seeing it — just then — his winkle, the twinkle of his shoe, gets caught inside a pock of dust; he sprawls forward, hands out, braced to fall, snarling as he goes. In that instant we read his face: a babyboy's face, like our own, no longer creased into a scowl.

'Heeeeeeeeeh!' we all screel, copying him, his tribe. Not being naturally tough, we must all act so.

Sneer.

'You almost got dirty,' says Winkie, laughing most.

Carrot, erect now, turns back, tightens his white fist. Listen now to the air whistle all around us. Over zoowards comes a low groan from . . . what? The elephant mourning, calling Africa?

'Mooooooooaaaan,' its hollow trumpet sings.

Carrot's fist is tight: pummel-tight. Air suctions round us . . . me. My laugh dries all fakey on my mouth.

'C'mon, son,' says Keely, Capt'n Keely taking charge of the situation. Inside Carrot's grey-green phlegm eyes I read the comic cartoon of Whopper's threat. We scuff along some further.

'What'd you know?' It's Winkie again, whine-slow.

'How come you know?' His eyes graze me. Soft-slime, snail trail. *'Who you done it with?'* This is Keelyboy.

Inside my eyes, like an x-ray, is his head. Ever since I first saw him I ache to have his head. Shaped at the back like a football, the perfect head. The way he carries it on his shoulders, just as if he is trotting back having scored a try. as if inside the soft moist globe of his ear he always hears a cheer. Is deafened by it. But gracious. His brown-brown eyes modestly looking down. He grins. But now is silent.

'O!' I say, then, 'o,' a smaller o, a tiny hole of o, hardly open. I lower my lashes again, bringing on night. I don't want to know myself. 'I can't say,' I say. I look down at my plastic shoes, rimmed with fuckmud. Plishplashy all round the soles. A new invention, plastic shoes. I don't know whether I like them, hate them. I want pointy shoes, like Keely. Keely has new pointy-toe shoes, which I stare at longingly and silently.

'Why can't you say?' wheedles Winkie.

'He can't say because it never 'appened. E's makin' it up'.

Carrot sends a punch, lightly, scaling off Winkie's back. Down his spine. He grabs Winkie's creambuns and gives them a squeeze. Winkie squirts away.

'Doaaaannn!' he moan-moans. He really hates it, I can tell.

'I do know!' I cry out hotly.

My cry comes out so loud, far away on the grass a squadron of gulls lifts up, ripples.

A thousand eyes watch us, tense.

'Come on,' says Captain Keely, suddenlike. 'Squadron prepare for surprise daylight mission. Take offensive position. Attack!'

He goes, one pointy-toe after another, leading us along.

We form behind him.

Pearl Harbor lift-off.

Into gullstorm.

Now, above us, white sky gets cut into a million black pieces. Wings break the air all around us. Whirlwing.

We run dodge-dodging the bombs-splatter.

Screaming, us.

Laughing with freedom, Form One Accelerate.

CLOSER TO THE sleeping beast of school, we walk-dawdle.

Seriously.

Lengthening the time till we hit the wood.

'What it feel like?' barely says Carrot. Looking down at his shoescuff.

Breathless.

It felt.

'It felt,' I say, closing my eyes, then going on walking.

Now I have them. I glance over to see Keely feel me with his eyes. His football-shaped head leans towards me, curving. The skin on his lips unseals in slow motion, like skin which is burning, being ripped apart. Soft pink inside there, small bubble percolating. His sweet, almost grass-smelling breath. I know it.

'Howudfeel?' his voice groans, prickpoint, expectant.

'Like,' I say, wondering how to describe it. Like. Like. Like. I close my eyes. 'Like I was inside a fountain but comin' out the fountain mouth.'

The eyes of boywatch stare at me.

Carrot's banana breath sneers all over me.

'Where'd ja put it?'

'. . . like an earthquake,' I say, convinced.

'Earthquake . . .' Winkie echoes. Happy to have me proved right. If he can stand in my shadow, he is protected.

I move away from him, leaving him rooted to his own shadow.

Eye of sun stares down at us curiously.

'. . . quake?' says Carrot, suspicious.

Beat of our feet across football mud. Thudbud.

'Ye-es,' I say.

There is a pleasant pause here, because I know I have reeled them in.

'Tell us then,' says Keely, anxious to get over-and-done-with-it.

Sometimes I don't know with him whether he actually likes me. Like now. I feel the warm spray of his eyeshot as it wets me sweetly.

'Tell us then,' he breathes down deep inside me, settling into me.

'O . . .' I open wide. 'It was a hot still day. It had been hot for weeks, months. Everyone went about their daily tasks. It was the first day back at school. Nobody suspected anything . . .'

'Like today?' asks Winkie cleverly.

'Now,' I say. 'Like *now*.'

We lift up our heads and look all around.

'Nobody suspects a thing,' my words murmur, treacherous creek. Lilylapping words lull them underground, into cavern echoes, where the words shiver up the walls, break into crystal stalactites, hang low over us, shimmering.

Listen, I don't say to them as I tweak the silver reins round their ears, pulling them underground with me.

A SOUND BREAKS open my dark.
A splinter burns. Footsteps thunder over the roof, which tilts, turns as I roll over in the surf of my dreams. Tide runs out.

I am in Ponky's bedroom. *Ponky*.

Night.

I hear, first, footsteps skittering across the tiled floor, then, as if catching a ball just a second too late, the hall door in-between closes. But it is too late: already in the kitchen I can hear the faintly high-pitched wheedling of Uncle Ambrose's wheeler-dealering. His voice is bright alight, and I can hear, too, the skid of Aunty Gilda's laugh. Her laugh is high, mounting like looking inside a shaken-up Coke bottle and seeing the bubbles chasing one after the other: arrow-bright, exploding. Other voices too, happy, crowd round her laugh, florally arranged all around it, fishfern and foliage.

I hear the fridge seal unslurp.

Moments later a bottletop spins across the lino floor. Giddy. Chairs scraping back. The patter of highheels tittering. Laughter, adult voices, joking. The splutter of a match. Uncle Ambrose has been to the races. Uncle Ambrose has been investigating his winning streak. *Uncle Ambrose has won*. I fall back into the soft feather eiderdown of sleep.

UNCLE AMBROSE IS inside the room. He has brought into the room all the smells of the night outside, the faint ordure of the horse track, the softer staleness of beer, the saliva in his mouth, of cigarettes and the busy glands of his eyes. He stutters in his enthusiasm, words falling over each other, tipping over hurdles as he persuades. This is Uncle Ambrose the refrigerator salesman. This is Uncle Ambrose who has a whiteware franchise, his very own showroom in town. This is Uncle Ambrose who has the first motor mower, the first electric frypan and pop-up toaster in the district. He has been to the races, we know. He has won. Won! Won!

Of course he has won, he is a magician, he pulls thousands of pounds out of a rabbit's hat, he changes his car constantly as he moves forever upwards, producing a Holden and changing it into a Vauxhall, he takes the Vauxhall and changes it into a Velox. And now he has produced the most wonderful of things, a bright red, no, a scarlet Jaguar.

'How's my boy?' Uncle Ambrose says to me, as the bed sags down. 'What's he been up to? Has my favourite boy been good?'

'I've been good, Uncle Ambrose,' I say. Thinking of the bright red, no, the scarlet Jaguar. I see myself getting off by the school gates. Linger, door half open. I walk away, casually, head held high, eyes closed to slits so I can just see. Through the fur, CarrotnKeely watching. It only has to be one. *Better if it is one.* Then they will be forced to tell. The truth.

Uncle Ambrose bends down, quick-attack, and buries his prickles on my forehead, a wet slug kiss. I resist my impulse to reach up, snatch away the snail. In the dark, we breathe.

'OK, everybody, don't keep the kids awake. They've both got school tomorrow.'

It is Aunty Gilda by the door. 'Please,' she says, and though there is a laugh in her voice, everyone knows she is serious. On the level, Aunty Gilda. Fair and square.

'Shhh!

Shhhhhhhh!

SHHHHHHHH!'

The adults sillybugger a shushing game, disappearing down a howling tunnel into silence. The lounge door closes. I know soon enough someone will break out the door, go to the fridge to get another beer. So the adults retreat, laughing and talking, letting leak into the world all their loose happiness.

I can hear Ponky's breath.

We listen to the adults' voices, high, excitable, careering. We listen to Uncle Ambrose's voice proclaiming, 'Bejeez I felt it in the end of my little finger, I could tell I was off on my lucky streak . . .'

WE LIE THERE in a mute conspiratorial silence in which we both read each other's telepathy, hard, cruel and unsparing, oblivious if not hostile to the sentimentality which adults clearly need to mask the stink of their failures and loneliness.

Bright and hard as the iris inside a flame, we lie there, staring up at the ceiling, waiting for darkness to snatch at us.

HOURS LATER, THROUGH the wall, I wake to hear them sing, *Show me the way to go home.*

If only I could.

The City of the Night Soil

Shushabyebaby don't you weep,
shoeshuffle your shimmy across the street,
rainaway future, fox chase the past,
this is the end but not of the last.

O, let's pretend, he said. Let us play pretend.

THERE IS A *house, a small blue house, in a long street, a very long flat wide street, a street as long as a streak, as wide as the world, rocking, rocking like a plane slowly turning, wings tipping; but this street never moves, except under the crowd of cloud which skitter their shadow fragrantly, flagrantly onto the bitumen burning under the sun, broiling and bubbling into pockmarks, which you pick with your fingertips, your nails drip black, black tears under a white sky, and a high eye of burning sun; and this is what is so very special about this place, the seaaaaaaaaaaaaaaaaaaaaaa, which surrounds every part of it, but the sea goes out as well as comes in, and when it disappears it appears so final it will never return. There is mud here for miles, and mangroves, and nearby, in amidst the mud and the mangroves, the composted lives of an entire city, for this is where the rubbish goes, this area, this is where the shit was taken to be dumped, and this is where the night soil, the night soil of a city was delivered, this is where the defecation of an entire town was sent to compost.*

So, naturally, it is a place rich in dreams, and nightmares, and visions grown from when men and women and children and animals and houses and trees and insects sleep; so, naturally, this place is for nightmares both generous and surreal; so, naturally, each moment of the day there are dreams both waking and sleeping; so, naturally, there is, like a balm, at any chosen moment in the day — that is, at a moment chosen by the moon — tides which creep in over the mudflats, like a pool, like a mirror, like a harbour, and so, in this area, wedged between a dump, a zoo and a loony bin, in this small triangle, a long wide empty road down which a bus whistles on its wires, to a projection, a peninsula, a point, a wedge, a dagger of land with sparkly, glittery waters like diamonds dancing on points, is a place known as Hungry Creek.

This is a small world, an entire world, an utter world, a pinprick, a freckle, nothing more, a dot in a series of dots, which close-up to your eye makes up the name of a word on a map, nothing more. An unimportant name, a place of no importance, overlooked, to the side, a joke, in so far as it is known. This is a place where occasionally a body is washed up on the beach. A woman, a lunatic, takes her own life. It is no loss. She has lived in the institute for the insane for all her adult life. She dies, aged fifty-six. She almost has no name.

Up the road from the blue house (but sharing the same night) there are electric shocks, there are padded cells, there are barred windows. Up the road there is a cinema with a waterfall curtain which changes its shades from raspberry scarlet to lime-green to gold. Up the road is a library, a wooden ark full of books, which at full flood floats you away from the surface of the earth, the dirt, the composting ordure: in this ark is something better than two animals of everything (they are imprisoned, at any rate, just along the road, at the zoo) — in the wooden ark full of books lies one hundred, no, one thousand, no, one hundred thousand maps for you to read: none of these worlds exist — none! Just think of it, the mysterious provenance of these maps to nonexistent worlds: each day people queue up nervously, anxiously, before the central turret in which, majestic and busy, the lady librarians live — even Miss Twist with her calliper leg spitting, 'Hsssst! Be silent,' be respectful towards books, the words, these maps which lie in your hand — trace with your finger a way out, an escape — read carefully, in silence, mapping out on paper yourself, this underground tunnel which will lead you away and out and far away and beyond until you reach that ether known as, known as . . .

what word can describe it . . .

. . . heaven happiness peace, perhaps. Yes! Peace. Peace is the ether, the secret heartland for which these maps exist, this is the secret for all of us; peace of which there is no more beautiful word in the language, not one with a finer sound, a lispier sibilance yet with a more profound reality: peace silence stillness.

Night

I AM INSIDE the dark empire. Every night it comes to claim me. I leave the world prepared. Under my pillow, a revolver. This is a smart little black plastic number, quite evil looking. *I am ready.* Even as I sink into sleep my fingers feel towards it, brush the hot plastic. I lie very still in my trench, knowing when he comes he will not be able to tell whether there is a body in my bed.

I have my plan. My plan is ready. If there is enough time I will get inside the wardrobe. I pull the door shut, slide the clothes along on their rails, school blazer crushed against my face. I crouch in there, hiding, staring.

He has his back to me, he moves intently, still, sensing at the same time if there is so much as a breath in the room. I do not breathe now. Nothing. But at that moment, as always, he stiffens slightly, under his fawn coat. I know then it is inevitable. Where I have sought to hide, I cannot escape. He turns quickly, face taut with power. He is smiling, lightly. Sneering. The power of his body is a wall, a wave, it comes towards me.

Either that, or I manage to get under the bed. I have heard a tiny sound, out in the corridor, which wakes me. I lie there, listening. Waiting to see if it is him.

Night surrounds me, packed tight as ice. Cold, I climb down onto the floor. It is lino under there, a field of dust. Breathing is hard. But I must try not to breathe.

Yes, gradually the door falls back of its own accord. He is standing out there, in his coat. He has pushed the door back gently, to look in. But I am clever. I have my gun. And I have arranged the bed secretsevens fashion, with my pillows.

I see now, as the door swings open, his shoes. *The shoes.* They are brown brogue shoes with a soft squidge of grey-yellow mud. He has come across the park. Pine needles edge onto the soles of his shoes. He brings into my warmsmelly room a chill scent of death, of the hole he has dug for me, the mud he has walked over. He lives in the night, he . . .

Shoes come closer. Right by my face. I open my mouth, ready to yell. But I know already no sound will come. I have entered the empire where nothing is as it seems. I am in the night empire, the vast space where you find out what really happens in the world.

There are two worlds, a long daylight world in which everything happens like a dull circus roll on a roundabout, everything coming back at the same time, each day, each night. Gulls in the evening flamesky, shimmering through, back to the old pine tree they restnest in. In this world I am not who I am, I am only pretending, badly, to be who everyone thinks me to be. I cannot even play myself very well, I forget the words and what he, Jamie, should be doing. This is because me of the nightworld, this longer eternal world, the one which waits for the daylight to end, is sitting there, powerfully. This me wants things which Jamie cannot have, is not allowed, shouldn't want.

I lie, under the bed, gripping my gun.

His shoes stand there.

I feel the bed above my head squeak as his hands *coldasdeath*, his ice fingers, fireflame through the sheets. He cannot find my body. Now it is the moment. He will either lose interest, and vanish as quickly as if he never existed: or the most terrible thing will happen. He will bend down under the bed and I will see him face-to-face. But he has no face. That is what is so terrible. For I have seen his face. And it is not there.

Like me. He has no face, in this dark world.

If he finds me, I will begin to run.

Each night this happens.

He finds me and I begin to run.

This is where we live, this world.

By day it is one thing, by night it changes into its true form.

What is true? Who makes up things? I know this world to be true, and real.

YET — WAKING UP, bursting into light — everything is so still, and I lie there, waiting to hear his footsteps running away down the street, running as fast as he can go.

But I hear nothing.

Once Upon

'JUST ACT CAJ.'

This is Ponky to me, as we pad off over asphalt soft as butter, her in front, slightly. It is a hot February day, one in an endless line, one after the other, so the whole city swelters and the tar bleeds on the roads, making little hillocks and blisters which we puncture, with our fingernails, letting the dark treacle stick to us, burning. Sometimes we scoop chewing gum off the road, little dried lakes of it, and carefully place it in our mouths, watching each other solemnly, as we taste the road inside us, teeth gritting on bits of tiny gravel. It tastes grey, like winter. But Ponky is clever like this. *She knows.*

It is she who organises me and Matthew to scout round the beach, after the big weekend days, the hot days. We go looking for threepences, which are such tiny moons of silver, crossed clubs, that fathers drop them out of pockets as they reach in for a dirty handkerchief with which to mop their sweaty brows. Mothers scatter them, having opened their purses, then turned, suddenly, to catch the tottering pyramid of their teenage sons, balancing, wobbling on each other's shoulders. *Look Mummmmmmm!*

We own the beach, Ponky, Matthew and I. On these hot days, everyone from the suburbs all around swills out to our beach. Right outside our front windows, families disgorge, taking out blankets, billies, deckchairs and rugs. Each trolley bus unloads another crowd who head off to the beach, quickly, fighting to get their own particular possie.

Down by the beach, three shops operate non-stop, selling ice-cream, raspberry, lime, pineapple drinks: the wooden shutters of the kiosk, which are padlocked all winter, are prised open and Mrs Baveridge works behind the counter, fierce in her make-up, never wavering as she hands out ice-creams, cold drinks, milk-shakes, cricketballs, oddballs, heartshapes, buzzbars, chocolate fish, TT2s, a never-ending stream to a queue which is constant, as if never quenched.

The sea becomes churned up by one thousand feet: old people paddling, courting couples glued together, children who hold toddlers. A sweet widdle piddle falls into the sea as all the sugar eaten by everyone leaks out of our bodies and turns the salty water into a grey warm soup.

And through it all, casually, effortlessly, people drop threepences, sixpences and occasionally, by way of an El Dorado, an entire shilling.

'Act caj,' Ponky gives the orders. This means, *act casual*. Ponk, alias PK chuddy gum, her favourite brand, is dressed in her usual rig-out: T-shirt; shorts; a cap on her head. Her hair is cut short as possible and she is tanned all over, a uniform soft brown, the only mark on her body (which I am allowed to see) the two white Vs where her jandal marks flare. She walks slightly ahead of me, as is only right for our intrepid captain. But she also occasionally falls back just to the side of me, so we are in easy eye range.

Today is the day we look forward to every summer. And every summer is measured by our degree of success. Because this is the day when the meat and packaging works put on a picnic for its workers. And on this day, they have races for the workers' children. We infiltrate, as spies. And naturally, as fast athletic children used to running, we win. And we win model cars, a bag of sweets, a paint set. But each year it is a testing time: can we pass?

Ponky doesn't wear today what she normally wears when we scout round the park. Then she wears her Davy Crockett fur hat (made out of possum skin), sporting the imitation rifle over her left shoulder. I was given this rifle for Christmas by my father — and which she swapped, saying, *'Can't I? I mean, you don't really want it do you, Jamie? I mean, it's not very good, it doesn't go or anything.'* All the time her eyes are on the gun, they cannot leave it. I am in her room and my eyes are on her doll, my eyes can't leave that either. The doll is so big and sits there, with a stiff lace dress on, its mouth so open you can see the miniature serrations of teeth, little pig fingers grabbing.

Ponky doesn't so much as deign to touch the doll. She despises the stupid doll, I know, even though I see her pretend for Uncle Ambrose that she, yes, she likes it. But Dora the doll sits on Ponky's dressing table, right by her bed, cold and unloved and I stand there, aching to touch it, hold it, dress it, talk to it. Couldn't it be my friend?

'You doan want it, do you, Jamie, eh boy, you doan want it really?'
I can hear Ponky's voice all low and simple, a tone she uses when she really wants something. 'Well,' I say. *'Well.* If you give me, maybe, some Juicyfruit and a hokey pokey ice-cream. Two cough-drops. A packet of cricketballs. Then,' disguised in the centre so she can't decipher it (or rather, so that the nakedness of my quest is more decently disguised), I murmur drowsily, burying my eyes in my toes 'if you let me play with Dora. Maybe then I might.'

But a strange thing happens always at Ponky's. A week, two weeks after Christmas, after Uncle Ambrose has made the biggest and best Christmas ever *for my little girl,* Dora the doll and all the other presents just disappear. Into thin air. 'Go back,' says my mother, 'to the shop,' pleased that she is not proven wrong, that safety does pay, that watching your pennies is important. 'Bignoise Ambrose,' is what she quietly says of him. 'A Bignoise. Everything of the biggest brashest and the best. But no substance,' Mum says. 'No substance at all.'

So Dora with her glass eyes and claw hands which never move (I don't want you anyway, with your stupid expression which never alters and your flesh which never warms), Dora goes back, away, disappears as if she never existed. But Ponky has my rifle. And together when we are on our own we run round the cliff-edges of the park, kings of the wild frontier. The wind blows. We are free.

But today is serious. 'Act caj, follow me,' Ponky says out the side of her mouth. She chews gum as she rolls on her feet. I know this walk. This is Ponky as boss, Ponky as the person who knows just what to do. She squints into the sun, from behind her sunglasses, as she and I silently, like spies, infiltrate the park: our park.

We know every aspect of the beach: the bins in which empty bottles are dropped, and which we will collect, early the next morning; the shop where, late in the day, we might score an empty packet of ice-cream; the swings on which we sit, going higher and higher each breath; the cliffs which overlook Hungry Creek, where stupid couples go to be alone, wandering along, heads joined together (we spy on them, under blankets, as they struggle). There is no part of the beach which to us is unknown.

Today, this hot perspiring day, under a merciless blue sky, is special. Mr Lamb had marked out the grass of the park, sternly, into strips. White paint thick on blade after blade of grass. The lines run magically away from him, seeming to come out of his very body as he moves along, grave and serene. We are all frightened of Mr Lamb, whose Maoriness has a kind of grave savagery, a severe dignity which is outside our understanding. But I know. The Lambs in their small dark house are in league with the trees, the stern roaring pine trees which guard the park.

These trees, so thin and gaunt, branches hacked off so they appear as nothing so much as leaning soldiers returned from some bitter campaign, stand on the very cliff-edges of the park, facing out to sea. They guard us sternly. Also, at nightime dreamtime, when the water rises up and washes over the peninsula and we all sink back into being the dream people the night soil people, these guards do not let us out, they stop us from escaping. In our faces they slam shut the iron door. The wind plays them mournfully, ice fingers plucking mournful tunes. I hear the screams of murdered souls at night. I hear the sobs of the lost souls whose bodies occupy the bin up the road. Through their needles soaks the blood of forgotten people.

But in daylight — and this is always the trick — in daylight everything returns to being what it is not. The daylight face finds them familiar. I touch them with my fingers and the soft pearloid gum comes out and sticks to my skin. Above us they creak. Soft needles cushion us as we, Maddy, Ponky and I, lie at their feet, in our own secret bunker. Talking.

'THIS IS WHERE there was a battle,' says Maddy. 'The tribe arrived in the faint light of dawn: it was still dark,' he says.

We see the dark.

'Their canoes pulled up silently at the beach. Blood stained the sand so much it was as if all the blossoms of the pohutukawa had fallen and formed a carpet on the ground: a carpet of blood.'

We see red.

'This is the site of a terrible battle.'

We see, under our feet, corpses, and listen in silence to the cries of the wounded, the dying.

We smile.

Matthew is my brother. Maddy. He is a Quiz Kid on the radio, much to my humiliation. I hate having a clever swot brother. He even wears glasses. It is a terrible brand on my flesh. But I listen. Ponky listens. She knows too, when no one is around, we can hear his words, which tell us things we do not know. Sometimes we don't know whether to believe him. Like now, when we lie on our backs and up, high above us, the trees slowly move against the sky. Creak and gently falls and flights a small needle, whirling round and round and round towards us.

'How do you know?' says Ponky.

'It's written in a book,' he says. 'In the library.'

'Tell us, Maddy,' I say the old words, rehearse the litany. 'Tell us.'

With my backbone I nuzzle into the claybowl softened by pine needles. Ponky, too, lets out a sigh and flops over on her front.

'Well,' says Maddy and he takes off his glasses. He is instantly blind, I see that. His tide-grey eyes look far away.

'The faeries and goblins wanted to build a bridge from this side of the harbour to the other. But the gods said they may do this only in night-time. They must labour —' (this word is typical of Matthew, a fancy, long, embroidered carpet of a word. Ponky's brow frowns: she hates fancy) '— only in darkness. So the goblins began to build.'

My eyes stray out into the silvern water. Black ridge folds out, and falters.

'What happened?'

I know what happened. But I need to be retold. Just as the goblins each night must labour again and again to complete this bridge.

'Tell us, Maddy. Tell us.'

'The goblins were working and slaving away carrying rocks on their backs and singing as they went,' he says, 'and the bridge was being built, they were almost there . . .'

'Almost there,' says Ponky. She grins. Her braces glint in the light.

'They could see, just about feel, they were reaching the other side of the harbour, when first one bird sounded . . .'

'A tui? Through the still forest?'

I know this story.

'And then another bird, and then the darkness started to fade away, and a faint light quivered across the sky, and still they worked on (they thought if they could only build the bridge they could then cross the harbour and escape the gods and run right away) so on they went working.'

'Fingers bleedin'?'

'Yes, fingers bleeding, backs aching, and the sun rose high and hard in the sky and a terrible a terrible thing happened then . . .'

We pause there, all of us. Maddy is kneeling so upright, slim and vibrating, his sightless eyes scanning far out to sea. I see a strange smile play and quiver on his lips.

'The light killed the goblins,' Maddy says then, folding downward. He put on his specs again, covering his eyes with glass. He is exhausted.

'So . . . the bridge was never finished,' I whisper for all of us, for I hunger for completion, for the bridge to be finished.

'And that is the sound you hear each night. It is the goblins singing as they labour to finish the bridge each night, condemned to work and work again and again, and it is their voices you hear, their voices singing, you hear each night, in the very pitch of night. You must listen!' Maddy triumphantly concludes.

None of us says anything. We suffer the pleasure of a story well told. Besides, I know the truth of what he says. I know the mysterious forces of daylight and night. I have heard the goblins singing.

My eyes find Maddy's, and I look at him and I see not my brother but a stranger. Who is he, Matthew, this strange changeling? Sometimes I think he is one of the faeries too. He knows what lies just slightly beyond me. He is my older brother. But I know it is dangerous to stick too close to him, with his glasses and stories and long words and silences. He is a Quiz Kid after all. Quisling. Gosling. Ugly words. Ugly wiirds. Weird.

BUT ON THIS day we, Ponky and me, having given Maddy the slip, do not even glance at the trees. Old friends, them, we know.

Our destination is the scrawl of kids over by the raceline. Even now, a gun goes off, a ragged line of boyshout struggles up through the white.

Watchit.

It is Mr Lamb. His brown eyes bullet us. We look down at the grass, searching for threepences, as we mosey away.

I hear PK humming and I do likewise, casual and treacherous. We thread round the edges of blankets, laid out on grass. Fat white feet imprisoned in sandals. A baby mewling on its back, a mother bent over on all fours, changing it. A ragged line of bigboys runs through playing tag, 'Get out!' one of the fathers stands up and bellows. He is a bigbelly dad, wearing a singlet, a small hanky on his head, face red. Mother says, 'Oh, sit down Dad, they're only being boys.'

We thread on. Down by the swings a boygirl war is happening. Boys behind the girls, waiting to push them higher, to let them feel the weight of their push, its power and momentum. The girls' thin squiggle scream. We move on, PK turning to me and pulling a face of horror, *'Uggghhh girls,'* she says to me, *'Yuuuuuuuk.'* I agree without saying to her I like girls, at least I like being round girls, they are very interesting with their secrets. Boys' secrets are different. Boys' secrets are cutting your flesh with a knife and always it is a competition to see who what how. But here, silently and casually, we have got nearer to the front line.

'OK,' says Ponky, captain of our operation, her face without any emotion whatsoever. She takes off her sunglasses so as to pass with all the other kids whose fathers cannot afford to give them sunglasses (nor Coppertone which is what gives Ponky her glorious even tan: *nothing but the best* says Uncle Ambrose when he is feeling happy, *nothing but the best for my girl.*)

'OK,' Ponky murmurs to me very caj, 'Just hang out round here, doan move too much and just say you're one of the Meatworks kids if anyone asks . . .'

But already an organising father, white sleeves rolled up, comes towards us. He is hot from organising, I can feel the blood thumping through his body. He has a handkerchief, its ends knotted, sitting on his bald skull.

'Blue,' he says to me. 'You in this race? What age are you?'

His hand hotdandles down my back, to the bottom of my spine.

'Ten,' my lips say, I hope caj. Behind him I see Ponk give me the OK nod, yeskid keep goin', she likes to talk American when she can.

'OK, Blue,' he keeps calling me, his hand thieving up into my hair where it rests hot and damp. 'Your race coming up.'

I feel his hand squeeze and caress round the ball of my head. I am used to this, for, without it seeming to quite belong to me, I have hair the rarest shade of russet red ('A true auburn,' says my mother nodding knowledgeably, as if she knew all along she would one day produce something of such consequence. The strange thing is no one knows where it came from. 'The milkman,' says Mum, and laughs oddly, everyone laughing with her. 'I don't know where you come from,' she says to me smiling mysteriously.)

'Hey are these kids ours?'

The man peers into our faces. We don't look stubby enough, stunted enough. Behind her Coppertone tan Ponk goes white. She goes chicken, I know.

'Son of Ray,' I lie, desperately.

The man's hand surges electricity up and down my backbone. He smiles into my eyes.

'That's the story, Blue. You speak up.'

'Hey, she's a girl!'

Her hat is taken off, face assessed. I see Ponk stiffen. She doesn't like this.

'Well, I'll be blowed.'

Laughter.

Ponk's face loses its features, she goes stone. *Don't worry, Ponk, I say to her silently, sending her a message. It doesn't matter. We'll win anyway. Just you watch. I will win something for you, PK.*

LINED UP, ON the white.

On your marks.

Get set.

My world explodes.

In a wave-wash, a face blur, I see the pine tree my tree smiling at me. Feet-thud, beside me another neck straining, air pulling in threads, ropes of it inside me, yanking me onwards as I lunge forward and break the white line. Oh, these people. If they only knew the practice I got each night, at running.

Clapclapclapclap! I am breathing all the air of the park and picnic inoutinout dragging it into me in all my excitement: I taste gum and hot tea and sweat and the water inside people's eyes and the warmth of their blood and all . . .

'But he's not one of ours!' a mother says. 'Whose boy is he? Whose?'

'Now, don't be a poor loser, Ima. He's here every year.'

He's here every year.

Now I see PK race. Easily, with a superb disdain, she heads off all the other girls. She wins with sleek ease, like a practised diver taking to the high platform.

Together, silent, mute, we head off to get our prizes. We don't risk speech.

We feel each other's triumph silently. Our eyes graze past each other. Inside ourselves we laugh. We have passed. We have infiltrated. We have pretended to be like everyone else. And, what is better, we have won. This is PK's lesson to me.

PRIZES IN HAND now we run riot and wild back down to the beach. Our togs are on under our shorts. Stripping aside our outer clothes, we run into the waves. We sink into the warm salt water, laughing.

But there in the distance is Maddy. Hide! Hide! We lie flat into the sea. I watch him slowly walk into the men's changing sheds. He is always going in there. What does he find there that is so interesting? I do not understand. We watch him go into the dark, then we continue on with our appointment.

Entering the sea I enter heaven. I lie back. I look up at the sun. The sun burns a scarlet aureole on my eye-shard. I smile. My face forms into a boat, and the sail on the boat is my smile.

This is how it used to be.

Once.

Ghost

IT IS THE morning and I am trying to make myself invisible. I'm waiting, standing by the Ezy-cleen Formica, I'm trying not to get in the way. Now it is morning, all the colour in the world has drained out, down the plughole of Aunty Gilda's new stainless-steel sink. All around me I feel the patterns of Aunty Gilda, Uncle Ambrose's urgent movements. I am in the way, I know it, just by occupying any space in their kitchen, in their lives. By being where once there was no one, the best they can do is walk right through me, like I am a ghost. None of us slept well last night. The visitors did not leave till two am.

All around is a sleepless suburb, accusing.

Now Uncle Ambrose is in the hall. I have silently followed him, with my eyes and ears, tracking his every movement, the small dog of my desire running right by his heels, nipping. But he doesn't see me.

Aunty Gilda, Ponk know to keep out of his way.

There is no conversation.

Only this race, this silent tussle, to get ready for work. And work is a wall, a Berlin Wall rising up high beside us, we live now in its shadow.

Bowl of rice-bubbles on the tabletop, glassy Formica under my fingerpads. Sometimes I like to trace the folds of the scarlet curtains placed under glass. But now it is chill to the touch, sending little electric shocks of dislike into me-who-doesn't-exist.

Uncle Ambrose, I silently say, willing him to remember the ride to school, in his red Jaguar. I am desperate.

In the hall he keeps his suits all in a row, a blue one, a brown one, a thin-striped cream one. Uncle Ambrose is so important his suits are kept inside plastic bags, being drycleaned endlessly so he is smart as a new five-pound note. Bustling into the kitchen now, his footfall is fretful, we all, goose-startle, streak out of his way.

His red eyeball, dry, accusing, falls on me.

'Hello, Uncle Ambrose,' I say into my ricebubble moonscape.

'You won't forget the hedge,' he says to me sharply. 'You didn't do the hedge. You haven't cut the hedge.'

Hedgeclippers snip, slash the heads off the leaves.

He orders me, his Hitler-soft face staring down at me, momentarily.

I realise in this second, and for this second now, he hates me.

The kitchen is empty. Mysteriously, Aunty Gilda and Ponky have vanished. They know what side their bread is buttered on.

He goes over to the kitchen shelf and gets out an Aspirin. He pulls some water from the tap. How slow time is as the water in his glass flows down his throat. He stands there, hand on the tap, one hand on the glass, letting the silver water flow right into him.

Uncle Ambrose, I don't say as I look over at him silently. Am I no longer his goodboy his ownboy? My cheeks hurt. I look downwards.

Soon, just as Aunty Gilda bustles into the kitchen, highheels running across the lino, and Ponky comes back in, we hear Uncle Ambrose opening the garage doors with a curse, then the sound of him backing down the drive. Just as the car passes the wall and the whole kitchen becomes occupied with the volume of carsound, Ponky's eyes lean against mine. Just for a second.

I lower my lids so she can't march inside.

I SLIP IN through the school gates, my head held low so I can keep in my eyes the image of me getting out, really slowly. It is the *Saturday Evening Post*, over at Aunty Margaret-Rose's, an advertisement, in colour, and the car door falls open wide, in front of the lit-up Southern mansion. A full moon like a lamp hangs in the sky. A bright slash of black marks the glittering marble floor. A thin, elegant and muscular young man stands beside the opened door. He wears a dinner jacket, a cigarette smokes elegantly between the semaphore of his second and third fingers.

And through the opened cardoor we can see a waterfall, a flood of dress, a ballgown all afroth as the coolly smart lady prepares herself for the immolation of the moment. Drawing the silky whisper of her wrap round her shoulders, she leans out, nervously, like a plant to sunlight. In one second she will have made that marvellous transition.

Under a thousand eyes, she will have been born.

B ALL SPLATTERS INTO a puddle.
Wet gravelly slime travels over my face.

A Cameo tribe boy leers into me, his stubby wart-fingers gathering into his palm the ball.

Bald ball, branding ball.

'Watch where you're goin', Noddy,' he says, bashing his bag into my legs. Banging into me so his legs tangle with mine, and I get a closeup of his hungry eye. Everyone in the world hates getting up early and, for hours, for a long time into the day, everyone is still snatched back into dreamsleep, except now they are sleepwalking, awake, eyes not really turned round from the inside of their skulls.

I know the territory of this world now. I know the points of danger. All narrow entrances and exit points are dangerous. Anywhere where precedence and order must be defined is to be avoided. The narrow path by the dental clinic. The long narrow track near the creek. A sudden converging of asphalt between two buildings.

Better to keep to wide spaces or, even better, to wander haphazardly, dreaming and lost, through the girls' playground.

INSIDE ME, INSIDE a small glass bubble of memory, lodged in there for all time, a capsule which still releases its potency, bleeding into my system so that, startled by the flush of its power, force of its imperative, I remember the day I invaded the girls' playground. I know yet I don't understand these imperatives. What I do understand is the logic of their overwhelming power: the way I am driven, like an automaton, to realise its 'quest', to comprehend, to enter the world of skipping ropes, chants, rhythmic incantation, leave behind the world of knucklebones and marbles and fights; this is not difficult, but different, different laws and rules, a different form of cruelty. But the world is cruel. Cruel in its indifference to all of us, masked by deceit, smothered by concern. I know this as I move along, swinging my bag against my leg, in time to my movement as I edge round the building so I can get my first,

yes,

my breath flares up through me,

yes,

there they are,

CarrotnKeely already in an energetic dance, feet caught off the ground, eyes alight, air whistling through their bodies —

the ball bounces on gravel

for one instant I conceive the wish that my body was that gravel and it felt the hotfall of that ball

bounce

bouncing off the ground.

SLOWLY, I COME nearer. This is brazen of me, to even think of interrupting their dance, they are so intent, CarrotnKeely, joined together in the web of their breaths as they interlock, and dance apart, patting the ball between them, diving and lunging, turning and dancing, catching all the early morning energy of the world in their footsteps.

Neither of them has time to notice me getting nearer.

Already I have left behind on the wooden seat by the classroom Winkie, who wills me to sit down beside him, not leave him.

But I am drawn, against my will, sleepwalking almost, towards Keely.

As I get nearer, Carrot lets out a yell, and dances round a Murray Halberg victory lap. I watch him acknowledge the cheers of the crowd, his hand raised above his head, flag of false modesty, thin lips creaming. Keely goes hahaaaaa, but bounces the ball anxiously in his hand, eager to keep playing, to get back to playing, to win.

I look at Keely, whose whole body is breathing an energy so swift it roars as it passes up through his body, from out of the earth, his earthbrown eyes shining, his cheeks reddened by the effort, his milkwhite teeth flashing against his brownbrown skin. His hair is neatly mother-tamed, then altered by the artistic flick of his own comb. He wants to be Fabian, he wants to be Jerry Lewis. He is neat, and treacherous, Keely.

Like now.

In slow motion Carrot has become aware I am standing there, held back by the white line painted on the asphalt.

Across this I can't cross. I stand right beside it, queuing.

I have rehearsed these words for so long now that when I say them, hoping desperately they have a kind of careless casualness, I know they are imprinted, embedded, formed, shaped, sculptured by my desperation.

'*Go, Keely,*' I copy him precisely, waiting for a miracle to happen.

Wanta game?

Wanta join us?

Wanta join onto us, into us, become part of us?

Yesplease.

But time goes slow-coach when it wants to be and this is now.

Keely's head turns just slightly as he follows Carrot's glance to me. His head is turning so slowly that I watch his eyeball swivel in a protracted arc, which circles round the earth, round the globe it travels so lingeringly so that, by the time it attaches its trapeze to me, I can feel I am turning into stone.

Sticksandstones

break my . . .

Carrot's eyes have travelled once, twice to Keely, and he pushes his hips out. I don't know what this means exactly, but I know it is not good.

I will Keely not to laugh.

Inside the stone, willpower.

He, Keely, feels all the magnetic force of this will, but he is also aware of Carrot's power. We both realise Carrot is talking, he has let drop the basketball down towards the earth. Yes. Now we know that whatever will happen (and it will change how we will behave from now on), whatever is going to happen will have to occur before that ball, hurtling, meets its own shadow as it rushes down darkly to meet the earth.

'Er, *go*,' says Keely, fingering the words with all the exaggeration of my learnt text.

'Er, *go*, Jamie.'

Ball strikes the earth.

In that second of impact, he makes me see how ridiculous the words are when you don't possess them, when you don't know the magic that lies behind them. Go where? Away from them? Into the earth? Sink beneath your feet, through the gravel into the dirt? Go where exactly?

Carrot has heard the thin line of ridicule in Keely's voice. In fact it is for Carrot, it is Keely being a housewife in a frilly apron, delivering him on a tray from the oven, still-warm, a full tray of biscuits. Now Carrot eats every one of them, ooze coming out of the corner of his mouth as he laughs up at me.

The ball leaps back into his hand.

He stands there, more beautiful than any statue on earth, possessing Keely.

The ball balances there, on his palm.

TODAY THEY WILL not ask me to join them.

But tomorrow, or the day after, or even on the day I arrive at school on the back of a brilliant red Jaguar, which snarls at them like an MGM lion; yes, then they will relent, and casually, to hide their humiliation, the very scale of their defeat, they will come and ask me to join them, to go with them, and, casually (as if I knew it would happen all along), just like that lady as she slides out of the car, and, adjusting her wrap in that second as she raises her head, faintly smiling, walks into the flood of camera flash, with them I will *go*.

A FILM IS running inside the school hall.
A film?
Not just any film.
A film about sex.
A sex education film.

There, on the shadowy white square, smelling dank and of the creek. There, between the thin silk curtains which blow with any furtive gust of wind, silvering in through holes in the asbestos walls.

There, in the hall which was, once, a resting station for wounded American servicemen, so we are told.

There.

THE SCREEN HAS been wound down, on its scroll, and now across its silvery surface plays knowledge so secret and hidden boys have to be separated from girls, and each of us, to enter, has had to provide a secret password: a note written in hand by one of the persons who gave us birth (or a guardian), saying they agree to their child witnessing a film about sex.

A film about sex.

How simple this sounds, beside the silver calibrations which tintinnabulate up and down our spines as we wait all of us, a lineup of boys, a sausage file of boyboyboy, jointed into each other by the rushing flush of eager anticipation.

What lies on the white? What is inside?

Each of us can hardly wait to get inside the doors, to drink of the deep and forbidden knowledge.

Now, sitting in the dark foisty moist of it, smelling of boy sock and the sweat under unwashed armpit, by Carrot's hot bananaskin (he is entranced, Keely too has raised his face up to the white screen). On this we have seen many acres of boredom. Across this we have trekked through wastelands and Steppes of commentary: peas being tinned; milk spurting and splashing into glass bottles; how baking powder is made; 'Look at the bother Dad gets into while Mother's out visiting!'; we have observed process and, cheerily, with an aching boredom, learned nothing.

But now, now is the moment we have all, unknowingly, been waiting for and the suck of the air all around us is soundful as we bloom towards the screen, each of our faces an open flower, waiting for the rain.

Rain on me, I pray, playing at knowledge.

Boomvoice, as always.

Diagrams.

Charts.

Little corpuscles.

And then the miracle happens.

A naked male body, presented side on to the camera. The row-upon-row of boy draws in its breath — sucks in, vertiginously, almost like a dog-growl. A howl emerges down the front, wave after wave of laughter flecks back, the tidal wave surges through the dark.

But my eyes are trapped.

This body has no head, this is what is so disturbingly fascinating. It is as if, so long as you have this thick hose thing, nestled in a strange black whirl of hair, a posy of springstreak, you no longer need a head, a body without a head, but possessing this thing — a penis, as the voice devoids it — you are complete.

The torso, entrancingly, begins to revolve towards us. The hall is awash with boyjuice, plashing and crashing all up the walls. We are drowning in its stifling struggled-for breath, in its longed-for groans; all around me boy is grabbing boy, hands rifling up backs and running down thighs, stroking members, grabbing crotches to certify that this thing does exist. The secret is out. The hall goes abandoned.

But I am struck dumb by all this — untouched.

For in one electrifying flash I have understood.

I have understood the power and energy of malehood. Under all their clothes every man carries this secret. This is one of the secrets of the world, so enormous and accepted that everywhere you go, wherever you go in the world, in every travelogue, men are cloaked to hide it.

This electrifying secret.

And in one moment, with a similarly inevitable swivel of the head (parallel, yet in opposite motion to the body), my head turns to gaze at Mr Pollen.

By the light of the projector he is stooped, an arrow of concern running down his face. He is watching the feed of film into projector, the bite of sprocket into sharp wedge. He is drugged on the drone of the machine, the heat which radiates off this metal object. In one second I understand why I have been brought into this dark temple of malehood. I comprehend that the body on the screen is actually Mr Pollen's body, in another image. I have now seen him, miraculously unclothed and, even better, not even possessing a head. Freedom whistles up and down my veins like buckets of gold being hurtled along a speeded-up mechanism within a deep mine. Yes, I comprehend. I have seen Mr Pollen naked, and I will always see him now, his body perfectly white, with that perfection of white which only black-and-white film can possess.

He is revolving towards me, then halts.

My eyes lay their tracks towards him. It is as if I have never seen him in my life before, but having seen him now, I will never forget him. More than this, he has a miraculous power over me, a magnetism, the desire to know more.

And Mr Pollen sits, ignorant of this fountainfall of love plashing all over him, squatting down by the projector light, irradiating his face as he stares, first downwards, then his gaze opens up, like a flower in slow motion, as his eyes travel to the screen. And then, unseen by anyone else, I watch a magic moment . . . he feels down and, one arm outstretched, he begins to wind back a shirtsleeve.

I do not watch so much as my body becomes invisible and I turn into an organ of sight.

The whole world becomes the revelation of his forearm, taut, muscular, wrapped round with ropes of veins, laced over by a fieldflow of hair. I can hardly draw a breath so suspended am I by this on-going spectacle. He continues rolling his sleeves up, over his elbow joint, revealing finally a view of the bulging muscle of his upper arm.

This act, brazenly non-sexual in his view, is for me so rhapsodically drenched in everything I have seen that I understand immediately that those muscles which wrap round his arms, and bulge, so satisfyingly rigid as he casually flexes his forearm, are simply poetic equivalents, hints and mere shadows, of that other miraculous secret, the one which is so extraordinary that nowhere in the world can it be seen.

P<small>ONKY IS NOT</small> home again when I return. This is a statement, an interruption to our silently agreed-upon rituals. It is removal, withdrawal. Dismissal. I cannot understand this, just as I cannot understand the arbitrary arrangements of the world, why things have to change. If we are together, why should we be apart?

This afternoon is a cool grey one, still, depressing. Outside there is no one but the bus passing and repassing up and down the road like the ticktick tock of a clock. I look at Ponky's empty bed, pick up her comics, let them fall. I stand there and try to stop breathing for a while, to see if this will change things. I burst out into breath, decide to go down the park to see what is happening.

Outside I don't even have a shadow. My toes whisper over the gravel, onto the grass. My toes know every mound and indentation of the footpath, the way it mounds slightly as it nears the roots of the pine trees, where puddles glisten darkly when it rains, where the ragged edge of asphalt breaks apart, like stale cake, into clay and then the grass.

But no Ponky now, Ponky is hidden from me, just as she now has to wear gloves and hats and stockings and blouses and a smock-like dress to hide the fact she was once a tomboy. Once.

I walk into the park, looking round me, vaguely and distantly, as if I don't actually expect to see any threepences.

The seasons have changed, from summer into that indeterminate time when it is too cold to swim, and the next summer seems so impossibly distant as to have fallen off the edge of the globe — will never return. I feel the forlornness of this, it bleeds into me.

Looking for threepences provides my reason, my only reason, as I wander off down the green gully of grass, towards the swings.

I swing back and forth so hard and high, small stars bleach into my sky.

I see in the distance Mr Lamb picking up rubbish under the pine trees. They slish-slash wildly across my horizon: distant harbour rises falls in earthquake; pine tree colossi wipe across my pupils. But it doesn't work. I am alone. I hear above everything the arid screech of the swing in its socket. Now it is no longer summer Mr Lamb doesn't oil the swings any more because the rain and wind and frost simply sluice the oil away. So, in an empty socket, screeching, oil-less and dry, I try to fly, but my hopes die.

Wander off, in a wild loose loop, knowing every part of the park, like a map of my hand. That tree there, the small kauri, is Matthew's tree (we have chosen one tree each). It is, typically for him, difficult to climb, its flesh smooth and viscous. When you reach its first branches, there is nowhere to rest: you must balance there, on the balls of your feet, challenging vertigo. You cannot really hide up there. You can only be daring, and dangerous, and unusual, all of which is Matthew. As well as, I suppose, the fact that nobody else even knows it is a native tree: he would always choose the special, the extraordinary, the one which holds history and its secrets.

(My tree is a wide blooming macrocarpa with a girth so enormous it appears to be elephants' legs all bunched together. It is not too high to climb into and, best of all, if you ever fall, you plump down soft on to a nestling bed of pine needles on which you almost bounce. You can spy from this tree, lying up there, unobserved. Or simply drink in all the sky. Through the hole in your eye.)

Maddy and I hide up this tree when we run away from home. But then time is so long we get defeated and return home, anxious that we had not been missed. Ponky's favourite tree is the giant pine tree which keeled over during a storm. The following day every child in the area was down there. It was claimed, and clambered on, and scored with initials, becoming overnight a source of wonderment.

It projected out into the tide. It became a bridge.

Her tree offered drama, crowds, money-making potential. Just as Maddy always wants the unusual so Ponky is so tuned in to what most people like that she always wants what Matthew calls the obvious.

Or the lucrative.

But no Ponky today. No Maddy.

I don't even go near our bunker.

It no longer exists.

I abandon the park and go over into the bus-shelter.

I WANDER INTO the trickly chill of the men's toilets, where words of savage want are scored into the wood. A wry sad piss smell coats everything and the light comes in the trellised window, like a condemned cell, a nun's room, a cell before the executioner's block.

Now it is empty I can investigate this site of so much mystery. Here on the wall, in the smallest cell, is a chart engraved into the wall, hardworked in pencil: Saul 7 inches; Dirk 8 inches; Geoff 15 inches.

I am not sure what this means, though I know, precisely, what it is about. It is part of a large almost unknowable mystery, a dark map, a world which we children have invented, and which adults know nothing about.

But outside I hear the silent tug and glug of power which announces the advent of a trolley bus. Distant at the moment, soon it will be there in a barrage of sound, a bash, a whoosh, a weird whirlpool of motion into so much stillness.

This means the driver will wander in following on his footsteps, a stranger occupying them until he stands beside me, creaking, and asks me, impartially, yet sweating in some part, a dimple of fear in each eye, would I like to hold his thing? 'No thanks, thank you though.'

I know that is no mystery. That is simply like an unflushed toilet, kack all over the floor.

I QUICKLY DIP down the stairs towards the beach. One hundred and five steps exactly, forty-three steps first of all, a landing, then a further steep run. These steps are thick with gravel chunks — crude, pockmarked, like a biscuit recipe with not enough mix in it. A metal tube is the single handrail, worn smooth by the hundreds, no, the thousands of hands which have rested on it. These stairs are steep, dangerous. You may fall and stub your toe, break your nose. After an afternoon at the beach, these steps grow even steeper. And the metal rail glitters like an eel, taunting.

My brother says the steps were made during the Depression. Hungry men built them. And some of their pain, their hunger has gone into the terraces where you are meant to lie, sunbathing — they are filled with sharp shells to press into your flesh, reminding you that you are lucky to be relaxing, you are one of the fortunate ones to be lying there, face turned up towards the sun. Steep stairs whispering, ready to send you sprawling, *you are at the poor person's beach.*

Down I go, down I flow past the changing sheds, of green corrugated tin, with their shower and in summer the efflorescence of naked men. Why is Matthew so often lingering in there? I don't understand. I do understand. One part of me does.

I pass by the whisper of its sound, the shower nozzle running silvery and silent, calling me in but I wander on by.

Down onto the beach.

The tide is coming in, overlapping waves sending in a sharp tang of salt, and beneath that the pickled smell of mangroves. Through the softer spools of dark, sprat storms etch the glass. Pohutukawas lean down, old women bathing, lowering their tresses and dresses, already damp and clinging, into the sea.

To the right the long white bow of the cockle beach.

I look at the sea, wondering mutely whether we will ever return to summer again. I mean by this, one of those summers by which Ponky and I mark the highwater mark of our happiness. I think of bottlefishing, of swimming under the sea. Keeping your eyes open, seeing the sprats inside the bottle. You have to kill them, bash them quick. An eye looks up at you. Sweetscented mixture of capture and release, those summers, oblivious birth leading into quick death.

But today the sea is too cold for bottlefishing. Besides it has all changed. Now Ponky has a fishing rod. Bottlefishing is something only kids do. Babies. Now she goes down to the rocks where bigboys go, where the mystery is strongest. She has penetrated this world and left me behind.

There is no bottlefishing any longer.

The day for sprats is over.

AT THE VERY end of Hungry Creek are the cliffs. The wind here is brisk, impatient, having travelled vast distances. I do not want to linger. I can see right up the harbour which opens out before me like tinfoil unrolling and falling.

A sudden and wild exhilaration overtakes me.

'Ponky, I don't care!' I yell into the wind, knowing the words are taken away from me, off me, unsnared. *'Maddy, I don't care!'*

I pause to see if there is an answer.

When I don't get one, I mutter to myself, whispering to the only person who can hear.

'MumnDad, I don't care if yous never come back!'

THEN, FROM HIGH on the cliff-top I see her. Spy her. Fishing with the bigboys.

A wicked spirit enters me. I want to yell down — *She's a gurl doan yous know it?*

But in that second, PK turns her weight sideways and I see in the bowl of her face such a slide and shade of vulnerability, of nakedness, I can't bring myself to do it. More than this, she makes a quick and funny grimace to me, which says *I can't speak to you now, don't tell on me, I'll talk to you later;* the hidden semaphores of meaning I have known all my life. She does this with her back to the boys around her who, grim with their own importance, do not deign to notice the countermovement of her dance — it does not fit within their severe diagramatics — but the second she has sent this message to me and I have received it she turns away from me, and I know she has already forgotten me.

AS I WALK along, my head hung low, I keep an eye out for threepences. But I see none.

Silence

AFTER SCHOOL THE next day I see him coming towards me, my heart flares up. It is as if I have never seen him before, so completely. Matthew. I can see all the suburb arranged round him, outside of him, an outer skin attached to him, and he is in its centre, cut-out. Matthew. I have never seen him before. He who is inside me and so much a part of me he is my own body, flesh of my flesh.

Now I see him, and I realise with a shock I miss him.

'Hi, Matthew?' I say, tentatively, shyly, uncertain about what drives him to see me.

'Hello, James,' he says to me smiling his awkward strange smile, like a coathanger twisted skew-whiff in a cupboard, the clothes falling off. This is Matthew. He is thin, Matthew, with the high, wide coathanger shoulders of our mother.

I can smell him, even as he stands there.

Aniseed balls. *Aniseed*.

He is my deep shame, my brother, a brother who, with a choice of all the sweets in the whole wide world (that is to say in the local dairy which alone operates at the front of the closed down hotel), my brother chooses the purple-brown sugar berries which give off an odd fennel-like smell. He always has a bag in his pocket, melting and falling apart, balls glued together. He no longer bites his collar, like he used to. Gnawing the edge of his collar, intently, nervously, passionately inside his own world.

Matthew.

Why have I got a brother like him, instead of another kind of brother? Nobody in the world likes such weird things as aniseed balls. My Quiz Kid brother, who wears glasses. He is different, my brother, and it frightens me.

Now I glance about us, spy-like, to see if anyone can see us together. He is leaning his maroon bike against his legs, as he talks to me.

This is so typical of Matthew. Other boys would put their bikes down. Other boys would balance their bike, riding their crotch on the seat, pushing the bike hard into the space between their legs, an odd smile playing on their lips. But Matthew stands there, his bike leaning against his body, his body a wall.

Nervously, in his excitement at seeing me, he pushes it back and forward. Though I am his younger brother, I feel older.

He is excited to see me. This annoys me. What annoys me is that I am excited, thrilled to see him. Waves of warm rush through me, to the end of my fingertips. I can't help myself smiling.

As we stand in the street, with nowhere to go.

We're too old now for the hollow under the pine tree facing the harbour, which was Ponk's and Matthew's and my own bunker.

'Have you heard?' he says to me, a little tense. 'From them?'

I look into his peeled-grape eyes, with their tiny burrowing pinprick. He owns all of me, my brother, he owns every part of my body. Cellophane beside him. So I cling to what everyone else thinks of him.

Brainbox. Foureyes. Aniseed. Poison.

We are joined together at the mouth.

Until we went to school, neither of us realised we spoke strangely. Forming our words correctly, even running sentences together.

Punch! This is the difference between us: I learnt, by watching what happened to him.

Punch! Kick! Thump!

Face down in the dirt, arm twisted behind his back.

'Lissen to how 'e talks. LA-DI-DA. Think you better than us? Think we're not good enough?'

I learn to slur my words and slouch my language. I learn never to put my hand up in class. None of this, he knows. None of this essential language of survival does he know.

Can I know him? He who owns me? In private, in our private hours, flesh of my flesh, breath of my breath, another hand or limb stretching out from my mother.

'You're always so quiet and good and tidy, Jamie. Stop that Matthew! Stop it!'

His toys spread everywhere. On a quiet moment he comes to me and pinches me and pushes his face into mine, screwing it up into a mask, a mask of hate. At other times, he becomes a magician. In the limitless ocean of time on which we sit becalmed, he swims towards me, causing ripples all around me to move.

This is Matthew. He holds a saucer of sand in his hands. He has the heads of a thousand cinerarias all plucked from the dark side of the house, the wasteland beside the garage. The heads are vividly purple, so rich and varied, purple, white, a blur of blueness and an intense shade so pure I can hardly breathe as I watch him, quietly, silently, his head lowered intently, plant the small flower heads. From under his fingertips a pattern emerges. I watch intently. Behind his fingers is scattered a floral pathway, so decorative even I understand he has made something exist which, once before, never existed. Better than this, he has re-shaped time. He has, magician that he is, boldly taken time and re-formed it so that it re-emerges under his thin, nervy, busy fingertips, with the bitten-down nails and the broad spatulate palm of a hand, with the high rising mont — that hand, with warts on it — with even these hands he has boldly fingered time, and rearranged it so from out of his fingers comes this fine cineraria sand dish, the smell of the flowers and the damp sand so potent, I lower my face down into it, it becomes a kaleidoscope, dizzying me as it breaks apart. He is a magician, my brother, so clever. But I cannot know him.

He is looking at me now, waiting. Leg banging against the side of his bike.

'You heard from them?'

Them, I know, means our parents.

I don't answer, I just shake my head, imperceptibly.

Beyond his head I see Mrs Beveridge whose eyes are like a sewing machine, stitching everything together, a consequence to a cause, a slip to an intended insult, a passing comment to an over-emphasised formal letter of complaint. She is a busy ticking machine of a woman, carrying with her all sorts of offcuts and odds-and-ends.

Her husband ran away from her. 'No wonder,' says Dad. She lives in shame in a house with beer bottles plunged upside-down into the soil for a flower border. This was done by her husband. Before he left.

She says, 'Hello, boys, missing your mum I expect.'

Mrs Beveridge is naturally interested in absences . . . and the pain they cause.

Her brightly blue eyes reach across space and try to find communion.

'G'day, Mrs Beveridge,' Matthew calls.

I mean this is what is wrong with him. He calls back to Mrs Beveridge who nods happily, chirpily like a tug boat in the wake of his reply.

'Can't be too much longer,' she calls out gaily, passing on, her day made.

Maddy's eyes re-find mine, invade them.

We look at each other, a slim bridge swinging between us, frail thread wound by a spider, suspended.

We inspect, from this joined bridge, the joint conspiracy of our parents.

It is apparent neither will return. Or worse, they are enjoying themselves without us.

The betrayal is deep, fundamental.

Within the tight weft of our family has come this coldness. Within the tightly packed encyclopaedia of our family, one so immense it runs on for more volumes than the *Encyclopaedia Britannica* (each page made up of breakfasts and dinners and moments on the back steps and looks and repeated sayings), certain pages have been brutally ripped out. Our continuity is threatened.

Now we know we are unwanted. Unwantable.

My eyes catch on Matthew's face. His face is changing, just as his body is beginning to thicken. It is as if there is some other monster inside the boy I used to know, and he is losing that thin urgent laughy sprite, who pinched me so viciously, whose elbows sharply dug and from the end of whose fingers flowery sandsaucers in a million kaleidoscopic shapes emerged. His legs are no longer so thin, or kicked and scuffed round the kneecap from being pushed into the dirt. His legs are becoming muscular. His neck is thickening. He is becoming someone else apart from the Matthew who I know.

Think I know.

His eyes glisten a little. Inside the pupil I see my own world returned to me, and I am standing there, waiting. Waiting.

'No,' I say.

I do not tell him about going up to our old house, the house we used to live in once, because Ponky is staying late at school, silently preferring it to hanging round with me, a kid. So alone, lonely, like a sick dog, I retraced my footsteps across the gravel, went up the drive, all the while expecting a face, a voice to call out. Turning the corner of the house, the back garden stared back at me, like the face of someone I knew once so intimately I expected to know them all my life. Blind now, deaf now. It looks back at me mutely, till a riff of wind lifts up a plum tree bough and sinks down into it, so the plum tree creaks out a greeting to me. No plums now, empty.

The clothesline rocks on its cradle.

A cloud passes down a window gauzed with salt.

In the far distance, high up in the sky, where a sun is suffusing a cloud, a single gull wavers, trapped inside the thickness of glass.

I do not dare to move forward. I want to call out hello to everything in the backyard, retracing my footsteps as if by doing so I am re-threading up a web of all past uses.

Instead I walk, uncertainly across the concrete backyard my father and his friends handymanned into existence so proudly, so that none of us would ever have to play in dirt, in muck, in mud again.

But now all I see is a single pumpkin upraised in its own shadow, awaiting its ripening.

A swift stroke of movement emerges from the bushes. It is Achilles the cat who stands there, indifferent yet watching. To him I am as the cloud on the glass, the gull in the cloud. I am the pattern of leaves under the apple tree, the small lichen attached to the very top of the clothesline.

'Achilles!' I call, overcome with joy to see him. Some spark incinerates in his green eyes. Does he remember all my cruelties towards him, *love me, love me more. Love me absolutely.* But he moves now, following his own fur footsteps across the concrete to me, a superbly indifferent arrow of . . . affection.

Yet there is still a small frisson of uncertainty as he comes close to me. He scents my abandonment. He criticises me for it. Silently. I bend down and pick him up, feasting for one entire minute on the heat-thudding blood-pumping furry warmth as his flesh pushes into me. *Mummy.*

I bury my face in his fur, crying unexpectedly, tears dragged out of me on thin burning wires. *I never meant. I didn't mean. I . . . I . . .*

Achilles twists in a shudder under my hands. He reasserts his independence, demanding gravity. I am lost again. I set him down on the ground, torn between establishing my own independence *('See, I don't care you horrible cat,')* and a bereft feeling of isolation and sadness which sweeps over me.

'I haven't forgotten you,' I murmur to him softly.

I tell Matthew nothing of this.

His eyes silently read all the space on my face. Time (of which he is magician) has become elastic. as if his fingers had come and moved across my face. What is he reading? Of how I unlocked the stormdoor and penetrated the woodsmelling heat of the back porch? Of how I went into the wash-house and looked down at the houseplants sitting in their own warm wet moss of water? How I turned the tap on and gave them a fresh drink? How I left the tap running until a sudden storm of indifference and cruelty overcame me and I wished to drown all of them, or take them outside and throw them out? Instead of which I turned the tap off and tiptoed out and locked the stormdoor behind me.

'Have you heard?'

'Heard what?'

'That they don't want us.'

Neither of us says anything for a while, then:

'How's school?' I ask in a downward descent every schoolchild understands.

'Alright. I came top in Latin. We study how Caesar conquered Britain.'

'I got to do a picture,' I say sullenly. 'For the bank competition. *Savings Bank*,' I say sourly, as if I am biting into a plum, unripe.

He looks at me sharply then, as if he has suddenly had a dawn of knowledge.

He does not know I have never told anyone my brother is a Quiz Kid. He does not know I have never told anyone I even have a brother.

'Do you?' he says. 'Do you want some help with it?'

'Don't know,' I say sullenly, kicking the gravel under my feet, so I see a scuffmark open up. I keep on kicking. *Don't know. Don't know. I don't know anything,* I want to say.

We hang together, tentatively, words having outrun us. We steal looks at each other uncertainly, each unwilling to ask the other what he is up to, at that moment.

'Do you want to go and have a look at the hut?' he asks me.

I see myself naked and feel the air coolly lifting up and inspecting all the finest hairs on my legs, my arms, my every part.

'I doan know,' I say, frowning.

'Come on,' he says. 'It won't take long.'

'I doan know,' I say, again, as I turn and start walking along with him.

'I doan know,' I say, when I stand there, naked in front of him.

But this requires no words.

Messenger

'WHAT'S THIS?'

Aunty Gilda is using an ice-cream scoop to mound out the mashed potatoes on the plate. I see this as a part of her modernity. Here, in her kitchen, where everything is made to fit, there are no preserves, no tins full of homebaking. Aunty Gilda is a working woman, eager and smart, wearing thin stiletto high heels, so high it is as if she is walking up to the sky, small skyscrapers stacked under each of her arches, rising up tensely, straining as she moves forward, always half-running, in little geisha steps. Late, Aunty Gilda is always running late.

She is not like my mother. Aunty Gilda has a waist so tiny and cinched in tight by a wide shining-black patent leather belt, and shellacked golden hair. She is smart not hard, brittle not strong. I like her. I think how terrifying it is, yet how interesting that each person in the world is different. The way they look at you, whether they see you or not, and what they see, and whether they like what they see.

Aunty Gilda is good to me, she does not see me as different. I am something known to her, familiar as the buses running up and down the road, the coin embedded in concrete outside the back door, which Uncle Ambrose and the men made: a Coronation coin which Ponky and I have never given up trying to wrest out.

Without Uncle Ambrose we relax. The back door stays open, onto the sunset, and something happens in the house — all the spaces become liquid and connected, as if you turn into fluid yourself and you might just slip out the door, into the light evening air, or wisp along the road to the shop to buy an extra tub of ice-cream; everything is light as air, light as hokey pokey, light as waffle, as hair-sprayed hair.

I am setting the table. Standing thoughtfully looking into Uncle Ambrose's refrigerator. Our fridge at home is white. Their fridge, as always, is smarter than ours. Newer, pastel green. And when you put your hand on the rocket handle, it opens wide. It does this with a kind of sigh, like a fat person stretching and yawning after a satisfactory meal. A slurp of happy rubber lips. The door, weighted down with its freight of goodies, swings back as you stand there, irradiated by the brilliant lights.

This is their Hollywood Bowl, this radiance which greets me. There are the bottles of Waitemata beer, ready and chilled for Uncle Ambrose's advent. These above all must always be lined up there, one replacing the other as it is drunk. It is my job, as serf, as slave who stays there, menial and skivvy, always to make the trek from fridge to wash-house where Uncle Ambrose's wealth lies stacked, cooling on concrete.

Ponk has her radio plugged into her ear and she looks out the window.

What does she see?

I don't know.

A SHADOW FALLS across the doorstep.

It is Mavis Crickwood. I look at her slippers. She is a woman who marches across to the shop, led by a cigarette always burning on her lip. Her hair is dyed a shade so astringent it gives the feeling all her intelligence had grown into her hair, into a set of angry lips. She has a smudge of rouge on either cheek. Warpaint. No eyebrows. Plucked.

'Gilda!?'

'Mavis!?'

The two women stare at each other across space.

'Come on in, Mavis,' Aunty Gilda says, inviting her across, and over, the backstep.

We can see Mavis's eyes are vehement with news, bulging almost in their sockets as her pupils strafe across the face, first of Ponky, then of me, then jumping back, cricketattack, to Ponky.

Already water is thundering down the spout into the jug (not a kettle like at home). Gilda connects water to electricity.

This is an emergency crisis summit.

Khrushchev to Kennedy.

Another look at us, the children.

'*I thought someone should tell you,*' Mavis Crickwood retracts a self-important breath: annunciate. '*Last night. Round about six o'clock. Just when it was getting dark.*'

More looks. Gilda follows Mavis's looks to us, which seek, hook to sheep, to corral us out of the room.

We sit there, changed, every pore in our body turning into an ear. We are moist with interest. Nothing ever happens to us, we think. We are hungry for life, waiting for it.

An old stale blush falls down Mavis's face, a dropped scenic curtain. Aunty Gilda, we know, wants us treated as adults: Aunty Mavis (everyone around us is an aunt or an uncle, a monstrous entanglement of family-which-is-not-family), Aunty Mavis will have to speak.

'*A face,*' she says.

'*In the steam. Looking in the bathroom window. At Brenda. In the shower.*'

Idly, carelessly, Ponky's and my eyes entwine.

The intensity of our glance betrays us. Instantly, it is as though each of us has already looked, which perhaps we have. Daughters in their late teens occupy a strange zone, somewhere between the very old, whose age conceals great secrets, and people like ourselves — stateless persons, caught in an in-between world, hostages as much as emissaries — it is no wonder that someone has activated all our impulses, which is to stare into a bathroom window, frosty with steam, and, wiping away the translucency, looked long and hard.

A delayed yet sharp intake of Aunty Gilda's breath.

Like a flare in the sky, her glance lights up over us.

Protectively.

But it is too late.

We have heard.

And now we see, through the mist of the bathroom glass, half turning as we dry ourselves, a featureless face, the intensity of a stare which itself is a form of robbery. It takes, does not ask. In fact it has already taken. Observing, it marks. Watching, it prepares.

Within breathing distance of us, like a light wind running down your back.

A leaf outside crinkles across the concrete.

We jump.

A soft slow shudder passes through all of us simultaneously. Our fingers splay back unconsciously on our hands. The hair on our heads becomes electrified and fibrillates, straining up into the air. In unison, our eyes meet and in them is the percussion of a single word, a single thought, the complete expression of horror, beyond which there is no other: he has come onto earth to express it.

Mavis nods grimly.

'Brenda couldn't see who th'dirty bugger was . . . but . . .'

Horton, she does not need to breathe it, the escaping air ventilating out of the puncture of her body does it.

'Horrrrrrrrton,' murmurs Mavis on a dying downward slide of breath.

'I'll kill the bastard if . . . I can only lay my hands on him . . .'

And now, now Mavis Crickwood has breathed it, we all know, individually and alone, he has been sent out into the world again, to terrorise us, to make each night now into a slow journey through fear, the ultimate ghost train, and there, at the end of each day, like a punishing mother, an angry father, like a lover, he waits for us.

'JUST THOUGHT I should tell you,' Mavis says now, a ghastly accomplice's smile on her face. Mavis the butcher from Buchenwald, blood dripping already, in congealed drops, on the lino.

She looks again at Ponky and me.

We feel ourselves go white.

'Keep your eyes open, kids,' her lips tell us.

From now on I know I will be frightened to let my lashes drop black.

My eyes are pinned open, bleeding.

Scuff of her messenger-of-doom slippers back over the asphalt.

'OK, kids,' says Aunty Gilda all bright, having drawn in a brilliant scarf of a breath, which rotates in her chest, round roundand-round so fast soon it is as hard as a golfball, 'OK kids,' she says, after a brief pause. 'You haven't finished up your tucker, but *you want some ice-cream?'*

We listen to her voice, half-diverted by a vision of a double-header, just dipped in molten chocolate, then sprinkled with hundreds, no hundreds and thousands of thousands. This is placed, in neat silhouette, against the shape of a head, looking through a misted-up window, staring.

We are struck silent.

Aunty Gilda's hand hesitates by the doorknob for the slightest second. But seeing we are watching her, our eyes attached to the momentum of her hand, Aunty Gilda boldly leaves the door open, refusing to speak to us right at that second.

It is when she is hurrying past to her purse — she, as if accidentally, with a sideswipe of her heels, pretending she is only at that second recognising what she is doing — boots the door delicately shut. And we sit there, in the sudden dark, sunset cut off from us, looking at each other, waiting.

Soon Uncle Ambrose will be home to protect us.

UNCLE AMBROSE IS talking. Uncle Ambrose is talking non-stop. He has come in the door, hat carelessly flung and hooked on a doorknob (none of us would dare to do this, as we know we might not hook the hat correctly and what would we serfs do if the king's crown fell, if the king's crown rolled across the carpet?)

'I bought, I sold, I said . . .'

Uncle Ambrose is on another roll. He feels none of our fear, our heartjump as his hat soars across the room and connects, magically, hooks then swings, nonchalantly, off the chrome doorhandle.

'Jamieboy, that's my boy!' is his carol, *'Go and get me another beer, buddy, that's my boy (my pet).'*

I go, goodboy/badboy/goodboy, over to the fridge and unseal the safe of their richness. Even the news, the burning news of Horton must wait for him to have finished the recital of his daily conquests, for we all know we are retainers in his court, dependent upon his charity and wealth, so we have to listen, nodding, agreeing, secretly moving in our own patterns round the room, dancing silently around him.

'Jamieboy,' he says, having drained the last froth, the last dribble of gold into him, he bangs the crystal glass down on the tabletop, misjudging the distance between the table and him so Aunty Gilda jumps a little bit — *My nerves,* she doesn't say, she is too busy not listening.

Thinking of, thinking of.

Ponky has stumped off to her room where she stuffs the transistor plug into her earhole, but she leaves all the doors open, I notice, even turning the lights on behind her as she trails into her bedroom. She does not want to be disconnected now.

I go to the fridge and unseal the banksafe, their food vault, and I stand there, surrounded by the whispers of dry ice as I stare into their cavern: here is their richness, reproduced in the mirror of my eye, in the sheen of my glance so that, in neat reproduction, on the surface of my eyebulb, I share these possessions, simply by looking.

'What's holding you up, Jamieboy?'

Behind me I hear the question.

'What's the hold up, sport, don't you know you have to run with something when it's hot . . .'

My hand swings forward, to grapple his nectar, grab his joyjuice, to obtain the bubbles which will froth up and foam out, down the crystal tube, then, aerating his fantasy, blowing him up a little wider, he will induce them into himself and infuse himself into being a magician who however briefly lifts up off the ground and defies gravity.

Like a little pasha to his sultan, I deliver the goods.

LATER THAT NIGHT it comes.
  The sound of footsteps.
  A door cranes open.
  The sound of two breaths.
  A knife whistles through the air.
  A naked blade.

A scream fills the night.

'O turn it down,' I moan softly. 'Ponky?'

She tweezers the sound away from me. But I realise I must hear the ending or I will not live. It will live inside my head always, waiting like a flower to bud and burst.

'No please,' I say then, 'I must hear the end.'

A lazy spurt of blue spray across our night. A saxophone drone then swing and sway all the nerve endings of the night. The powerlines outside weep. Black tears. And night falls all about us in its sequinned want.

'Ponky,' I whisper, 'you asleep yet?'

'Yes,' she says, annoyed.

'Ponky,' I say after a while. Because I know when her adenoidal breathing connects up. 'Ponky,' I say, 'You think he get inside?'

I glance at the window which lies in-between us, separating us from each other. He could easily break the glass, and reach in.

But instead of an answer there is something worse: the slight groan of her outward breath has met the inward suck of air into her lungs; matted, fretted, frayed and straining, the air moves into her body. She is sinking down under the compressed weight of night. Her fingers, with their bitten nails, fall slack around the transistor. Softly the radio tilts and leans against her pillow. I hear the slight pock of a bubble of saliva as one balloon of spit opens and closes by the very corner of Ponky's mouth. Then her trap falls open, her lips do a quick lick, she grunts once, turns like a happy whale and whooshes off to explore the limitless ocean depths of sleep.

Storm

'No!' says Uncle Ambrose, *'No! No! No!'*

He is never a man to spend one word when he can spend twenty, so he goes on, banging the end of his stainless-steel steak knife on the tabletop, *'No! no! no! no!'* Ponky does not smile, her face takes on a Mongoloid quiet. She hides her glance, does not even sit at the same table. I understand she is used to this, which is almost a new production for me.

'You haven't clipped the hedge closely enough. It needs . . . Uurgh!' Uncle Ambrose's moist lips let out a splutter of exasperation.

A dull purple flush begins to bleed into the veins which trace another mask over his face.

I have never seen this face before.

It is ugly.

I see the big holes at the bottom of his nose, opening and closing like a dangerous fish. He is swelling and undulating, his scales opening and closing quickly, with agitation. I feel the weight of his eyeball, cool and slippery, as it drags down my flesh.

'When I was a boy I . . .'

The clippers feel awkward and heavy in my hands. I push and pull them open and shut. The hedge is an eternally growing beast so that no sooner have I clipped it all along to one end, where I stop, exhausted and hot, to look at what I have done, achieved, than at the other end it has started growing again.

Maliciously a sharp twig leaps out and snaps at me.

Tony Lamb walks by, airy on his flat dirty feet, his blackblack eyes sparkling an insult to me. *You thought you was a fairy princess,* he does not say, adjusting himself inside his serge pants which I know do not have underpants, I have seen his thing, dangling down there, looking at me.

He laughs at me, as he wanders by, licking with his tongue all over a fast melting ice-cream which leaks over his hands, his fingers. Then, standing still, his legs planted wide apart, his horny flat feet feeling the distant thud of the heart at the centre of the earth rinse of its blood as it runs up into his crack, he begins to slowly lick, one after the other, so slowly I feel his tongue travelling all over my face. He begins to lick his dirty fingers, which I know have been up inside his pants, feeling for himself and then down round the back where he has been playing intensely and moistly, fiddling and riddling a tune he plays constantly, a smile coming and going on his face.

He cheekily laughs up at me.

The straight line of the hedge breaks apart, and continues growing.

'. . . and I never once!' says Uncle Ambrose banging his knife against the table again, so the peanut butter glasses with the FLOWERS OF NEW ZEALAND on them jump up into apostrophes of fear.

'I never once!' he says to me, 'ever had the money to ride a bus to school. I didn't have a bike. I never so much as expected a ride. No one had a car. No! I walked three miles to school barefoot. Through the frost without so much as a shoe on my . . .'

I sense Ponky's lips moving along in time with his breviary, though she knows to keep her face without expression. I feel, without seeing, Aunty Gilda's eyes sending to me a chocolate log train which whispers to me: don't answer back to him. Listen to him in silence and he will run out of s-t-e-a-m.

So now we all sit there and listen to him, and I feel a break of bleakness rinse all through me. I look down at the jigsaw puzzle and see all these pieces, some of which are parts of Ponky's face, her smile as it used to be, Aunty Gilda's false eyelash, Matthew's tongue all purple from the aniseed balls, an airline letter, imprinted with a plane, and I see in the sky my parents' plane lifting off and disappearing in the sky.

I call to it.

I watch this for a long time, until there is nothing left.

A fly spot on the green ceiling.

'What you got to say?' Uncle Ambrose is asking me, insistent.

'You listening to me, Jamieboy? You better. You better listen to your Uncle Ambrose when he talks to you. *Otherwise. No more Coke. No more sweets. No more halfcrown falling heavy and flat in the palm of your hand so you can go off and sit in the flicks. No more flicks. No more nothing.'*

No more, I know, I want to say to him. I know this already, as the last plane sound dies in the room.

I know this. No more no more. I know this.

But as he waits for me to speak, I wonder if I do.

'Right,' Uncle Ambrose snaps. 'Tomorrow. That hedge. Cut again. Straight. Neat. Shortbackandsides. You hear me? You hear me?'

'Yes, Uncle Ambrose,' I murmur, looking down at the scarlet silk curtains which seem so far away, trapped behind glass, I can no longer really touch them.

Yes I hear, I do not say.

THAT NIGHT PONK and I make sure the window is fastened shut, that is, open on a slit so small only air can come in. We do this with a kind of manic nonchalance, with an intensity which fails to disguise our fear, our anticipation. As I sink into the black, slink in the back, I keep eyeing the slit, feeling for my gun, sinking forever downwards as we wait for him.

By nightfall he moves and wanders round our streets, quietly testing window fastenings, pulling on stormdoors, looking inside letterboxes, the eye inside the keyhole.

He is everywhere, because he is nowhere, and even if he were caught, and placed in the deepest cell, inside the furthest prison, behind the highest wall, he would float out through the keyhole, shimmy round the chill iron bars, he would join himself, in a miasma, onto the air, blow on the breeze till he finds himself invisible, at which point he can manifest himself as he stands there, laughing to himself diabolically, just down the road from the picture theatre, in whose dark he has changed back into himself. Now he stands at the top of our street, throwing his glance down the long street of my nightmares, the one which allows no crooks, no beds, no dips.

He stands there, poised, about to launch off down towards us.

And crushing his cigarette out under his shoe, the lone spark gambols, frisking along the asphalt, glimmering up into light, one planet in the solar system which glows brilliantly, then sinks down into darkness.

We are walking, Ponky and Matthew and me.

It is an afternoon so fine and still the sky has disappeared into the pure white of sun. The whole of heaven is a white aura dazzling down on us, sucking into itself all sound, apart from the strange suctioning sound of our feet as we seek to lift them out of the tidal mud. We are on the forbidden side of Hungry Creek, that narrow inlet which runs into a crinkle of mangroves, in which is hidden the creek: Hungry Creek.

Beyond it lies the reef.

This is forbidden territory for all of us because this thin vial of silver, which lies now so meekly and slim, threaded onto the glittering viscous mud like a phial of quicksilver, can grow into a fierce force which, having trapped your feet in the mud, flows over your face and forces itself down your throat, drowns you.

This creek demands babies and toddlers attracted to its tameness. Each year it gobbles down the flesh of some innocent leaving behind a mother covered in shame and tears so terrible they must leave Hungry Creek and go and live in the bin where you see them hanging onto the wire as you ride along the road, calling out to you as if you are the child that they lost.

We are walking out towards the reef, led along by Matthew, who has been there before, he tells us.

He is leading us intrepidly.

Ponky wants to go there, to prove that she has done it. Because all the local kids have walked over to the reef at low tide. Which means crossing the creek. They have found fabulous things there. For the reef is not merely an encrustation of rocks (not merely the bridge in which the ghosts of a thousand dead goblins lie, to reawaken each night) it is also the dump.

Here is left the remains of what many thousand upon thousand of people think is no longer valuable. There is no end to what is no longer wanted. It is like a catalogue of lost souls, the detritus of the city, it is like the dandruff shaken out of the huge head of the living.

It is treasure.

Matthew tells us this.

He changes what some people see as meaningless into objects of value, to be sought.

A bank vault was discovered, its door blown open and mysteriously full of nothing. Matthew has already shown me the jewelled brooch he himself brought back as booty. It is intricate, a webbery of gilt on which are embedded a scattering of stones; pink stones, the palest of blue stones and stones which are a curious, yellow-green colour. The fastening on the back no longer works, but this only adds to its curiosity. Its uselessness becomes a glittering star of uniqueness.

Matthew has told us all of this, as he leads us on.

I don't know whether to believe him, my brother, or disbelieve him.

My feet are sinking now into the mud, which is warm on the surface, but cold, cold as death underneath. We know, hidden under the mud, are broken bottles, septic tins waiting to implant into our blood systems the serum of poisons, illness and lingering painful death.

So each footstep, as you sink downwards, is a tentative sensing out to see if you come into contact with any hard object.

The mud is now up to our calves.

We can no longer walk. We have to struggle against the mud, forcefully.

We grow tired.

'What happens if we strike quicksand?' asks Ponk in a small, yet concentrated voice.

'Don't fight it!' Maddy says. 'If you feel yourself sinking,' he advises, 'you have to stay still as possible, but put your arms out wide: like this.'

And here, embedded in the mud, he stretches his arms wide apart, palms out flat.

For one second, he looks strangely emblematic, and I see the creek behind him, the mud pillowing down smoothly. It has a sleek shininess as if all the bereaved mothers in the world have come there, to the banks, and polished the banks with their knees as they tried to wash away their tears.

Is that what Hungry Creek is? A torrent of tears?

Flowing out of the dark huddled landscape.

We stand still, so still, just looking at it.

I turn round and look back at all the houses, roofs, telephone poles.

I can see washing on the line of Mrs Beveridge: white sheets hanging still. Surrender.

Five sparrows in a line along the top of a tin roof. One hops along and replaces another. It is so far away and silent.

Now strands of deep green speckle the jade. Clouds overhead rearrange their shapes, shuffle their strands all over the harbour surface.

It is then we realise what has happened.

The mangroves are sinking beneath the harbour.

The tide is racing in.

The creek grows thicker.

The mud settles round our legs, turning to concrete.

The tide now runs towards us, with soft and surreptitiously gleeful slurping sounds.

What will we do?

The creek licks its lips.

I wake up.

It is Uncle Ambrose with the first electric shaver in the district.

He is singing to himself under his breath, he comes into our room.

'Out of bed out of bed, you kiddies. The early bird catches the storm.'

I feel today I will be lucky.

A ND SO IT happens. I have no control over this, and this is the magical process by which life instantly changes, trips over itself, invents its own despair and hallelujahs afresh.

I have no control over this except: I am there. Magically I am there, as I knew I always would be, in my dreams — *waiting*.

I have not been delivered to school in the scarlet chariot. But still, this does not matter so much because it is about to happen. As I dreamt it would.

But not *how*.

Carrot has come to school early and there is no Keely. No Keely to be attached to his Carrot, so he, insufficient, feeling he is lacking his full half, mooches about, his hands buried deep, deep in balls of agony inside his pockets.

He kick-kicks his winklepickers along, as if, in tumbling the gravelstone, he is trying to find Keely. His grey sky is lowered, he scowls a little loosely, till the gravelstone, *of its own accord,* leads him towards me.

He is now, with his left hand, as if this hand had no other connection with his body, bouncing the foursquare ball.

The ball bounds down to earth, repercusses up back into his hand. This is his heartbeat calling out to Keely.

Keely's disappearance covers all of us, is the air we breathe.

Carrot's snot-yellow eyes glance over at me.

In one instant I sense he is alone, as shy as me. As curved and carved into strangeness as I am. I am made stronger, some part in me relaxes, opens wide.

Yet everyone else in the playground, in this instant, is made invisible, soundless.

I can hear the gulls over in the tip biting into the rubbish, beaks plying plastic. I can hear ants eating. I can hear the underground sound of worms moving through the soil.

O, Carrot, I don't say, for I understand I must appear indifferent, so he cannot hear my heartbash. Or perhaps more precisely, so no one else in this playground may sense my milkshake of excitement. All must happen silently, and furtively, in the severe patternings of a set dance.

So the gravel magically untumbles towards me, revealing, at once, a path which was eternal, pre-existent, simply awaiting this instant to be discovered. (Yet the real mystery is that it is equally possible this path might never have been revealed.)

Feigning surprise, Carrot's eyes dart towards me, the object to which he is being driven.

The ball leaps and falls from his hand, taking on its own life.

At this second, though Winkie is talking, I sever our conversation, turning into stone beside him.

My eyes flick-flicker towards Carrot's, entwine and ensnare his eyes out of his head, so his body is drawn, mute, following on behind my ventriloquist's stare towards me.

Ah, now we are situated exactly opposite each other, though Carrot, to show he is not impressed, stands with his hips slightly to the side, ball bounce-bouncing into his palm where, for one oscillating second, fraught with enormous implications, he scowls down to me and murmurs:

'Keely's not here, you wanna play with me, fuckycunt.'

Winkie beside me changes into a Christmas tree, his lights flashing.

'I do, I can, I will,' he cries out fast.

But I am walking, I am beside Carrot, instantly we have married.

To the improbability of our encounter, to its frank impossibility, we have pledged a wager.

Of course, I understand neither of us must show any feeling.

It is his job to get me into the foursquare box before anyone notices that, in that second, the whole fragile infrastructure of game-playing, inside the playground, has altered. With one swift twist, a new dynamic is being introduced.

I comprehend I am strictly on offer. Winkie has got up and trails after us. He is waiting for my downfall.

INSIDE THE BOX, inside the white lines, possessing the space which is set aside for CarrotnKeely, Carrot — as if to show everyone I am not Keely and therefore he owes nothing to me —

Carrot sneers slightly, and for one second his face falls into cowboy indifference. He taunts me with my own unimportance, my reduction to nothingness — just when I might be given the chance to leave it, I must recognise the full weight of my insignificance. Accept it.

He lifts his hand up, and with a powerful thrust he sends the ball whistling towards me, hoping it will strike me in the face and this nightmarish moment will be over. The moment in which it looks like every game in the school might halt, at some subliminal alarm, all other children crowding around us, yelling and screaming for Carrot to eclipse me.

But just as the ball grows larger, as it lacerates the air around it, some electric and secret energy flows from the asphalt under the soles of my shoes and I enter into the magic dance.

THE BALL IS sent back to him sooner than he hit it to me. This is as much a shock to him as it is to me, and I gasp. I open my mouth and from out of it flow a hundred thousand coloured streamers.

This is suicide.

Inside Carrot's eye clouds a storm. Yet his return and my attack are so swift that he instantly realises he cannot afford even the luxuriance of thought. He must engage simply to stay alive. Winkie, Winkie beside me is whistling, *'Go, Jamie,'* he sings, *'Go, Jamie, kill Carrot.'*

I, who can barely understand what is happening to me, give myself up to the strict energy of our dance.

Each attack, I defend. Each return, I attack. So we dive, and swoop, and circle through the air, our eyes catching on each other, as our limbs answer the stroke of the other. All the energy of my waiting to be asked is expressed in that game which I quickly and almost superbly win.

Carrot does not stop to ask me if I want another game. He simply starts again, furious. So we begin again, and fight again, and make love to each other through our opposing movements.

This goes on for so long the hundred thousand coloured streamers have enwrapped themselves round every ligament of

Carrot's limbs and I can feel him, and smell him, as if he is already changed into being me. And effortlessly, though he himself is only just sweating to realise it, I control him. I begin to open my mouth, to let out my very first laugh. With surprise, we hear the bell go.

And when the bell has finished its last peal, echo dying across the most distant perimeter of the playground, and everyone is draining indoors, it is at this second, we notice Keely is standing beside us, has been standing beside us for a long shadow of time.

His face is white, beneath the pale suntan he always has, his natural half-Maori glory.

His mouth is dry as his eyes flick-flicker back and forth from Carrot to me.

As Carrot catches the ball on its final bounce, breathless and pale himself, under his skin of silvery sweat, his eyes turn to Keely and Keely does one of his Fabian-cool film-star motions of attractiveness. He takes out his slim comb and runs it through his hair. Effortlessly he draws our eyes to his beauty, his summation, his control of niftiness.

But now his timing is all wrong and the managed flick of the comb as it mounts up the font of his hair hesitates.

'G-Go, Carrot,' Keely murmurs the password to Carrot, and Carrot murmurs back, breathless, after two solid heavy heartbeats (ones so immense he can hear them, inside the dark shaft of his consciousness, like a Big Ben gong strike, one after the other which intimates from now on he will have to acknowledge me), 'G-G-Go, Keely,' he murmurs. Then in one swerve so expressionless it cannot survive language, he bounces the ball towards me so I have to catch it, and without me saying a word, risking a word, risking them seeing I do not yet possess their language (dare to), I simply return the ball to Keely who gathers it into his captain's clasp, and then, understanding graciously that to maintain his power he must appear to lose it, he bounces it back to me, and I, understanding the elaborate yet wordless rhythm of our ballet, return it to Carrot.

Carrot, wordlessly, examining in his sublime defeat, returns the ball to Keely, who s‿ away from gravity and the eternal victor, the bea‿ all-time captain leads us, his team, behind him, pᴜ blissfully exhausted, into darkness.

THEY DO NOT talk to me for the rest of the day.

Letter

...iting for me. He is standing there

...rawing he has done for the Savings
... looking at it.
...quisite strong blue-white card, one

I gaze at the way it is un...udged, the figures and words clearly and cleverly drawn.

A wise owl prepares for the rainy day.

Done in brown pencils.

It is far beyond my own ability to draw.

He holds this here, as a love token.

'For you,' he says. 'What you think of it?'

I think of how it is cheating, how he has done it for me. I think of how my brother is so good at drawing and painting and doing everything which is clever with his hands. He simply has to look and observe, his head oddly on the side, holding into himself a strange mute stillness. No wonder he needs glasses, he looks so much, and so intensely.

It is only at these moments he keeps still, for most of the other time, all of the other time, he is jittery and stuttery, as if the words are stuck down inside his throat and can't quite burst out. But I know this is because he has so much to say. He knows so much, my brother, he has read book after book from the library, consuming knowledge, absorbing facts and figures: this is how he has become a Quiz Kid.

My brother who all the other boys at school aim to trip up, then let him fall in the dust, and laugh at him. My brother who gets bashed up, and comes home with his knees bloody and his glasses broken. Tense, shaking like a bomb about to go off, smelling of aniseed on which he lives, his snotty fingers covered in warts, working out mysteries.

I know this, I know all of this history which trembles through his fingers as he looks down from the picture he has drawn for me and then up to me, expectantly.

I do not know what to say, as I look over at him. He has ridden here as fast as his legs can go, as fast as he can get to me, the second his pencil finally left the drawing. He has held the drawing, rolled up into a bundle loosely enough, on the bars of his bike. There is a faint imprint of sweat, the pores on his thumb still marking the outside of the cardboard.

'But they'll know I didn't do it,' I say, trying to buy time.

'No they won't,' he says. 'They don't even know you.'

Everyone knows the assessor is an art teacher from another school.

'But,' I say, my fingers itching. 'I didn't really do it.'

'Don't you want to win the prize?' he says then.

'Yes but,' I say. 'Yes but.'

He pauses and looks at me. He begins, very very slowly to roll the scroll back up. He does this so slowly my eyes have a chance to catch on his and I put out a hand, 'Oh, don't put it away just yet, I haven't finished looking at it.'

His fingers stop, and he holds the picture in front of himself. Where his head and chest are is the picture.

I look at it and dream, not so much of what I might do with the money if I win it, but of what it might mean to win. I dream of how KeelynCarrot and others will be forced to admire me and . . .

I dream of this for a long breath of silence, absorbing into me the fact that Matthew is standing there, awaiting my verdict.

But already it seems my decision has been made for me. He has made my decision, by doing such a beautiful drawing. I know I could never do a drawing like that. And he, knowing it, has done it for me.

Now he reaches across and gives it to me.

Silently.

Yet the moment it is in my hands, its weight changes and it becomes heavy. I am trapped by it, I sense, as I look back at

Matthew who is looking at me intently, as if he expects something, by not expecting anything.

'Be careful,' he says now, fussily, 'not to get your fingers on it. Where are you going to keep it? Have you got a roll to put it in? How are you going to carry it to school?'

'I'm only going to keep it for a while,' I say defensively, pushing his hand away. 'Till I decide. I haven't decided yet. I haven't made up my mind.'

He looks at me, and is hurt. I think: *good*, I have hurt him, he will keep away now.

I walk off, carrying his drawing.

'Jamie,' he calls out to me.

I turn behind me and see him standing there, with his bike.

'Can't you say thank you?' he asks, a strange look on his face. His eyes, I can see his eyes very clearly, as though we are very close. His eyes are the very palest grey turning at points into green. They are like the tide his eyes, the way they change colour, and sometimes they are grey and warm and soupy and othertimes they are cold, so hard to get in.

'Can't you thank me?'

'What for?' I whine, but in a tone of voice which is stern also, with non-recognition. To my Quiz Kid brother, who wears glasses, and reads books.

'Why?' I say to him. 'Why do I have to say *thank you*? You *gave* it to me. I didn't *ask* for it.'

Which is true.

'I know,' he says. 'You didn't ask for it. But I did it for you. I did it for you,' he says then in a heated way. He has come closer to me. I think he wants to snatch it back. I can see his eyes, which are almost crying, but I know he wouldn't cry in front of me. Not any longer. No more.

I pull the paper away from him, so he can't snatch it back.

'So what,' I say insolently. 'So what. I didn't ask.'

He just looks at me.

'You heard from MumandDad?' he asks then.

'No,' I say. 'Course not.'

'Why of course not?' he says, suddenly interested. Now it's like he has forgotten about the drawing.

'Well, they don't want to think about us. Why should they?'

The logic of this is pretty unassailable.

'Why shouldn't they?' he says to me. 'After all they are our parents.'

I shrug. I don't know what to answer to that. 'Maybe they won't come back,' I say. 'Maybe they like it over there. I don't know,' I say, angry at having to think of all this. 'They better buy us some good presents,' I say warningly.

'Do you like staying with Ponky?' he says to me, sharp and close.

'It's OK,' I say carefully. 'How are the Balles? You like staying with them?'

'It's OK,' he says, as if it doesn't matter. 'It's only three weeks now,' he says to me.

'It is not,' I say, angry. 'It is three weeks and five days. *And*, I glance down at my watch. 'Four hours. *I know*. I'm counting. Not like you.'

He sighs then. He says, 'You will use the poster? It took me hours, *and* I had to buy the card myself.'

'I don't know,' I say coldly. 'I haven't decided yet.'

We look at each other. Matthew turns his bike around and starts walking away.

'Well you tell me if you don't,' he says to me. 'Because I can use the paper again.'

I wait until he has gone, then I unroll the card and look down at the paper very carefully, admiring his subtle colours, the way the yellow on the feathers fades into brown, with soft and curly little strokes of purple pencil. I look at these fine flicks of lacework, of inspiration in action. This is what I could never do.

I let out a long breath, knowing I have done something hopelessly wrong in, first, accepting the drawing from Matthew, then not thanking him. I should have just returned it. But, I think, as I turn about and start walking, *he shouldn't have given it to me.*

He shouldn't have spent five hours writing me a love letter which he then put in my hands and asked would I accept it. I didn't want it. I didn't ask for it. He did it. He gave it to me.

And faintly in my mind's ear I can hear CarrotnKeely saying, *'Wow, Jamie, you won the competition, you're really neat, can I sit beside you in art class? You want to walk home with me, Jamie? Can I come to your place?'*

Can I stay the weekend with you? Sleep in my bunk, Keely? Put your hand down there? Please, Keely. Yes please.

Listening to all this, not listening to the words inside my heart, I walk away with my brother's love letter in my hand, being careful not to smudge it.

Sleep

I DON'T KNOW who heard it first. Sometimes I think it was both of us, simultaneously. And the instant we heard it, we both knew it had happened.

He had arrived.

He had come.

And the look of shock on our features — this was what Ponky and I now exchanged as we lay there, turned to each other.

It was as if we had both glimpsed a dead man's face and recognised the face for the very first time: *it was our own*.

At the same time, and in the same simultaneous impulse of fear, our eyes moved towards the safety of Uncle Ambrose and Aunty Gilda's bedroom.

We both gauged the distance: could we make it?

He would have to get through the window.

Surely this would take a moment?

But in another sense, we knew it did not matter.

Horton had super-human strength. The mere occupation of space by something as insubstantial as wood, as glass, as plaster would fall away, explode into its essential nothingness so that he could, pincer-like, lean through and claim us.

Take us back.

THE BLINDS RATTLED again, impatiently.

We were running.

We were running and screaming, at the same time.

We were screaming and running and running and screaming.

It was so long, that run.

When we got into the hall, sound came out of our mouths. Up till that time the scream had been growing inside us, resounding in our throats, echoing to every part of the suddenly abandoned torture chambers of our bodies. Now it gouged up our throats, pulling our gullets apart painfully as the sheer volume of our terror blasted out.

Aunty Gilda sitting bolt upright.

'*Horton, it's Horton!*' we screamed. *He's come to collect us.*

Aunty Gilda awakened into her nightmare.

We were beside ourselves, hysterical, still running on the spot, even though there was no further for us to go.

'*Horton!*' we kept screaming, though I realised, with a shock, our voices were only whispers, *they were his whispers:* his voice was in our throats, his breath had taken possession of our bodies.

We turned to Aunty Gilda.

Aunty Gilda had aged in one second. She had become a hag so ancient she had sat on rocks watching fleets of ships going out to sea, and sinking, within her sight. She had witnessed troops marching off to war and returning in casket after casket. She had witnessed mushroom clouds, and with a painted toe traced a human silhouette on a blackened pavement.

So when she spoke, the voice which came out of her mouth was one other than her own, recognisable only in that I could hear inside it the song of her hysteria, as if the faint tintinnabulation of her laugh had reversed itself and turned into an almost haggard anxiety, joining disaster to catastrophe, bad luck to ill fortune.

Yet this voice compelled. And her eyes, I felt her eyes looking at me, beseeching even as she commanded me.

Her wiry grasp closed round my wrist, and pushed me slightly forward.

'Jamie,' she said. 'The baseball bat. Get it for me.'

The baseball bat? Back into that room?

I can't I can't I can't, I sang to myself, under my breath, gazing away across the prairie of carpet to the door.

Ponky, come with me, come and die with me, Ponky.

'I can't,' Aunty Gilda, I whispered out loud. 'I just can't.'

We all stared at each other, in the whiteout of our powerlessness.

'Well, kids,' she said then rising up, blooming in that second into a nemesis. 'We'll have to do it together. Come on.'

The bravery which lay behind her conviction was beyond anything I knew.

'On the count,' she whispered now, converting it into a game which Ponky and I could understand.

She was our general. In that second she had obliterated Davy Crockett.

'One, two,' she whispered, then on the count of three, she opened her lips wide and out of it came a cry so terrible Ponky and I simultaneously felt the hairs on our heads rise up. Our eyes came together and met as this tribal cry — of defence, of anger, of outrage — merged and then blew Horton out of our blood systems in one seismic wind so immensely powerful we found it forced open our own mouths and we too were screaming out loud in our fury at being awoken into such panic. It was blowing us across the carpet, we were being blown before this tribal wind and before we even knew it, or could resist it (we sensed resistance was hopeless), we had breached the bedroom and moved out into the open territory of the hall carpet.

As if magnetised, the baseball bat leapt into Aunty Gilda's grasp.

She swung it once, twice through the air.

Her cry was more magnificently chilling.

Then.

'Open the door, open the door,' she murmured softly, seductively, as if she — she who had seen *South Pacific* more times than anyone I knew, sitting in the very best seats — understood the nature of theatre was to deliver the greatest effect, yet to undercut it at the last moment by something spare, low-key and personal. So she, the general, ordered me, the private, almost in a whisper, to snatch back the door so: brave now, individually heroic, inspired by the sheer lunacy of her leadership, I yanked the door back and, flicking on the outside light so it flooded the grass outside with a cruel white shade which we knew would kill all the spirits of darkness in which Horton dwelt, we found ourselves running out onto the dark lawn, all three of us screaming at the tops of our voices, emitting our terror so that what was inside us bled out and fled out and joined the real world of appearances so that the horror of what was not real and only imagined would be forced, in this instant, to leap into the real — or cease to exist forever.

THERE WAS A boy there.

He was standing in terror. Raised up high on the pedals of his bike.

He had his hand up at the window.

He was wearing a school uniform.

It was Matthew.

'Horton!' we screamed as if the word itself made every horror manifest.

'Horton! Horton! Horton!'

'Is Horton about?' my brother asked naïvely, gazing about him, oblivious to this fundamental fact. Because everyone knew in Hungry Creek, when Horton got out, all you could do was retreat inside, and close the doors, lock the windows, lie low and wait.

'I didn't know that.'

Instantly, our horror converted itself into relief, tinged with hilarity. Because now Matthew became terrified.

'Where is h-h-h-h-he?' Maddy stammered, looking about him into the dark.

'What're you doing here anyway?' Aunty Gilda thought to ask, and I knew by the return of her voice to the known routes of sound we were safe.

'Yeah, Maddy, what you up to?' asked Ponky almost fiercely, resenting the fact she had had to show herself in slightly less than a heroic light.

'I I I . . .' my brother stuttered.

His head turned slightly on its side as, in his urgency, the words failed to come out. I looked at his mouth turning into a spout, formed and pursed.

His shoulders were hunched and his whole narrow frame seemed to be contorting as he tried to get out whatever it was he wanted to say.

In the end he could not speak.

His hand rose up, trembling.

I looked down.

It was a letter.

From Australia.
Soundlessly he offered it to me.

'O! MADDY, YOU dunce,' Aunty Gilda laughed, so returned to her old self that she ruffled Maddy's hair, and he beamed back at her, at that second, like this was the sweetest sound, or word, he, a Quiz Kid, a brainbox, had ever heard.

Aunty Gilda had her arm over Maddy's narrow back as we wandered back up the steps we had, so recently, spilt down in terror.

'I think we all need a strong cuppa, Mutt.' She used Ponky's nickname for me. I always assumed PK's nickname was somehow inaudible to her, an invisible calligraphy parsed between Ponky and me, a form of morse code. But now, I did not mind. We were comrades. I even felt the odd prickling of pride. 'Get out the sugar for us, will you, Mutt pet? And plenty of it.'

'You were trying to give us a scare, weren't you?' I asked Matthew all cross, letter tightly held in my hand. 'Weren't you!'

But somehow I didn't mean it.

WE BEGAN TO troop back inside. Laughing amongst ourselves to still be alive, have limbs, breath, eyes to glance at each other. We now noticed that we were outside in our pyjamas. This caused even more laughter. Ponky threw the baseball bat up into the sky, turned round once, and caught it.

But as we came up the stairs into the light, Ponk, Aunty Gilda and I suddenly realised that we had to confront an undeniable fact, something we had blotted out at the time.

We had seen Uncle Ambrose bolt out of bed.

As if at that moment we heard, afresh, the turn of handle as he shut himself in.

He had hidden inside Aunty Gilda's wardrobe.

He had abandoned us.

Just at this moment, Uncle Ambrose chose to make his entrance.

Our laughter cut off.

Ponky, Aunty Gilda and I did not dare glance at each other.

Robed in an ornate blue silk dressing gown, cord laced round his pudgy midriff, he stood there, glowering at each one of us in turn.

'Who was it?' he demanded.

We all, as if in one movement, looked downward.

Even Aunty Gilda judged it better to remain silent.

'Time you was all in bed,' he said to us tartly.

Maddy stood up uncertainly, pushing his chair back and sheepishly making ready to go.

'I'm v-v-very sorry,' Uncle Ambrose, he stammered. 'I was only delivering a letter. Express delivery,' he said. 'I knew Mutt was waiting for it.'

In the strange circumstances, he too had taken to using my nickname.

I glanced at him warningly, then swiftly lowered my eyes. There was something more important — if somehow indefinable — at issue here.

'Why don't the lot of you go back to bed,' he chivvied us. 'And you, Matthew, don't you ever let me catch you coming up here so late at night again. I don't care what you got to deliver. Understood? Boy? Understood?'

With a stooped head Maddy nodded, taking his glasses off, polishing them then placing them back on. This had the effect of him taking a good and scrutinising look at Uncle Ambrose in his state of fallen majesty. For he had looked dethroned, no longer in his suit and smart hat, emerald winking on his little finger, but in the strange, even feminising garb of a silk dressing gown.

Aunty Gilda even tittered.

In a flash, I saw Uncle Ambrose on his annual trip down to the tide. Though Uncle Ambrose and Aunty Gilda lived only one hundred yards from the beach, they never swam, no matter how hot the weather. The only exception was a king tide. Under a full moon, Uncle Ambrose ambled down the road, in this same silk dressing gown. This was strange enough, though it seemed to have its own logic — darkness, night, a dressing gown, the queer lunar intensity of the moon. But it was when he undressed and revealed his body, white as a pupa, I grasped something else. Because, on these nights, Ponk swam as far away as possible from Uncle Ambrose. She abandoned him. And he was left there, standing on his own, glaring at anyone nearby, as if their one aim in life was to splash him.

The terrible truth was Uncle Ambrose could not swim.

There was nothing or no one more pitiable on earth to Ponky and me than someone who did not feel at home in the water.

And it was him.

I seemed to hear the splash of water across the warm surface of a moonlit sea as Ponk put stroke after concentrated stroke between her and her father.

I glanced at Ponk now. Her face was blank.

'Hear me, boy, or were you born deaf?'

'Yes, Uncle Ambrose. I mean no, Uncle Ambrose.' Maddy let out a small, almost clerical cough. 'That is, Uncle Ambrose, I wasn't born deaf . . .'

'Get out!'

Maddy disappeared into the night.

BOOK TWO

LIES AND THEIR NECESSITY

Dad

EACH WEDNESDAY, WHILE my parents are away, to keep the beads laced on the necklace, I go to running. This is to make me into my parents who carry within them as they age and forget, and frowns bury the young looks on their faces, twin memories, slim and silvery. One is of the young man fleeting along, his leg raised up as he bursts through the tape. The other of a young maiden, her body following through the master-stroke of her golf-club so that, as her hips cantilever round, she seems to be caught in a perpetual slow-revolve: revolving towards the camera flash as she goes up to the front to collect the cup which is and always has been forever engraved with her name, simply awaiting her hour, and her arrival.

This is what my running is. I must run, again and again, over the same length so that I may arrive at the correct hour, and there will be presented to me a small silver cup — the first of many — on which will be engraved my name. This will be the true beginning of who I am. It is only at this moment James Caughey, as my parents meant him to be, will exist.

I know all this from the silver treasury which lies on the very top shelf of the kitchen dresser, behind glass: the cup after cup after cup engraved with my mother's name, my father's name; small bowls, large chalices, tiny eggcups, each one as if to bespeak of a vast long table lined with people who that moment, in a sudden gush of hush, have risen to their feet, glasses charged and the solemn words are for us spoken.

IN MY MIND, within a little sealed bubble, an image exists of these cups always on the top shelf. I see my mother and myself taking them down every so often, smearing the dense pink paste of polish over them carefully, covering all the yellowed and tarnished mirror surfaces with the dimness. Each concave surface, every minute inset and recess must be covered. The tiny black podiums, some already blistering with age, must be treated with care. We do not want to reveal they are made of wood. We wish to keep the stark contrast between the whiteness of silver and the blackness of ebony. My fingers, behind the polishing cloth, feel out and follow the braille of their names. This is what made them, my parents, who they are. Mentally and forever they are bursting through tapes and delivering the master-stroke . . . except now, it is over. Now. It is over.

It is not forgotten. No. It is now buried deep within me, waiting for its ordained moment to surface.

Hence my duty to be always here, at the starting line, crouched over and waiting, tense, my legs shaking a little, waiting for the gun.

Waiting for the gun.

It is dark now, it is the beginning days of winter, and we the sons and daughters drawn out of the warm houses all over the district must show we can toughen up, and bear the cold, and watch the fiery dragons that fume from out of our mouths without so much as a cry, or murmur. This is, I know, the military camp for it. This is, I know, an internship in being turned into a man. We are all here, boys and girls, in a forced apprenticeship, one which will change us from being who we are, with still soft, unformed features, as if another creature is buried in our flesh, into people with faces in which are embedded the importance of breaking through the tape, of noting who comes second, of disregarding, in the silent swoon of victory, the rest, yet remembering always to have a kind word, a memorising glance for those who cannot win.

But we must learn swiftly, we must learn hard. We must crash into gravity and when it wallops us in the face, we must raise our faces up and, our mouths full of dirt, (bleakly) smile. In this is our true learning, in this lies our victory.

I am forever running my parents' race.

I am to win my father's race.

I am to win for my mother.

I am to be my father as he wins the race.

This time he shall win, and I will be merely a fleshy figment moving its shadowy shape over the sharp blades of grass.

My feet will fleet over upturned blades.

My toes will pass, without really touching, the swords of green which poke up to spike me if I so much as falter.

When I run, I see nothing or no one.

I simply release what is in me of my father and it runs, wild and powerful, towards the tape.

If there was no tape I would simply keep on running until perhaps I had moved out of the known world, and into some foreign place I no longer knew — or it no longer knew me.

ON THE LATE summer nights, when winter has not yet made its hasty invasion over the hills, leading its army into our midst with a roar and an apparition of overwhelming strength, sending us scurrying back into our houses, closing the doors, pulling shut the windows, sitting within as the wind blasts overhead, shaking the wood on the walls — on late summer nights a soft crease of peace opens itself like a hibiscus flower. We are like ants guzzling round the stamen, burying ourselves in the soft silken darkness. The tides lap in and fill up all space with their ululating lips, creating a lyrical song which sweeps us all into softness and laziness. On these nights I find Keely amongst the boys. He is a stranger to our district, he knows nobody here, and nobody knows him. He is dependent on me, and I am his king.

We come together and wrestle. We cannot stop ourselves. Magnetically, we must clash and try to find in our flesh some token, some image we cannot yet define, so we leap on each other's bodies and hungrily invade every space, every nook, every cranny.

O, I am astride him and laughing down into his face, I hold his arms wide apart, pinning them down by my knees. He tries to raise himself up, and in doing so his face swerves like a firerocket past my shoulder. Cinders, sparks, illuminations blaze right through my eyes, into the soft moist dome of my skull. His flesh, his smell, the roar of his heart, of the blood coursing through him — how can it be contained in another covering of flesh? Why can't we just create a small slit, like you do with a penknife, to swear eternal brotherhood? Why can't the blood of my entire life flood into him and his into mine? What a joyful release this would be, what a divine levity would overcome me. Some eternal lightness would lift me up, freeing me from the deadweight of being forever and always who I am. Can I not be freed?

He flips me over so the lights and the faces and his body swish past me in one violent slide, and now his legs are wrapped round mine and his hips lock onto mine and he grinds himself into me again and again and he tries to force himself, all his blood and his life into me. His face hangs over mine and together our mouths open wide, as wide as a crescent moon lighting up the whole sky, and into our mouths, from his mouth to my mouth, from his eyes to my eyes, flows every river and tide in the world and briefly the oceans move all over the planet and we have been flung far out from the gravity of the earth and for the sheer infinity of a second we exist, light, weightless, as we truly are, or might be.

IT IS AT this second the loudspeaker sparks into life.

This is so abrupt, heralded by some sharp splinters of sound, then a sudden shrieking scream so intense everyone stops what they are doing and throws their hands on their ears; and in this space, introduced into the gap of silence, in-between silences, I hear a name and realise that I must struggle back into the body and clothes and face and walk of that person.

For I am, I am Jamie Caughey.

Instantly, a form of dread, a drop of poison suspends itself over my head. It hangs there, a sword about to pierce my skull.

I unlace myself from inside and around and through Keely, who rolls off and lies there on his back, panting. He stares up at the stars, as if his face is the earth and the light from the stars must irradiate his nothingness. I feel his body tremble as his breath flames backwards down into an even rhythm. I am already standing up, giddy.

Without saying a word to each other, Keely and I have separated forever. He can no more protect me than he can accompany me as I follow my shadow as I move towards the lights. Around me everything is broken into the sharpest fragments, tears and rips, of a brilliant funereal whiteness. High above our heads, on long stalks, are the sports lights which award to each of us a deepened shadow so every human is made into a mask.

I wish now I was standing behind the security of a line. Why am I not at the beginning of a race? I prefer that white nothingness, that state of suspension when I hang there, waiting for my inside to explode.

Instead I thread my way towards the officials who stand near the bottom of one of the lights. Mr Carroll is the head official, I know his thinly whipped intensity, his rabid bad temper as he is surrounded by the brewling brouhaha of two hundred children. He is an old athlete. He wears his long skinny legs naked, unashamed of the thin daddy-long-legs which waver into nothing. He has a red cauliflower face, with lightning thrusts of purple, of congealed blood stopped in his veins. I know, under his towelling hat, his head is so bald it is painful to see. A chrome whistle dangles where his heart should be and restlessly, restlessly he paces the grass, flattening it down as he turns, revolves, spins on the ball of his feet like an animal caged and tied to the stake of the winter light. His whistle he blows, anxiously, forever.

'Boys of the fourth grade line up!'

'Girls of the fifth grade, prepare yourself for the one hundred yards!'

By his side, married to him, is Mr Barnett who is loose like a bag, the string of which has snapped. He has slack flails of black hair covering the naked soft spot on the back of his head, and these hairs, escaped, sprout out the top of his shirt. He sweats and looks as though he wishes he could apologise for the hair which keeps on growing: out his ears, up his neck, behind his shoulders, along his arms.

A gun goes off, splattering the air and I hear, behind me, the desperate thump of feet scampering across the crust of earth: burst of air within lungs as air is held in; the grunt of the loser as he lorries up the back-straight; the laughter of those on the sideline, identifying as always, carelessly and without any thought, with the winner.

Who naturally must never speak.

Mr Carroll cannot wait. He has raised the microphone to his mouth. I see he is a general now, staring into the dark-veined heavens of war. His eyes strobe the battlefield as the microphone comes closer to his mouth. His dreadful utterance is poised on the end of his dancing tongue, to be delivered into the dark like a hurtling cannonball which will drag all sound with it, whistling towards me so voluminously I must duck as it roars overhead. I feel myself: am I covered in cinders? Is that smell my eyelashes burnt down to my eyes?

As if separated from his mouth, which I see moving, the entire sky becomes lit up with his disembodied voice.

'Jamie Caughey! Report to the official's table. Your father is here for you.'

Your father.

My father. Who never comes to see me here. Here? Is he back from Australia? What special meaning is this? My eyes run ahead of my body, terriers scampering through the ankles of the crowd, side-dancing and lurching towards the podium.

Dad? Here? Now?

As if suddenly the straits between Australia and New Zealand have been turned into a billiard blanket which now is being furled up and rolled away before my eyes, I imagine my parents silently and swiftly coasting towards me, loaded down with wonderful things from Australia — electric frypans and pop-up toasters and transistor radios and new clothes with labels from exciting foreign places, cocktail coasters snitched from the plane — I see it all, I sense their imminence. Yet where I visualise my father, as if I can see cut into this scene all around me an exact shape into which he might fit (slightly stooping yet with broad shoulders, the thin athlete's legs which had carried him peerlessly to victory after victory, the arrow-shape of his head, his long limber elegant fingertips, his bony toes clinging to the composted pressed-down soil of Hungry Creek) as if his body is the keyhole and my sight is the key I search for him so quickly and completely it is as if the entire globe has revolved round once, entirely, in one second, in a violent whirl on its axis bringing me back to this point when I realise: my father is not here.

Uncle Ambrose is waiting for me.

'JAMIEBOY!'

I walk towards him, past Mr Carroll who does not even notice what is occurring, his general's eyes strobing through the battlelit darkness.

This is my father?

This is some mistake.

But as I near him I know and fear what will happen. He comes to me, and crying out loud, *'Jamieboy, you be my baby boy!'* he clutches down on me and kisses me and I am standing there thinking this is a mistake. I am not who I am. Nor is he. But in that second of hesitation, of prevarication, of uncertainty about what to do, I have left it too late. I have accepted his kisses. I have accepted the fact he is who he is not. He is my father now.

And so he must kiss me.

Shame

'YOU HAD BETTER invite everyone,' says Aunty Gilda. 'It's better than leaving anyone out.'

Fair Aunty Gilda, fair and square Aunty Gilda, our hero.

She is looking down, slightly doubtfully, wearying away, as if in her imagination the pivot of her high-heel, the tiny eye of the steel-cap, is boring into the ground, the rough scoria which coats the clay drive which passes up the side of their house. Their flat, they do not own their home. It is only rented. My mother says this.

Aunty Gilda has already said, 'Well, Ponky love, you can't have more than thirty'.

At her twelfth birthday.

This is impressive. But I understand that is what is owed, almost as fealty, to going to a private girls' school. Just as I know Ponky can no longer attend the local tennis club, or go to the local church. Everything that Ponky does from now on is going to be focused beyond Hungry Creek. I understand this, but feel a little of the wry perception of one left behind.

Thirty guests to a birthday party!

But.

'I don't think we can fit in Tony and Myrtle,' Aunty Gilda is saying in that special voice which even I know presages an important announcement. (This voice has a raw nerve running through it, naked, like electricity running along, unsurrounded by flex.)

'But Matthew and Jamie will be?' Ponky says with a small quiver of fear in her voice. Yet sullen too, slightly.

'Oh yes, of course,' says Aunty Gilda quickly. 'That goes without saying.'

They are sitting out in the kitchen at the table. I am lying on my bed, putting paper clothes onto Ponky's cut-out dolls, the ones she has never touched. The contempt of her fingers isolates them. I dress them in going-away clothes, afternoon-tea clothes, a visit to the ball. And now my fingers hesitate . . . before party clothes.

There is a small eddy of silence.

I try not to listen.

The voices take up again.

'We can only have thirty guests at the very most,' says Aunty Gilda then, her face lowered as she ticks off a list.

'Are we sending out invitations? Carole Jennings did for her party.'

'We need a present for everyone who attends. The golf club is hired. And the picture theatre.'

This is so grand it is spell-binding. Booking a golf club. Hiring the entire picture theatre. I have never heard of such grandeur. In one bold move, Uncle Ambrose and Aunty Gilda aim to supplement their initial advance (sending Ponk to Richmond View) with taking over the main entertainment places of Hungry Creek. This single stroke of quasi-ownership shows such ambition that I understand instantly how far-reaching Uncle Ambrose's and Aunty Gilda's (and Ponky's also) sight has become.

'We'll show . . .' and here Aunty Gilda's voice loosens its tenseness, that of the careful strategist, returning to the soft lagoons which we all know and love and bathe in '. . . We'll run *Around the World in 80 Days.*'

Ponky breathes out, 'Neat-o!'

I hear her throw something slight (a paper clip?) into the bin.

'Gottcha!' she murmurs lazily.

'And then everyone can come back here. To play,' Aunty Gilda says, completing the outline of her small Napoleonic campaign. I hear her stand up and the insistent beat of her high heels across the lino floor. She is busy, running out the back door, jingling her car keys as she runs.

'Pet, get some steak out of the fridge for dinner.'

I slip off the patio dress and put on the tea-dance frock. Smiling confidently, the paper doll looks back at me.

Ready and prepared.

'WHY CAN'T TONY and Myrtle be asked?' I say casually. Not revealing I am a spy.

Ponky doesn't answer at first. Then she pulls a face like she would like to shrug the whole thing off. We are walking down the rocks. Ponk had come into the room and whistled to me.
I dropped everything and followed.

We are no longer frightened of going out.

Horton was captured over by the swamp. In the toitoi over by the dump. Nobody gets away here. Everyone knows that. We are an island and nobody, no, nobody ever escapes. This blackness is in our blood flood. It is the moistness inside our bone. This is our marrow. Nobody escapes. This is the ghost laugh, the rictus inside the skull. Nobody ever escapes an island.

So, for the time being anyway, we pretend we are free.

Horton is captured.

And nothing ever happens.

Again and again with the dull reverberation of a weight pressing down metal.

This is why PK's birthday is such a major event.

'*Why?*' I ask, screwing up my eyes so the tide looks Chinese.

PK's face grows grave as she looks at me and I wonder what she is about to say. Disclose.

Then I am surprised.

'*Sophie Bensky has said she will come.*'

She says this in a special tender tone. One she hardly ever uses. Almost a reverential whisper. She glances towards me quickly, perhaps to cover up what she has just revealed. A fresh pink flush, just as if she has been slapped, falls over her cheeks. PK seems to plead with me not to laugh. But I am silent.

Bensky.

I know the name just as everybody does in our town. I have seen it written, three storeys high, in letters on the side of a building. Neon burns it into our eyes. Trucks carry it down every street. Radios pour its name, over and over again, into the open funnel of our ears. Inside every kitchen it makes itself at home, sitting on the side of packets, tins, bags.

I leave a space of silence as a form of a prayer mat.

Then I whistle. Low.

I look out at the sea.

It is heading towards low tide. The wind has disturbed the tidal drift so the sea is Karitane brown in a wide ring, out from the shore.

There is a small figure in the distance, bent over, legs akimbo.

Tony and Myrtle's mother.

Mrs Lamb. Digging for shellfish in the mud.

She is the only woman in the whole of Hungry Creek who would do this.

'. . . So?' I leave the hook of my question mark hanging in the air.

Sensing the huge differences in our world, between this place here, and the Eastern suburbs, where ladies lie down on sand made of mink, listening to transistors and laughing while speed boats draw silver threads back and forth across the horizon.

I see in my eye a beach ball bounce.

Then I wake up.

There is a faint dank tang in the air of mangroves, or is it pooh?

'You and Maddy wear shoes and socks,' Ponky says heatedly, as if Tony and Myrtle's mother can hear what she is saying, its treason. She leaves a long stretch of silence. We both look down at our feet. We are wearing jandals worn in so they have become soft and comfortable. On the pad of each jandal lies the imprint of the soles of our feet.

I see Tony's bare feet splayed out on the footpath, the undersides of his feet are going to hoover up any chuddy. His toes spread wide from grabbing at the surface of the world as its spins round and round on its axis.

Tony and Myrtle never wear shoes. Not real shoes, bought to fit their feet.

So.

And.

But.

Tony and Myrtle's mother stands up to ease her back. She is a big woman. Her thin dress ripples in the wind. It is wet all round the hem. She seems to sense us there, so far away from her. Tiny as a full stop.

The Regina Hotel has never looked as closed and blank.

Ponky has her penknife out. She is cutting her name into the clay, laying claim to the place.

'I don't believe there is an L,' she murmurs then quietly.

'Doan you?' I draw all the letters out in a low groan of surprise. Because this means Ponk is giving up thinking we will win the Coca-Cola Contest and, best of all, the Prize.

'All I ever get are Cs,' she says in a black voice.

'It was rigged all along,' I say. 'I knew it.'

She doesn't answer me and her thin blade gouges out a rough, wild Y, its tail slicing off in a trail of dust.

It looks desperate, somehow.

She flicks the blade back and looks at me closely.

'You would of taken me to Honolulu if you'd won, though, eh, Ponk?' I ask.

It is important. More important than if she had won. 'I doan need to meet him,' I said. 'The King.'

Ponk had told me she was sure she would run into Elvis on the sands of Waikiki. We had rehearsed what she would say to him.

'I doan know,' she says, looking into my face. 'I guess so.' Then in a different voice, cooler, harder. 'I hadn't decided.' She looks straight at me.

Then she says softer, a little hesitant, like she is about to say something to me, ask me something, maybe even confess, *'Jamie?'*

'I don't mind dressing up,' I say shyly, in a low voice. I like dressing up. We often play dressups in the hut. Maddy and me.

She says nothing for a moment, as if she is baffled.

Tony's mother is just standing there, on the beach, a lone figure, the wind rippling her wet dress.

Both of us feel ashamed for some reason. Fall silent. Hope we fade into the rocks, turn into camouflage, mangroves growing out of our ears. The sky rearing so high over our heads is one big ear listening to us.

'You got to promise to wear shoes and socks, Jamie,' Ponk says, as if she doesn't like what she is saying but must. She knows, just as

Aunty Gilda knows, what must be said. But it seems, at the same time, this is not what she was going to say.

She snaps her penknife shut.

She walks off.

'Hey, Ponky!' I call when she is a certain distance away. 'That's not a problem. *I promise.*'

As I come in the door Aunty Gilda calls me to her.

She is cutting the potatoes for dinner and I watch the slim knife scrape the skins. Revealing their whiteness, moist.

She drops them into water.

She does not look at me when she speaks.

'Jamie, if anyone asks you about the red car . . .'

She is silent as the knife digs into and flicks out an eye.

The dark rot falls onto paper.

She rinses the potato under the tap, then goes on speaking as if she has just remembered I am there.

'We've decided not to use it for a while.'

Her words form carefully, moulded by pre-thought.

Her eye falls upon me. I realise the seriousness of what she is saying — not so much what she is saying, but that whatever she says — and its meaning mystifies me — is important. I read that in her eye, which has no laughter.

'It's going to be parked in the back garage for a while,' she says. 'But don't tell anyone. If anyone asks . . .' she says, leaving a trail of questions multiplying in the space of her silence.

I want to ask why so I can make sense of this, but I know, just in the seriousness with which Aunty Gilda returns to her potato, knife skurfing and slashing, that the sense must not be questioned. She is in some hidden part angry and perhaps even miserable. Her lips, her scarlet lips are a little worn by being rubbed together and they are clamped shut and slightly down-turning on the corners.

No birds of freedom fly from them today.

'OK,' I barely murmur.

I shrug-shrug my allegiance.

It does not matter.

'I'll wear my shoes and socks for the party,' I say softly, running the sheer fabric through the goldring of my love for Aunty Gilda, my admiration. Because she often seems to me like a cut-out doll, always so carefully dressed, so perfectly turned out. Not a thing out of place.

She turns to me, Aunty Gilda, looking surprised at finding me there, and she breaks a bleak smile.

I seem to hear a gull cry, piercing.

THE NEXT DAY I stumble by the garage up the drive. The doors are shut. More than this, they are locked.

This has never happened before. It is so novel I go over to the padlock and pull on it.

The great wooden doors groan outwards, shriek, then, jointed together by the steel heart, they refuse to come asunder.

A warm gust of moistness fluffs out and down my throat.

I cough, caught on all the smells of old plaster dust, oil soaked on concrete, hot tin, and the sweet epiphany of kikuyu grass bleeding white in the shade, but still moistly growing.

I split my eye through the crack.

In the warm dark I can just see a slit, a slash of scarlet. But in the shadows it is hard to see.

Yet it is in there.

Even under a blanket.

I give the door one vicious pull, which sends a peel of thunder inward.

Above me birds rise up, spiralling, screaming, squawking.

As I turn I see the oily blackness of a myna bird, its yellow beak poised in thought.

A Hard Word

NEXT WEDNESDAY IS my appointment. What began as a simple interruption now takes on the form of a ritual, one I must await with dread, refusing each time to believe that it will happen. Praying that it won't. Or, if it does, some magical tongue shall fall from my mouth, and deliver me into the arms of truth.

Wednesday comes as my appointment and I await the inevitability of the hour when the loudspeaker first crackles into life, sending searing sparks scalding through the dark, then the black flower opens its heart, its dread stamens call for me: Jamie Caughey, *your father your father your father is waiting for you.*

Dad.

Like a tide it carries me, but a black tide, a chill tide, the creek has overflowed. The sportsfield is under water as I lie, carried in an eddy past the faces and the flesh and the legs (I am carried just slightly underwater so I can hear all the sounds, of chatter and voices and *you said* and *he did* and *I won* and *she ran* as I drift towards him, my waiting father).

I see him from a long way away. He cannot see me, standing there, wavering on his feet, caught in some inward storm of the emotions. He stands in a circle of light, naked, I see, even though he is dressed as always as the salesman. He is better dressed than any man here, his clothes are his armour, speaking of success. But to me he is naked, as he stands there peering out into the dark, waiting for me.

'*Jamie Caughey, your father is waiting.*'

So I am carried in that tidal drift towards him. Yet now his appearance brings with it a complication of troubles. For subtly and stealthily about me I have begun to notice things: looks of consternation, faces frozen in the middle of a question which does not yet possess the words. The words. *I know these words. I know.*

I know, simple as they are, they can possess a power so terrible that lives turn shipwreck and bodies carry dead flesh and hope is so lacerated it can continue on living only by bleeding, and mending in the dark. I know these words. They have after all attached themselves to my flesh. Cissy is my name. Sooky is my heartbleat. Stab me with these words. *I know. I know.*

I know the explosive potential in a word.

As I am carried into the circle of light I see Uncle Ambrose turn into a fountain overflowing with wordwordword, he gushes, he flows, he flutters the word paint all over my face, trying to pour it plashing down my throat so the wordword will fountain back into his. His need, he is needing and alone, I sense this, and pity him.

I feel the dry tear of sweat at the back of his heart and how this lone trickle falls down, undevelops. He is alone, in all the world, in his circle of light, and I am to come to him. Not understanding. Not knowing. Knowing only this. He is alone. And he has mistaken me. (Just as he, Uncle Ambrose the best salesman in Hungry Creek, the man who buys me the first ticket to the moon, is simply this man here now, with a strange smell flowing from his damp chill fingertips, just as a rim of gas-blue fear runs over him, so melted and mown down by this other flame, he wants to burn me, melt me into him, so our skin is joined.)

But he does not understand.

He is not my father.

Yet as I walk and think of this, Ponky's face forms before me, Aunty Gilda scurrying along on her high-heel stroke, turning, over her shoulder calling out to me, *Jamie, sweetheart, you're my darling pet, hurry up, we're waiting for you,* and Ponk's big fat slab of a face comes and leans against me, soft and warm as our old mog, and she murmurs, *hey, Mutt, let's go bottlefishing, eh?* And then she turns back and pads off, turning over her shoulder, '*Act caj,*' she murmurs out of the corner of her mouth, rolling along off down the rocks on the thick soft cushions of her feet.

Act caj.

Them I cannot betray.

This is my heartbleat.

It is I who must save them.

This moment of decision comes to me and lasts as long as I

walk towards Uncle Ambrose. And now, having arrived there, having reached the very edge of the circle of light, in which, burning slowly, he stands (a guy stuffed full of objects, toasters and cigarettes and Coca-Cola bottles and sweets and tickets to the pictures), around us, stealthily, the eyes have rearranged themselves to form a tightening circle, and now, though the sound of danger is shrill I realise he, my uncle, can hear nothing.

He throws his arms wide apart for me, then makes a rush towards me, a kingfisher stab for the centre of my flower.

BOOK THREE

STRAIGHT IS THE GATE

Girls

ON HER BIRTHDAY, Ponky is dressed as a girl.

I cannot stop looking at her.

She does not know how to walk. Or sit.

An odd, defensive look has fallen over her face, a brute mutiny, a mask of steel which reveals only a slight flush, a fallen scarlet which taints her chalk cheeks.

Her eyes avoid mine, or when they concuss, she dares me to smile, to speak, to say the treacherous words: — *How nice you look.*

She despises me for even hearing the silent whisper of her thoughts, those tiptoeing mice. Like a big sullen tomcat she swipes them away with a clawed paw. She snarls inside her foil of stiff lace and muslin, the pink ribbon woven so carefully through the broderie anglaise, her usually bare feet (splayed flat and comfortable on the hot asphalt, feeling through the soft tar to the heartbeat of the universe, the throb of all growing things, the lull of the tide, the shift of the wind, the sound the piperfish make in the sea as they sliver through the springtide), now those feet are encased in brilliantly shiny black shoes, which do up, like a lock, in a bright nodular button. They are doll's shoes for humans, just as she is encased in, dressed in, entrapped by a doll's frock for a mutiny.

Small white socks, ruffled down and threaded, again, with the ghastly insult of pink. Candypink, coconut-ice pink, the pinkiest of pinksin echo of the hideousness of what her nose defines as the stinkiness of stink.

AUNTY GILDA IS stern in her admonitions. Her dressing of Ponk has had all the high seriousness of a religious ceremony. We have arrived, at last, at the unavoidable importance of an occasion: and Ponky walks through her bedroom door, behind which I heard many arguments, ultimatums, sudden rebellions quelled by yelled appeals, of remarks about how much everything was costing; *how it is all for you; how it is only one day; how she is being asked to do it only for her mum and dad; how it isn't much to ask; how it is a lovely dress anyhow; how Aunty Gilda herself had always dreamed, always, of having a dress like this when she was that age but . . .*

My ears had heard the long litany, like the drone in a religious service which leads up, through its own stasis of boredom, of a held pattern, to that moment of revelation when the door falls back and out of it comes: Ponky, eyes down to the ground, as if in the pattern of the carpet she is tracking a key that might unlock a meaning which will help her pass through these minutes of hell.

I KNOW I should say nothing. If only I could become an ornament sitting up on the pelmet. Or the white telephone before the mirror which returns to Ponky a many-reflected image of herself, as if, because this is her day of all days, she has to divide up into many beings, rehearse what is about to happen later: how she will appear at the head of a long table, a small crucified smile on her lips, as we all sing happy birthday to her in one humiliating drone; how she will open all the presents, awarding a word of congratulation expressed through a gust of surprise to each bearer of gift; how she must keep an eye on all the guests making sure nobody is left out and that everyone is having a good time; how the party is less a celebration than a serious social test which she must, on all accounts, pass, for this is just the reason she is attending a private school, to be successful in a wider social world than her parents know.

In this sense she must turn into an explorer, but not of that world we know so well: Hungry Creek. No, now she must study blindly and mutely other things, learn the minutiae of gloves and petticoats and high-heels and how the red lipstick slides, unguent, out of the gold tube. How in all these things she has to break apart from being the one Ponky whom I have known up until this point, the Ponky of fishing and the flicks, and become another Ponky altogether: one who holds within herself any number of contradictions and suppresses whatever has been natural and easy to her (and to me) and become someone more suitable to the person who is wearing those clothes — that dress, those shoes, the tenor of pink, the consuming aura of white — assume the proper modesty which befits stiff petticoats and the almost-communion-white bodice (ones ironically I myself might like to wear, for at least a little, experimental while).

Yet I can see, even as she uneasily walks along (like someone fresh out of a painful operation), the heels of the shoes throw her off her natural lounging balance. She can no longer lope along, unseen, with a rifle leaning on her shoulder, or chew an invisible roll of gum, like a wad of tobacco, in her mouth.

'Mum!' she cries on an intake of a breath.

But Aunty Gilda, like a top on a crazed journey, spins by her, touching her privately on the bare arm, her painted glittering nails resting fleetingly against her daughter's flesh.

'Now, Priscilla,' she says to Ponky, as if by the formal use of her name she is reminding Ponky of her new invention.

Don't fence me in.

Ponky sees in that instant just as she hears, in her name, that the area of movement is restricted, made tiny, in effect is ending. Just as she is caught in that dress, so she is captured behind that name. Just as now, for the rest of the day in front of her (and for what lies beyond that, neither of us can foresee, or bear to look ahead) she has to continue to be this new creature, a girl from a private school, a young woman in apprenticeship to her first formal birthday.

PONKY CAN'T EVEN trust herself to sit down. I look away. I know if she sees me looking at her, this will be so offensive to Ponky as to mark the final perimeter of our friendship. I realise I will have to spend the rest of this novel day alone. I can no longer appeal to Ponky for hints, clues, ideas on how to behave, how to get out of difficult situations. We are both, and profoundly, on our own, more separated than we have ever been at any other moment in our life, or, as it was now becoming: lives.

AND, IN FACT, girls are already coming through the door in a cluster of white and cream and pink, like fallen blossoms, their faces even wearing little touches of rouge, eyebrows discreetly plucked and pencilled in. There is the shrill intensity of their chatter, the sounds, like crystal breaking, of their shrieks on seeing each other, as if they are discovering each one for the very first time (at the same time rehearsing their future lives as society women, with all the inventive falseness, the assumed intimacy which cloaks actual enmity). Indeed, some of the little modoms, as my mother would call them, can be seen looking about Aunty Gilda and Uncle Ambrose's flat with cruelly assessing eyes, eyes which meet with each other in silent mockery, only at the last moment to find that in the centre of the flower, as if within the heart of a ruffled and many-petalled camellia, is an arrestingly dark-skinned girl dressed in a uniquely soft shade of pink, through which is threaded slim ribbons of silver.

This girl is clearly of some importance, so different are her looks (to me she looks part-Maori, with that luxuriant lush darkness of textures, soft hairiness on the head and eyebrows, the density of black in her large eyes and the surprising, yet natural, redness of her lips). This unusual girl has lurched to a halt on the checked lino and, looking about her in surprise, holds everyone — her court of admirers — about her in mute silence as they await the delivery of her verdict. In that second everything is held in balance. (Ponky's future in the school, her social acceptability, whether she will be invited to other girls' houses), but the little princess in pink flushes an acute swarthiness of colour (almost as if her hidden essence has increased and multiplied) and cries out, laughing, doves flying out of her mouth in a whole flock, this way and that, darting, flapping and cawing, sending into the air whole perfumes of feathers and leaves and blossom-petals:

'Why, it's so pretty, it's just like a doll's house!'
'O, Sophie! Trust Sophie!'

The other girls fasten on her pronouncement with such fervour it is as if she has a unique way of looking at the world, in which, in fact, is condensed the essence of being a Bensky.

The crisis is over.

The party will be a success.

LIKE A FLOCK of gulls now they move towards Ponky, who stands bracing herself to face them much as a general might await the arrival of an army who might yet prove to be the enemy as much as they might be neutrals arriving with the news of a truce. And, as if in silent mimicry of this, these girls begin to hand over to Ponky wrapped boxes, parcels tied with vivid green and blue and pink ribbons, and small intricate shapes in circles, enigmatic packages and undisclosed treasures.

This act of obeisance goes on through all its arcane rituals of greeting, kissing, handing over, opening . . . until finally Aunty Gilda, laughing as she spins all around her daughter, directs the little flock towards the glorybox of Ponky's bedroom.

Yet, seeing me standing there stiffly in my long socks, shoes I normally wear to church, a boy amid all the girls, she calls out to me, to introduce me, to include me, *'Come along, sweetheart, give your Aunty Gilda a hand tidying up all this paper,'* and small birds, as if in duplication, run out of her mouth. And the air all around me becomes lost in a vast flock of birds, thick with them, as if an entire race is shifting from continent to continent, and I am now caught in their mass migration.

AS ONE SHRILL beast we have moved from the golf club, on the eery privilege of a bus set aside purely for us, to the grand institution of the picture theatre. Hysterical with the amount of sugar surging through our nervous systems, we have stamped our feet and hurtled up and down the sticky carpeted stairs of the theatre, claiming every inch of space.

Inside us now nestle continents of jellies, seas of fizzy drink (passionfruit, raspberry, lime, lemonade), islands of brandy snaps, floating icebergs of meringues, lamingtons, plains of white bread and sweating butter sprinkled all over, like the stars of some highly coloured cosmos, with hundreds and thousands.

The sugar surges through our systems, changing us into one all-slithering hysterical monster.

But even in the dark of the picture theatre I cannot help looking at Ponky (at the rigor mortis of her smile which I alone diagnose as not being genuine), at the same time entering into a further and deeper confusion as to why Ponky is putting herself at such pains to maintain this strange unreal smile, one which indicates she no longer recognises me or knows me as myself (which is all the more disturbing as there are so few boys present). My brother had come late as had Ponky's cousin Ben, and we had become the objects of brief intense inspections, as if the curved beaks of wonderfully terrifying tuis had come towards us unerringly and bent down and, savagely, luxuriantly, thrust their prows into the soft open heart of our flowers. This they ravaged intently, sucking into their interior all our pollen, before, distracted by the sight of another flower centre nearby, these extraordinary and enormous glittering birds had stretched their wings, momentarily cutting off the sun, plunging us into darkness, and moving on, excited, cawing to each other, to inspect a further flower, and, sitting, their claws attached to stems, sending out raucous victorious laughter echoing through the universe.

WHEN WE ARRIVED back at Uncle Ambrose and Aunty Gilda's flat, Uncle Ambrose stood on the top doorstep and, barring our entrance to the interior of their house (which they must have sensed could not withstand such a small typhoon of destructive feminine energy), he called out, 'Gwirls gwirls gwirls' (in his slight even feminising stammer), and he stood motionless, his palms turning outwards, as if we had to read in them a stigmata, and, again as if he were directing traffic, he called us all to a halt. He announced that he was about to institute a game of hidenseek, with much hidden treasure.

Like mercury splitting apart, like a brittle pane of glass shattering in slow motion, then suddenly turning into fast speed, we fractured, screaming and shrieking, diving for cover.

I looked about me, feeling strange. I didn't know who to run and hide with. Nobody had chosen me. And also, under the impact of so much sugar, so many sweets, so much attention, the little modoms had reverted to a savagery which was quite at odds with their virginal white dresses. Faces were flushed, hair undone, the white dresses were now marked with grass, stained with spilt drinks. One plump girl had become a bossy hysteric while another cowered, whimpering behind her, stammering and unpopular. Others made sounds which were exactly like the sounds any other local kid would make: barks of pleasure emitted from their guts; their pupils rolled in their eyes; faces flushed and glazed; and their hair, released from plaits and ribbons and hairbands, now fell over sweaty brows. Anxiously bitten nails drummed the wood. Pushing, shoving each other remorselessly, these daughters from the other side of town now seemed no different from . . . from . . .

. . . I saw on the other side of the road Tony and Myrtle.

They had come up to watch the birthday, much as you might watch a passing procession.

They were simply observers.

Silent, wordless. Shoeless.

Should I wave to them?

Would they wave back?

Would it lead to worse complications?

They might come over, hesitatingly, or even boldly, simply walk over the small concrete fence no higher than ten inches, stepping right over and walking inside Ponky's place, just as they had done on many occasions before.

It was too risky.

Like everyone else, I pretend they aren't there.

'Pssst,' I HEAR from behind me. *'Pssssst,'* again.

I turn on the balls of my feet. It is the princess of the eyelashes, of the laughing mouth.

'Come over here,' she whispers to me.

Her skin is so evenly brown it is like the most perfect tan in the world, in fact it is beyond a tan, it is the quintessential colour of all skin for which my own white and freckled skin is just a poor preparation, a layering which I might hope to scrape aside and reveal underneath this warmth of colour, which is so intense it aches inside my mouth to eat it or lick it or stick it inside me so it might come out, drench out of the pores of my skin, covering me with sunwarmth and brownness.

She is blacklashed and blindingwhite, strong teeth stuck into redgums. She is blackeyed so enormously that I can see inside her pupils, curved round the horizon's global shape; the lawn and wooden house and in the distance little white flecks like fallen blossoms of all the girls.

I understand in that second she controls all the world in her eyes.

Younger than me she is wiser than me.

She smiles at me, she sees me, she does not look beyond me.

When I crawl closer she makes room for me.

'My name is Sophie,' she says seriously.

'My name is Jamie,' I half-quibble burying my voice back down inside me.

She looks all over me.

'Let's escape,' she says then. 'Let's escape.'

'AHHH,' SHE GOES, running onto the green pelt of the park. 'Ohhhhh,' she goes lying sideways as we go rolypoly down the bank flashing sky eye peer and peek inside our skulls and find our laugh we screeeeeeeeeam as we rollpollrollpoll smell of crushed grass sticky paspalum-juice and the hot rich dank murmur of earth.

She jumps up, Jillinthebox, her pink dress lopsided and now stained with the grass. She wants to break, to make the pink dress turn into another flower. All the time she is laughing and dancing and running ahead of me, saying, *'Tell me, tell me.'*

We are on the swings swinging the sky up and down inside our eyesockets, balancing the world on our tongues as we laugh . . .

'Go higher!' she says, *'I can go higher than you.'*

We swing with such vengeance the entire framework of the swings begins to shudder, the shriek of the unoiled sockets calling to us. Our vengeance is harsh and we beat the air with our blur, bluesky greengrass and beyond the fringe of black bark of pine tree the calling waving of wave upon wave upon wave.

'Tell me,' she says. *'Tell me everything. I must know. I must. I must know everything of this world so I may conquer it.'*

We are giddy and slow and simply sit on our swingseats, waiting for the wirrld to ungiddy itself from the centre of our storm.

'I feel sick,' she says.

And I say, *'I feel sick.'*

I say and she say and I say and together, then, we go and throw ourselves on the warm breast of the earth and drink down into our insides a long cool draught of sky.

We hear back there a shrill whistle and Uncle Ambrose goes, *'Gwirlgwirlgwirl,'* in a high screel of stop!

'Let's not go back,' she says, sitting up, feeling better. *'Let's explore.'*

EXPLORE WHAT? MY hand? The lines on it? This is what this world is. I have only to open my mouth and the words drop out, like bobbles of water on a powerline on a frosty morning. I do not even have to speak to describe because I have lived here so long and breathed here so long that there is not one mound of earth not one nodule on the bark of a pine, not one rubbish wire basket, not one faded TT2 wrapper shaking in the wind I have not been.

'This is the pine forest,' I say, 'in which the souls of dead people play. This is the bridge the goblins hoped to build but . . .'

And I repeat everything my brother has told me, tulled me, sung me, tilled me: I am his field and now I am growing I am growing miraculous flowers and she is now settling into my heart.

'Can we get there?' she says, nodding to the goblin bridge. 'To the treasure.'

'Only when the tide flows out,' I say, grave as a statue casting a deep shadow. Now my words turn into writing-in-bronze round the bottom of the war memorial. This statue was given by gracious permission of Councillor Waters, who sat on the Council 1921-35.

She smiles all across her horizon, lighting up the trees with her sun.

'Eh?' she says to me. 'Eh?'

'Good eh?' I say back.

'Good eh?' She says back to me.

We run now screaming, escaping from the shapes left behind, the shadows of ourselves who are still standing at the final bus-stop in the world.

We run screaming till we stop.

'Can we, let's us, you and me,' Sophie says, 'go over to the reef?'

I LOOK AT her shoes. They are made of white kid, so dainty that they are made from the inside of an arum lily.

'You're not dressed right,' I say sternly. For it is not easy to enter and become a member of our unique club — Ponky Maddy and me.

'I've got,' I say, boasting calmly, 'I've got a record from the dump which plays advertisements from many different radio shows. Ponky and Maddy and me play radio announcers. We've got at least five records,' I say airily, rich as Croesus. I've got, I've got, I've got . . .

'O,' she says turning her sun on me, full of admiration. 'O, can we go there please? It sounds, it sounds . . . ,' then she says it, 'heavenly. You will take me with you?'

We are standing on the cliff-edge.

'That is where lovers jump,' I say.

'How many?'

'Many,' I say. 'About two.'

She gazes down the cliff. A long way down we can smell the beach, tinny and strange. For this is the rubbish dump side. Where lies the treasure.

'They were crushed,' I say in an offhand way. 'Their legs went into their stomach. Never walked again.'

'O,' she says. 'Shall we jump? Kiss me,' she says. 'Come and stand close here.'

She walks out. To the cliff-edge.

I, who hate heights because I know the enticement of plunging, now feel no fear.

I walk towards her.

'Come on,' she says, and she laughs then a pure wild laugh, *'Come on,'* she says *'Come here and kiss me. Let's be lovers who jump,'* she says.

She is looking out to sea; I realise in one instant I could push her down. I realise I cannot stop myself from murdering her and getting in her car, and then driving away, perhaps even becoming her, but instead, just as I get right up to her, halting my momentum forward, she turns, sensing me there right near her and the sea glittering all round her head, she turns and seeing me so nearby she simply smiles to me and says to me as she has learnt in the movies, in a low voice somehow right at the back of her throat, so I learn in that moment I must go to the back of her throat with my tongue to retrieve it, she says, *'Kiss me, handsome, kiss me, handsome. Hard.'*

And I do.

SILENCE NOW AND deep into shock of the impact of my tongue inside her, slithering on the cliff-edge, we hung we hang we in space the sun and air around us breaking apart into separate atoms exploding, and the bright hard sun dashing on each crashing miniature wave so the tide turns into one million little mirrors all pointed towards us. The shadows on everything stream away like long strands of hair in a river. The heartbeat of the earth attaches us to the ground, our toes curl round the nodule of pohutukawa root which clings to the side like a dragon half-way down, crouched to catch us if we fall.

As we unseal, her face comes away from mine and unlocks the shadow, so I am blinded, and, standing there, lost in vertigo, I waver back and forth over space. But her hands, her small birds, have picked me up by each piece of cloth on either side of me, and pulled me back from the brink.

'Lie down,' she says

I lie down

'Do you love me?'

'Always.'

'Forever and ever?'

'Ever.'

'My real name is Lorna Doone and one day we shall marry. I love you forever, write to me under a *nom de plume*.'

We go back to kissing again, and gradually it is happening. I am both taking off and burying in, I am rising up and losing all weight. From inside the pith of my skull starts a pure burning wire of fire which flares down from the dome of my head, down my back, kickstarting my heart, and then, in one enormous roar like a plane across a sky drowning me out in its noise, this spurt comes out.

Shaken and wet, I look down.

'Take me to the reef,' she says. 'There is more.'

Boys

'I KNOW,' I say to Keely as he stands there. I look into his face, which is half-turned towards me, caught there, like in a photo.

Without knowing why, without arranging it verbally, there we all are over at the transit camp, two sets of gangs, boyboys and girlgirls, ranging round each other.

Form One Accelerate.

Nobody organised this, nobody made a time and a place.

It is as if this place, this time was already within us, formed from the instant of our births. It is simply as if a clock has gone off, an alarm clock, and each one of us has awoken to find himself, herself here inside the transit camp.

Across the road from the dump.

It has been raining forever. Hanging clouds like wet washing.

There is no sound but the grader over at the tip. It grates the air into sharp scallops.

Is that a zebra I can hear running?

Or the shoes of Cora-Lee? We are all here, keeping our secret, mute, yet rebellious appointment.

The girlgang is led by Zeena, whose dress at the top is already swelling and tight, straining against the fabric.

Zeena's face is dirty-bright alight, and her slack lips, which are pastel-painted, always loll open. Is she squinting up at the picture screen? Or laughing? Or buried deep within her scowl? She wears brown shoes, whitened by tennis-white.

They are her pride.

Zeena is the girl who knows everything, is the repository of all knowledge. She is sullied by this knowledge, she, who must be the container of it all, and carry it, not on her head, which is where we all, anyway, see it, but secretly within herself: sullied, soiled, a used stamp which can no longer stick.

Angel is her deputy in knowingness.

Zeena and her best-friend Angel are always curved round

each other's ears down which they pour hot exciting spurts of words.

I catch some of them, *'Frenchie, feel, pantie, root.'*

I run the magic terms over my tongue trying, willing to make them feel at home.

Please know me kindly. Frenchie, feel, pantie, root.
I will know you.

CARROT HAS LED we boys along on his low-swinging hips, which he jerks back and forth in an undulant dance, flickering his eyelids as if he is undergoing a heart attack and letting out bleat groans which make him sound like he is a cowboy shot down, writhing in death throes.

Keely goes: *'HaaaaaCarrot haaaaaaaCarrot,'* but watches attentively.

Carrot says to me, between hard-bitten lips, 'I seen Keely in the backrow of the Cameo and he has his hands round Zeena's tits. I seen this,' he says to me, serious and professional, a bearer of hard truth.

I look into his doubting.

'So?' I say, hard and wild. I have learned this language, this tongue, which is all mocking disbelief and sharp not-knowing.

Not knowing who to trust and what is true, I trust to knowing nothing.

'So?' I say, meaning: impress me.

Carrot has lured along Winkie, which is no wonder, Winkie only wants to be included, wants to find out, he doesn't want to miss out. He is different from me in some profound way. This I know. I can hear this in the difference of our heartbeats, as if his heartbeat bangs to a different music than mine. Whereas Keely? I am always listening for it, just as I listened and watched for the ballfall during foursquare. I am always listening for it and trying to learn it, and match it and copy it. *Copy it bright copy it light, make it mine all through the night.*

'I know,' I say. *I know.*

'O?' Keely doesn't say. I can feel the relaxation of his body right through my own. I wish now I had brushed my hair like his, so it fell, in a wide awake wave all across the top of my skull. I wish I had hair like his, combed back along the sides then glittering with Brylcream so its black darkness winks in the light. I wish I was inside his mouth, or even his eyes, which turn to me and look at me, all over my skin and clothes and body and face. I wish his eyes could go inside.

'. . . Whaaaaaa?' goes Keely who is so cool he chews gum slowly even when he has none in his mouth.

'What the fucken hell,' breaks in Fainell who in this crisis has come along with us, boy with boy.

Fainell sometimes leans his eyes against my face, and I find myself looking at his hard blue eyes, and all the scurf of pimples which ruffle round his jaws. His face permanently red, as if ringing in his ears all the time are words boys scream out at him.

Often I see him turn taut and give the fingers and scream back other words. This I hear and do not quite understand. This language is mute.

I see him pushed face down in the earth, rubbed. But he rises up and is curiously strong. He does nothing back, he stands aside, he does not fight, he does not even look at them. He walks away. And when he is a long distance away he turns and screams. They chase him then hotly. I do not know what happens. I do not know what happens. When they catch him by the bridge. I see him being carried away by the boys, he is upside-down, being dragged, his head hitting the stones, jerking as it hits. The boys all gloating and groaning over him as they drag him down round into creek-darkness.

All this is in his eyes, his face, his permanent flush. Yet this is what surprises me with Fainell. Nobody has whiter skin. His skin has an almost radiant whiteness, beyond clouds, beyond the snow which none of us have ever seen. He is whiter than a page, on which words are waiting to be written.

'Hah fucken hah,' says Fainell to Carrot who has crept up behind him and, placing himself behind Fainell's creambun, begins to flail away, fluttering his eyelids and letting out his dying injun moan: 'Ohhh . . . ahhhhhh,' he mimics. 'Ooooooh aaaaaaaaah.'

We boys all stand in a circle, listening.

Fainell says, *'What d'we do? Who's going to go first? Which girl?'*

'Where's the girl?' say Keely, who, beneath his tan, his beautiful brown skin which is so fine it is like the covering of a foreign landscape I wish to visit, Keely is a strange yellow. His lips dry.

'Where's the girl?'

We stop, prick-alert, and listen.

'Ooooaaaaahhhhhhhhh,' snarls a tiger, pettishly, full of stalled fury. Inside her cage I hear the padded threat of her paw. I hear the hot gush of elephant piss. I hear overhead the clouds lock together, shut.

Where's the girl?

THE TRANSIT CAMP is where the communists are stalled before they can enter our land of freedom. We throw stones on their roof, chanting. We call them commies and run away from their ghost faces. Faces in which are outlined, in a scrawl of wrinkles, concentration camps and horrors we cannot even imagine. But seeing them, we laugh. We throw stones and run.

It is good to be free.

'HAH!'

We turn, startled.

There behind us, massive as a tower, laughing to herself, is Stumpy. Five foot nothing, kauri-stump legs planted apart.

She has a tight and straining bodice, too, but it bears no correlation to her face, which is stern as a ship prow bearing into storm.

Stumpy is famous for out-staring Mr Pollen, winning by continuously staring at him in one long unbroken stare so immensely heavy in its weight that Mr Pollen in the end staggered away from it, as though he was bearing the impact of a spume of water from a fireman's hose. This is the power of Stumpy's glance. Stumpy who can push over a boy, ram against a would-be man, with such brutal force all boyboys gush and part around her, an invincible rock: Stumpy, with her kinked hair and lard legs, and plain fat scone features.

She sometimes talks to me.

But today she just goes, *'Hah!'*

And the derision of her sound is such that all we boyboys turn to her, revealing in that second, opening out of ourselves as if being peeled.

'Hah! Ugly fat cut,' sneers Carrot low.

'What's that, littleboy?' says Stumpy.

'We're looking for the girl,' says Keely all aslant with curvaceous dimple-boy charm. I watch Keely being duplicitous. I have seen him use his charm on every living thing. He has even used it on me, once, when alone. But I have seen him charm and tame boys men girls women dogs cats telephones. Keely possesses this charm which lives inside him. *I wish I wish I wish.*

Stumpy turns behind her and creates a significant pause.

This pause grows so immense it overwhelms all we boyboys so we group together, innocent as a group of virgins being rounded up for ritual slaughter. We pass between ourselves many anxious flutters of glance: Winkie to me, me to Keely, Keely to Carrot and Carrot, forgetting he is always cool, falls ashen white.

Stumpy turns away and whistles low and luxurious: almost a bird love song.

From out of the grass, so close we had no idea they were nearby, stand the girls.

Zeena and Angel, haughty in their looks, and last of all Cora-Lee. They crowd the silence and we boyboys look at the girlgirls. This moment glows and grows and stretches across the bridge of silence. For long seconds it looks like none of us will dare to step a foot on there. Then Carrot, scratching himself down there urgently, like he's got an itch, mumbles furiously:

'Who's gunna go first? Someone's gotta.'

Zeena leans forward. She is like a flame which sucks towards her all the oxygen in that day. Around us trees, plants, clouds whistle. We boyboys are clinging on to rocks by fingertips, whistling in the wind.

Zeena's bold eyes gimlet each of us. There is some blindness in her glance, some elemental force so strong it can differentiate between all of us, or none. It doesn't seem to matter.

Her hips thrust forward, legs apart, imaginatively she sucks on the long silent cigarette of cinema and blows the smoke into all our eyes.

We see her genie.

'OK, boys,' whispers Stumpy, swiftly becoming our umpire.

She is about to blow the whistle.

'Who's it gunna be? Who's gunna step forward first?'

There is a long pause of silence here as Winkie turns to glance at me quickly, and I traipse my glance to Keely who ricochets it to Carrot who, coming awake, as if from a long trance, goes to make a sound, but the sound has died in his throat.

All that comes out is a pathetic whimper, the cry of a lost boy.

His features round his nose dissolve, and before our eyes he melts down to his winklepickers. We all of us see he is not there.

'I wull.'

The words cut into the air, rearrange all the sound and sight and tastes of our lives around them. Heads spin on necks. All living things fleck past, lost in speed.

Who is this being *who wull?*

I see standing there, face drained of all blood, blindingly white, his fists rammed tight into his shorts so I can see, behind the serge, the pumping agitation of his knots — I see standing there, his legs splayed apart in answering dance to Zeena: Fainell.

Fainell!

'If yous wanna root I'll rootcha.'

At these words a low sounding whistle passes through all the girls. It is like the sound of a pyjama cord being whipped out of the top so the material falls with a whooshh downward.

'Oaaaaaaaahhhhhhhhhhh,' goes the cry.

But its sound flecks back and smacks, hard, in a whiplash, into Zeena's face. It digs its claws into the little black pin-pimples by her rounded nose. Her eyes widen and take in the boyboy who is offering to root her. Her eyes try and accommodate Fainell, who is now doing a dance in front of her, his legs wide apart, like she is the ball bouncing already up into the cup of his palm.

But she doesn't move.

'Where we gunna do it?' asks Zeena in a thin voice, knowing that she must not hesitate.

Her eyes braise the surroundings.

'I doan lie down on grass,' she says plaintively. 'Nor up against a rock. My shoes might get dirty,' and with a small gesture her fingers fall open to disclose down below her pride and joy, the one moment of her immaculateness: her whitened shoes.

'Nobody must touch Zeena's shoes,' says Angel firmly. She nods hard, bright, her eyes flamey. 'OK?'

Handmaiden to Zeena, she stoops and wipes away an imaginative grass clipping off the shoecap.

Zeena's lips move dryly.

'I'm not gunna do it with all yous round.'

'How we gunna know you did it?' Cora-Lee raises a point of logic.

'Yeah,' says Winkie. *'Yeah.'*

'We've got to see,' says Cora-Lee professionally.

'I'm not gunna do in front of all yous,' says Zeena. 'Not for all of yous.'

There is a pause.

Crescent of boyboy held by circle of girlgirl.

'You dunno how to do it, does ya?' says Fainell then through a slit in his mouth.

He lets out his laugh and empties it all over us.

'I does so,' says Zeena, backed up by Angel, who jumps forward and says hotly,

'She does too. I know it.'

'How you know? You done it too?'

This is Carrot, reeling the corpse of his courage back.

'I don't have to say,' says Angel coolly. She blows the smoke of her own imaginary cigarette into Carrot's eyes. And smiles enigmatically.

'You've not done it, bitchcut,' Carrot says then suddenly exhausted.

For one instant boyboy might attack girlgirl; we all hang there ready to break.

Stumpy looks round at all of us, pale. She realises she does not control any of us.

A lion then roars, oh roars ancient and riotous and mellowly angry at being behind bars. The lion roars and roars and roars. But is content to be entrapped.

'Hah!' now Fainell yells. *'Hah! Hah!'*

The hot lava of his scorn pours out and molten runs into every one of our stinging orifices converting us to rock — the basalt of shame, we stand there trapped in whatever position we found ourselves when the lava overcame us, so we may be found centuries later (in actual fact, only several moments), each one of us caught in a characteristic posture: Keely shimmering on a half-turn, raising his eyelashes to gaze into the mirror which is the world; Carrot slummocking down into his shoulders and gazing inwardly as if to extract from his fetid interior some glint of passing intelligence; Stumpy leaning forward as the sails of a ship blowing before a storm; Winkie blinking in an in-between state, neither seeing nor not seeing, his hands half sliding out of his pockets but not free; Cora-Lee positioning her face like a camera so she may get the best exposure; Zeena, her face splayed back, body arched prepared and ready to receive what is coming towards her — a blow, a caress, a bad word, a free ticket to the flicks; and Angel rising in a half-curtsy as she stands up from protecting Zeena's white shoes with the forever wide-open fan of her dress.

We stand there, frozen, monuments to uncertainty.

Fainell alone is victoriously living.

He leans forward with a superb arc of disdain. He fingers and feels in the moist dark for something, some weapon, some pen with which he may do his celestial sky writing.

He withdraws from his bag, with a sigh, a bottle of ink.

Radiant blue.

Inside the glass its colour washes everything.

In our bleak-and-white world.

And as he raises his hand up, so we, each one of us, stand up out of our lava shells, not so much who we were, several minutes ago, but who we shall now go on being.

Fainell's hand is raised as high as it can go and, seeing each of us staring at him, caught, trapped by the very speed of his momentum, he releases the bottle.

The bottle shatters.

We watch in silence as the blue heavens ripple across Zeena's white shoes, then sink in, staining.

Zeena sobbing.

Broken, she collapses inward.

'Yous stupid bugger!' cries out Angel.

Zeena is shaking. Zeena is sobbing. Zeena, like the bottle of ink, is shattered.

Angel puts her arm round Zeena's shoulder. Cora-Lee flocks in to comfort her as she is carried along by the outrage of the girls, who all look back over their shoulders saying, *'Fainell, trust you to make a mess of everything. Trust you.'*

Fainell happy unhappy proud depressed shrugs.

Last to turn and go is Stumpy, who, with a curiously enigmatic smile, looks over all we boys so that, in an instant, we become shorter and younger and more hopeless under the storm of her ironic glance.

She just says a single word now, a small drop which falls on the crown of each of our heads, right on the very centre where your hair radiates out from, in all its whirls: this drop falls, chill, precise, uncomfortable:

'Huh!' she says, reducing us to nothingness.

Prize

'Yous a dirty rotten little stinkin' fart of a cheat!'

'We knows you dunnit.'

'I didn't dunnit,' I say staring round at the faces.

It is another day, always another day, an endless stream or train of them hurtling us along even when we want to cry stop! please slow! please let me sit awhile and think of what it means, how it fits together, but there is no time for slow, for sitting, for thinking now, days pour over each other, the other deleting.

Uncle Ambrose is a pinprick in my pupil, a freckle up inside my sleeve (one I hardly recognise — that is me?), my finger-domes feel for home, then, recognising the shape, the raised indentation of a wart I worry it as I turn round and look at the circle of faces which surround me.

We are outside the art class and I am rolling up, the scroll of my painting with which I have, I have (my brother has?) won.

This spurt of redred blood fountains away inside of me, gushing all scarlet, unknown to them all.

Winkie and CarrotnKeely and ZeenanAngel glare, and even Stumpy frowns as she looks at me, biting into and angrily eating the very last quick of her nail. She spits it out when my eyes catch hers, rub against their deep brown. But all of them, through my eyes, are lavishly painted, dripping wet, with red.

I cannot hide the faint trace of a smile, which lingers all over my face as if it is the original purpose or shape or impulse — the one that is made to tie my features all together, tie them down, nose to lips, eyes to mouth, ears to cheek — all of it briefly one map.

I have won.

I have one.

I am one.

My eyespray washes them but the crimson-dash splatters hard against their statue stillness. The liquid runnyruns down their folds and cleats and eddies out, in scary fingernails of scarlet, through their toes.

'Didja paint that paintin'?'

Stumpy turns towards me on her pivot. Her face is terrible with implications, hung with them, garlanded and heavy.

'Didja?'

'Nah, we knows ya didn. Ya can't paaaaaint like that.'

This is Carrot, who, with his crouchback digit, achingly, runs the crayon over paper, racked with disbelief that anything might come, amount to anything under the switching intuition of his fingertips. And where may it lead? To a plumber's apprenticeship? He scowls as he screws up the paper. *Useless bloody useless.*

'Jamie is good at art,' says Winkie, squeaks Winkie. I feel a frown grow down my face, cut into it, two sharp slashes by my brow. *Winkie, please don't speak please don't say a word you cannot defend me. Not you. You not.*

'He's a cheat,' breathes out Angel, luxuriating in all the words which at last, at last are spoken.

A breath passes through this group who tighten round me.

The word is said. Why does this change things? Can I not change things again by saying:

'I am not a cheat!' Hot and furious and angry.

Yet what can they read inside my eyes? They march their army into my arena, bivouac down and prepare for a long and bitter siege.

Cora-Lee is angry, trembling, for it is she who feels the barb of my victory above all, with her pretty little swerves and soft pastel fadings and gatherings of glitter (all copied from the *Australian Woman's Weekly* from the coffee table at her mother's hair salon — Diannes for Hair, Appointments Not Necessary — written in curvy black Italian-style lettering faintly peeling off the glass under the impact of sun).

Cora-Lee is trembling with indignation at the prize she has not won.

Zeena is more furious than she should be, knowing each of us is looking down all the time and seeing her shoes sprayed all over with bluejuice, broken there by Fainell.

He stands outside the group, watching me, smiling.

What does that smile mean? Why is it so strange, so enticing? What does he know here? I feel his smile like it is a gull above me, circling in the air, feeling the wind under its wings, drifting.

'Come on, Caughey, tell us the truth.' It is Stumpy. She has pushed past Keely, turning him on his edge as she comes towards me.

'Ya didn't paint that pitcha coz you couldn't a,' Carrot speaks up now bitterly. 'Who done it for ya?' he asks suspicious.

Stumpy holds out her ham-fist.

'Give us it,' she says.

Prison warder.

I put the roll behind me. Of a sudden I sense how desperate this is. If I unroll the painting they will turn from looking into it, being blinded by the passing flash of Matthew's sun and, eyes no longer in their heads even seeing me, they will come towards me, from all sides and, finding no one in the middle, finding nothing there, they will turn on whatever is left of me, and chase me.

Bash me.

My fingers calliper about the roll. I feel its smooth chill cardboard shine enter into the bones of my fingers, making them porcelain. My eyes are marble. It is I who am a statue now.

They will never get my fingers to unwrap.

'Give us it,' says Stumpy again, each word weighed down like stones tied to my legs. They are taking me to the creek, I know, they are taking me to the creek into which glass hardness they will throw, weighting me down with stones so that, sinking I will go: met and eaten by the eel which waits for me, its mouth craned open so I will slide in. Then its snag teeth shall grind shut . . . too late. I am inside.

This circle of angry eye and dry throat and fist all gather together into a pummel.

'But,' I whine, holding the painting behind me. 'Why should I give it to yous? It isn't yours. It's mine. I don't have to hand it over.'

'Hand it over, Noddy,' says Zeena.

'Cissygirl,' hisses Carrot. 'Give us it. Or we'll all give it to you.'

He tries to dive towards me but I turn. I kick out with my shoes.

There is a moment here, a precipice of shock.

Ugggghhhhhhh goes the air through this little laced circle, tightening round my throat, trying to strangle all the air out of me.

'Let's drag 'im down the creek,' says Carrot then through dry, thin lips. His eyes yellowy-snot green as they glint at me.

It is at that second I see inside him, inside his eyes flow and have flowed all that time the waters of the creek. That is what is inside him. Not blood, not tears, not hot and indecipherable yearnings. No, inside him are the waters of the creek, speckled with frenchies, laced with entangling clouds of seaweed, which flutter and smile at you through the glass, invitingly. *Jump me, cross me, it isn't far. You can get from one side to the other,* he says, always down there, in the dappled dark.

Keely is standing on the other side, too, by Carrot. Light fingers its blossoms, moisture butterflies all over us. Periwinkle rugs soften the curves of the valley all around us. Creepers invade ancient trees, weighing down the sky with their green closeness. We are doing nature study. Nature Study. Carrot is doing that thing with his hips.

'Come on, Jamieboy,' he says to me whispering softly, as if inside my ear, my mouth, he is lying on top of me as we play on the grass, rolypolying against each other, *'Come on, Jamie, come over here.'*

He entices me to jump the creek.

'O!' I say. 'O?'

Not wanting to let them know I am frightened of this gash of sleet which rumbles slowly and darkly from hidden sites to sea. Lumbered with rubbish from the tip.

'It is narrow here. Jump.'

'Heeeeeeh,' goes Keely when Carrot grabs him from behind and pretends, they pretend for me to be lady and men lovers.

When Carrot sees something suddenly. He dives down into the periwinkle.

'Hah!' he cries triumphantly.

In the light, he holds up an opalescent old balloon.

'Aaahhhh,' says Keely, of a sudden silent.

'Oooh,' says Carrot putting it on his ear like it is an earring. He pretends to be a lady, walking, swishing his hips from side to side.

'O, Jamie,' he says, *'O, Jamie, my sweetness come over here. I have something tasty for your dinner.'*

He speaks in a high, funny voice.

'Haahaaaa haaaa,' I laugh but instead out comes a creak, dry and rusty. 'Haaah?' I end on a funny dry note.

Carrot holds the balloon out to me.

Come and get it, Jamie, he calls to me.

Keely joins in, under the dapple dark.

I look at us. All three of us are coated and speckled as if wearing a magic costume. All our living flesh is moving with the slow wave and toss of trees overhead. We swim through silence. Now I know. This is the silence of the beginning of the world. The animals from the zoo, their cries, provide the decor.

This is the beginning and this is one of the moments.

'Jump!' says Carrot then losing patience. *'Come on, Keely,'* he says to his lieutenant (it is strange under the trees, down by the creek, it is Keely who is Carrot's handmaiden here, all relationships go into a strange reversal, nothing is as it seems on the dry and open paddocks upstairs). Keely is changed into a strangely subdued character, like he is silently waiting and listening for Carrot to address a certain word to him at which point he, he, he . . .

Danger smells. And I smell it now.

Carrot starts his winklepickers marching off, picking through the periwinkle, dragging with him all the speckly spaces of light. Keely is simply pulled along in his wake, washed after him. As he goes he turns a mute face towards me, but already I can see his eyes are sealed shut, or if open, they are the eyes of a drowned man.

I see in that instant Keely has been lulled to the bottom of the creek and all its dark coursing has passed through him. Eels have made themselves at home in him, not even knowing they have swum in through his open mouth and out through the eye in his behind, not even knowing they are slithering, not between the dank earth banks of the creek, but his chill fleshy body. Old bits of rubber with stickiness dry in them, rusty needles, photos at the last stage of their holding an image, half-eaten crusts, the dead bodies of rodents swollen by their sleepy transit through Keely's blood stream. All this I see and sense as Keely turns his blind eyes from me.

I am seeing the face of a drowned man.

Carrot has almost dragged Keely's wet and stiff body into the undergrowth so he can masticate, at leisure, on all the remains of his warm, blood-heated brownness.

And for one instant I stay there. But I know, unless I move, the patches of light which trance restlessly, again and again, all over my skin will join together, or rather, fleet apart and a chill cloak of darkness will fall over me, and I will be dragged into being nothing, not even existing, simply part of the silent trees, and the soundless forest and the whispering creek.

'*Ohhaaaahhhh?*' I cry. '*Carrot? Keeeeeeeeeelllllllllly?! Wait for me, eh. Yous fellas wait for me, eh? Eh?*'

No answer.

I must jump.

I move back, to get a good run up.

'Hand it over, Jamie,' says Stumpy, implacable.

'Yeah,' says Angel. 'Let's get him, dirty rotten little lying cheat.'

'I,' I say, wanting to turn round truth and balance it on my palm.

Look at this prism.

I begin to run. My feet take off for me. I am praying for flight.

'*Tell us then. Didja do the paintin'? Who did it for ya?*'

'*We only want to know the truth,*' says Cora-Lee the journalist.

My feet begin to hurtle towards the creek.

Uncle Ambrose please save me, please drive towards me in your scarlet Jaguar, let the door fall open with a heavy somnolent creak, let the smell of leather upholstery sumptuous and rich be so dense everyone around me goes into a trance and Stumpy lets out a sigh, as if within a really good dream, a long deep happy one, as she murmurs slowly and thoughtfully, 'Is that walnut on the dash?'

Run Jamie run.

I converge all my powers on leaping across the creek.

Inch by inch the creek widens before me. It changes into a leering embrace, a welcoming smile, opening itself before me as it fleets wider. Down below (as now I am in mid-air, having gathered behind me all the energy of a giant spring — and in that second I know I have left everyone behind me: Uncle Ambrose; Ponky; Aunty Gilda; even Maddy — but mid-air I see in my hand I hold his painting, this is my torch, this is what lights my way) eerily and still, I see an eel, in a patch of sunlight look up and watch my traverse — its eyes, Carrot's eyes, greedily try to snag my shadow and eat it. A laugh bursts from my lips. It is only shadow, I want to say. *Welcome, welcome*, says the eel, *come closer, come closer, I will not harm, just touch me, just put your fingers there and feel how warm, how hot, are you cold? I'll warm you, don't worry, you needn't worry.*

But it is too late, the momentum of my jump is such that I am already hurtling towards the other side of the bank.

'You couldna paint the pitcha. We know. Just tell us. That's all we want ta know.'

Wet clay, tentacles of periwinkle rise up to greet me, jump into my body, thud into the bones of my leg. But Carrot was right, Carrot was true, he lied as always — to where he was trying to seduce me is in fact a soft marshy eddy of the creek, carefully cloaked with weed so it looks like hard ground. Cold acid water burns through my shoes, grabs my legs by the muscles and begins to yank me, hard, desperate, into the creek.

Uhahhhh, the breath fights to battle up my gorge. My fingers grab hold of the clay, I pull myself, my body all along the pug, feeling its chill embrace welcome me, offer to fold itself over me and give me a long sleep.

For one second this is enticing.

'Carrot? Keely!'

I see them standing there, behind a thick engorged trunk of a tree, laughter skimmeying up and down their bodies like rings running so fast their faces are blurred into masks.

'Heeeehhhheeee,' skimmies Carrot.

'You lied to me, Carrot!' I cry, as I pull myself out of the pug. The wet clay unsucks from me with a last sore kiss.

Then I cannot stop this, my voice is louder than ever, more true because this is the heart of my hurt. *'You you lied to me, Keely. You did.'*

And I see in the distance Keely goes still, untying his laugh from himself, trying to unlace from around himself the tight black thread of Carrot's ownership. But, as much as he struggles, Carrot keeps up his laugh.

'Fall in didja, Caughey? Eel get you, Caughey. That'll teach ya.'

You lied to me, Keely, I don't say now because my eyeshot funnels straight into Keely's face and down into his warm hot burning insides where it rips apart vessels and lets bleed my hurt. I can see the soft shudder of the impact on Keely's face.

'Come on. Tell us what's true,' says Angel then, angry at my continued silence.

But my eyes are on Keely's face who, seeing me look at him, turns his face slightly away from mine so his eyes do not risk any concussion, risk any contamination. In that instant he sells me. He decides I am too risky to know. What I want is beyond what he can give, in front of all these people.

Can I tell them I cannot tell them? Can I tell them what is true? I cannot tell them. You lie, Keely, you lied, you lied, you lied.

This is the power of my heartbeat, its secret motor.

In the distance I have not even noticed Uncle Ambrose has driven away.

He was never coming anyway.

The circle closes.

But, at the very last second, as the hands rise up and the bags begin to swish towards me, as the eyes widen, then narrow into slim slits out of which, too soon, will shoot burning arrows, as the boots fall back to dig, with luscious vengeance, into my legs and shorts — as all of this goes into a sedate musical dance and I prepare myself to go St Joan to the stake — why why do I think of Fainell as he emerges back up the banks of the creek, his face eerily white, in his defeat an invincible victor, possessing something nobody can destroy (except perhaps himself)? With all these thoughts streaking through me, a sound leaks in.

A single long sharp sound.

It is the school bell.

It is the message which subliminally jerks us out of where we are, and, unknown to ourselves, sends a message hurtling through our blood streams that we must move on to the next classroom and begin again, begin forgetting again, begin learning again.

So in this second everything freezes.

Then crumbles.

'Lying cheat,' says Carrot to me, whispering into my ear as he brushes past me. 'You're so fulla lies and skite you wouldn't even recognise the truth if it run over you like a bus.' Then he narrows his eyes and smiles at me and pours down my ear a spurty hot draught. *'Come back down the creek. Soon. I got a present for ya.'*

And he winks.

Truth

IF I SAY something is true, then why isn't it? If words represent actions, why can't something be true, just by saying it? Aren't words the truth?

KEELY GAVE ME the eel like a present. He placed it in my hand.

'It wants to feel you,' says Carrot screeling. I am in shock and I walk towards our classroom, which is empty, natch, since we are all on Nature Study, 'studying nature in all its wonder'. I do not know what to do with the eel, which keeps squirming its head round to look at me. It terrifies me. It eats me.

I see the aquarium, our class aquarium, which is a bold square of glass so thick it is shaded green when you look at it in a certain light. Inside the greenglass is the pretty universe Coralee and Angel have created. There are dimply crystal necklaces growing up onto the surface. There is oxygen weed daily placed in there to keep the water clean. Goldfish transfer their rainbow essence all over the glass. And at the bottom, on the lunar pebbles, Coralee has placed a Chinese bridge, an old man, a courting couple. It is all so pretty.

As soon as I see it, I comprehend. I will place the eel within, so it shall live. Besides part of me is already no longer there. I want to go back, go back and find out, find out what KeelynCarrot are always doing down there by the darkcreek.

I slip the eel in and run away.

They are nowhere.

Nowhere.

I keep hearing their laughter under the trees.

You lied to me, Keely.

And when I come back into the class, there is a small knot of people gathered round the aquarium. Coralee is sobbing, as she holds in her hand the dying moments of a goldfish. I see its mouth open and shut for the last time.

'Someone has murdered,' sobs Coralee.

All around our shoes is a welter of thick water welding shame and crime to us.

'Who done it?' cries Stumpy furiously. 'Who wrecked our class project?'

I open my mouth as if to say, to speak. But Mr Pollen now rushes in.

'What's the problem? What has happened? What happens when I leave you on your own, trusting you all to use your time beneficially?'

We comprehend in one moment the special length of the word is used to flay all of us. And, indeed, because he has given us special trust, we all of us feel more wretched.

'Someone done it,' says Angel shrilly.

And as she speaks she stands aside revealing the big eel dead inside the aquarium. It has thrashed all the water out in its last moments. In its fury. Its face looks congested with anger. Its jaws are open. Eyes glazed but looking, looking at me.

I shudder.

Already there is a terrible fish smell. Stagnant. It smears its shame all over me.

'Who done it?'

'Who done the terrible thing?'

We won't tell on you, if you don't tell on us.

'THE PERSON ONLY has to speak up,' says Mr Pollen lightly, dandling his words on his tongue, as if they dance on point.

There is a long moment of silence and I wait for the words to come up my soundpipe to sing the tune which will explain everything. I think I am saving the eel, that it will live, that it will be added to our class exhibit. I don't think it will kill. I think it will live in water. In water, the divine essence, the thing which gives us life.

Without water we die.

BOOK FOUR

OPEN SESAME

Wonderful City

HE IS WAITING for me there, by the bridge. Standing with his bike leaning against him. Casually, I turn, slowly, to spy if anyone can see him.

No one.

He tenses a little when he sees me, and smiles, almost. I almost smile back but my lips form stiff and I sigh, almost apart from myself, so the words slide out in a moan:

'Whatcha doin' heeeeeeere for?' and the word here takes on the skid of a long deep groan, like the lick of a wave sliding into the chute of a cave and echoing up and round the walls, before slithering out again.

Low.

He says nothing, but gets on his bikeseat and begins to ride off. He is silent, and his knees, I see, have been scratched with blood, which has dried. And by his eyes is a soft flowering bruise, which has changed the mask of his face, as if a giant thumb has been pressed into his wax and gouged out and into it another shape: as if the native shape of his face is not good enough.

As I push down the weight of my pedals, desperate to catch up with him, I moan low, *'Wai-it,'* (like it is two words and each one is a swingbridge towards him), *'Wai-it for me, Maddy. Don't leave me be-hiiind. Please.'*

'Whatcha up to?' I lie all offhand when I bike-bike up to him. We are on a crest. Wind fingers through our hair, flacking our shirts and pasting secret smiles on our faces.

'Watcha up to, Maddy?' I lie urgently at the same time so he knows he may undress whatever is inside the vacancy of my mind.

For now I know there is nothing.

'You thought of what you're wearing for the fancy dress ball?' he asks then. Accusingly.

He explodes this in my mind. I watch, from a far distance, the explosion happen. It is a fine explosion, in tiny shivering sharp spears of metal all firing out from a central point of contact. In it I see faces: Stumpy disbelieving; Keely watching me close; Carrot picking his nose, looking at it intently, rolling it into a small bullet between thin crouchback fingers, flicking it at me.

Dust darkens the air.

I have seen something I cannot quite name.

Is it chance? Luck? Hope? Escape?

Or rather, what I see has no name yet. Is the missing word.

So this is his mystery as he keeps silent, pedalling beside me, he who knows the missing word, carries it before me.

He starts to ride away from me quickly, laughing.

The streamers float out from his mouth and flash through the air. His legs pump.

He carries the word away from me.

'Waaaaiiit for me. Waiiiitttt.' I moancry as I stand up on my pedals pushing.

He turns to me and laughs.

'Catch me,' he cries.

We race now laughing, air tearing down our throats and blasting into our faces. Now the roads and houses fleck past us and we control all the slide of earth which lies on the rock, resting on our tongues. Turning sideways, tears roil from the corner of our eyes, dragged out by the pen of the wind.

He relaxes and settles back on the hooked bikeseat.

I do likewise. Copycat.

We coast now silently.

Past a blackbird on a swaying powerline.

Its beak follows us. Knowing eye glints.

NOW WE HAVE fingered down into our part of the street. It is as if we have not so much come to a house than the place has opened up its fur and we have entered into the soft moist space of it, its density of associations, and we come upon it so unexpectedly it takes on the satisfaction, the surprising satisfaction of completion.

Outside our house he says, 'Let's go into our place. I've got something to show you.'

As always with him, as if I have no will or he has invented my will, in all my vacancy I follow behind him and soon all there is is the sound of a bumper rattling on the wheel of a bike as it rides over the small indentation at the bottom of the drive, where the concrete parts from asphalt, and soon this splinter of sound is softened, then multiplied then lost in the striated echo as it shivers up and down the sun and shadow stripes of weatherboard. The eery cackle of the cabbage tree palms send out a greeting. We turn the side of the house and there it is, our world, our sleeping beauty which has been staying there, awaiting this moment, for its rebirth.

The sound of the key sliding into the padlock. It shivers up my spine and unlocks something in my head. Matthew's warty hands, capable and febrile, finger the key, which is small, brass, intaglio. He has had one hidden all along. Under a brick, by the lemon tree. He has been using the hut, at secret moments. And now he has drawn me here.

'We'll work on your costume together,' he tells me, almost sternly, yet casually too, so I do not take fright.

I note he says your costume as though it already exists and I see it there, now, ahead of me, already existing, my fate. I hunger suddenly, acutely to know see touch and then get into this costume. It hovers before me, behind that door.

The costume. Which costume? What will he make of me?

'I doan wan nothin' special,' I groan blackly. 'I doan wanna stick out,' I say looking at him suspiciously.

I pick at my scab intensely, frowning.

'I got into terrible trouble because of that owl you drew for me,' I say to him harshly.

A blank look settles on his face. Impact of my explosion. Then, I see the bruise on his cheekbone swelling outwards. His collar is torn away from his shirt: I smell the particles of dust, all the powder of his fallen world, shaken and ground into his pants.

He has been fighting again. That mysterious and horrible fight, where he is picked on. I see his glasses have been taped up the side. Where they are broken.

As if he sees my eyewater has just rinsed them, he snatches his glasses off and holds them in his hand. He looks down, sad yet defiant. He gets out his old snotrag, and polishes clean the glass.

'But you won though?' he asks me slowly.

I leave a long trail of silence. Then I say, in a voice which is not quite like my own:

'Yeah. I won,' I say, *but I lost too. I lost everything,* I doan say. Everything. Cause of you.

I'll make you the most beautiful costume on earth, he doan say. *I'll make you a costume which will carry you up into heaven. We will leave this dust behind.* He doan say.

I am still suspicious. He knows things wider and more different than anything we know in our world. He is a Quiz Kid after all and has dragged all the spangly and awkward intelligence of half the globe into his brainbox.

'What is the circumference of the globe?'

'How many days did Captain Scott survive?'

'Name the state capital of Alaska.'

He knows everything yet nothing. Nothing that KeelynCarrot know in the faintest brush of their most careless fingertips. They know everything here, which is what I want to know. Matthew may paint the best owl in the universe, the most owliest of owls but it doesn't count.

'We'll decide on the costume together,' he says then, key in hand. 'I've got an idea,' he says, secret and darkly shining.

'O,' I follow into him.

For, away from KeelynCarrotnPonk they fade into the tiniest dot on a pore on my finger. They count for nothing but a pair of watchful eyes and a down-sagging mouth.

'What costume?' I murmur then, restless as a wind through the apple tree, lifting each petal and letting it ruffle and fluff and then settle down again, grateful and graceful.

'You have beautiful hips,' he says to me then. Intently. Creating me in that instant.

Who am I?

I am beautiful hips.

'Like a fashion model. Suzy Kendall,' he says knowledgeably. Nodding.

I nod too.

This is my brother. I am numb partially through gratitude, yet also because it is my face my body my mind that is this soft wax which his masterful fingers plunge into and swiftly pass over, moulding and pushing, melding and warming, changing the inert into what becomes the surprising incidents of meaning.

And I ache to change.

All around me I can sense the surprise of the garden that we have come back into existence again. The apple tree. Rhubarb, strawberry patch. Stealthily watches Achilles, the cat. Sentinel, he sees us, then decides we are so unspectacular he only galvanises open a yawn and out of it comes his boredom, his greeting to us. Pink flower mouth. Folds close its petals. Achilles slummocks down and rolls over, presenting his belly to us. He stares at us mesmerically, from upside-down.

MY BROTHER NOW stands key pricked on lockeye.

'What is it?' I ask suspiciously. 'I ain't goin' in there if you doan tell me.'

I curl my toes round inside the worn imprint of my feet at the bottom of my sandals, for at this point when I might be bidding farewell to the person I had been, I want to cling, for one last time, to the imprint of who I have been.

But the key, the golden key, has slid in as far as it can go. I hear the tiny pock of the knock as the key hits the metal. Now, as if inside me and I feel all its movements, the key turns and connects with secret and hidden combinations so that, in a second, the padlock springs ajar. The sound of this is so shockingly precise, so like Maddy; in that instant, over by the sailing club, the gulls mistake the moment for the sun falling off the edge of the earth. They rise up in one swoon and hail and frail over the sky, darkening it with their scream: the air turns into whirlwind, and the ladybird hesitates on the viscous glitter of a lemon; the insects nestling inside the sheeted folds of a blossom pause; the cat who has been licking his inside paw over and over again stops, rolls over, stands up groggily and looks about him, mystified.

What new pattern is this?

HE STANDS NOW inside the hut, its fecund smells reaches out to welcome me: the waxy smell of old linoleum which has been warmed and become soft in the heat of the sun; the grannysmith apples my mother stores there; the dry papery smell from the hundreds of books (for this is our library) — it is as if the papery fibres of a forest of trees, from which the pages come, have swollen in the silence and the heat and in some fundamental way returned to being trees and wood, and emit now all the highly scented earth-sourced smells of the forest, drawing up from the moist forest floor all the cries of the earth: the Amazon momentarily flows through our hut; plus a faint scent of staleness, which comes from the track of a human finger as it passes line by line down the page; I can smell swelling out to me all the pouring out of thought and dreams and idleness as the eyes pause before the words, transfiguring the little black serifs into entire worlds, into avenues and tunnels of escape; smell too of the earth under the hut scented with shade and unrealised promise, and the grass by the door where, each morning when we sleep there, my brother stands and pisses open a beautiful green carpet.

HE STANDS INSIDE there and waits for me cautiously, opening and shutting books as he pretends he is not waiting for me. He does not need me but I read in the small vein pulsing, fluttering with excitement by his glasses, he is anxiously awaiting my single movement. He now lays his glasses aside, wounded bird, and turns his face to look at me.

His eyes are sightless.

Just as mine, soon, shall be.

Soon we shall both be operating by other senses, as if we are mute unformed beings revolving still inside the womb, attached together.

I do not pause, indeed time has taken on the strangeness of non-being and it is not a question of walking in there so much as shortening the space between us and realising its inevitability.

'I gotta have a say,' I say, furious, knowing that I will not.

I walk inside and pull the curtains back along the severe wires and open up the sky to see what is inside.

HE HOLDS THE magnifying glass there.

'Hold out your hand. *There,*' he says. 'Now keep it still.'

I look down and see a small petal of fallen light, a hidden rainbow quivering, a flower, an insect being born: then *pain*.

'Ha!' he cries vaunting. 'Ha!'

I rub it, tears in eyes.

Saliva he puts on my hand.

'That is the sun,' he says. 'The power of the sun.'

'I won't hurt you. Truly,' he says to me.

I stare at him and into him. I cannot understand this intoxication, he who knows of the sun and can make glass turn into flowers . . . of pain.

I doan trust you, I doan say as he licks my hand with his tongue rasping me like a cat.

'This will heal it,' he says lingeringly.

NOW HE REACHES for a book I know off by heart.

The Film Show Annual. The Wonderful City and its Famous Inhabitants.

He inspects the cover intently, then blows off some imaginary dust very carefully.

I let out a low expiration of air.

'You take a look,' he says to me then, pretending to be calm.

'I've got an idea from it,' he says very impressively.

I am breathing slow now, for I have the book of all secrets in my hand.

With a blunt finger, as if summoning up a talisman, I pass my fingerpad then lay my hand flat (as one would to open a secret door) on the cool surface of the dust-jacket.

I close my eyes and await the magic slide as I move into a trance.

For I am travelling now.

Escape

I KNOW EVERY page in this book. I know the order in which the pictures happen, just as I have read and absorbed into my system every single word. The minute I finish the book I usually return to the front page — or back — and begin all over again.

I loved the way everyone seemed to lead lives of such careful artificiality, with human beings, or rather film stars, posed in luxurious and somehow unreal sitting-rooms, pool-side gardens, or even sets imitating throne-rooms, log-cabins, gambling-dens. It was a world as strange as the circus, as wonderfully unlike the world we lived in, so at one and the same time my brother and I received the welcome intelligence: here was a world other than the one in which we were embedded, imprisoned and forced to exist.

We ate into the words and pictures — we did not differentiate — like hungry borer in dry heat.

I turned as I always did to the page which was my favourite. This was a photo-essay on a young actor called John Saxon.

I looked as if for the first time at the photo of him running through curiously shallow water (one of the studio backlot lakes), then I slowed down to gaze at his body, erotically wreathed with muscles, his togs so white and tight against his dark hairy legs. I always found myself gazing at the togs as if within them or behind them lay a key to understanding the moods and feelings which had plunged me deep into a trance. Blundering after understanding and elucidation I turned to the words — words which I knew almost off by heart like a prayer or a mantra.

JUST AS I began to read I glanced uncertainly at my brother, to work out where he was standing, what he was doing. I saw his lowered face cloud and momentarily sad as his finger ran up over his bruise, and I reached out and took his hand away, *'Doan do that Matthew,'* I whispered almost low and painfully, *'It don't help,'* and joined together in that point of tender misery I smiled at him. He looked away.

Now I began to read:

It took me some time to realise fully what was happening to me after that day a man tapped me on the shoulder as I was walking along a New York street.

'I am a photographer,' he said. 'How would you like a job as a model?'

The casual tap on the shoulder . . .

Only a short time passed before I was answering a long distance call from Hollywood.

How . . .

'*How,*' I took my eyes off the page, unleashed them from the mesh of the words which held me, every time trapped, entranced, '. . . How . . . you going to . . . ?'

I was breathless, I realised. Now I raised my face up, which I felt was burningly hot for some reason (I was excited by what I had read, or shamed by the disclosures I was making by choosing John Saxon as my favourite star), my mouth was dry and my lids forced back over my eyes which I felt were bulging (yet lazy at the same time, languorous) . . . how?

The great mystery of the world was being presented to me, and I in turn presented it back to my brother.

Without bothering to answer me, or as if answering me was not necessary, Matthew simply reached forward to the book, took it out of my inert fingers. In silent concentration, he ruffled through the pages. There was an eddy of silence. He looked down at the pages which I could not see. This powerlessness, and anticipation were so delicious to me that I wished for it to go on longer. He was so silent I seemed to hear, outside the door, an apple blossom detach itself from its stem and I heard its movement through air as it swayed and whirled down and landed with the softest bruise on impact, on an upright blade of grass: then behind me (for he was standing just slightly behind me, so he looked over my shoulder inducting the words at the same time I was) — as I turned slowly to look at him, and gazed right into his face — at that second I felt a strange discovery overtake me: *he had become John Saxon*. He had taken on all the dark firm beauty of the young man, and in that second I became, not delirious which was how in one way I felt, but actually powerfully sane, as if I was seeing my brother for the very first time.

Yet now John Saxon was leaning towards me, and coming so close that I fell into a state of nulled fascination. I could neither move nor speak, I was ashamed at my silence; I had taken on the mute, almost pitiful, stance of the adoring fan before a film star. I simply made a small gasp, as if my incomplete knowledge of the world was being punctured, as the real fleshly face of this small demi-god from Hollywood came closer (with real lips clearly visible). This glance passed over me, then, receding as swiftly as if I had been subject to a seizure, he returned to being my brother who now simply handed the book back to me open at a page, and tapped the image lightly.

'*I dreamt this up for you,*' he said.

Famous Inhabitants

SCREEN TOPNOTCHER YUL Brynner plays Herod, sultry King of Egypt in Cecil B. De Mille's spectacular THE TEN COMMANDMENTS . . .

I stared in silence at the picture.

I took in not only the out-of-focus backdrop of the Sphinx and the perfect Hollywood sky, but my eye became fastened, even shocked, by the sheer drama of the man who occupied the central vortex of the photo: the explosion of a beautiful man.

I glimpsed in that instant the body of Mr Pollen and his shadow up on the screen in the school hall (the body without a head), but here, in this photo, the man had not only a head but a savagely beautiful face. He was powerful and masculine. I looked silently at his hard midriff, his columnar forearms, the perfect circlet of his thick neck. I saw they were encircled with gold, studded with jewels, and given such a heightened curvaceous form that you became aware as much of his nakedness as you did of his costume.

His head was shaved — in itself strangely disturbing — and he was wearing a weird kind of crown, formed smooth like a hood of what even I could read, and felt, as if it was forming inside me, as the flange of a hard penis.

I gazed down at Yul Brynner, marvelling.

He looked so fierce, so proud. He was the epitome of all that was manly.

Yet I could see he was wearing a short skirt, what appeared to be a metal brassière, jewellery and make-up.

Suddenly, I understood everything. *Cleopatra* was the film of the hour, the pre-publicity was drenching our town like a tidal wave. And my brother, with his sensational sense of what was current, what would be on everybody's lips, had gone to the very heart of the matter. He had divined the invisible current which moved the insensate surface of all matter. And he had chosen for me a costume which was so clever as to be bewitching in its ambiguous choice. For though the costume was that of a man, as authenticated by the centre of all fantasy in our lives — Hollywood — it was so like a woman's as to reach out into a strange middle ground, one which did not exist in our daily lives, but only existed in such a magic place: a book. Or in Hollywood.

He was undercutting everybody. And he was doubling the outrageousness by offering to dress me as Cleopatra, or rather a sort of slim gilded ephebe; for clearly in this world of Egypt, or was it Hollywood? men dressed as lavishly as women. Yet the sheer fact this came from a book (and from our favourite book, with all its surreptitious pleasures) meant this choice was authenticated, even — like everything Maddy did— studiously worthy, esoteric and seemingly sanctioned by secret powers.

I knew I was looking at some quality Maddy possessed — it was diffuse and even faintly frightening, rare and foreign, something like individuality, or genius.

I stared down at the page silently, weighing up the danger. Yet some excitement, some sense of the imminence of escape, pouring and plashing through the veins in my body, coloured and heated charging through me as the knowledge overtook me: I could be wearing this costume, this dress, with make-up and jewels. I felt a strange lightness overcome me.

'O, Maddy,' I murmured.

I looked down at the picture losing focus. But as I did so a strange thing happened. Because on the facing page was a large closeup of Kim Novak. She was directing a smouldering glance over her shoulder, her pullover suggestively pulled down so her shoulder shone. Her lips were parted and her eyes glazed with come-hither. The odd thing was, as I gazed down intently, the photo of Kim slid across the page and hovered, in superimposition, over Yul the king.

I became lost in reverie, and it was as if Yul had opened up the hard vault of his chest and revealed inside it the hot invitations of a soft and yielding Kim, a vixen with sharpened fingernails behind whose gleaming eyes lay, in turn, a metal hardness, a double-edged ambiguity, both masculine and feminine webbed together, inseparable and never to be apart. Was this what everyone and everything was?

Something itself and yet within it something else again?

And then within that, something else again and again?

Was this the secret?

'*This?*' my dry mouth formed the word which yet would not come out. There was no force of air in my diaphragm. It was as if all the air of imagination had been taken up by what I was looking at (as if I was in the desert and a hundred thousand men in glittering chariots had raced through me, leaving me dazzled and exhausted).

'*This?*' I said again, so that my voice came out strangled and uneven, running up and down the register improbably.

'*This?*' I said a third time, and turned my eyes wonderingly towards my brother, to see if he was really insane or, in fact, by a reverse process rendered into a sanity so intense it mimicked the lunacy of the insane. I knew this was dangerous.

'*This?*'

He remained silent as the Sphinx printed on the page.

O, Keely, o, Carrot I moaned in my mind as I saw, even felt them grow fainter and fade away into total silence. Ponky, too, had become swiftly irrelevant. None of these people could deliver me to this state of rapture, this conceptualisation of the missing word.

Taking the book from me, Maddy held it behind him and took on the strangely deflective look of someone in whom all knowledge resided and who must impart it with due ceremony, and only at the right time.

He pursed his lips slightly and then said to me almost casually:

'Oh, yes. We shall have to take measurements.'

Disguise

I RETURNED TO Ponky's in a state of exhaustion. Aunty Gilda was sitting in the kitchen, reading the newspaper. This was so strange I glanced down at the page. It was the page in which court trials were written up. There was no sign of Ponk.

Aunty Gilda looked up from the newspaper surprised to see me.

In that instant I caught the last beam of a reflection on her face: it was a worried look, tense, which instantly disappeared before my presence and she assumed an almost unnatural sprightliness behind which she quickly hid whatever was worrying her.

'How's my Jamieboy, then? Been having a good time?' she asked as if that was the only time possible or allowable to be mentioned. Then she saw something in my own face, and because she was a sensitive woman who loved me in her own way, she simply said in a softer voice, 'Go and wash your hands, pet, we'll soon be having tea. Just us two together.'

I left her in the gathering darkness of the kitchen; the seasons were swiftly changing and what was, only a few weeks before, a room wreathed in autumnal sunlight was now only getting the reflected heat off a single plaster wall. As I trudged into Ponk's bedroom and threw myself down on my single bed — recognising in it the only home I had in the world — I heard the sound take up, slightly nervously and anxiously, like a tongue touching a hole in a tooth, again and again, repetitively: the sound of the ice-cream scoop Aunty Gilda used to place dollops of mashed potato on the plate.

AUNTY GILDA'S INVENTORY of my day had long since evaporated into silence. I had told her nothing about what happened in the hut (not out of dishonesty but because I could not comprehend what she would make of it, I wanted to protect the tender novelty of it, the fact the entire scenario was in its opening moments meant I wanted to shield the infinite possibilities, nurse all its futures in marvelling silence).

The only sound in the kitchen was the knock of our stainless-steel knives on the plates. We were having luncheon sausage, Watties tomato sauce, mashed potato and Birds Eye peas. That this was Ponk's favourite meal on earth only emphasised, in a melancholy way, her absence.

I noticed also, but only dimly and even thankfully, that Uncle Ambrose was not so much not home but not even mentioned, as if he was the furthest person from Aunty Gilda's thoughts. Yet looking into her face, as my eyes did simply by the dint of the fact of having to look at something — someone — I could see Aunty Gilda's face was scrawled over with lines, and she looked old. I looked at her underslung jaw with the faint jowls of incipient middle-age, the bulbous nose, the thin, usually overpainted lips.

Now her lips were unpainted and there was a naked kind of vulnerability in her glance.

Suddenly, as if seeing my eyes were spying on her, her own eyes turned to me and there were a thousand oscillations of thought, almost as if Aunty Gilda was seeing me anew. She assessed me, her eyes taking on a distant look. At the same time, as if she could not hold it back, a deep sigh ran through her body, and some sediment of melancholy, of worry settled as ballast in her light and effervescent spirit.

Her hand reached out across the table and I, half involuntarily, put my hand out and we held on to each other, in complete silence.

I felt through her body some ebbing vibration, some tidal pull which flowed into me and was made neutral, or stiller by my sheer elemental blankness about what might be upsetting her.

I simply squeezed her hand back, once twice and my mouth fell open; I was about to vow eternal allegiance to her, spread out before her the carpet or cloak of my eternal admiration. But the words did not come, perhaps did not need to come.

'Jamie,' she said to me, and giving my hand one reciprocal squeeze back, she withdrew hers and went on slowly eating. But her eyes returned to me. 'You've been enjoying it here, haven't you?'

'Yes,' I said not allowing the smallest pause to enter into the equation which might open up any amount of uncertain emotions and complexities. 'I miss my Mum,' I said to her then in a naked husky voice. I hung my head, embarrassed to be expressing this.

'Well, pet, she won't be away too much longer,' Aunty Gilda said. Then she added something which seemed to be a non-sequitur: 'Everything turns out alright in the end.'

And she let out another deep sigh, which, in effect, acted as a cancelling out of her last statement.

I looked at her, wondering what she meant. I myself felt tired, exhausted, as if I had begun a long journey and had only reached the very first post.

As I got up I glanced down at the page Aunty Gilda had been reading. I did not so much read as receive, almost without thinking, a collection of words which went . . . *receiving a stolen automobile . . . changed ownership papers* . . . words which meant nothing to me.

The pepper shaker obscured the rest.

Aunty Gilda had got up and gone over to the taps. For a while she simply let the tap run and stood there, looking out the window. I could not tell what she was looking at and the room was filled with the silvery music, melancholic and rustling. Then she seemed to wake up.

'Ponk's been over playing tennis at the Benskys' house,' she said.

There was a strange thin note of pride in her voice.

She rinsed her own plate. She cut the water off. I drifted over to her with my plate.

Then, as I got to her, I upended the plate, and held it before me like a mirror; I returned to childhood by licking off all the smeared remains of the tomato sauce, as Ponky always did.

Having rendered the plate back to an immaculate whiteness, I handed it over to her.

I sensed her hand might come over and rest for a second, ruffling the hair on the top of my head.

Just at that moment, the back door opened and Ponk lumbered in. She was in a good mood, she was whistling to herself the theme music from *Laramy*. But instantly, on seeing her mother and me standing so closely together, her whistle cut off and with an abrupt,

'Hi?' to us both, in one word making it clear that she did not differentiate between us and we were both criminals in stealing away what had once been her own exclusively, she walked into her room and momentously closed the door behind her and locked it.

She stayed in there till eight o'clock, making sure I missed our favourite serial, which had become the sole basis of our communication. She was sick of having me round. I knew it. And I did not blame her. When I asked her what had happened in this week's instalment she just looked at me and, after leaving a long pause in which I felt stupid and suddenly young to be even asking, she said blandly, 'I forget.'

KEELY ASKED ME at school, 'What you going as, Jamie?'
I looked at him and pretended not to hear. This was so strange for him that he stopped what he was doing — bouncing the ball back and forth into his hands, catching it then sending it spinning round and round on his fingertip — the ball fell down through the hole in his concentration and bounced away.

Instantly one of the bigger boys got hold of it and gave the ball such an energised kick that it leapt away in a giant spurt, revolving through the air even as I heard a low moan, of pain, almost grief, ticking away in the back of Keely's throat.

'Ooahhh?' he cried.

And as I looked at him I saw a flush of humiliation rise up over his features, rendering him no longer the most beautiful statue on earth, but rather something waxen, melting down, no longer having a strong centre but turning everywhere, all over the playground at once, appealing to everyone — anyone — even to someone as unimportant as myself.

I looked away.

'What you goin' as, Jamie?' he whispered to me. 'You gotta good idea?'

He left a brief pause in which I found my lips did not — would not — move. Now I had my own slightly miraculous secret. To speak in daylight would . . . endanger it. Secrets like this could only grow in darkness. Or behind curtains. In shade. Night was their secret hour, their appointment. Also, I knew Keely would be the first one to laugh at me. Then steal it. He would emerge on that most sacred of all nights, the night to which all our nerve-endings were feeling, possibly even dressed in my costume.

Anything was possible.

'O, Keely,' I moaned for it was horrible, in one way, to see him so nakedly before me, and realise he was almost, in most particulars, the same as me: just different in his own way, which up until then had been so enticing I had always been willing to lose myself, abandon myself gladly, as if I could climb into being him. But now the faint image of the costume, seeming to cast a residual glow, began to make him less attractive, less, curiously, as if he was there.

'Hey, Noddy,' he murmured to me, but low and sweet, like he was pouring something honeyed down inside my ear. 'You get the ball for me? Then you play with me. Just us two together. Eh, Nod? Then you tell me your secret.'

I continued looking at him for such an intense length of silence that he went a deeper red. He took refuge in pulling a Jerry Lewis face, crossing his eyes and making himself appear buck-toothed.

I was still seeing the costume, or rather the ghostly and luminous afterglow of the photo of Yul Brynner.

When it became apparent I was not answering, he looked at me again, more intensely. Almost not believing I could not be seduced by the flint of his charm, he walked off. He did this doing his locally famous imitation of Jerry Lewis being a paraplegic. His legs splayed out, arms jerking like a spastic windmill, mumbling and gibbering. Normally this would garner for him attention and applause. He was used to being loved, Keely; he had become an addict to it. So much so he did not notice when it was withdrawn. And at this point, to further deepen his humiliation, Fainell, who happened to be loitering down the far end of the football field, saw the ball coming towards him. Nonchalantly, he paused. He saw Keely advancing towards him. He watched Keely's display unmoved. He walked right round the ball, so he faced towards the tip.

Keely now abandoned his Jerry Lewis imitation and began running straight towards Fainell, calling out, *'Hey don't, don't, don't.'*

Just when Keely got within several yards of him, Fainell raised his leg back and with one enormous kick (a kick saved up through all the hours of his humiliations, a kick which emerged through one of his dreams), he sent the ball arching high and twirling through the air.

For one moment everyone in the playground halted, realising some fundamental change was occurring, its shadow fleeting over us, darkling and deeping our knowledge of how things were (how the anarchy was patterned within us) until the ball began to sink, sink ever deeper until we saw it become lost in the overgrown trees which masked the creek.

Nobody said a word.

THAT NIGHT AT running Uncle Ambrose did not appear.

When I got home, he barely noticed me. The fact it was Wednesday had totally escaped his memory. I was not sorry. In fact, I was tiptoeing past him, as he stood, looking out the front window, slightly concealed by the curtain when he turned sharply, saw me and asked in a subdued, almost human, voice, 'How are you, Jamieboy?'

Should I hesitate, should I answer? Should I simply go to him and bury my face in his flank, or chest, as I would have done with my mother when I sensed she was sad, or uncertain? This nudge always said: *Remember, you have me.* Instead, something made me pause, some uncertainty about what might follow (he might try to kiss me, for example, something I didn't particularly enjoy, though in another way I only minded it in the way I disliked a plate of khaki silverbeet on my plate in wintertime). It was all relative.

So this evening we stood apart from each other, just looking almost shyly at one another. I sensed he wanted me to walk towards him but instead I found myself saying, 'I'm back from running, Uncle Ambrose.'

At this a wavering flush ran up over his face. I caught, I thought, the glitter of a tear in his eye. Was it humiliation? That he had never come to give me a ride home in the scarlet Jaguar? Did he recognise this? Or some other adult emotion I could not readily name? I understood that adults had emotions which were different to those of children, or at least ones which were more difficult to read. I also understood, from my mother, it was a form of impoliteness to look too deep.

'How-how'd you run?' he asked in a curiously lowered voice. He glanced towards the bedroom where I knew Aunty Gilda was. 'You . . . win?' he asked me in a voice with no liquidity in it.

At that moment a car passed down the road. He turned quickly and looked out. He jumped back behind the curtain. Catching me looking at him, just the very last of my glance which instantly faded away as I sought to deflect his glance, he smiled at me, a little ruefully, a little embarrassed, and placed his finger to his lips.

'It's a game,' he whispered to me. 'We're in hiding,' he said. And with this he leant across and turned away the shade of the lamp which lit the wall behind him.

I liked this game. I lingered there for one second longer. He looked at me in silence and both of us listened to the car pause outside the house. This went on for a long time. He smiled at me. I smiled back. Then I became bored. I walked quietly across the carpet and reached up and kissed Uncle Ambrose on his brow. I always chose a particular, safe spot, between his wiry eyebrows. He lowered his head towards me, and as I drew away I heard a faint sound come out of him, out of his entire body, it was like a sigh, not so dissimilar to the one Aunty Gilda had issued. I diagnosed, almost subliminally, he was in some form of pain, not physical, but I knew enough now that adults (humans) may feel a psychological pain as acutely as anything physical. His arms came round to gather me into him; this was what I feared, I did not want that, so like a silvern shadow I slipped out of his clasp saying, 'I awfully tired, Uncle Ambrose,' and he said nothing to me, just nodded and I knew his eyes were following me as I tranced off, with the lethargy of a growing boy to find rest in my bed.

Flame

I WATCHED MADDY take the slim stem and stamen out of the matchbox. He was anxious and angry as if he could not wait for the starting up of the magic. He was hungry and starved for it, and I shrank inside myself thinking: it may not go well.

IT NEVER GOES well when he is like this.

But now he holds in the cup of his broad spatulate hand the flame which, dancing and slim, outlines all his flesh with warm scarlet: and by magic I see the frail bones within his flesh, the web and barb of them, a flail of ligature holding together and supporting the worn cushions of his meat. The lines, too, on the sandhills of his hands enchant me momentarily.

I hold my breath because I know he holds in his hand my death. The flame.

We have been forbidden to play round with matches in the hut, told to use them sparingly and always to a purpose.

He is priest-like as he turns, flame webbing in his hand.

He bends down before me and opens up the heart of the small black heater.

He holds the match, nudging it against the wick.

'Turn the wick up higher,' he barely says to me. Knowing that words, and language, can be sparingly parsed between us, since at all times there is always a moving sentence, a golden link, a chain, a silken web, an invisible line moving between us.

'Not too much,' he says to me then harshly, so, feeling the brand of his contempt hot on my flesh, I moan.

'It isn't too much.'

And at this point a swift crease of gasoline, raw and indolent, fills the air: we breathe it in intently and the small flames eddy round the darkened quiff of wick, and dancingly, in an absurd little procession, the flames leap round in a circle, and upwards and outwards flower.

Black fumes and flames stream upwards.

Across the sloping hut roof beautiful moths' wings quiver, grow, take their shape.

Veins.

Maddy's grey eyes stare into mine as his lips form an enigmatic smile.

I know he is asking me: shall we burn ourselves to death? Shall we make a suttee fire for ourselves like the maharajah's wife in *Around the World in 80 Days?*

Further than this, he is asking me: will I burn along with him in the flames?

Leisurely, he kicks the door shut.

Now the room takes on a warm fetid darkness. The strange shadows from the heater re-form our faces: bring them into a startling closeness.

'Maddeeeeeeey,' I moan and let out a punctured, stifled cry. 'You trying to kill me,' I say softly. 'Not before the school ball. Please.'

He laughs then, for I know he has been showing me again the magic of the magnifying glass: it both causes pain and creates beauty even as it explains and elucidates all mystery. Or rather the mysteriousness of all living and inanimate things are invested with their right and proper spirit.

He laughs. Powerful and possessive. And more than a little mad.

'No,' he says to me then. 'Not today. Not at this moment. But at some moment. In the future. You will not escape.'

A frill, a thrill of fear pierces through me. It opens in my veins, and flowers through each pore in my body.

'Like Horton?' I breathe.

'No, no,' he says laughingly then. 'Not like Horton at all.'

'How then?' I ask.

Tell me.
Tell me.
Tell me.

'TURN AROUND,' HE says.

'Why?' I say to him whining. 'Why? I doan wanna turn around.'

'You have to undress.'

'Why?'

'Because it is the costume. I have certain parts of it ready.'

I am silent. He has stood up from the heater.

Our eyes are level. I search in his eyes for the missing letters, the missing word.

'Where?' I say glancing round the hut.

'I have hidden it. It is a surprise,' he says then urgently so that I understand and partake of the miracle, 'You can't see it all just yet.'

No, think I, I must earn it and suffer for it.

'You want me to turn around?' I ask.

'Yes,' he says. *'I have hidden it so I may produce it like a magic act and you must understand there are proper forms and rituals to which you are an essential part but you must learn to play your part. You are clumsy and know nothing: you must first of all begin to understand that. You must leave everything outside this door when you enter here. You must swear eternal allegiance.'*

So this afternoon, this play pretend night in which we wrap round ourselves the solemn and rich garments of the crisply smelling soil of night the dark, this pretend afternoon I must undress totally and stand there before him as if I have just been born, for I am being brought into birth under his fingertips, and first of all I must learn to stand naked and vulnerable in front of him, so that I understand my own poverty, and also, my own richnesses. He will investigate them for me so I understand the meaning and uses that these can be put to, then he will invest me with dress.

He will create for me the first real garments I have ever worn. The first and freshest ones since I struggled out of my afterbirth. For he makes me understand now, in the sharp uplift of breath as it races up my windpipe, and as the pupils blossom in my eyes, he is dressing me as I was always meant to be dressed, he is making nascent what is always implicit; this is his magic touch, his ability to read and translate and spell out, even blindly, even dumbly, with fingers that have been blunted by being rounded into fists with which he must defend himself. He is bringing out from my body a layering of wings and a unicorn horn, of all magic things he is singing as he brings them to birth through my flesh.

'You mustn't hurt me,' I moan. 'You promise.'

'Turn your back. Close your eyes. You must stand still. You must . . .' and here his voice is so still I have to strain to hear it, '. . . you must hold still and not move, and . . .' here his voice again finds its perfect form, its flower, '. . . trust me. You must trust me.'

In all my wirrrld of warm darkness I stand there.

The flame from the heater is no more naked than I.

It peoples the dark with warmth. Through my lids.

'Don't peep. You must not move. If you do so, you will spoil it.'

He is savage to me with his word. His sword. Just think by adding a single hissing syllable what a difference you slice.

'I will tie you up if I need to.'

Tears burn in my eyes.

'But I'm not,' I wail. 'I'm not even moving,' I say.

And the dark takes wings which are scarlet, the softest pinkiest red so bled I am inside the silent heart of the world.

I feel his breathing inside my own chest, its hollow barrel, but I realise it is my own breathing, falling in perfect symmetry with his.

'Hurry', I say. 'I'm getting giddy.'

'Lean forward,' he says then sternly. He is almost frighteningly close behind me. I feel the soft featherings of his breath on my back.

Cold speckles of saliva spray prickle tickle.

'You won't hurt me,' I say then. 'It's not a trick is it? You won't tie me up and then leave me here. Will you?'

He doesn't even answer me. Instead, he takes my hands and places them against the top bunk.

'Lean against that,' he says sternly yet simply. 'For your balance.'

'It won't take long, will it?' I moan. 'Ponky's waiting for me,' I lie then. 'Ponky and Aunty Gilda. They're gunna take me into town. To the five o'clocks. We're gunna see *How the West was Won*. Cinerama. Curved screen. The latest. So don't take long. Promise.'

Behind me I hear the key turn inside the lock.

As if the key within me is turning.

I feel his breath on my calves, warm. The hairs on my legs prick out.

'What you doing?'

'Relax. You've got to relax. It only works this way.'

I am almost whimpering now, with pleasure. 'Please, Maddy,' I say. 'Please. Maddy.' I no longer know what I am saying please for, or about.

About my calf muscles he binds silver wings, made of oven foil. He tightens them, the string.

'Too tight?'

'Yes,' I murmur peacefully. 'Too tight.'

He loosens them a little.

'Not too loose,' I say then out loud so our voices startle us.

'*Phhssst!*' he hisses to me and we both hold still.

Outside it is a leaf falling. Coming to its natural rest.

That is all.

'You're not allowed to look,' he says to me again.

'No, I say.'

Now across my shoulders and then round my waist, brushing against my nipples so chill I let out an involuntary cry.

'Shut up, you stupid fool,' he says to me then, like in a spy movie.

'I'm sorry,' I murmur. 'It's just that it's cold. What is it?'

'You'll see soon enough,' he lances into me solidly.

'Hurry,' I murmur now to Matthew. 'Please hurry I don't think I can wait any longer. Please hurry now.'

'O!'

But he must take his ease with me.

Now round my thighs and belly, round past my behind my buttocks, round by my stamen my thing my cock a soft warm tactile darkness brushes against them all.

The air has turned velvet.

I feel — still without seeing — that the air round me is being restricted. It rushes up, seeking an entrance to my centre, he tightens whatever it is round my hips, firmly, so I am suddenly thrust forward, losing my grip. He laughs then, with a full round ball of pleasure.

'Wake up,' he says then. 'Wake up. Cleopatra. Queen of the Nile.'

And I unseal my eyes, take off my bandages. My flesh fresh stings as the adhesive is peeled off.

The sight of the hut, its wallpapered walls, the books on the shelves, the pictures from PanAm calendars pinned up, the drawings of my fashionplates in chalk — it is as if suddenly I can see, removed and separated from me, all the images of my childhood around me — yet I am losing them all at precisely the same time; I am giddy and the room sways sideways.

He catches me and holds me upright.

Still.

I see in his eyes the fire of love, of pride, which has freshly, fleshly this moment created me.

'Here,' he says to me then. 'I will get you a mirror.'

And as he turns away, I realise he is in his own trance as equal to mine, that in some senses he can only come alive to the extent that he creates me and that in a strange tangential yet utter way neither of us may be complete without the other. He says to me:

'It isn't finished yet,' he murmurs proudly.

'But I still haven't said I'll wear it,' I warn him. 'This is only a try out,' I say to him, or is it to me? 'This is only pretend. *Isn't it?*'

Dark

IT WAS DARK the following afternoon, threatening rain. I was inside at Ponk's, playing with her cut-outs then growing so sick of them I packed them away, not realising this was the last time I would ever play with them. I had made myself a cup of coffee, feeling quite adult. Now the cup lay empty on the bench. I watched first one, then two, then four ants emerge and begin to make their way towards the cup. I killed one, almost abstractly, raising my forefinger up to my nose so I could smell it. It smelt of rain. I licked my finger clean, eating it. I thought about what it tasted like.

I wandered away, off through the shadowy interior, back into Ponk's room. I turned the radio on. I turned the radio off. I turned the radio on. I turned the radio off.

I listened. Eyes closed.

There was the faint ruminating echo, the tug and whistle down the trolley bus wires.

A window somewhere closed.

In the near distance I could hear the over-animated women's voices of an afternoon radio serial:

'Well, if that's the way you feel, Olwyn, it's goodbye forever.'

As I strained my ears to listen, another woman's voice replied:

'No, don't say goodbye, I beg of you, Alicia. Just because Gordon . . .'

A newer sound emerged. More close at hand. It was a car drawing up. I opened my eyes. Ponk's bedroom in all its hyper-detail rushed at me. The pink organdie curtains. The little bowers of flowers in the wallpaper pattern. I felt briefly yet intensely homesick.

I looked out through the curtains.

It was Mr Webb, the local policeman. I recognised him. I watched him lock his car door and his eyes scan the front of the house.

I ducked down below the windowledge.

Mr Webb's footsteps (so grave and measured, so like, I think, the sound the feet of an executioner might have made) moved over the gravel footpath then hit, with a smoother percussion, no less dramatic because they were coming nearer, the concrete path which led to the front door.

I crawled on my hands and knees, fast as a spider, out into the hall then, behind one of the moquette chairs in the living-room, the room furthest away from the front door.

I hunched myself up, wrapping my arms round my legs.

There was first one, then four knocks upon the glass pane of the front door.

I had begun shaking, as much through suppressed excitement as fear.

The pause between the first knocks and whatever might come next was so extended as to be almost a trial — a form of test — about who might make the first sound. I sensed he was listening deeply. It was not beyond Mr Webb's powers to have a form of x-ray vision which would diagnose, not so much my physical presence, as pick up the oscillating vibrations of my guilt: at not answering the door.

His next knock was abrupt, thundering into the interior with so much violence that I jumped. I leant my face which was hot, moist, against the coarse moquette. I saw my own face in the chrome arm of the chairs. I saw a boy's face, white, freckles drawn in a loose map all over it. *Africa*. I looked guilty. The metal frosted over with steam from my breath.

There was an unendurable silence.

Though I had no idea why he was there, I wanted to jump up and scream out, 'Yes, yes, it was me who did it!'

The next sounds were disassociated. He must have been out at his car, without having made any transition from the back door.

The car door slammed.

He drove off.

I got out and, continuing the charade, which by this time had become enjoyable, I crawled on my hands and knees and crept under the bed in which I slept at night, happily breathing in the dust and falling instantly into a sweet deep sleep.

FIRST OF ALL there was the sound of a key nudging round the interior of the kitchen door lock. It knocked so bluntly, so inaccurately at first, on awakening, I was convinced someone was breaking into the house. I thought Horton was out again, but some rational voice in my head told me that Horton did not require keys: he ate through the wood, or simply flowed through the gap under the door, or emerged inside the lightbulb hanging over your head.

Footsteps in the kitchen. I recognised the sound of the footfall. I rolled out from under the bed, and rubbed my eyes, I stood up. Stretched.

I was covered in dust.

I sneezed.

Uncle Ambrose came into the hall, quietly.

'It's you Uncle Ambrose!' I cried out, smiling.

He was swinging his key in his hand, looking at me pensively.

'You're all covered in dust,' he said to me. 'What you been up to, Jamieboy? Playing games?'

I shrugged.

I wasn't sure what to tell him about Mr Webb's visit. Perhaps it had all been a mistake. A wrong number. It would slip out easier to Aunty Gilda. Uncle Ambrose, as if sensing such a thought passing through my mind, came over towards me. He reached a hand out and his fingers ruffled through my hair.

'What say we clean you up? What say we have a bath, eh? Nice and fresh,' he said to me as he disappeared into his room, to hang up his suit jacket.

I waited there uncertain about what to do.

A bath in the middle of the afternoon seemed a strange, an unusual rite. But I was covered in dust from under the bed. And who knew, really, what strange customs were followed at Aunty Gilda and Uncle Ambrose's house. It was a bit like having the cutlery on the table without a tablecloth. You could never be certain how other people lived. *'You must do what you are told.'* I heard the faint, the last shadow of my mother's voice lingering on the air. *'I know I can trust you to be a good boy, Jamie.'*

Uncle Ambrose went in and turned on the bath.

A good boy.

'How about a bubblebath, Jamieboy,' he called to me, exultantly, 'I think you'll like that.'

THE WATER, THE hot water, flooded out with such force the bathsuds foamed up instantly, crackling in the still air, joining effervescent bubble to bubble until soon the entire bath was afroth with the perfect whiteness of a film-star bath.

I stared down at it mesmerised: it had the pure whiteness of Jayne Mansfield's hair and teeth: it even had the unreal emphasis of her exaggerated bust. I knew she had a heart-shaped swimming pool, which seemed to me the epitome of chic — the unreason of chic, the unattainability.

Uncle Ambrose had, as befitted someone who was rich, scattered a liberal amount of bathsuds into the bath.

He did not so much ask me to undress as offer the opportunity to me.

I had no compunction in unwrapping myself.

I wished to wear the film-star's ermine.

For this was what I saw it was: I saw in my mind's eye the soft sling of a white fox fur which luxuriantly, like a living animal, curved round her body, suffocating the white-white flesh of her neck. I could feel and hear the stamens of fur moving in the light: I longed like an animal to re-enter that fur covert and feel the fur brushing against my face. I saw the film-star's stole had slipped off and lain there, down below, awaiting that moment when my slim and eager nakedness would sink below it, through it and then emerge under it, wearing it, at which point I, too, would be ready.

'Ready?'

There was something drugged and still in the atmosphere of the bathroom. Almost subterraneously I heard him go to the door and the slight echo of a key knocking round as it carefully turned in the lock — for one moment like a fish moving downstream I attempted to reverse myself, but the irreversible motion of the water surrounding me, pleasurable soft silent moving, nudged me further on.

Now everything became very slow.

I felt in that instant, as my clothes fell away from me, the eternity of two patterns floating in towards being one pattern, which was readable: the sound in the universe had dropped away and I was intent, alert in a way I had never been before, and every hair on my body was flowing with energy and my eyes became holes into which flowed and curved the entire world: now I understood.

But understood what? This was what I was about to find out. I knew this. I was now, I understood, for the first time, alive. I felt a delicious will-lessness, which at the same time was protective; just as, the instant after a sting, or a cut or a burn, there is a momentary numbness before the great pain exacerbates the system. In my blankness, I witnessed everything in the bathroom: the taps; the doorhandle; and above all the small window; I saw the small dots of rust on the chrome tapheads, I saw the faded brushstrokes left by a paintbrush on the plaster wall and finally I saw the whirls in which the world outside was reproduced in the bathroom glass.

I worked out, as a passage of survival: if I could become like that glass and held there I would survive. It was simple. It was so simple. That simple.

'The water will be warm enough in a tick. We don't want to hurt you,' he said and reached in and felt.

'It mustn't be too hot, or too cold.'

He spoke to me tenderly.

I did not know whether I was nodding or not. I was trying to assume the naturalness of the moment as I continued to work out, experiment with what exactly this moment actually was. So standing there naked I felt preternaturally aware, over-aware, as one prepared for some great mystery.

I was about to step in. I was arched, my leg poised. I was about to leave the safety of land and step into the strange world of heated water, of glittering, faintly evanescent bathbubbles.

'What's going on in there?'

The sound of knuckles rapped sharply against the bathroom door.

The lurch of returning to my body was so severe it was as if two worlds were colliding.

I was momentarily deafened.

My return into my body was violent and rough.

I felt winded by the impact.

I seemed to possess no power, I had lost the power of locomotion, and I could only turn my head slowly sideways and, the door unlocked, saw a stranger standing there: Aunty Gilda. Everything became rushed and awkward and jagged.

'Put your clothes back on, Jamie,' Aunty Gilda said to me in a voice which was strangely terse. I saw her eyes playing fleetingly about my body.

Slowly, with the real exhaustion of one who had made an immense journey, yet not reached any destination, I began to dress again. I felt drowsy, yet deeply mystified, for Aunty Gilda, with anxiety in her face, her voice like a whip, had forced Uncle Ambrose into their bedroom. The door had been slammed shut, and in there I heard subdued but raised voices.

I waited, uncertain about what to do. Then I grew bored, and slipped out the door. I went down the road. I went to the top of the steps which ran down to the beach. A faint smell off the sea, warm and almost fresh, told me the tide was coming in.

I felt a strange lethargy.

I stood there and breathed in the sea.

With my eyes closed I began to walk down the steps.

Vacant

SILENCE AS WE sit there threading the crêpe streamers together.

Miss Jaye, our art teacher, has taken the scissors and, raising them high to show us how they may cut, she then applies the sharpened edge to the soft dull tissue of crêpe paper.

'This is how I want you to do it,' she says. 'Neatly, orderly and carefully.'

We are sitting in the empty hall. Round us is crowded the enormity of the coming event, the possibilities, the mutations, the costumes, the secrets (of which I own just one).

We are sitting inside the pattern of a window, replicated in sun on the dusty floor. Form One Accelerate sit on chairs and manufacture, as a special favour, a badge of our intelligence, streamers. Out of boxes they come, from out the end of our fingertips.

In each of our mind's eye are the shrunken remains of old streamers, still attached to their rusted drawing pins, too high up to be taken down. So they mourn past gatherings, accreting dust and forgotten laughter.

What we are webbing will be new. The world always begins with us.

Even its mistakes.

'This is how I want it to go,' and dexterously Miss Jaye takes several cut and slashed ribbons of coloured tissue paper and she interweaves them. She does this once, fast, so we are amazed at the cascade of Chinese lanterns that fall from out of the end of her fingertips. Then she, smiling serenely now as she floats over our heads, in her own celestial balloon, does it slowly, showing us each stopping point in her intricate manoeuvres.

'Here, this way, then this,' she lowers her head knowing for once we are following her. Now we tumble down sense and knowledge, following the dance of her fingertips. A smile plays upon her lips.

'So and so and so,' she murmurs low.

Miss Jaye lifts up and announces in a soft tone she must now vacate the hall, but has the highest expectations.

'What is the plural of ox?' she fires out.

'Ravens,' answers Stumpy darkly.

Miss Jaye sails away.

We are left alone again re-forming inside ourselves our forever fixed manoeuvres inside the transit camp.

My chair is slightly further away from the others, just cutting into shadow. Zeena and Angel sit together, boldly in the middle, proud and unspeaking. They do not deign to bless us with their words which, however, shuttle like termites, unseen, through the woody corridors of our minds.

Stumpy sits on her own, threading a thin excuse of a streamer. Her mind is not on the job (she is dreaming of how she will come in a monk's uniform — her father's old dressing gown — not as a nun, but a monk. She is sitting there dreaming as she hears her own vespers echo through tunnels and snake through the catacombs as she carries along the essence of her own spirit, a small and sturdy flame that no storm shall quench, no draft of chill air).

But glancing up swiftly, her eyes fall on me.

She blushes, and partly scowls, as if I have crept right into her warm thought tunnel and made myself at home.

'What you going as?' she asks me quietly so no one else can hear.

My fingers interweave pale mauve, radiant ink blue and a soft carnation pink. My head on one side.

'Don't know,' I blandly say. 'I forget.'

Carrot sits there his legs splay wide apart, randomly snipping with the scissors pieces of crêpe paper. It is important he illustrate how useless this is. Like tears they fall. Zeena and Angel stir from their underwater depths and gaze at him.

'Wha?' says Zeena.

'He makes rubbish,' says Angel. 'He's nothing. A no account. What you coming as, Carrot?' she asks drily. 'A ghost?'

'No,' Carrot says simply, so caught out he forgets even to lie, 'Keely's coming as a ghost.'

Serenely they ignore and look through me and don't see me. A translucent or is it vacant window?

For long, drawn out seconds, we lose ourselves and each other, and each of us becomes a pattern of coloured crêpe paper interwoven in all its complexities to form a slight bridge. We can hear the soft winnowings of our own heartbeats. And this is the miracle, without us thinking of it or trying for it, our hearts all start to beat in a rhythm which our fingers duplicate so that around us and out of us stream the paper ribbons, inch upon foot upon yard upon chain upon mile, each one appearing another inch with the unified beat of our silent heart.

How pretty we look from a distance.

How lost.

'OH, JAMIE!'

It is Aunty Gilda catching hold of me in the corridor. It is afternoon, after school and I am sliding out the door, on my way to the hut. I glance now at the door.

Shut.

'Now listen, Jamie . . .'

I am caught, 'Yes,' I say, she hesitates a little. I see, up by her eye, under the powder, a small vein throbbing. Almost like a snake uncoils.

Her eyes search my face . . . for what? I don't know.

'I want you to make me a promise.'

Yes Aunty Gilda my heart throbs. Yes. I will make any promise.

She opens her mouth then and out comes a fiery flower, which opens in front of me and I stare into its heart.

'We won't tell on you . . .' (About what, I think, staring up at her, then assuming, on an instant, yes, there is so much not to tell about me, how I don't set the table right, cut the hedge straight.) *'. . . If you don't tell on us. We won't tell on you. If you don't tell on us.'*

I think about this seriously, in the dark of their hall. I realise the house is listening. The world stopped. And I am in the heart of her flower. It has grown to cover the entire world. Wall to wall. And everyone is listening. My parents' movement in a distant street halts. Aunty Gilda's face, high above me, my sky, is contorted, she too is strangled for breath.

Waiting.

But I am only trying to work out what this means.

What this means.

We won't tell on you, if you don't tell on us.

I blink.

'I want to know who did it!'

I hear Mr Pollen's voice, insistent.

'You only have to tell the truth.'

His eyes bore down the desks. I feel myself grow hot, then small.

'I want to know who is so stupid as to put an eel in the class aquarium.'

Everyone is still. They know it is me. Of course it is me. It is I who did it. But nobody will say I did.

I will have to speak.

I.

That slim thin letter.

It was me who did it.

Me.

But it was Carrot who trapped the eel.

'Look what we've caught,' he kept yelling. He slid it into Keely's hands, *'Hold it, feel it, it wants to feel you.'*

That moment under the trees.

Keely starts to murmur to me, *'Take it, Noddy, take it take it.'*

And I fall into his eyepond. So softly worn.

But it is cold. Freezing cold. Underneath.

This is their trick.

To pay me back for winning the bank competition.

They have lured me down to, down to the creek and there they have given me my prize.

For you, Noddy. You.

KeelynCarrot run off laughing.

The eel is alive inside my hands.

I can tell it is dying. Its small snagged teeth, greypus eyes on the back of its head staring at me, saying to me *you hold me in your hands, but I control you.* It slithers in my fingers, all oily and snot-slick — sends flicks and flashes of power through me as its boned back hooks round to snare me, gash me, rip me open so it can throw me down on the asphalt, gush down my throat, rush inside me, eat its way through me, chewing into my innards and then growing into a million swarming maggots.

Inside me, eating.

I get up to the class. Nature Study. I see the aquarium. *Water.* Its natural element. It shall live. I walk towards the glass box, slide it in. I run off to find, to find CarrotnKeely who are naturally nowhere. The trees laugh in my face, slap me with silence.

And when I come back into the class, the aquarium is empty. The class's goldfish lie upon the floor. Mouths open. Dying. And inside the aquarium is the eel, its monstrous jaws open, its eye staring at me in accusation.

'Jamie!'

Aunty Gilda pulls me back and I look up at her, swallowing hard.

'I never meant . . .' I said to her huskily, hanging my head. 'I didn't mean . . .' She gazes at me waiting. I hear the second hand on her watch jump and uncatch its latch as it hurries along. Now time is scurrying, racing along, carrying me with it, bewildered.

'Do you say yes?' she asks me, as always, fair and square, only trying to find out.

I am not sure what I have done.

What *cannot* be told.

I feel my head not so much nod as sway slowly from side to side.

'*Good*,' she says. 'Good boy.'

And the moment rushes on.

I am caught in its storm.

The door slams shut.

She is gone.

I RUN ALL the way up to the hut. Maddy turns to me when I get there and nods.

'Sorry I'm late, Maddy.'

'Sit down,' he says, nodding to the small stool which is exiled from our kitchen.

I sit. I am out of breath.

'I got the rest,' he says to me casually. *'Everything.'*

'O,' I answer him as casually. It is important that nothing, not the weatherboards of the houses nor the tape on the powerlines nor the lichen on the lamp-posts nor the tar which blooms in tongues hear what we are saying. We both understand that what we are passing between ourselves effectively re-orders the layerings of ordered meanings in the world: and for this to be made public is to threaten the waves with turning backwards and the sun, which has sailed into a cloud, with reversing itself and moving in a contrary, novel and yet perhaps more pleasurable direction.

But it is only pretend. We see.

This day he reveals his miracle: a tube of lipstick.

Our mother's lipstick.

Now he unfurls the scarlet.

I gasp at the sheer temerity of his invention.

'It is . . . make-up,' I murmur. My eyes move down and possess the propelling shape of the tube of lipstick.

'It's Mum's,' I say mutinously. I turn my eyes to his and a shade of flush falls down, slips down the bones of his cheek.

'I sneaked it from inside.'

'We not allowed back inside the house,' I say sternly. 'We promised.'

He shrugs then.

'It's not important.'

We stare at each other wondering what new mutiny is opening up.

'I'm not allowed to wear . . . ,' and I leave a small pause here, a genuflection to the enormity of the gap which lies between realisation and actuality: promise and performance, 'I'm not allowed to wear . . . *make-up.'*

I whisper this low in case the weatherboards part and eat whole this secret.

'O,' Matthew says and here I hear the bored urbane tone of voice he uses to diminish Ponky and me with one of his Quiz Kid utterances ('O, but in Paris they drink wine with every meal. Or in Utah they drive on a different side of the road.')

'O,' he saunters his word path towards me, laying it down sedately so I can taste and experience every milli-quarter inch of it; how much further he has travelled than me, how far ahead.

'O, but the kings of Egypt always wore make-up.'

In one swift flash so powerful it is both like a hallucination and also a flash of multicoloured lightning (in which the colours green and purple feature vividly), an entire landscape opens up before my gaze. From side to side of it is the photo of Yul Brynner as the king of Egypt as seen in our Hollywood Album. This is overlaid by more current photos of Elizabeth Taylor, enchantress and seductress, taker of husbands and Queen of the Nile.

These images are imprinted on my brain so intently and intensely I realise, in the aftermath (again as if one were recovering from an illness, the first instant you realise you are getting well) it will be perfectly alright to challenge all the rules of the everyday world we live in and by. If Yul and Liz can do it, I have a precedent which is so enormously powerful as to be ungainsayable.

I sense a nascence of power so immense I know I will do and risk almost anything to appear before CarrotnKeely and Stumpy and all the others brazenly wearing make-up: for the simple fact is (a detail my brother has subtly introduced to me) it isn't me myself wearing the make-up, it is actually Yul Brynner's face, beneath which is my own, and I am only, as it were, wearing Yul's face as a mask to cover my own unformed and naked features.

But I know at the same time, I will be wearing eye make-up of a completely exaggerated sort, my lips will be thick with women's lipstick, I will be wearing a small dress, I will for all intents and purposes be as much a queen as a king.

This is in almost flagrant disregard of the rules of our universe: the laws of the power poles and the grid of the lines which run between them, of the tar which bleeds in the squares of concrete on the roads. This of itself, by a perverse logic which feels for the first time utterly true, persuades me that what my brother and I are doing (or rather I am doing at my brother's behest) is absolutely and completely right.

'We'll have to have a trial run,' I say intently, with the small hard voice of a peasant hugging his single gold coin, already having made up his mind to make a purchase. 'I doan wanna look no fool,' I say lightly.

'O no,' says Matthew airily then. 'You certainly won't look a fool. That is the last thing you will look.'

I stare back at him, dumbfounded by the sheer enormity of his gift.

We look at each other in the resonance of shock which follows the seemingly simultaneous understanding of this single fact: for if I am not a fool, does it not instantly make everyone around me into precisely that?

Smiles trapeze from our lips.

We begin laughing then until all the hurt from the world empties out.

'You know Uncle Ambrose,' I say to Maddy.

Maddy's face is so close to mine and I glance at his face. It is intent. Trance-like as the eyebrow pencil traces its tribal hieroglyphics across my face. He pauses and pulls the pencil away.

'. . . Maddy?'

He does not answer.

I smell his breath and how comfortably I am inside its zone: faint tang of aniseed, and that other warm, living breath, as if flowers and plants could grow and effloresce in his presence.

His seriousness, his distance though, make me aware I am part of a ritual. He is withdrawn from me, a small scimitar of concern embedded in his brow, he is drawing the curved marvel of a line.

He pauses and glances, quickly, like the dip of a beak of a kingfisher into the pool of the paper on which I see the brazen beauty of Yul. Another one of Liz.

Again the eyebrow pencil takes up. Its weight leans into me, like an older brother.

'Doan move,' he says, serious as a jeweller cracking a diamond. *'You know.'*

'Yes, I know Uncle Ambrose,' he says heavily.

I see Maddy's lips are formed in a strange shape as he concentrates.

'I doan like him,' I say simply. as if the words coming out of my mouth are formed, invent their own discovery.

He looks at me seriously.

As if at a new idea. Or one which needs be looked at from different angles.

Or is it simply my painted-on eyebrow he is looking at?

'Why?' he says in a flat voice.

'Why.' I say. Thinking.

'Why not?' Maddy says.

Why not, I think. I look at Maddy. I am robbed into silence. It rises up and coats me.

'I don't know,' I murmur. 'Why. I just. Do. Don't. Like. Him.'

He says nothing.

'They'll be back soon,' he says then.

I sigh. 'I doan think they ever come back. They sick of us, Maddy. We two orphans, eh? Maybe we'll run away together.'

'Where to?' Maddy answers in a level, unconvinced voice. 'We tried that once. It didn't work.'

The truth of this is so heavy it returns me to silence.

'Uncle Ambrose,' I say, Maddy's face moves in front of my own, like my eyes are planes and below me is his landscape. 'Uncle Ambrose,' I say again.

But there is a long silence.

You like me, Matthew, don't you? I am your Jamie, aren't I? Tell me you love me. I like to hear it. Please.

But this is all said by silence.

'Maddy,' I say, 'I just want to tell you something important.'

Maddy looks at me now, for one shaved splinter of a second. 'What?'

'The Jaguar has disappeared.'

He was silent a long pause, considering. Eyebrow pencil poised. 'Has it been stolen?'

'No.'

'What does Aunty Gilda say?'

I shrugged, not trusting words but trusting that my brother's glance would pierce through my skin and drag out the words I would need.

His eyes stayed on me, pensive. Then his fingers, as if his fingers had their own tempo, their own demand, and must keep working to soothe some savage pain in his own heart (his own hurt), his fingers went back to tracing the eyebrow carefully.

'He probably just sold it,' Maddy said then, a little absently, as if the thought hardly merited being followed through to a conclusion. 'For a big fat profit. You know Uncle Ambrose. He's got gold dancing in the end of his fingertips.'

I looked ahead at the PanAm photos of Brazilia and Hong Kong By Night I had cut out and glued to the wall: they were blurred.

Everything seemed a blur right now.

Or was it the make-up, caught in my eyelash?

'No,' I say after a long time, long enough for the thought to lose the hidden barb within it, to appear, almost, just almost casual, but not really. 'No.' I murmur low, like Aunty Gilda or Uncle Ambrose might be just outside the door, listening. I reach out and play with strands of Maddy's blackblack hair.

He shifts his head emphatically, and shoots me a look of annoyance.

'It just disappeared forever,' I say then, to no one in particular. Into air. Into smoke. Into sky.

I think then of how I asked PK and she said, 'What car? It was never our Jaguar. We were just borrowing it. And now it's gone back.'

'Mutt the Dreamboat,' she said, half-pie smiling. Walking off. Whistling. Down the rocks.

Maddy does not think to answer he is so busy. All he does is nod just a little, to tell me he has heard, and he lets out, like the spill of water from the top of a saucepan filled to the brim — with the precious water which are ideas — a soft yet definite grunt.

'Mmmm,' he murmurs suggesting words cannot be trusted. 'Don't move.'

I hold still. I hold quiet within me the strange thoughts which dwell, like luminescent eels which travel by night in a dark dimpling pool. The lights on their noses, by their eyes, which sprint down their tails, dimple and dash through the surface. On the far side of the silent creek a crinkle of water unwraps its sound, disclosing a smooth and liquid susurration. These eels have spawned during the sunny hours of daylight: and as the sun has sunk they have, instantaneously, burst — like fireworks, like streamers from a whistle — into one million forms of sentient life: eel breeding eel until the entire width of water, the creek, is one moving thickness of them.

I am thinking of how perhaps I encouraged Uncle Ambrose to call himself my father, because, after all, I have said to KeelynCarrot my father has a Jaguar. Is this what happens with words? When you do not tell them true, they curve round and capture you, inside their own net?

Is it not all my fault?

Don't tell on us and we won't tell on you.

'Maddy,' I murmur.

'No,' he says to me then. 'Be silent.'

'Matthew!' I said again in a note of alarm.

But as if brandishing before me the poker of burning fire, Matthew now unfurled the bright scarlet lipstick which was to daub my lips, the lips of a king of Egypt, or was it queen?

'Put your lips together and keep silent,' he said to me in a peremptory kind of voice.

I felt a kind of despair, as if I sensed how finite his discovery of me had proved to be, that he had found out everything there was of me to know, had voyaged round and through me, right into my interior, and returned there, now, the conquistador who was quintessentially bored.

'Pucker up,' he said to me impatiently, and he held the lipstick scented so strangely, full of artificial scents to mask the very basic reality of unguent wax.

It was right by my lips.

So I pushed my lips together as, at the same time, all the muscles of my mouth fought to form the words: *Matthew Uncle Ambrose is turning up at running pretending to be Dad. He asks me to take a bath in the nuddy with him. I don't know what to do.*

But it was as if he himself had taken a strange drug which made him oblivious to what was passing through my mind, so I felt a kind of bleak disillusionment, even as I underwent the insecurity of leaving my old self behind and being changed and changing into this new creature, I felt all the disillusionment of a cast-off lover who must survive through the act of being made love to (he could not hear me, he could not hear the words above all in the world I wanted to tell someone).

So I felt the heavy weight of the scarlet drag its way across my mouth, and each pustule of muscle became coated and drenched in a thick waxy falseness.

'This is critical,' he told me sternly. And he leant right into me.

Imprisoned in this way I could see in extreme closeup his face. I saw the intensity of his glance, the grey-green pupils focused so intently they hardly moved, the fine black lashes, and I knew he loved me yet he could not help me. I felt a fundamental sense of aloneness.

The lipstick left my lips.

My brother leant back and surveyed me critically.

'I've made your lips bigger than they naturally are. Though you have good lips,' he told me in the impersonal voice of the professional beautician who must not spend too long with any one client, but hurry on to others.

'Matthew?' I said.

'Try not to talk,' he said to me. 'Try to speak as little as possible. That is, until you get in the door.'

I looked at him in silence.

'It is terribly important you make a great entrance,' Maddy said to me. *In that moment, you will understand how I have changed your life. In that moment you will understand that at long last the limousine has arrived . . . and you are within it . . . and it is that final moment . . . before the car door opens . . . and you shall get out.*

PONK AND I were preparing for bed. There was only one day to the Costume Ball. As was our custom, I had changed into my pyjamas, re-opening the door which signalled I had changed. Ponk lumbered into the room (her room) taking up all the space, it seemed.

She was wearing slacks, a jumper, and a frown.

I was about to climb into bed when she surprised me by murmuring, as if she had only thought of it, at the last second, 'Hey, Mutt?'

Something about the level of her voice made me pause. In syncopation, she turned her radio on, and its sounds rose up the walls, filling her room with an ambient softness. Her face was curved into humour.

'That was real funny, eh, how frightened Maddy was by Horton?'

She slung out the line of her humour. I ate the bait. Ignored the hook. For I missed, like a long and persistent ache, the balm of her friendship. And at this moment now, for this moment, it looked like she missed it too.

'He was really frightened, eh PK?' I said obediently. I mimicked Maddy's look, making glasses with my fingers. And we began, together, laughing.

'But it could of been him,' said Ponk, eager to defend Maddy's honour.

'He could of eaten us down to the bone,' I said simply. 'We might have been found, down the beach, under old Ma Kirk's boatshed, a little heap of thighbones.'

PK grinned at the macabre image, appreciatively.

We liked to cheer each other up with images of unspeakable horror and cruelty. In this way the real blows of life were somehow diminished and brought back into scale.

'You need me to help you and Maddy take the costume up to school?'

I knew instantly this was the real heart of why PK was speaking to me. I gazed all over her broad face, feeling an almost unspeakable lurch of love, of old and nearly lost fondness for her. I could see, as one sees under the tidal surface, the bottom of the sea — sand, the irrigations of rock, of pools, crabs, even the old crockery sewerage pipes with which we were familiar as people are with ancient ruins — I could see Ponk's face as it was when she was more of a child, more as I was . . . or used to be.

She even grinned at me her engaging, even sassy smile. I wondered instantly how she knew about the costume. What she knew. Had Maddy perhaps taken her up to the hut, as a special treat? Or boasted about it?

'How you . . . ?' I murmured softly. I was crouching on my knees on the bed, looking up at her brightly. But I knew from the sudden shadow passing over her face (like shade on the water's surface, caught from the sun), I should say no more. Ask no more. It was all part of the mesh, the web of secrets in which we lived. Which held us and made us. And unmade us, too.

She simply breathed out that long low sound, which said many things. Don't ask me how I know, she might say. I know everything. I know nothing. I know all. I am all. And yet I am nothing too. She might have said all these things.

I lay back on my bed. Her bed. Uncle Ambrose and Aunty Gilda's bed.

'I won't be here much longer,' I murmured softly to PK, as a caress. Because in some way I knew how to caress her too: it was as you stroke a dog you love, by running the flat palm of your hand over the soft slide of dome between the dog's ears, and you feel within all the liquid love of its intelligence.

'Hey, but I can give you a hand,' she said low. 'I can double you up on my bike. It's no trouble.'

I thought about it for one moment. And I knew she could not come. Not on this ride. Just as I had not been able to go with her, when she went down the road with her fishing rod, to fish with the bigboys.

A road opened up before us. Diverging.

Not trusting myself to speak, I felt my head move slowly. Sway into a shake. She simply observed this, and said nothing.

For one moment the radio played on, covering over all our embarrassments, melding over our wounds and placating the tidal roar of want, of hurt that beat so insistently in our hearts.

Our eyes could not look at each other for a long time. Neither of us could risk ruining whatever it was that lay still between us.

Then PK turned, grabbed her pyjamas and loped out of the room.

WHEN SHE CAME back in, she had a kind of fierce brightness.

'Hey, Mutt!' she called to me. I looked up over the top of the historical romance I was reading. She was standing there in the clean and ironed pyjamas of late childhood. Already she had outgrown them so the bottom of the pyjamas reached down to her calves.

She was holding the baseball bat.

Secure in the knowledge that my eyes were on her, she threw up into the air — high and wide — an invisible baseball, and as it zoomed down to strike the bat, she brought the bat towards it with all her new and adult strength and together we watched this ball, which existed only in our children's imagination, hurtle away with such savage and yet serene confidence that we watched it actually become small — a tiny dot — then finally disappear altogether.

'Yeah, Ponk,' I murmured to her softly, our old prayer, 'We win every time, eh, Ponk? We win.'

Crown

'CLOSE YOUR EYES,' Maddy said.

It was the day of the ball and I was standing in the hut.

I closed my eyes. I closed them obediently. I wanted, I wanted to go back, to go back inside, to go black, to lose consciousness. As I did so I swayed backwards, in a swift fall into unconsciousness and felt his body, warm, confident, behind me.

There was a slight knock, of concussion, some current of electricity passed between us, then I lifted my body away from his.

I kept my eyes closed.

In this darkness, I felt something being placed on my hair, on my head. It was stiff, damp. It smelt of glue.

It was the crown. I knew.

'Open your eyes, Maddy breathed from behind me.'

I looked in the mirror.

THE CROWN WAS made of papier mâché. Maddy had glued on plastic pearls and the small baubles which usually hung on the Christmas tree. The rest he had painted gold. Like me, Maddy had a natural propensity for all things gold and glittering. But the only gold paint he could afford was a small pot of paint, full of impurities of green and grey. We both imagined something like goldleaf — the effulgent even falshy goldness which leapt out of Technicolor films of the Queen's Coronation coach. This paint, however, was thin. as if in defiance of the obstinacy of the liquid to live up to all the brilliant associations which go with 'gold', Maddy had piled on as much paint to the ridge of the crown as it could sustain: yet the sheer weight had turned the papier mâché a little lumpy and soggy in parts. It had sunk under the mass of paintwork.

And I saw suddenly, under the gold, the leftover cardboard from my owl drawing. I carefully said nothing as I observed this imaginative failure. I knew by blurring my eyes the effect would be better. Besides, I could see he had generously layered on as much gold paint as he could afford.

The tiny tin stood empty: symbol of the expanse of his heart.

'Maddy, it very good.'

He was standing a little to the side of me, caught in an indecisive moment, somewhere between disgust at his failure to create a better crown, and appreciation for the facility of my compliments.

'You very clever.' I added. 'Very very clever.'

The crown scratched against the back of my neck. I could smell the piquancy of glue — wallpaper glue — which was not even dry. As always with Maddy, he had been running behind in his plans which had obviously grown more and more ornate as he had visualised the costume in greater and more expansive detail.

Inside the crown it was damp and warm, even soft, so I moved round in a spheric embrace, the perfume of wallpaper glue. But it was unchivalrous to look at the materials Maddy had made the costume from — canvas, paper, cardboard, Plasticine and oven-wrap silver foil — these momentary detractions were like learning a new language: I positively embraced the rasp of the helmet against the soft tissue of my neck I was so eager to pass from those slightly embarrassing moments, when you first put a costume on, to when you become the costume — you simply become the spirit which animates its outer surface: I suddenly felt drunk on the powerful essence, the purity of this spirit, as if it were alcohol passing my lips for the first time.

Maddy would not allow me to look at the rest of the costume. He told me to stay still and keep standing in the same spot. I had buried my feelings about Aunty Gilda, Uncle Ambrose, in the mounting excitement I felt at being so changed myself — it was as if I were parting from all the dilemmas which surrounded me — as if I were sliding away into an entirely new world — simply via a change in costume. But my metamorphosis was taking too long.

I changed feet in impatience and let out a long bored sigh.

My brother was so powerfully near to me, his forehead creased in a frown as he tried to tie on the breastplate: all I could smell was Plasticine.

'Maddy!' I sighed like a bored child, which in essence I still was — it was the cocoon which I was soon leaving — 'Maddy, hurry up,' I said, 'I got to go weewee.'

'Wait!' he said. 'Hold on. Won't be long.'

I looked down at the breastplate.

Skilfully, with hours of careful mechanical work, Maddy had laboured to create small lozenges of gold and silver. Only by staring at them more intently did I recognise they were old paint tins cut almost roughly, even dangerously, into flame shapes. These were attached to a canvas backing. There was the power of engineering in this, an ocean's width of work and careful thought.

But all this was to recognise the ordinary fabric of the world — and I recognised I was leaving that soil, embracing that foil.

He tied the back on firmly — the metallic wings of my breastplate clattered unevenly: he put the dress on me, old curtains from the living room, I felt afresh not only the wonderful alcohol of the wickedness of a boy wearing a dress but, less abstractly, the insecurity entailed in wearing a dress: the strange freedom of having nothing containing my thighs and that vulnerable and tender ridge which ran between my legs exposed, right up to the moist centre of my being.

My stamen fell against the soft green velvet drowsily, and shifted, instantly, in a jerk.

I could feel the air fingering all over me.

Maddy held the cloak out behind me — a gaudy Egyptian tablecloth my father had brought back as a spoil of war. This had already doubled as the cloak for one of the three kings in the nativity scene at the local church, where Maddy had served his apprenticeship in terms of costuming effects, decor and historicity.

Now I was more or less complete.

'I'm still holding on,' I said to him faintly.

He held the mirror up for me, so I looked into it and for the first time saw the person I had — or would — become. The change was so electrifying that I gazed at myself for a long time in complete silence.

A veneer of sophistication had been placed over me, a kind of pouting beauty, hard and entirely self-contained — so different from anything I natively was that I opened my mouth and let out a great laugh of joy which seemed to force itself up from my insides and then crush up through my gullet dragging my insides out with its sheer force so it was only in that moment, as my laugh died away, that my transformation — of my inside becoming my outside — became complete.

Maddy stood there, holding the silver mirror.

He has delivered me into the mirror.

As in a dream it slides down the ceiling, capturing a window, the books — all the worlds I have known are shaken free and then delivered back to me.

I am struck dumb. Plunged into silence.

He looks into my face, his breathing is close and he . . . now his eyelids flutter a little and a strange white look, powerful and entrancing, comes over his face, *yes lets pretend lets pretend we are far away from here* his fingers sing, *let us hop upon a barge and be slung through the slow and heavy gold, the sun a sequin in a copper silk sky*, he sings and a shiver walks up my back, a delicious taste opens inside my mouth and I feel my left leg, the upper flank, shake of its own accord again and again.

Impersonal, his eyes brush against mine.

'Let's pretend,' he murmurs quietly. 'Let's pretend.'

And I hear on my lips the word the song the plea in my heart I answer him back as he holds still the mirror.

'Yes, Maddy,' I murmur, 'let's pretend, eh, let's pretend.'

My brother throws open the hut door. He lets out a cry of victory so profound, so elated it would have been recognised by anyone as the cry of the successful inventor.

BOOK FIVE

THE MISSING WORD

Discoveries

MATTHEW HAS ALREADY exhausted every avenue of discovery in my body. I realise this as I stand, bored and naked, in front of him. We are in our hut, standing close by the bunks. It is mid-afternoon, the summer before last.

'Turn round, Jamie,' Matthew says to me, not unkindly.

I know this game.

'Let's pretend,' he says. 'Let's pretend . . . you're a girl.'

'But,' I say.

'No,' he says. *'Let's pretend.'*

'But I . . .'

'It's only let's pretend,' he says impatiently, taking my clothes off.

'But I'll have my turn,' I'd say suspiciously. 'When it's over. Won't I?'

'Of course,' he'd say laughing. 'Of course.'

I turn round, feeling all the cool air circulating over my body. Delicately it lifts up each minute silvery hair and plaits them in a soft, febrile dance of nervousness. Each pore in my body is opening and closing, the hair on my head fires with a kind of dull metallic brilliance. I no longer have eyes. Sight has been replaced, or changed, into an accompaniment to tactile sensation, a keen feelingness, the rawness of all new inventions.

I know this game.

His hands have travelled all over my body, discovering it, sculpting it, making it exist so that, invisible up until this moment, I stare down with surprise and find I have toes, knees, a waist, hips, a dalk.

He has invented me, explored me then exhausted every part of me.

It was at this point I discovered the two boys, Dirk and Geoff.

All this happened last summer.

They lived over the back fence, separated from us by an old plank wall. Like Matthew and me, they were brothers. This was perfect, as if we were the only form of twinning in the world, as written in the Bible: Cain and Abel; the two animals who walked into the ark.

So I brought him my captives.

Secretly, I had recognised them from athletics, where their father was a trainer. Already their tender bodies were being shaped into an apprenticeship of men's bodies, so they could grow into broad chests, strong arms and supple legs.

Now it was our turn to reinvent them.

IN A CIRCLE we stood and, silently, in awe, stared at these engorged tubes whose crests rose thick to flesh-lips, neatly wedged flanges. We were amazed at how similar, yet how different, was each of our dalks.

Their tensile apprehension was a miracle we all shared, in an almost mystical silence.

My brother pulled his away and let it thwack hard! against his belly. This sound, of itself, sent a shake, a shimmer through all of us.

Obediently, each of us did likewise.

Then we turned our eyes to Matthew.

What do we do now?

He had a flushed intent shine on his cheeks. Beads of sweat dimpled his upper lip. His eyes had a steely miasmic look. Or was it the reflection of my own eyes in his?

'Lie down on the bunk,' Matthew said.

He pointed the bunk out to Geoff, who had silently been picked.

He had been chosen.

Geoff's speckled lashes quivered but, as if he had no will of his own, he simply raised his pale green eyes up to Dirk, his brother, to see if this was what he should be doing. Receiving back an order so severe and simple, Geoff laid himself face downward on the mattress ticking, only at the last second thinking to turn his head slightly sideways, so his nose wasn't lying right into the pillow.

He turned his head towards the three of us.

Seeing us staring down at him from a height so colossal as to make him feel he was lying at the very bottom of a chasm, Geoff simply let out a slow long breath, of exhaustion, of defeat, of acceptance for whatever was to come next, then he rearranged his face to the wall, and turned his head from us.

'Rope.'

Matthew spoke curtly to me.

I handed him the coil. He bound the rope quickly and efficiently round and round Geoff's wrists.

Dirk and I, by a slow groaning movement forward, as if a door had been suddenly opened and we two, like flames, had fluttered and torn in one direction, Dirk and I glanced at each other, uncertain about whether we should admit this excitement to the other. Dirk answered me with a single, dazzling smile, the smile of a boy who was discovering new tricks.

His front tooth was chipped, I saw, in a bold sabre-like shape.

Dirk shot a triumphant look over at me, as he grabbed his brother's ankles. Geoff's ankles were scarred and white from being knocked against the chain of his bike. They were hard with callouses. Yet beside them was a tracery of veins, purple it seemed, against his olive skin. A delicate fannery of line. I wanted to blow on them.

Matthew meticulously showed off all his boyscout knots, which Dirk and I followed with scientific curiosity: the curiosity of all true learners.

Geoff's flesh was white where the rope cut into the fleshly mounds of his bumcheeks. At the same time I could see, almost as if in a hologram from all the summers past, the sharp white outline of his swimming togs.

It was part of the allure of his and Dirk's masculinism, of their being conscripts of the world of sport that their hair was astronaut-short, even shaven so that to the fingertips it felt a wry prickle (running your fingers up it the wrong way sent shivers down the small of your back, running in soft fans over your buttocks till the sensation concentrated, in intense contractions, fibrillating away in quivers right into your moist excited hole).

But an added enticement was that their togs were the latest American models, cut off in straight lines across their thighs, boxer shorts whose looseness made the exact definition of their dalks more of a game, more of a search-and-find expedition. My brother's and my togs were old-fashioned ones, tight-fitting, metallic in sheen . . .

I had made friends with these brothers who accepted me almost without question. Yet with what pity I received the intelligence that the most exciting advancement Dirk and his older brother could offer me was to crawl under their house on hands and knees till we reached the dimmest part, by a chimney, where the light of a bright sunny day filtered through skirting boards in hairs of heat, lighting up a small lunar world of old shoes, bottles with spiders in them, broken bricks.

I had had to undergo serious and searching questions before I was allowed into Dirk and Geoff's secret world. I had had to swear eternal silence but so intent was I on adhering myself to these acolytes of the sport world that I would have sworn anything, lied about anything, given anything away.

Finally, when I was allowed to crawl through the odd powdery clay under their house, over-heated and palpable as the world of secrets, this was the great climax of Dirk and Geoff's mutual discoveries — an infantile one which made me pity them as much as I understood, almost with cruelty, how easy it was going to be to make them mine (or my brother's and mine, if necessary) — for Dirk orchestrated his brother, as if his older brother was his plaything and minion so that, at a prearranged signal, Geoff crawled upright into a squatting position, reached round covertly with his left hand and yanked his pants down over his shining, ovoid rump.

I gazed at this palely brown piece of flesh (the colouring of his skin was what I found most intoxicating about Geoff — the faint tawniness, its opaque waxiness, the way its range of colour was so different from my own skin which, once having burnt, now broke apart into freckles: his skin had all the beauty of the shell of a brown egg).

But having arrived at this great moment, Dirk, Geoff and I had to wait for several long seconds of anti-climax until, small shudders of delight running through Geoff not unmixed with terror (since Dirk had in his hands a switch of narrow bamboo which he used as a branding whip), Dirk reached rudely forward and pushed his brother over by his shoulder so that we could see more clearly the dilation of his hole, and we witnessed the production, moment by moment, of a phial, an elongated globule of shit.

This movement was done in grave silence, profound as it was gleeful.

I watched the distension of Geoff's hole as it grew in size, forming small lips round the excrement. Dirk reached over and laced a companionable, even brotherly arm over Geoff's shoulders, as if to illustrate how proud he was of his brother.

Now, exhausted by this production — out of nothing, of something — Geoff turned a face over his shoulder to me, displaying all the wonderful gift of passivity which he was offering, wrapped in wonder, seeking to read in my eyes an affirmation of the marvellousness, even uniqueness, of this strange rite.

The shit detached itself from his hole and fell, in a soft, plump curve into the dust.

Dirk and I stared gravely at Geoff's behind, noticing how his hole had sealed shut, into a furled suddenly exhausted bud.

The soft filtering smell of his ordure began to fall back and scent the dust under the house, fanning out and entering our nostrils so that we knew we would have to leave the underside of their house.

Dirk promptly began to use his switch as a whip, forcing his brother (whose abjectness struck me as intriguing) to spider along on his hands and knees, his pants caught around his thighs.

Dirk simply laughed at his brother.

After this I knew that I had to deliver these ripe and willing captives to my brother as soon as possible.

The fact was, until this was achieved, everything about the boys' house acted as an aphrodisiac to me. I could not keep away, breathing in its extreme cleanliness, the absence of carpets, the jet-fighters on the wallpaper in the boys' room which were as a vacated temple of their bodies, the solemnity of the bread-and-butter pudding placed on a tabletop by their pious mother, the bowing of our heads for grace: the very simplicity of the rituals of their household became a forerunner to that moment when Geoff could be bent over and Dirk, my brother and I could take turns in experimenting, with branches, pencils, ballpoints and fingers with the dilation and expansion of Geoff's pliant and supplicant hole.

After all this, exhausted by the sheer energy of our invention, we would untie the curtains, unlock the door (secrecy was a necessary part of this cult, of these rites), and leaving the door open we would lie back on the bunks, Dirk and his brother relegated to worn linoleum at our feet, and we would begin to talk about our favourite movie stars.

Death

PART OF GEOFF and Dirk's attractiveness lay in a strange fact. This was that their uncle and aunt had been drowned when their car plummeted off the ramp as it boarded the North Shore car ferry.

All of us were familiar with the grave and important world of men which allowed them, with such indifference, to fling down the steel ramp that momentarily, and even magically, formed a bridge between earth and vessel, allowing cars to pass across a wide gap of air, down below which lay the sea.

As children, gripped by a dark apprehension — that apprehension which brooks no logic — we knew that it was an unreal supposition that a weighty piece of metal like a car could successfully pass through space over such a thin piece of metal. We knew as if within our clenched innards that the real destiny of all this testing of weights and space (accomplished by men with laconic yells, strange signals, even a dense exchange of enigmatic movements suitable for the ultimate ferrymen) was a very simple one: that, at that climactic moment when your car mounts the first slight incline of the ramp, then enters onto that narrow strip of metal which is a bridge between shore and vessel, at that precise moment, the full illogic of the sea (its hidden demons which we know so well as children who grow up in the sea) will suddenly rock the boat.

In a swift movement, the boat slides out to sea, the metal ramp slips along the concrete with a hideous rasping shriek, sending a shower of sparks up into the air.

Now all is happening too swiftly for decision. The ramp pauses briefly in mid-air, as if in disbelief at the situation, then it crashes into the water which greedily slurps the car downward, accepting it gratefully like a bite out of a particularly fresh doughnut it has been eyeing hungrily all the time.

There is a stunned silence as onlookers rush to the wharf's edge.

They can see the maroon top of Geoff and Dirk's uncle's car (a 1954 Vauxhall) as it sinks. They stare down at it, feeling a terrible impotence; no matter that a man dives in fully dressed, no matter what anyone does, the faint maroon imprint of an object sinking through dense water begins at once to darken, like a bruise which will be left in someone's consciousness forever and at the same time growing fainter, until it is clear in the complete silence of the scene in which everyone waits, for two figures to break through the surface, gasping air into their lungs as other figures, now in twos and threes, dive into the tide to retrieve them, that the silence only grows deeper, more profound.

The bubbles on the surface of the water no longer fume.

The heroic diver has grown tired from trying to gain access to that hidden depth.

From a far part of the city a siren may be heard.

And in the calm surface of the water every on-looker reads the fact that a tragedy has occurred and they have become an accomplice by the fact they have been there: as a witness.

THIS TRAGIC DIMENSION added immeasurably to Geoff and Dirk's stature. When my brother's and my eyes turned to glance at them, even covertly, we saw, even felt, the last minutes of their uncle and aunt, witnessing for ourselves that moment when one turned to the other and, their hair flowing out in tendrils as if they were being changed into sea beings and ceased to be humans, they cried to each other, and began clawing at the car doors, only to find the doors would not budge.

Surprise

ONE DAY NOT long after we started our games, things didn't go as we expected. Or rather our games had reached the limits of our invention and we had all collapsed onto the lino, happily enjoying our companionship with the dirt and dust, laughing at nothing, at anything. At nothing.

When I looked at Geoff's face, he was crying. Quietly.

This surprised us, so we all felt a thrall of shame overtake us, shame on behalf of him, that he, a boy, should allow us, other boys, so private an entrance into his inner being. The hut fell into a silence so total that it seemed we could hear the flow of the hairs on our arms moving in time with each of his sobs.

We were at a loss to know how to deal with this situation.

Dirk stepped over his brother's body then snaked up his underpants. He said nothing. He stood there looking down at his brother. Then with his foot he placed the flat weight of his sole against his brother's pelvis and rolled his brother over so Geoff lay there, looking upwards. We all looked into his tear-streaked face, it was like the face of an idiot, no longer handsome, all beauty stolen from it. His mouth, which only minutes ago had seemed so greedy as if he could not pack and slobber into it any more pleasures, sweets, laughter, now seemed a loose gash, like an old paper bag so fingered it had frayed and was on the point of falling apart.

But Dirk, standing up so high above him, wearing only his white jockey underpants (which I could see had a small stain of shit in the fold between his legs, at the back), smiled down at his brother in consolation.

'Don't worry, Geoff,' he murmured to him softly. 'You can do me next time,' and his foot now travelled up to his brother's face, and he held his brother's face there, just as we had seen cowboys do in the movies.

Geoff slumped his face sideways and Dirk then rested his foot, lightly, like a conqueror, on his brother's head.

This was their brand of tenderness.

'I -I -I,' Geoff was hiccuping by now, but a strange dim smile was also playing over his features. 'N-n-next time,' he said.

At this point Dirk did something strange: a whole luxuriant yawn overcame him so he stretched every part of his body in slow motion, it was as if I was seeing all the bones in his body glutinously change their position inside the sack of his flesh, to find a more comfortable relationship, and then he took his foot away and began humming to himself as he went on dressing. He got to the third bar of 'Broke My Dentures' when he stopped, and slipping his shorts up over his thighs he said, 'Yumyumyumyumyum.'

He spoke in an off-hand kind of way perhaps to cover up how much he was excited by our games. But his attempted nonchalance was broken by him firing a glance first at my brother, then more lingeringly at me. I saw him upside-down at this point. I hardly knew how to interpret this glance.

'Come on, Geoff,' he said to his brother then, 'We're late for footie practice,' he said. 'Dad'll be angry.'

Geoff said nothing, he got up on all fours, then began, silently, to gather his clothes up.

'We weren't laughing at you,' I thought to say to Geoff as he paused before going out the door.

He had brushed away his tears. His face had a naked, fleshly look about it. His eyes, which had servilely never left the lino during the whole time after he began crying, now raised slowly to look into mine. I seemed to feel inside me the lever of his glance, as if I held a levitating machine which was, of its own accord, raising his glance quarter inch by quarter inch. Finally, his eyes looked into my own, and I felt a flood of almost bewitching power because I knew he would come back to the hut, to take part in our games, that he had accepted everything as it was, and that he would soon by lying there again, face downward, a blank page for us to write our futures on.

Before going out the door, and as if to recoup some lost prestige, he grabbed hold of me — but in such a loose, fond way as not to startle me — and, gathering my head in a rugby hold, he ran his fingers through my hair, letting the pad of his fingers send a primitive kind of energy into my scalp.

He caressed me secretly.

My brother and I watched him walk off through our back garden, recognising in his body that attractive imitation which he already had off pat, which all the boys who played league affected from an early age on, this was the rolling gait of the older boys.

But just as Geoff seemed to find his proper footfall, he walked directly into the whiplash of the apple tree.

It drew its fingernails of pain right across his face.

He yelped, reduced to the pliancy of a puppy, the source of all his attractiveness.

At the same time he turned round, darting a reprimanding look to my brother and me. We saw him reduced to being not a tough youth, a footie player but a soft and unformed baby who wanted anyone (my brother, me, his mother, his own brother) to quickly kiss him better.

So we looked at each other across the space, none of us moving till Dirk's voice came from the other side of the fence, he was lost in the mass of the Chinese gooseberry vine, its tendrils and dark furry weights of fruit:

'*Geo-offfff?*' he called and half-whined, 'Pop'll give us a hiding if we late for footie practice,' and the way he said *footie practice* instantly recalled Geoff into being the older boy he aimed to become. He turned away from us, hiding his child's face, rejecting my brother's and my rituals as children's games.

The last we saw of him was his behind, struggling as his legs fought to get over the barrier of the back fence. My brother turned to me, looked at me briefly, then turned his head away.

'They'll be back,' was all he said.

Worm

'Aren't we gunna play stiffies again?' Geoff asked sullenly.

'It's my turn,' Dirk said aggressively. He tried to push his brother out of the way. 'Aint it?'

'No,' said Geoff, insistent. 'It's mine. You promised,' he said almost shyly. And looked down.

His look of hunger made his skin, usually so burnished, take on an acrid yellow colour, so the small creases round his eyes appeared as minutely rustled as wet tissue paper. His faded-green eyes, too, had an empty look, like the sea at low tide, when the mud below is clearly visible, and when you put your foot in, small puffs of mud rise up and fluff out the aqueous space into dimness. He raised his hand up into his mouth and began biting at the quick round the nail.

I was amazed at how he seemed to be turning into my brother (all his nervous mannerisms had been spawned onto him), whereas my brother — standing very still, so still I sensed something momentous was about to happen, he seemed to represent the force of imminence itself — simply stood there and looked, not at Geoff, but as if at that moment he was looking right through Geoff, as if Geoff were an empty pane of glass slightly smudged so my brother had to concentrate all the more intensely to see right through; and it was as if he were seeing there, in that unknowable space in which lay all diversion, all entertainment, all filling in of the vast and abstract weight known as time what we were about to do: in fact he seemed to tremble with the force of the knowledge which was passing through him.

Looking at him I felt that same depth of being impressed (while at the same time on guard against the sudden immersion into shame which I knew I would feel if anyone else saw the nonsensicality of the games we were playing); while I hung there, awaiting what my brother would say next, Dirk let out a little rustle of exasperation.

He had a limited concentration span, he simply wanted to do, to explore, to feel, to apprehend and tussle to the ground whatever sensations, excitements, delights and incidental food were coming his way.

'It's my turn,' he said sullenly. 'You made a promise.'

'We haven't made a pact,' my brother then said.

He spoke lightly, but distinctly, with startling clarity. This was at such variance to his habitual stutter, which erupted in the face of challenging situations, it was like my brother had inside him a new voice, a voice of such complete certainty it persuaded simply by the fact of its existence; it was this voice which indicated he could always see slightly further ahead than any of us, that he could make up tricks with rope, with paper and card and paint, even invent stories and tell us how the world spun on its axis, why water did not cover the world, how there was a winter, summer and spring and who Hone Heke was and sundry other essential tales.

'We've got to swear on oath,' he says. 'Eternal brothers. Forever and ever.'

I listen to the deep maroon carpet of his voice.

I see before me unrolling and opening further and wider and deeper a long continuously existing pathway of carpet. Small golden fleurs-de-lis sprinkle this, like stiff and slightly artificial flowers. A slim rod of brass, like a sceptre, keeps the fall of plushness taut.

'Like the Queen,' I say. 'On the way to her coronation.'

I glimpse up the nave through overarching vaults the small concupiscence of our quartet, all dressed as brides, or better still, as virgin boys, all of us with our own particularly shaped fleur-de-lis, which we leave uncovered in our nakedness.

My brother barely nods. It is so serious.

Dirk, who when bored and simply absent-minded allows small bubbles of saliva to foam at the very edges of his mouth, now makes a small ppppppping sound, of agreement or disapproval none of us can tell. I feel an overwhelming awareness of his raw red pleat. I watch his lips, slightly cracked from sun, stretch their pinkness into an undulant smile.

'I swear,' he says. *'Bloody. Bugger. Bastard. Bum.'*

Then he stands there, smiling round at all three of us.

Standing in the nave.

'No!' my brother cries now in positive anger, his voice echoing the length of our abbey. (That we are only in our hut is immaterial. My brother has taught me this: what we are surrounded by can change with the slightest will, the smallest smudge of a fallen eyelash.)

My brother says, pointing to Dirk: 'He must be punished.'

Immediately, a laugh explodes out of Dirk, a sort of milky pappy staleness of air as he curves away from us and tries to make for the door.

My brother simply leans forward and shoots the slim bolt home through its groove. As if in some subterranean way we all four of us feel that bolt drive its way along the slightly greased alley so that, as our eyes meet, it is as if the bolt joins all of us together, runs through each one of us and makes us connected.

'Jamie, pull the curtain.'

I grow and grab the dark.

Dirk, feeling the shade fall on him, has gone still. Like a rabbit. But Geoff, a smile cracking open his pumpkin, leaps forward. He grabs his brother in his arms, from behind, his arms pressing into Dirk's throat tightening.

'Bloody bugger,' he says, copying.

In the sudden and illicit half-light of the room he yanks his younger brother back so his feet leave the lino momentarily.

'Not too hard! We mustn't kill him,' my brother commands at the sound of Dirk's gurgling. *'Yet.'*

All three of us, with an abstract grace, watch the purple darkling of Dirk's face. His veins ride up.

My brother has in his hand, as we all know he would, the coiled snakes of rope. This rope is new, bristly to the touch. If you run it quickly through your hands, it spins the flesh off and leaves behind ribbons of blood, searing snakes of ache. It is coarse, and cuts into your flesh when tied.

If escaping, when climbing down, you must go slow.

This we know.

'Please. Maddy. No.' Dirk gulped, when Geoff released his hold just slightly. He was speaking as perhaps he knew he was meant to. 'Not the rope. Please.'

But his please, I noted, had a special note of entreaty to it.

Behind him, Geoff's face had taken on a strange gleam, his brown flesh taking on another lustre. A cruel look overcame his usually slack mouth. He was grinning.

'Hah, Dirk,' he said. 'You're the idiot now. Eh?'

He turned round to me and Maddy for reassurance.

But we were silent.

My brother, kneeling, first of all pulled Dirk's pants down in one quick humiliating pull. Dirk, as if to protect himself, pulled his pelvis in:

'No,' he half moaned, half whimpered. 'No,' he said again, but whatever he was going to say next was cut off as my brother span him round and began tying his wrists together. He did this silently. He seemed, in fact, to be briefly lost to us all, as a small frown played down his forehead.

For one moment, his eyes passed over my face, and I shivered because I didn't know whether he recognised me, whether I was next for this new game, or whether what we were doing was part of the swearing of eternal allegiance.

Dirk's hands were tied behind his back. My brother's fingers had felt inside the tightness, testing that he was not hurting Dirk. But Dirk was grizzling like a small boy, pretending to moan but in such a way he displayed all the hammy exaggeration of a bad actor. Actually, he was moaning too much, and swaying his hips back and fro, almost like an island maiden about to be sacrificed in a silent film. A small smile played round the raw edges of his mouth, between his moan.

His eye caressed each one of us. He was hungry now.

Geoff was squatting at his feet, pulling his grey boxer shorts out from under his bare feet. He took Dirk's underpants and, displaying a small yellow stain to us, he made yukky sounds. He held the underpants right by Dirk's nose.

When Dirk opened his mouth to yell out, Geoff stuffed them in. His face was full of glee.

I noted he looked briefly intelligent. When he caught my eye, I looked away.

While this was happening, we began to be aware that Dirk's dalk had begun to stiffen, first of all filling out, then rising up until it went through all the degrees, quite speedily, like in a time-lapse film, from half mast to fully erect.

It lay flat and hard against his belly.

A series of quick shivers passed through him and then he became solemn, the proprietor of a stiff. At this moment I saw our cat staring in through the window, head slightly on its side, trying to make sense of this strange ritual happening inside.

Silently now we three began to undress, without anyone saying anything. There was only the swift snap of the elastic of Geoff's Jockey underpants as my brother impishly pulled them back and let them make a satisfying hard smacking sound against Geoff's bent behind.

Geoff, obligingly, grinned.

'Thirrrrl,' Dirk struggled to say, through the gag of his underpants. I knew he was saying the worst word he could think of: *'Girl.'*

'What do we swear to?'

We now all stood there naked. One by one our cocks had risen into columnar hardness. For one long second, we feasted our eyes, as we had done so many times before, on the strange individuality of each of our secrets. Although I knew, logically, these had nothing to do with the fecundity and earthiness of root vegetables, somehow I could only think of a hard fresh cauliflower (my brother); a slim stripped leek, long and shiny (Geoff); Dirk's was like a nobbly carrot, blunt and aggressive; my own was made of green jade, an asparagus cooked to perfect succulence, still snappy but soft to the teeth. In every detail it seemed perfect, like a replica fashioned by the most exquisite of craftsmen, as did all the other boys' secrets which surrounded me. This was how I saw it, as something almost separate from myself, like a new shirt, or the towelling shorts my mother had made for last Christmas.

My brother swiftly drew out his penknife, a knife with a thick pearly handle, which boasted a bottle-opener, a corkscrew and many other conveniences. It was bigger than the knives we habitually played with, but it was heavy with practicality, rather than menace.

I shivered.

'We've got to swear eternal brotherhood,' my brother said now. 'We protect and look after each other. Offer help and come to the aid of each other. Utter secrecy and silence. Forever.'

Utter.

Mutter.

Stutter.

Nutter.

Looking from one to the other of us.

So saying.

He slit.

A red flower.

I shivered to see the thin lip go white and then scarlet.

'You'll bleed to death, Maddy,' I murmured drowsily. For a kind of sleepiness had overcome me. I felt as if instantly my veins had become clogged with honey and I needed to go to the toilet. My eyes longed to fall shut into a divine kind of slumber.

'No,' he said to me almost abruptly. 'No. We live forever. Once. Once,' he said to me, 'you do this.'

There was a pause.

'You gotta do this.'

And he held the blade against my pulse.

I saw down below, through our joined arms, our matching dalks; I wanted to laugh: they looked like two old men coming together for a natter, old men who would always meet up, to argue, dispute, fall out, make up and discuss.

But my brother was serious. His eyefall cascaded all over me, I felt a kind of terrible disdain in his glance, as well as — perhaps worse — a kind of rapt appeal. We both knew unless I agreed, the other two brothers who were natural cowards and reticent before all new experiences would not do so. They were standing there like peasants before the door of a church through which one could glimpse blazing candles, gilt, the strangeness of incense, and all the other wonderful peculiarities of closed sects, mid-service.

I nodded just imperceptibly, whimpering at the same time as I leant forward, and put my hand, for strength, on Maddy's shoulder.

'*Baby,*' said Dirk contemptuously, having at last spat out his underpants. My brother and I froze. But in that instant, as if miraculously, blood popped its diamond and ruby diadem up through the strange white mark, almost as if drawn by chalk, which ran across the outer side of my wrist.

I felt now a sharp pain.

Maddy grabbed my wrist and he licklicked it.

His eyes my eyes.

I looked away. The saltiness of his saliva caused me to whimper again. But more than this, I felt the contempt of Dirk who, standing there wrists tied together, was looking at me. Yet when I looked at him more closely I saw something else in his eyes. There was a kind of wild exhilaration there, a daring. His truth burst out.

'*I'm gunna tell,*' he murmured.

As if to render him silent, Geoff held out his own wrist mutely, offering himself up to make up for his brother's mutiny. At the same time his eyes moved over to look, in a worried glance, into his brother's face.

My brother, almost nonchalantly, slit Geoff's wrist.

'Turn Dirt round,' he commanded, instantly changing Dirk's name, so we understood how meaningless Dirk's threat was.

Geoff and I jumped to obey, spinning Dirt round so fast he fell sideways so he tumbled over into a humiliating posture, his head and shoulders resting on an old kitchen chair. His tied wrists writhed on the slightly sweating curve of the small of his back.

All three of us laughed, almost uneasily, as we looked down at the raised vulnerability of his bumcheeks.

Leaning down Maddy quickly knicked the back of Dirk's wrist.

A curl of blood unwrapped.

'*Quick!*' Maddy said.

Maddy held his wrist out. I lay my own against his, still sticky with his saliva. I felt the bird's breast of his pulse against my body. I shuddered, I didn't know why. I looked into Maddy's face to see what was readable there. I couldn't quite read it. He, Geoff and I, then Dirk all lent our small wounds against each other.

'Eternal brothers.'

There was the satisfactory fall of silence.

'Together forever.'

Achilles, seeing my eye rest on him, first of all attacked his coat, licking it with concentration, then, turning sideways while remaining sitting upright, cascaded away from the glass.

I watched him stalk away through the daisies.

For one moment, sensing me looking at him, he turned round and sent an immense sequinned gaze right into my heart.

'I'm gunna tell,' said the formed hard voice of Dirk, who had been left propped up in his downward facing position. His voice had the blood-filled density of someone looking downward too long.

My brother now pulled him back upright. I could tell Dirk was dizzy. He simply stood there, rocking back and forth on his feet. But as he regained his sight, he looked naturally downward, to the point of gravity . . . and what did he see, what did we all see, but the columnar strength of his cock looking back up at him, so strong and firm it was as if muscular ramparts held it forever up, a thick broad arrow which occupied all his living cells, his actual intelligence, independent from his own body, so his slight, but nuggety body, the body of a nascent scrum forward, seemed merely an attachment to it, a loose vagary, an afterthought.

'Gunna tell,' he said again, edgily.

Geoff abruptly leant forward to him and, with his fingers, playfully flicked Dirk's cock so it banged against his belly, and immediately it stood out harder and fuller — more in a begging question.

'Tell what, Dirt?' Maddy said with such simple force, a blush began to rise up Dirk's face, and as it did so, a strange and parallel thing began to happen: his dalk began to lose its columnar stiffness, it began to retract, and so that by the time Dirk's face was dyed a strange dense red his dalk now hung, slack and downcast between his legs.

'Tell what?' My brother said again with his characteristic dryness.

Geoff let out a vindictive guffaw, or was it victorious?

Dirk looked at him threateningly, and even tried to tussle with the ropes.

'I no say a word,' Geoff said simply. He went to the door and, pausing for my brother to unshoot the bolt, he quickly went outside.

I glimpsed him totally naked. With a shock I realised he had short legs. I had never noticed these before. I wondered what any neighbour would think if they saw him.

Under the apple tree, he bent over, momentarily and with complete innocence revealing to us the soft bruised hole in his bum. Quickly he was back in the hut. My brother shot the bolt and we saw what Geoff had in his hand.

It was a worm.

I looked down at this strange blind thing, squirming into mid-air, palpitating and retracting its rings as it moved about Geoff's blunt fingers. Immediately, I was struck by how this worm seemed like the worms which we all carried, as boys, and men: it had the same blindness, the same moist pinkness and somehow overwhelming and vulnerable nakedness. I had seen them bloated with rain. I had seen birds pulling them from the earth. And now Geoff went towards his brother.

'Whatcha gunna say?' he demanded of his younger brother.

His brother said nothing, then his eyes moved round the hut, from Maddy — the source of all this witchery — to me, and then to his brother. For one second I saw the worm and Dirk's cock in motion. It seemed it needed only the most incidental excitement for his cock to start into life.

'Open wide,' Geoff said, electing to pay his brother back for a small lifetime of insults.

Dirk made grim and threatening sounds.

'But Dirt likes eating worm,' said Geoff softly.

I lent down and, my fingers passing by the extreme heat given off by his cock, I sent a column of warm ticklish air into Dirk's ear. His mouth, as I knew it would, fell open. A swift series of clicks happened down his throat, almost begging noises. His cock jerked up into the hard repentance of erection.

Geoff very succinctly placed the worm in the open hole of Dirk's mouth.

I kept blowing hot air right down into Dirk's ear.

Dirk seemed oblivious to what was in his mouth, as he squirmed and laughed and protested and cried out in rage, all mixed in together. But then, on closing his mouth, he realised what was in it. He immediately tried to spit it out, in spraying belches. But Maddy had caught hold of his head and was singing softly, in an almost sweet tune:

'Dirty must eat the wormy. Dirty must eat the wormy. Dirty must eat the wormy.'

Obediently, Geoff and I took up the chant.

Flushing again mutinously, Dirk's jaw began to work.

We three gathered in front of him and watched him with a kind of exhilarated glee.

'All of it,' Geoff ordered his brother, giving his behind a quite brutal, even proprietorial, whack.

Dirk's eyes moved to his brother and they stayed there for a long ominous moment. His jaw began to work, and we watched him in complete silence, as he swallowed with difficulty, then tried to cough the worm up, spattering saliva and worm out in all directions.

While this was happening my brother did a strange thing: he pulled along the curtain so that a pale white light entered the hut and bathed us all.

I was amazed that the ordinary light of the world still existed.

For a long second we looked at ourselves in complete silence.

We were brothers.

Underwater

THIS WAS OUR favourite game.
   Our longest running serial.
   How to escape.
   From a sinking car.

WE ARE LYING there in the warm shallows, little ripple of waves nibbling along the backs of our legs, hitting us softy, with sweet lips, where our legs meet.

It is summer.

The veil of water on our backs is transparent enough to be like a glaucous container which magnifies the sun's strength so we feel its powerful imprint bearing down, stern and fabulous, rendering us (Ponky, Maddy and me) into a drowsy almost half-drugged state.

'What would you do?' I ask.

We watch the silent and even peaceful twirl downward of the car as it moves, irredeemably, towards the bottom.

PONKY AND I both know this from bottlefishing. We are pliant with the arcane knowledge of how one takes a preserving jar (hopefully with a narrow neck), how one ties round its mouth strong white string, then attaches a length to a floater. You fill the bottle with small snitches of white bread. You swim out to a peaceful part of the tide, far away from other swimmers, you claim a part of the sea. And then you fill the bottle slowly with the tide and let it peacefully, in a slow drone of fall, sink.

You leave the bottle alone.

You may lie on your back on the tide's warm surface, but silently, and without motion. You must become as a lull of the waves, as the silent traverse of a cloud passing the sun.

The voices of people on the beach become thin, shadows scrape off the earth.

The floater suddenly agitates. It bobs under the weight of fish nibble. This is when you turn into a hunter.

Turning swiftly over, you penetrate the surface of the seaworld and, your eyes open, feet kicking powerfully, you enter another world.

Up above the sun lances the surface in prismatic spears, the soft sable bottom drifts and shifts, but you can see (your heart begins to pump with victory) inside the bottle, oddly enlarged is a small collection of fish. Diamond darts, rainbow scales, a moving fulcrum of dart and tinsel thither-hither, they hang, a cloud of sprats, an apprehension of intelligence gathered round the mute now disappearing white bread.

But as you approach (you the monster) dragging your own darkened shadow along with you so the light of the sun is momentarily quenched, this is when you must make your shark dive. You must attack the bottle before all the fish can withdraw. But already the school, the cloud of apprehension, has tinted and turned and glinted and flashed away into and along the vast corridor of the underwater world.

In the distance you see the strangely whitened legs of an elderly swimmer treading water. Your lungs are bursting. Your hand closes about the top of the jar. Inside a fish, two fish desperately try to engineer a rear movement. But you burst up through the water, into light; into sound; into warmth; and you carry in your hand the catch: one hundred and seventy sprats over one afternoon.

Ponky has taught me how to kill them with least pain. This is emetic. You simply dash their brains out in one sharp whack, swinging them by their tails. The rock becomes glutinous with a faintly red blood. Scales fall off. Tails stop twitching. Eyes become cloudy. Bodies stiff. Thus we experience death and overlook it for our own convenience.

But in those moments, of flying underwater, we have both, Ponky and I, watched the weighted bottle sink. We have witnessed miniature Titanics first of all fill partially then become weighted as a surge of sea gushes in then the weight begins to pull the vessel downward, downward, until now sinking, now falling, now twirling and catching the last rays of the sun, sending out a fitful glint of light, like a last cry, or whimper, now sinking further downward, always downward, turning and revolving, spinning downward as if the bottom of the sea is a magnetic core, as if all beings and things may find their natural destination there; to lie among the shattered sewer pipes, the old shoes, the lost bottom dentures. In its traverse Ponky and I witness again and again the final agonies of Geoff and Dirk's uncle and aunt.

'WHAT WOULD JA do?'

Ponky turns over, her back a special brown.

'You have to wait,' she says. 'You have to wait till the car fills with water.'

She has this way of talking when she is imparting information. There is a generous heart in it, like the dark part inside a flower. But her lips form seriously, too, so you know, in your heart, you must listen, and listen carefully and slowly.

I feel a shiver running its silver slime all over my flesh. I shudder. *But how? How not to?*

'You mustn't panic,' she says. 'Above all you must not panic. You must wait patiently. Conserving energy.'

I think of this.

'You must wait for the car to fill with water.'

'How do you breathe?'

'Air is trapped inside the top of the car,' Maddy then says authoritatively. I check a small rinse of annoyance inside me, that he is being a brainbox again, without my knowing anything.

'You only need a small piece of air,' Ponky says. 'Trapped.'

Trapped my lips say. *Trapped*.

'Yes,' says Ponky slowly so I know I have to listen, 'You must not panic but wait patiently.'

'Water pouring in,' I supply the imagery of panic.

'Yes, you must sit there and wait until the water reaches almost the roof.'

'Then the weight of the water inside the car equals the weight of the water outside,' says Maddy slowly and bored.

'I know!' I cry out hotly, like you do when someone provides the answer to a favourite clue, thus spoiling all the joyful repetition of known responses, given in their right order, by the right person. 'I know.'

The pressure of the external water must equal that of the internal water — then click! — a door shall open.

Ponky's voice is now so low I must strain my ears to hear, as if in diminishing all sound down I too am straining to float out past the open car door.

'Now!' she cries. 'Now! Now you must push the door open and with the last piece of oxygen in your lungs, you must start your swim to the surface. But slowly!' says Ponky wisely. She even raises her hand, in a strange almost judicial gesture. 'You must swim to the surface slowly, even though your lungs are busting.'

'Otherwise you die of the bends,' says Maddy, losing interest and rolling over to feast his eyes on the light blitz fed directly into him by the sun.

For a second, none of us says anything. Ponk goes back to bashing out the brains of fish: quickly, efficiently, so, as she says, they feel no pain.

I get up, separate myself from gravity and pull all the world in with me as I slide off into the tide.

Changing Sheds

DIRK IS TAKING his swimming togs off under water. He struggles them off in quick excitable tugs. Up above on the surface of the sea he spouts water out, like a whale.

We have run down the pink asphalt path from the changing sheds.

Dirk is laughing and wrenching his togs down at the same time, almost delirious with giggles. He has slipped his secret out from under his togs as soon as he gets under the water and now he shakes it about, screaming with laughter, drunk on the freedom of having shaken his secret out into the world.

We all take turns in diving below the water. We spout out the sea, screaming with laughter at the sheer celerity of our secret.

For we have just come from inside the changing sheds.

In there is a zoo of secretiveness, the very collection of all its covert forms, growing up like mould in the dank wateriness and wry pissy smells.

Here we glimpse, with carefully noncommittal eyes, vast donkey buttocks of ancient men, white as clotted cheese and somehow bestial as they bend, winding down their soggy old wool costumes from Before-the-War. There are also those other men whose heads turn like antennae in the shade and, with one expert flick of their wrist, they open out the misshapen dangle of their elephantine protuberances, smuggled up into dark rings of hair which blossom against the whiteness of their flesh.

All men — and even their subservient slaves: boys, growing up with aching slowness to mimic them — all men have this other x-ray on their flesh, the shape engraved over their nakedness (the ghostly shape of their togs) so, in the changing shed, it is as if we glimpsed how we might see them out in the sunlight, in broad daylight, if we possessed Superman's sight to penetrate all things, to look beyond everything covert, to the true heart of the matter.

But Dirk, Geoff, Maddy and I know the rules of the changing shed, which is that one must always affect a total seriousness and that all momentary dalliances of glimpsing and staring must be done in a carefully choreographed casualness — this is the hidden music of this room — all men are drenched in its sound, and the speech which emits from their mouths is as if it comes from underwater it is so exaggeratedly slow and impounded by the sheer weight of being hearty — these naked giants stand there with their idiotic protuberances so casually commenting on the weather, or the score, something they always keep as a game to ululate among themselves, so as they move towards the shower (that man there with the suntanned back stroked all over with a dark coppery hair, his almost phosphorescently white bum, and that man there with a v of hair running into the small of his back like an arrow pointing down to his pleat) — they flack their towels over their backs and — all the while to cover their nakedness, convert their secrets into a null thing, they keep up a never-ending conversation about passes, catches, scrums, tackles and other prevaricating rigmarole by which men touch men, so relax and open are they, so knowledgeable are they about the arcane laws of this game — of men not touching men.

WE HAVE EACH of us placed this world inside our eyes letting our pupils grow wider with the sheer casual intensity of this world of naked men, taking place inside the darkened ellipsis of the changing sheds.

We also note the glancing blow of some strangers who register our presence, and dance a slight mocking smile upon their lips: these men, too, we know, we know that they know we know. They welcome us to this world of unpeeling and unshrouding, where some men edge a wet dank costume down their legs while they hold, tensely, a drooping flag of towel across their secret, whereas other men simply peel away as unwanted the shade over themselves and turn so swiftly that their dangle whirls outwards. They walk their nakedness across the concrete, whistling.

'Hey watchit, Blue!'

As you run into their legs, feeling the light whip of their hairiness as it twitches across your face. Their fingers thieving through your hair.

'What's the hurry, Blue?'

We fill our lungs with all the oxygen of this world then race out into sunlight, blinding ourselves so we can carry the litmus of everything we see and do not see and imagine and know, and then flow throw ourselves in the sea. Here we float the ideograms and hope to fit into them.

'LOOK!' CRIES DIRK now, and we dive down through the aqueous depth.

For we know on the summer days the busy days there is a world down below the surface completely different from the world above the waterline. One world is strangely magnified and densified so it is as if space is given an added dimension. Flesh becomes statuesque, bled of blood and changed into a strange greenish pallor, moving with a poetic, aquatic slow motion. There we see couples bobbing on the surface joined together but as we cut down through the waterline we see them jointed in together, in one clung octopus connection, moving in abstract judders, like a fish on a hook.

We surface gradually, with all the mischief of a thief, and see the couple (not yet engaged) serenely thinking their secret is hidden, a flagship of deceit. Down below again we see the man's hand slide down and in the strangely delayed world of underwater — that province of wrecks and drownings and cars sinking slowly downward — we see the man's hand struggle to release his secret from his togs, but the whole weight of water, we know, would render him ineffectual.

A different law rules down here.

Underneath the surface.

We see old breasts floating, and the varicose-veined legs of ancient women nobbled as they bounce up and down on the ocean floor; we see hands making covert adjustment, and one day we swim underwater, holding our breaths and see, yes, the soft effulgence of yellow piss flower and bloom out of Mr Casper the councillor's togs. We witness his deflowering. (Up above he is grave with dignity as he attempts to direct the traffic of the entire beach, raising his hand in noble gestures, upholstering his slack body with the invisible robes of plush velvet and dyed rabbit.) Yet with what joyful vehemence down below does he piddle! The craven smile of all tricksters distorts his noble face on the surface. 'What a beaut day,' he yells out to Mr Lamb, converting the area of water around him into real estate.

This knowledge we throw off as superfluous as we dive down, screaming and giggling to look at the white greenness of Dirk's bumcheeks, all dimpled with little craters and mountains, with threads of sun-shade flowing all over them. His cock hangs out, semi-hard at a strange angle, like a railway signal half paralysed. Its head, with the slit eye, looks suddenly comic and . . . alone.

Geoff dives down and pushes himself through Dirk's legs. He upends him. As Dirk sinks I see his face, the wreck of his face: his pretended upset. But then as he layers back into the soft eiderdown of sea, as he sinks, laughing, I feel his eyes reach up towards me, and in them is a form of gilded wire, so for one long moment we hold in perfect stillness.

The nub of his cock is the last thing I see.

Geoff alone stands there. He serenely smiles. And he places his hands on the very top of the sea's surface, balancing.

The Secret History of the Beach

THE BEACH IS full of secrets and we penetrate every one of them. There are temples on this beach, shrines which have a special place in our new brotherhood.

Geoff, Dirk, Maddy and I know every one of them, for we, led along by Maddy, have investigated them, lingered before them, sat in them by the hour, waited in them thoughtfully and read every message on the walls.

One of the chief temples is the bus-shelter.

This shrine, as is perhaps suitable for such a notable, yet somehow sublimely anonymous and overlooked building, is a cross between a municipal amenity and a building carefully shaped to suggest holidays, beaches and freedom. On one hand it is painted a thick municipal grey, yet its roof is luxuriantly tiled, the ends of it, Maddy has pointed this out, arch up into little municipal gods: spirits guarding the temple. (Typically, Geoff, Dirk and I have not seen these gods, or rather, in seeing them, we have no way of comprehending what they might mean, their significance, so we have, as it were, undone what we have just seen, carefully unstitching any embroidered meaning, preferring the comfort of eternal blankness.)

But Maddy has instructed us on what we are, in fact, seeing so now we nod, knowledgeably, not even knowing what we are agreeing to, so greedy are we for knowledge in any form. This temple has been, perhaps, carefully drawn up by a weary young architect, hoping to make something of what is really only a tram terminal, by giving it a slightly elegant shape, deep eaves, a tiled roof, he has also created two deep bays in which there are seats for those who would be eternally waiting.

The fact is, however, these bays exist only as a form of waste space, a necessary separation for the ablutions of each sex.

We had of course crept into the women's toilets which offered much less interest than the barnlike nature of the men's toilets.

Open to the salt air, the doors had pointed palisades which gave them an embattled look, as if we were in fact in some kind of redoubt.

Each time we entered this little side chapel, we would look for new words, new scrawlings, new and inventively desperate or covert messages. The urinal was always covered with a beautiful green slime, water running perpetually as if it must be ready at any hour, at any depth charge of night, to receive new pilgrims searching for what lay behind or within the secret of all secrets.

We would hang around this toilet and the bus-shelter until boredom just about became a frenzy. Then we would laugh, scream, sing whole operas in complete gibberish, poking out our tongues, distending our eyes, until, overcome with vertigo, we would drop back into silence. At times like these we would turn to the walls again.

For the fact was the entire wall of the two bays was an illegible scrawl of writing.

Crowds in summer would take refuge in the bays, having come up off the beach only to find the bus had sailed off without them. At this point an almost sublime exhaustion would overcome them, an exhaustion perhaps like that of mythical gods who had spent a day creating the world.

On overcast or wet days, there would always be people in the bus-shelter, mournfully looking out at the rain like pilgrims who had arrived at a church only to find the religious event had been cancelled or was already over, and they had, forever, missed the miracle. We locals would look at them with eyes so superior we affected not even to see them. Or we would walk by, our faces averted as if from shame at their lack of knowledge to arrive at the beach on a wet day.

It was established you had not really visited the beach unless, one, you had cleansed your soul in the tide, two, you had rewarded the flesh by feeding into it as many sugary substances as you could intake, as if to signify this visit almost had the nature of a religious holiday or high-day, and, three, you took revenge on the eternal unseeingness, the always renewing energy of the sea by scrawling some message on whatever surface was available, lodging the fact that you had, in fact, been there: that you were not, as the sea always whispered, immaterial.

The walls became like an informal visiting book, a wailing wall, a via dolorosa as well as an eternal love letter, a plea of physically acute angst. Every inch of it had been covered, bedizened, bedecked and scribbled upon. But such was the universal urge of everyone who came to the beach to mark their presence there that words spilled out everywhere you were likely to go — from the terminal to the corrugated tin changing sheds down by the sundecks, onto the small metal surrounds by the bins — words were even scraped by the end of a stick into the sand almost in an effervescence of desperation, knowing they would be obliterated soon by the tide; yet such was the force of these words, of people carrying words and needing to express them, that the cliffs where the land met the sea, at the very end of Hungry Creek, were themselves carved all over with words, arduously, with a penknife, over a whole afternoon, or a series of afternoons, a single letter, or an elliptical message in the form of a word only the inscriber could understand.

GEOFF, DIRK, MADDY and I would trail off down to the cliffs as part of our ritual, having again inspected the words on the busshelter for any new entrants. Here we would go to the next station of our inventory: the lone and spectral cathedral of the pine trees. This was a part of the park which looked out to the reef, and, possessing such high cliffs with no access to the beach, it was seldom visited.

This area was sacred, given over, almost by common consent, to courting couples. In summer, it was our joy to creep up behind these couples, from tree to tree. We would watch these sexual wrestling matches for long intense minutes. We had no idea what was occurring under the blanket but occasionally one of us would break the seance by snickering out loud with sheer pity at the misery these couples inflicted on themselves.

Sometimes Dirk would throw a carefully aimed pine cone. The third or fourth pine cone always brought the situation to a crisis.

Our safety was based on the fact that when the young man leapt up, there had to be such a concentrated series of adjustments, buttonings, pullings down and up — the young woman inevitably sitting up, dazed and pulling her top down, this was before a bleak and mute anger would colour her cheeks — that while this mini-tragedy of thwarted lust was happening, we would screel away across the green, just about making ourselves ill with the amount of ridicule bubbling up from our insides and cascading out in wild percolations of laughter.

Men and women, the drama of maleness and femaleness, never seemed so absurd, so pitiful.

On quieter days, we would pass by the empty banks, renewing, within the perpetually running cinema inside our eyelids, the many comic scenes of passion we had seen there, as well as purely educational and even erotic glimpses of thick engorged dalks straining to escape tight fabric, or the loose bowl of a breast with its central nipple, staring at us like a surprised eye.

On these still and empty days, when only a wind sped over the park, we might pause, for genuflection, before the hollows under the pine trees, then move on down to the beach itself.

The beach always had a special quality in its off-season period. It was then it was returned, unconditionally, to the local residents. Its cool emptiness was like a mirror image of a world unoccupied by humans. The empty wire rubbish containers rattled. The changing sheds were ghostly and abandoned shrines, as if the pilgrims and travellers had passed on to more clement lands.

OUR VISIT ROUND the shrines was made complete by our final point of call. The beach was so popular at the height of summer that it needed two changing sheds (or four depending on how you saw the sexes). The better known was the tin shed right by the bus terminal so those crowds, deposited by the tram and later the trolley, needed only climb down the steep hundred and five steps to a vast waiting corrugated-tin shed, a kind of immigration system not unlike Staten Island where immigrants from distant and rejected countries could enter and then, on exiting, emerge out into the desired new world, one they could only enter at the price of being returned to a shy demi-nakedness.

But further along the beach (and perhaps saved for those who had cars) was a superior changing shed, made out of roughcast concrete and the same heavy overhanging eaves as the terminus. This changing shed had a different ambience entirely, it was discretely placed off the beach and lay back, like an exhausted person, into pohutukawa trees, as if this person wanted only the solace and privacy of lying there, blissfully alone, gazing up through the trees to the moving panoply of clouds.

This changing shed was always our last point of call, our final search for the absolution of incident or event. Usually, however, this final stop in our search coincided with the fact that the changing shed was a hundred yards from Geoff and Dirk's house, and our own, which in turn intimated our time together was nearly over. Nothing had happened. Again. Again and again. We had only our own bodies to inspect, willing that at these moments one of us might be able to invent, out of the surprises of our own flesh, some incident. We might, at this point, undress and look, with searching eyes and hands, all over our respective bodies, or we might, because we were drugged on boredom by this time, merely look at each other with unseeing eyes, and with barely an exchanged word, as if in common consent that the miracle this day was not going to happen, amble off back home to our respective homes, carefully continuing to say nothing to our parents which might illuminate them with knowledge of how we spent our time, how we explored that endless quagmire and invisible quality which surrounded us on every side and ambushed us day after day with such ruthless efficiency: time.

An Event of
No Consequence

AND SO IT happened. Or didn't happen. Nothing happened, as I tried to tell Geoff. But he would not listen. He was rendered incapable of listening. What had happened? What had made him no longer listen to my voice? He broke our secret. This is what happened. Or rather, this is what did not happen.

IT WAS AT the very end of summer, that time before school starts. We knew we were going to different intermediate schools, so we had a dim forewarning that our world was ending. But in one way, we hardly minded. We had been stripped, scoured down to the very bottom of boredom to such a degree that first of all Dirk had disappeared, 'I gotta go and play footie,' he muttered mutinously, having screwed up his courage. Geoff stirred beside him, turning the empty cup of his face from his brother to my brother and then to me. An almost lewd look passed over his features and he said in a dull voice, a thick voice, he wanted to go over to our hut, but once we were there, Maddy kept looking away, as if he had discovered something, something else somewhere and he only stayed a little while, and I said with a sigh to Geoff why didn't he put his clothes back on, I preferred to go for a walk down the beach, and so we did and this was, this was what didn't happen.

A man came out of the changing sheds, the roughcast concrete changing sheds, yet so casually and naturally it took us a while, Geoff and me, to realise he was naked.

He began walking back and forth in front of us, slowly, brazenly. The tide was out, it was a chill day in early autumn — there was no reason — no reason at all for anyone to be on the beach. Yet here he was, this man, breaking the commandment that no one shall walk naked on this earth.

What had driven him there, to that appointment, but exactly the same interest in intercepting the knowledge of those secret words, those codes as us? We had arrived at the same point, the same church, the same vessel, that dimly dark salt-smelling room which the air of the beach infiltrated and made cool, even cold as if to hush the fevers of the flesh. He was a tall thin man, not well made, walking slowly back and forth, completely naked.

It was seeing someone so completely in the round, in a proper perspective, a head attached to the body, a penis attached to the flesh, feet attached to the soil of the world (even if mediated through a path) which astonished us.

Gravely even gracefully, he conducted the passage of his penis as it bobbed along as he walked. I had the faintest impression of a small smile on his lips as he turned to look at us.

Geoff and I were hunched together, the two of us on the bank which led away from the beach. The bank was soft with fallen pine needles, all auburn and shiny, gripped between our toes as we squatted down to watch.

He walked back and forth three times.

Geoff and I were plunged into a silence so immense it was as if we were sinking under the water, but joyfully, inertly, with the pleasure of weighted bodies; we were seeking above all to reach the bottom, which we would know by some sonic boom, we would bury our squirming toes in the soft mud which we knew lay at the bottom of the tide, as if it were the underlining of the beautiful quicksilver on its top. We were blissfully sinking and losing contact with the surface of the world which yet surrounded us on every side, we were swooning and turning with the knowledge we were being handed by this stranger when, wrapped round each other as it felt, as if Geoff and I were intercoupled and clinging as we joyfully sank down to touch the bedrock of knowledge, yet just at the point when our toes might have touched the ocean floor, when a key might have turned in the lock, I felt Geoff beside me stir, and a low moan wired out of his mouth.

I smelt fear, the brimstone of panic coming out of every pore in his flesh. It was metallic that smell, ugly.

I looked into his face; we were suddenly back on the outside of the world, on a bank at about an hour before sunset, the sun was pouring a particularly sharp cordial over everything, so all flaws, all indentations and pits and pores became raised up, catching and carrying their own flags of shadows, and I could see, just as I could smell, Geoff was rigid with panic. I felt his muscles ride up and tauten. I felt him rise up on his haunches, his head already turning, like the mouth of a trumpet, towards his house.

I placed a hand on his legs to stop him, to slow him down. But already, like a startled hare, he was scrabbling his way up the bank, pulling himself along as he made strange gibbering noises: the noises of a startled idiot. I turned quickly to look towards the man (to apologise by glance for this break in the solemn and distant ritual which we were partaking in) but the man had gone; he had gone as absolutely as though he had never existed.

The beach lay empty.

The sun sparkled on a field of mud.

A gull stood on the edge of a rubbish tin, looking at me aggressively, as if I wished to steal the last morsel of summer food from it.

But I was scrabbling up the bank, too. I caught hold of Geoff's legs on the bank and tried to pull him back. He kicked out at me, once twice, so hard I lost my speech. Instead I threw myself on him bodily, winding him. It was only as I lay on top of him, weaving my legs through his and forcing his arms back over his head so he raised his neck up once twice and tossed his head from side to side, that a slow and furtive consciousness came back into his face, that he was seeing me, that he saw me, that he knew me. He looked at me for a long moment, as if seeking to find out what intelligence I could flood into him, what meaning I could make of what we had just seen. I was so rhapsodic, I simply squeezed my hands around his wrists once twice three times, trying to force silently into his body all my excitement, my sense of sinking down and almost touching the bottom, of my feet rebounding from the floor of the world and sending me, like a rocket fisssssing towards the surface; his head fell, exhausted, to the side and I saw him looking at my hands tight round the boniness of his wrist.

My hands unclasped. He lay there exhausted and silent and the big bruise of his eyes moved up to my face.

'Wha . . . what?' he murmured to me. I heard in that second the extreme dryness of his throat. The very huskiness of his question made me feel, momentarily, nearly mad with a lunacy of power. I looked down into his pallid face. He was no longer beautiful. He was no longer brown and tanned and formed into a soft rawness.

'Wha . . . ?' he kept saying to me.

I looked away from him.

From where we were lying, on the very cusp of the bank, I could see the neat line of houses all looking back at me, separated by the grass and road and powerlines. In fact, I could see Mrs Beveridge walking her bike along, for all the world like a clockwork toy, like a woman in the weather clock regularly making her appearance as part of an overall scheme. Soon I knew a bus would come streaming down the road, bringing the same workers, who would say the same words in parting as they got out and departed; what was the connection between this world and what we had just seen?

Where lay the connection?

We lay completely still. I began to hear, then feel that Geoff's breathing had taken on a more regular rhythm.

When I looked over at him, he was starting to sit up. He looked like someone who had just been hit by something.

'We must not,' I said to him intently, 'say anything. Do you understand?'

He looked at me without understanding. Without intelligence. I felt weariness overcome me. I wanted really to be on my own, to think through what had happened: to restore to its miraculous and untouched image, like a religious icon on a stand, the completely naked man; I wanted to look again at this image which remained as a litmus on my brain. But I could tell, looking at Geoff, this would not be immediately possible.

'But wha . . . ?' His slack mouth opened wide. As it did so I saw a slim string of saliva joining his teeth to his tongue. Inside his soft warm cavern I saw his tongue lying there, struggling to form the word — a word — whatever word it was he needed to say . . .

'Wha . . . wha . . .' he kept on repeating, like an engine stalled.

He fell into a long silence. It was as if he had fallen back into a swimming pool, having released his hands from the metal bars of a ladder. I watched his entrance into the water. I watched his floundering.

'Look,' I said to him as I threw him a lifebuoy, 'Look,' I said to him, 'it was nothing, nothing happened, nothing actually took place. If we tell, if we tell . . .' and I myself fell into the same ring, the same aura of clotted silence.

I raised my eyes again to look along the road. The houses all seemed so prosaically still, even pretty. Late afternoon light was engraving the glass windows a pure lavender, with a shrill even tender pink running along the gutterings. The powerlines wavered in a slight breeze and I heard, overheard, the siren of birds' wings as they began to move in a flock towards the largest pine tree in the district, their nest for the night. I knew if we did not return to our respective homes soon there would be questions. It was important we inserted ourselves back into the moving vehicle of ritual which surrounded us on every side as seamlessly, as wordlessly, as possible.

Geoff was now sitting upright. He was even yawning. A divine stupidity slid down over his face as effectively as a motorised door sliding down, covering over all light. I calculated exactly what this omission would cover.

'Geoff,' I said to him, 'We gotta swear. You know. Like Maddy made us. Eternal brothers. We gotta make a promise.'

I knew how important it was to keep our childhood world separate and uncontaminated from the adult world, just as I knew, as firmly, that there could be no understanding, no commerce between the two worlds, only the unknown dynamics of catastrophe.

He turned and looked at me and I knew I was seeing, inside his eyes, that complete emptiness which marked his native receptive state.

'Wha?' he struggled again to make sense.

'We got to swear,' I said to him. 'Eternal silence. Not tell parents. Only trouble. Too much trouble. Understand? *Comprenez?*'

I used a word we all knew from the movies.

He nodded slowly but I knew, I sensed he was not convinced. Inside the emptiness of his eyes I saw the wire of doubt, just as I saw reflected in them the nobbled exterior of the vast old pine tree, the veteran of all pines.

His nod so slow I did not know.

'Agreed?'

He nodded again, slowly.

I did not know.

He got up slowly.

'Brothers forever.'

'OK, Jamie.'

'OK, Geoff.'

'See you.'

'See you,' I said, letting my words fade in the evening air.

WE ARE SITTING in the back of Geoff's father's car. We are being driven up to the police station. It is night. My father and Geoff's father sit in the car with us. There is a terrible silence sealing over everything. I turn to look at Geoff. But as my eyes catch his, he almost shrinks from me, as if I will hit him. I try to catch his eye again, to speak, to warn, to tell him to stay silent.

But something has happened.

What was kept inside our own world has now been breached and broken into. The end of a spear has been lent into our flesh, and now our innards, slippery and hot, viscid and smelling of shit, will plop out onto the floor. Now strangers called adults will feel their way through our insides, trying to find treasure but instead slowly killing us as they pull more and more from our bodies.

This intelligence I try to pass silently to Geoff.

But now, I comprehend the true limits of his lack of intelligence. He simply presents to me, as he has done at certain other intimate moments, the flat plate of his face. It echoes with emptiness. It is like the beach at the times of ultimate flat tide, when you never believe the tide shall come in.

THE SINGLE EYE of the bulb, without a shade, swung slightly in the garage which is the policeman's office. Mr Webb stands there. Everything is stiff with importance. Papers are flicked through. The cap is taken off a pen. The slow calligraphy which forms along a line. Words extracted from Geoff who speaks in the voice of a husk, a shadow. He does not dare look at me.

Our fathers, like centurions sentenced to become executors, stand behind us in the shadows.

I am asked too.

I feel the creak of my father beside me willing me on.

The words I find are all incidental. 'A man. He walked. Naked. Yes. Naked. No clothes on. He walked. We ran.'

That is all I can find inside me to say.

'*Did he . . .*'

The adult men hesitate here and surrender between themselves the knowledge each of them must know, intimately, at some parallel point in their own lives.

'*Did he . . . come closer?*'

'*Did he . . . touch you?*'

'*Did he touch you . . . in private places?*'

Geoff's lips I can see are moving to form a word which will be so calamitous, so vastly repercussive in its explosive effects I find my own voice speaking out:

'No. He walked. He walked back and forth. He had no clothes on. That man. He just walked.'

There is a secession here, of breath, of disappointment maybe, of relief, from the three old men, I can see them now as they were, three old men staring at their tender captives.

'No touching? No private touching?'

I do not trust words here.

I nod. I shake my head. And hear the knock of the car as it hits the ocean floor.

Yes, this is what it is about. The water pouring in.

And waiting.

'Geoff. Do you have anything to add?'

We all wait and then there is the sharp intake of a breath from Geoff.

Like a sob at the back of his throat.

He is crying.

The men all stand up immediately. Papers rustle. Cap put back on pen.

'An upsetting incident. Overtired. Time to get some sleep.'

The men all bury the moment hastily.

Earth is piled on earth.

We ride back home in the importance of a car. Geoff's father and my father talk about the score. That game which is being played forever in men's eyes and minds and pockets, the one they plan to finally win and which will forever set their minds at rest.

I sense Geoff is looking towards me. But I do not look towards him.

He reaches out to touch me.

I do not look at him.

I hear him sigh, deeply. He has settled on the bottom of the ocean. He will not survive. He will stop breathing soon. This I know. He will remain there forever for me, a small skeleton locked in the metal shell of a car, moving softly and even sweetly with the ocean currents, seaweed flowing in and out of the sockets of his eyes and where his brain once was, that tender dim bulb, a single crab has made itself at home and dances across the mossy ivory of his skull, doing a victorious dance, claiming all his space — forever.

Padlock

EVERY AFTERNOON MR Webb cycles down to my parents' house and I am ushered into the front room. This room is never used and I sit there, guilty, alarmed. Mr Webb brings books of photographs for me to look through. Photographs of faces. Men. Each afternoon I am invited to choose one. The one who looks nearest to the naked man on the beach.

I look at the faces frozen forever in the flashlight. A frightened face, an empty face, a face at the first moment of its dying.

Face after face.

I am aware of Mr Webb sitting so close to me, his kneecap straining the serge, creaking. He tells me to take my time.

My problem is I had no awareness of the man's face. If it were his penis, yes, I might be able to reproduce it.

I had seen that in intense detail. But not his face.

Randomly, with an eery ease, I choose a face.

Any face.

Afternoon by afternoon.

This goes on for one week, two weeks.

Then, perhaps matching up the fact that none of the faces coalesce, the visits from Mr Webb cease.

Nothing is said.

BUT THE HUT is padlocked.
The back fence grows taller.
Our faces have to avert when we see Geoff and Dirk.
We become strangers.
My brother and I are watched.
We are spliced apart.
Brothers no more.

EVERYTHING IS FORGOTTEN, and like a pact broken, a truce ignored, we move apart never to come together again, except at certain moments, in a lingering, even calculating glance.

Accepting the illogic of this — the end of the pursuit of words, the incomplete conclusion of their search — we numbly and dumbly accept the edict.

AFTER ALL WE have no idea what it means.

Coda

Ball

THE SPOTLIGHT IS roving the floor. Like an eye it is, a wide open eye of white brilliance. It lights the darkness of curved head. Feathers briefly catch fire, implode on the dance of a sequin. We are all drunk on the music, on the immanence of the word. It will happen, we know it, all of us now, as we join in the dance.

From the moment I entered the hall a widening wave and wall of sensation opened up around me.

I can only see the clumsiest of costumes: cloth unironed, taken quickly out of a dank smelling box; material unpinked from cellophane where it has lain, unbought through all the seasons, fading and losing its true colour. My brother has placed new eyes in my head and from beneath the weight of the papier mâché crown I can see there is not one costume in the room, the hall, the school (quickly it widens to become the universe) which is so intricate and arcanely perfect as mine.

Yet I understand I wear it only because of the perfect epiphany of all accidents.

More than this, it creates consternation.

Comprehending that surprise is the best form of attack, my brother has presented me as a source of astonishment:

who are you
what are you
what are you doing
what are you doing here?
I am Cleopatra, Queen of the Nile.
This is a costume ball, isn't it?

I BECOME AWARE that for the first time in my life I am truly naked, that in fact I am not even wearing a costume but that I am parading, perhaps like that man of so long ago, amongst them.
Miss Jaye stares at me, suddenly struck by something which has only just occurred to her.

I wave. Regally.

Mr Pollen's eyes cannot stop following me around. I await the ecstasy of surprise which will come when he recognises me.

There is some powder in my veins, some madness has leapt from my brother and set me alight, this night.

I am a fizzing firework, I recognise this as I follow behind the trail of myself as I dance across the floor. Girls queue to dance with me.

I nod graciously, picking out Stumpy as my favourite partner. Together we dance in a slow rhythm, outside time.

Keely comes past, dressed as a ghost.

He winks at me, conspiratorially.

More than this, he backs into me so I feel, all up my body, through my cloak, the warm percussion of his flesh. He does this once twice . . . and the third time it happens I read on the curve of his eyelash he is hungering to dance with me, to be with me, together moving. But in the dance, in the sudden dark, it is a spot waltz, he is replaced in the queue by Carrot; I never recognised he was so short. I have to bend down, as if from a skyscraper to see him over the ledge. He is grateful that someone, at least, acknowledges he exists.

'Go, Jamie!' he calls to me, as we jostle together, arm to arm. I read in his eyes a burning sea of admiration, and I simply say to him, 'Don't you mean, Noddy?'

These words are so cruel they curve round into the flick of a whip which rips the mask from his face leaving behind drips of blood: his eternal sore. I conceive the power of words and dance away laughing.

Still the light is dancing.

And then the needle is lifted off the record.

We lurch to a halt.

A card is held up.

A Queen of Hearts.

Everyone on the right side of the hall has to walk off.

I am safe. But more than this I have become aware of a silence forming in me as powerfully present as if an ear or an eye has opened within my stomach. I am listening for that pause, I realise; at last I have come to comprehend it and it has in fact already occurred around me and I am moving, almost miraculously, inside its magic bell.

It protects me and sings about me, as if another and personal spotlight has come on round me.

Is this what I have been waiting for? For this movement, this motion towards being? Is this the climb which has silently been happening inside my blood? Flood? For one second I comprehend something: the M is joining to E, this is what is soundlessly happening during this dance, as the white light bounces round over our heads: yes, part is joined to part and a form of wholeness, hidden behind the choreography of costume, is happening.

Is this not how the whole of life should be? Ideally. In this revolving softly, lost dream, this slow awakening.

As I sink, I leave all the sounds of the world and I begin, in the concentrated spell of a sinking car, to listen.

Home

THE DOOR HAS swung open.

Inside I see Maddy crouched down, putting away the costume. He looks at it, worn. Somehow in the daylight it does not look so good, and I see and sense each grass blade is watching.

'I bought you something. A present. *Which hand?*' I say impressively.

He just looks at me. I look into his face.

What do I see there? The peeled-grape eyes, the white skin, but something more in this even grey light. He looks tired, as if he has been up late at night, at night forever, as if he is an elf, working by moonlight.

For one second I felt impatient.

Now I knew the words, they had ceased, miraculously, to have much meaning, much value to me. I felt light, almost tipsy with the sheer weightlessness of the knowledge I no longer had. Or sought.

The strain of looking into the light had made him squint, so for one second he appeared to be blind.

I saw how daylight had robbed him of his magic, like those goblins who had been caught building the rock bridge by the fiery light of dawn.

I felt a crude power, a dislike of magic and arcane methods.

He seemed unhappy.

I knew I would have to seduce him again into compliance, with softnesses and kindnesses (arts which I knew off by heart), so I could effortlessly anticipate what he might want and he, the starveling, would rise to my offer always, gratefully, and together again we could continue our strange journey.

'Which hand?' I said to him, standing before him. On the carpet so close I could smell his aniseedness. He struggled for his glasses, but I shook my head. He held still.

'Which hand?'

I insisted he play the game.

He looked from one to the other, in that second, by accepting my game, slipping back into a comfortable world of childhood in which there were surprises as well as tricks.

'You were queen of the ball last night,' he said to me offhandedly as he uncrunched up and rose to his feet.

It was at this point I made a discovery. In the five weeks my parents had been away I had overtaken him — he my older brother — in height. This strange coming together, yet finding ourselves apart, caused a momentary concussion of silence between us. We both looked at each other wordlessly.

I looked down into his face, and the quick whip of a laugh escaped me.

'I taller than you!' I cried out, as much to the world of statistics as the measured quotas of love and affection.

He leaned forward and, cradling himself into my body, tried to reach behind me for his gift. Without blinking or altering the mirror of my face which was right in front of his, our breath intermingled, I placed the chocolate bar in my left hand.

I laughed into his face.

'It for you, for you, for you,' I kept on keening as he struggled to get my hand to leave my back.

I saw his face darken, and fracture, and a spool of unhappiness leak out of him. Immediately, I saw how my action, which was only meant to make my giving of the chocolate more of a game, was touching some vulnerable part within him. In fact, he seemed this day more vulnerable than he had been for a long time — moody as if I had done something to him, or not done something.

I sensed he was about to cry.

As if he was seeking to blot out the undeniable fact that now I was taller than him, he threw himself against me.

We were falling.

We were falling sideways so our world became unbalanced.

We landed with a hard jump on the floor.

He was on top of me instantly, raining down blows on my face. Yet as soon as he began this I began fighting him back. Furiously, we attacked each other, rolling over and over each other as he fought to get hold of the chocolate.

'Maddy, Maddy, stop, stop, Maddy!' I cried and I tried to hold him and clasp him still.

He seemed to see me after a time. He softened.

We were both crying.

'Drop it,' he said. 'Go on, drop it.'

His face was so closed, so unhappy, my fingers loosened.

Instantly he was off me. He ripped the silver paper back, and, as if he was a starving man and this was the first food he had seen in days, he began cramming it inside his mouth. Only towards the last, did his eyes — greedy and hostile — flicker towards me. He did not stop chewing.

There was only a single piece of chocolate left.

I watched his eyes move from the chocolate to me, then back to the chocolate. His jaws began to slow down. I watched his Adam's apple swallow.

'It's for you,' I said to him slowly. 'I brought it for you. A gift, Maddy. To thank you. It's all for you.'

'. . . Me?' he asked me. I saw inside his mouth a runny brown wetness.

I nodded.

His hand, already almost up to his mouth, hesitated and his eyes flew to my face. I felt he was seeing me for the first time that day. His hand slowly placed the last piece of chocolate on the edge of the bookshelf.

He went on chewing, swallowed, then we both sat there in silence.

It was as if there was nothing more to say to each other.

We both looked out the door: at the ragged tufts of unmown lawn, speckled with paspalum and daisy; the washing line staked to its own shadow; the cat, reclining against the weatherboards of the house, half in the sun, half out, gazing regally into nothingness.

For one long moment we both gazed out at the world which contained us, the sound of gulls' wings overhead.

It was as if, down on the beach, we could hear the turn of the waves: as if the tide had gone out as far as it could and was now beginning that tidal flow by which water all over the globe re-arranges itself.

A warm salty smell began to filter through the air.

Maddy began putting away the helmet, placing it back on the hat block.

'You don't own me, Maddy,' I said to him. 'Eh?'

'I got a letter,' he said to me as though I had not spoken.

'Oh,' I said, heart quickening, then turning over in a sudden dump.

'A letter? From . . . ?'

He gave the smallest inclination of a nod.

'They coming home,' he said.

As if hearing us, the cat stood up and, head down low but eyes concentrating on us, began making his way towards us. His tail made one or two leisurely flicks, almost strokes of recognition. Achilles entered the hut and sat down a small distance away from us.

'You don't own me, Maddy?' I said.

Maddy leant forward with the last bit of chocolate and he held it out to me.

I took it and, broke it into two, handed the smallest bit back to Maddy. Simultaneously, we both placed the chocolate on our tongues.

He smiled at me.

'You don't own me, eh, Maddy?' I said again.

The cat was staring, serenely, into the future: enigmatic eyes blazing with content, fur fluffed out and not exactly looking at anything but absorbing the whole room through its skin, each stamen of fur faintly vibrating — his large glittering orbs — miniature globes, reflecting the room, the bars on the windows, the sky — the universe — and as if in sympathy with his union with all things — Achilles broke out into a ragged theme of a purr, which took up its own momentum and now grew louder, more regular, more of a hymn to peace, to silence, to ease and —

'They come home now,' he said. 'They come home.'

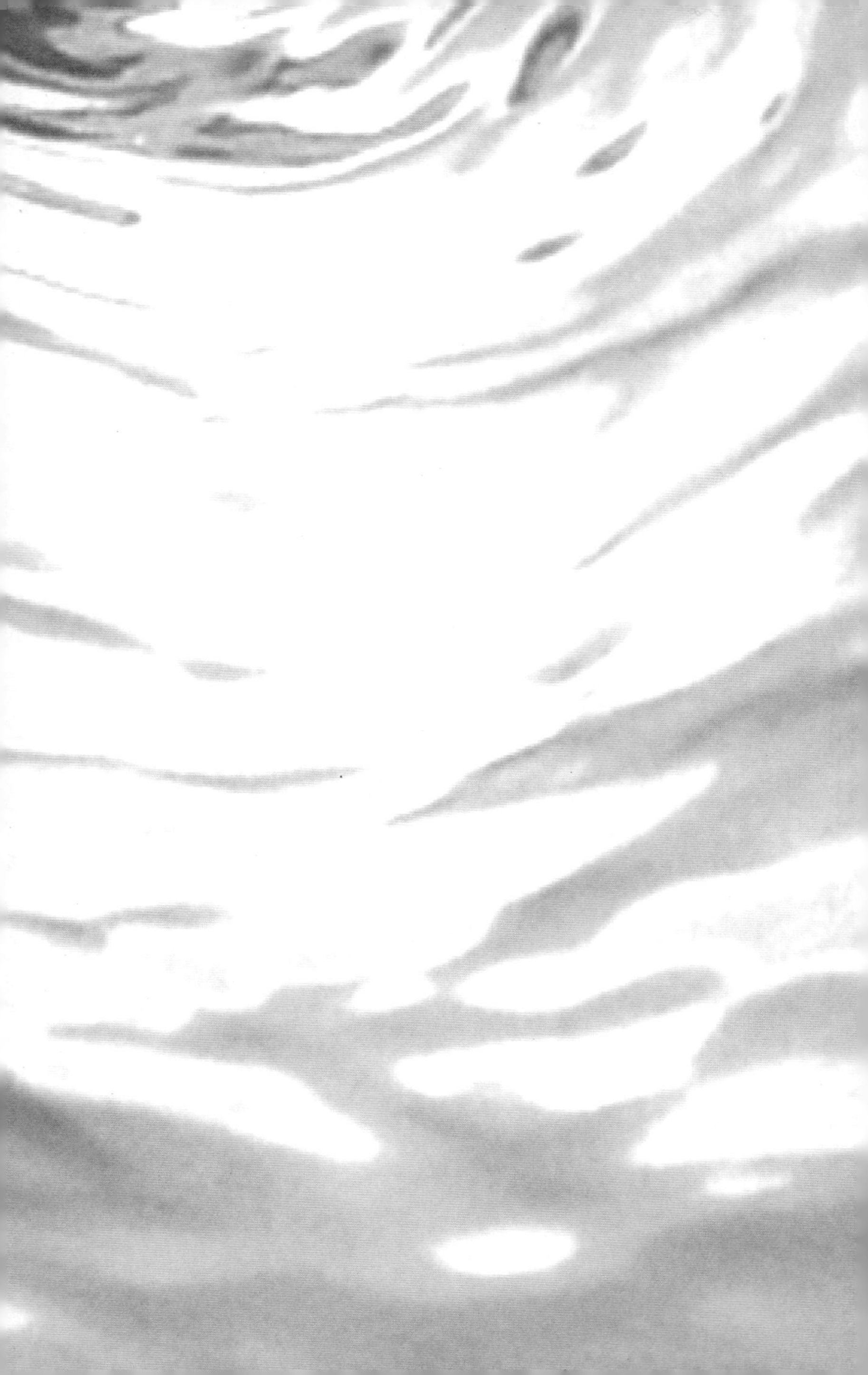